Degas to Picasso *Creating Modernism in France*

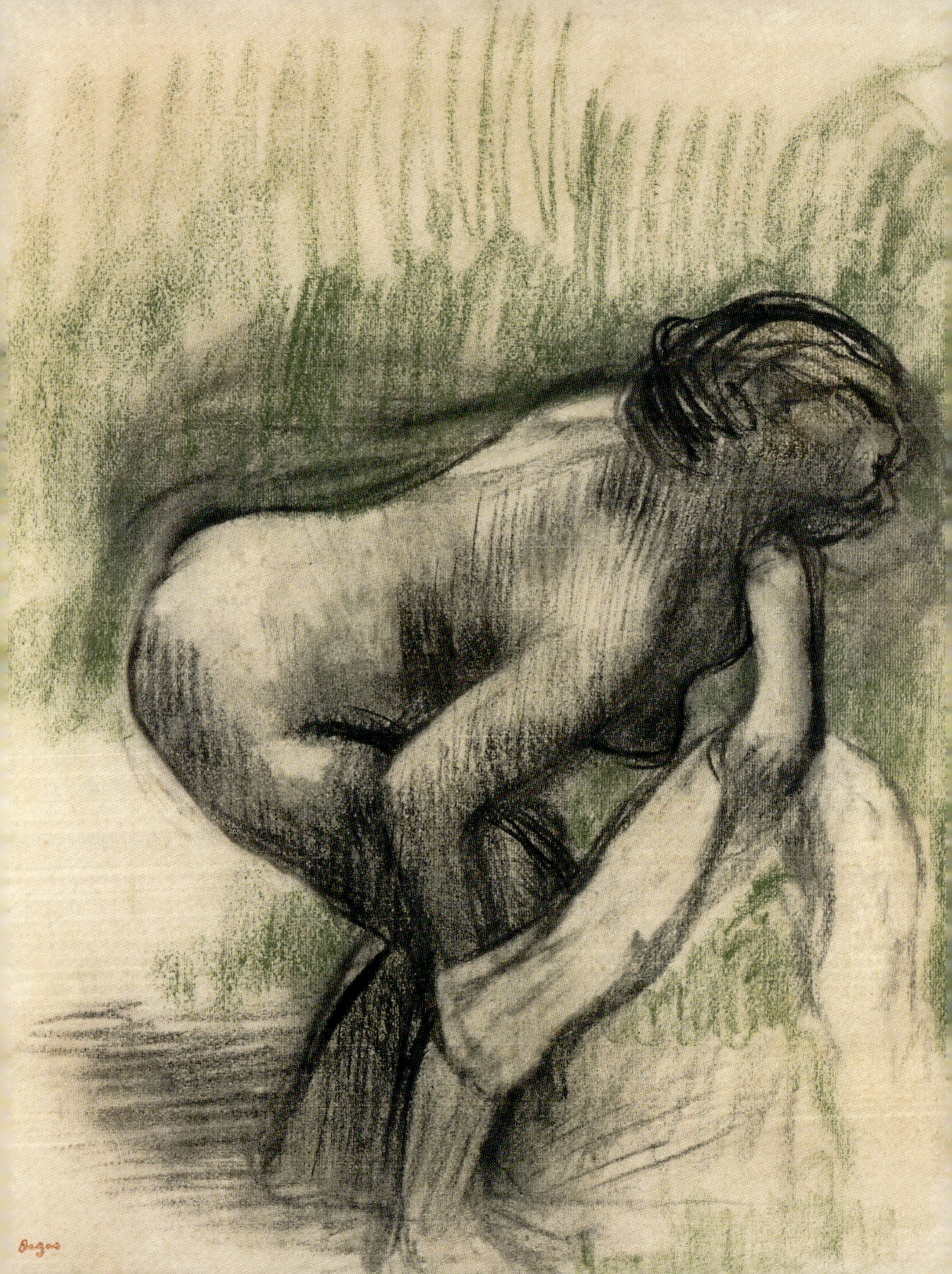
Degas

Colin Harrison
with Jon & Linda Whiteley and
Ursula & R. Stanley Johnson

DEGAS TO PICASSO

CREATING MODERNISM IN FRANCE

Works from the
Ursula & R. Stanley Johnson
Family Collection

Ashmolean Museum
OXFORD · 2017

ASHMOLEAN

DEGAS TO PICASSO: CREATING MODERNISM IN FRANCE
10 February to 7 May 2017

British Library Cataloguing in Publications Data
A catalogue record for this book is available from the British Library.

ISBN: 978-1-910807-12-5

Catalogue designed and typeset in ATF Garamond by Dalrymple
Printed and bound in Belgium by Albe de Coker

Front cover: Fernand Léger 1881–1955
Mother and Child (Mère et enfant) [cat.107]

Frontispiece: Edgar Degas 1834–1917
Woman after her Bath [cat.44]

Back cover: Pablo Picasso 1881–1973 *Study for 'Three Musicians' also known as The White Coffee Table* [cat.96]

For further details of Ashmolean titles please visit:
www.ashmolean.org/shop

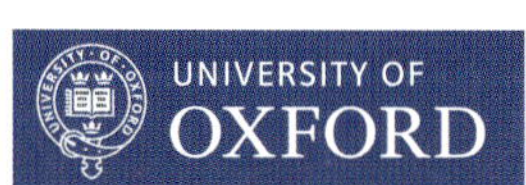

Foreword 7

Collecting the Art of France:
A Moveable Feast 9
Ursula & R. Stanley Johnson

The Art of Drawing in France:
From Neo-Classicism to Cubism 21
Jon Whiteley

CATALOGUE 39
Colin Harrison, Jon & Linda Whiteley

Notes and References 193

Bibliography 196

Copyright Credits 200

THE ARTISTS

Jean-Honoré Fragonard 1732–1806

Jacques-Louis David 1748–1825

Louis-Léopold Boilly 1761–1845

Anne-Louis Girodet-Trioson 1767–1824

Pierre-Henri Révoil 1776–1842

Jean-Baptiste Isabey 1767–1855

Jean-Auguste-Dominique Ingres 1780–1867

Jean-Louis-André-Théodore Géricault 1791–1824

Ferdinand-Victor-Eugène Delacroix 1798–1863

Honoré Daumier 1808–1879

Jean-François Millet 1814–1875

Théodore Chassériau 1819–1856

Eugène Boudin 1824–1898

Camille Pissarro 1830–1903

Louis-Auguste-Gustave Doré 1832–1883

Édouard Manet 1832–1883

Edgar Degas 1834–1917

Paul Cézanne 1839–1906

Odilon Redon 1840–1916

Claude-Oscar Monet 1840–1926

Pierre-Auguste Renoir 1841–1919

Mary Cassatt 1844–1926

Vincent van Gogh 1853–1890

Georges Seurat 1859–1891

Pierre Bonnard 1867–1947

Henri Matisse 1869–1954

František Kupka 1871–1957

Georges Rouault 1871–1958

Jacques Villon 1875–1963

Raoul Dufy 1877–1953

Albert Marcoussis 1878–1941

Albert Gleizes 1881–1953

Fernand Léger 1881–1955

Pablo Picasso 1881–1973

Georges Braque 1882–1963

Auguste Herbin 1882–1960

Jean Metzinger 1883–1956

Roger de La Fresnaye 1885–1925

André Lhote 1885–1962

Juan Gris 1887–1927

Marc Chagall 1887–1985

Marcel Gromaire 1892–1971

André Masson 1896–1987

FOREWORD

The century before the Second World War was one of breathtaking artistic experiment. During this time artists, throughout Europe but above all centred in Paris, constantly sought new means of expression, exploiting novel subject matter while also taking advantage of new techniques and materials. The invention of lithography in the late 1790s, for example, encouraged Géricault, Daumier and Manet to portray the horrors of war, or expose the pretensions of politicians and plutocrats, with ferocious immediacy. The development of man-made coloured chalks gave the Impressionists a valuable alternative to watercolour in their search to capture the instantaneous. This exhibition, selected from the Ursula and R. Stanley Johnson Family Collection, gives a powerful sense of these artistic experiments and advances. At its heart is a choice group of works by Picasso, Braque and other artists as they were developing the language of Cubism, as well as oil paintings and works on paper by artists who exhibited at the first public showing of Cubism, the Salon des Indépendants in 1911.

This is, of course, in many ways a familiar story, but it is one that is surprisingly difficult to see on the walls of British museums. The Ashmolean is not alone in its paucity of mainstream European modernism; our individual works by Picasso, Braque and Matisse are all from a single bequest. The great scholar and collector Douglas Cooper once lamented that for the British:

> *Modern art, in order to be acceptable, had to appear traditional, decorative and easy to understand. Thus, no-one collected Fauve or Cubist pictures; very occasionally single pictures by Picasso, Braque or Juan Gris might be bought by a collector, virtually never by a museum; and significantly, not even one representative collection of Matisse was formed between the wars.*

This reluctance to acquire works by 'progressive' artists has meant that British museums are remarkably lacking in Cubism. Nor was Cooper's own incomparable collection acquired by the Tate, where it naturally belonged, but dispersed after his death. The collection's core was snapped up by Leonard Lauder in 1986, and now forms part of his recent gift to the Metropolitan Museum in New York.

We are therefore enormously grateful for the opportunity provided by this exhibition to go some way towards rectifying this situation. The Ursula and R. Stanley Johnson Family Collection has been assembled over the last 50 years and ranges from Old Master prints to late Picasso drawings. In its focus on works on paper and the particular revelations provided by drawings, the collection provides an individual and personal survey of the principal moments and artists of the French avant-garde.

It cannot be easy to relinquish, albeit temporarily, so many treasured objects, and I would like to offer my heartfelt thanks to Ursula and Stanley Johnson, as well as to their children, for their generosity in enabling us to share their collection with the public at the Ashmolean. We thank them sincerely for all their support, and for the help they have provided in selecting and preparing the works for the exhibition, as well as for their contributions to the catalogue. Thanks too are due to Suzanne Varkalis, Eric Leech and Lukas Hall for their invaluable assistance with the practicalities of the loan and for photographing the works, and to Declan McCarthy for overseeing the production of the catalogue. We are also, as ever, grateful to the Friends and Patrons of the Ashmolean Museum who have also provided support for the exhibition.

XA STURGIS
Director, Ashmolean Museum

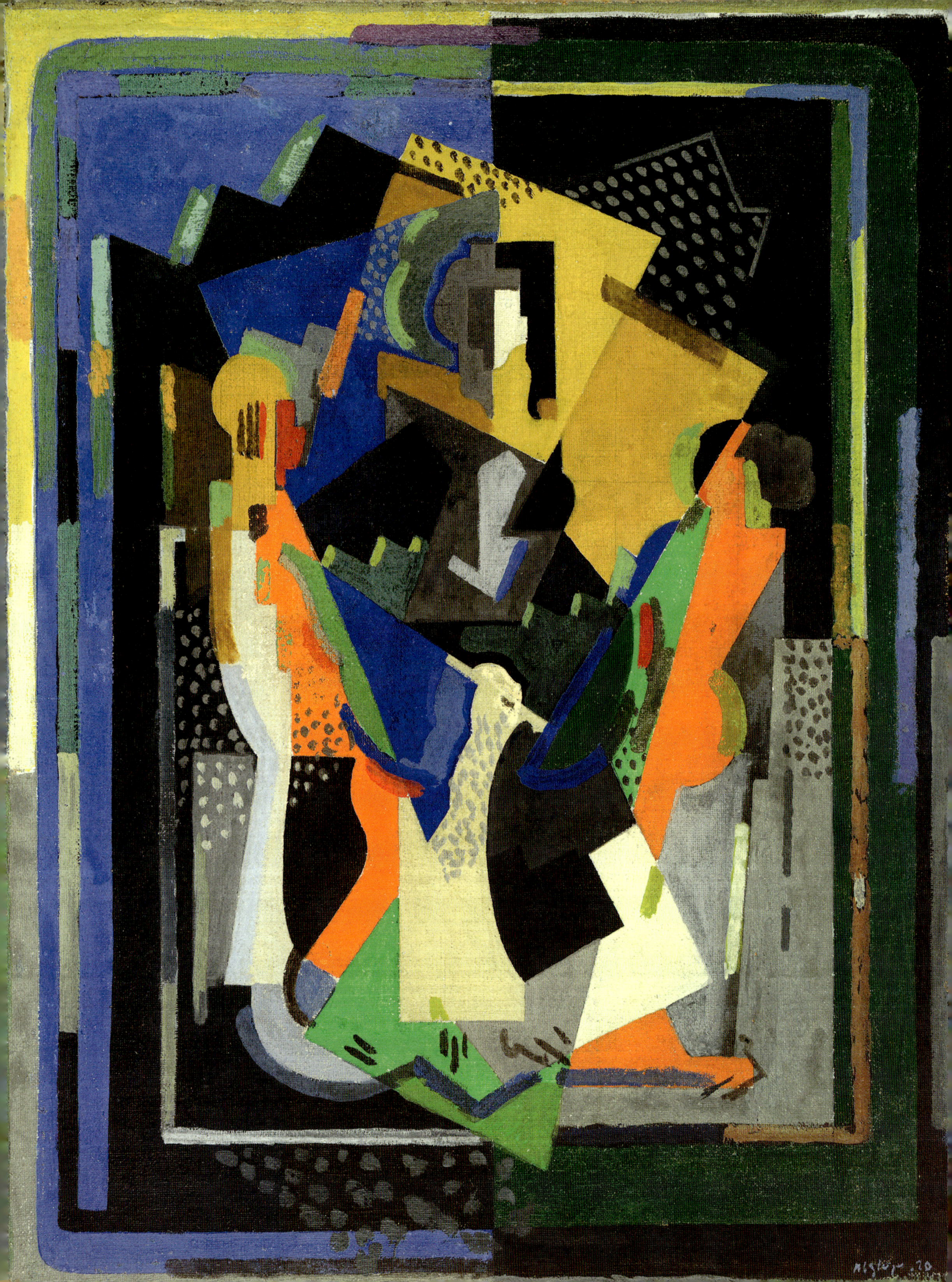

COLLECTING THE ART OF FRANCE: A MOVEABLE FEAST

Ursula & R. Stanley Johnson

On ne voit bien qu'avec le coeur.
ANTOINE DE SAINT-EXUPÉRY[1]

It was while studying in Paris in the late 1950s and 1960s that we first began to collect art produced in France from the late eighteenth to the mid-twentieth century. As expatriates – one a young German from the Rhineland, the other the proverbial 'American in Paris' – we were privileged to participate in an exceptionally intense period of artistic and intellectual creativity. We had as our guides eminent figures such as the Renaissance specialist André Chastel at the Institut d'Art et d'Archéologie and philosophers such as Jean Wahl, Gabriel Marcel and Maurice Merleau-Ponty at the Sorbonne and the Collège de France. Although we attended brilliant lectures and participated in challenging seminars, much of our time was spent looking at and talking about the art that we encountered at first hand. The echoing rooms of the then-uncrowded Louvre, the Bibliothèque nationale, Jeu de Paume, Musée Nationale d'Art Moderne, Marmottan, Carnavalet and many other Parisian and provincial museums and galleries became our second homes – while our actual home, at least initially, was a typical student's garret in Paris's *5ième arrondissement*, up six flights of stairs with no proper bath or even regular hot running water.

Right from the start, we found that we were particularly attracted by the spontaneity and intimacy often found in artists' works on paper. It was therefore no surprise that many of our first forays into collecting focused on drawings. The drawings we have acquired over the years range from artists' initial thoughts about a specific visual problem to highly finished compositions intended to stand as works of art in their own right. Some are rapidly executed sketches and others much more detailed compositions, sometimes produced for or after paintings, sculptures, prints or even other drawings. Our collection reflects an appreciation of drawings as both autonomous expressions of artistic creativity and as critical elements within a more extensive process of experimentation and planning relating to an individual composition or project. The decision to concentrate on drawings executed from the end of the eighteenth century onwards was based in part on our growing interest in the art and culture of these centuries, but it was also driven by what works were available – and, crucially, affordable – to two young students. Already by the early 1960s it was increasingly difficult, with a few rare exceptions, to acquire fine drawings from earlier periods even without budgetary constraints.

Our initial attraction to drawings produced by artists working in France was matched by a growing interest in other types of works on paper. We thus began to collect engravings, woodcuts and etchings by old master printmakers from Northern and Southern Europe including, among others, Martin Schongauer, Albrecht Dürer, Lucas Cranach the Elder, Jacques Callot, Rembrandt Harmensz van Rijn, Giovanni Battista Piranesi and Francisco de Goya. Over time we added prints by modern masters as well, concentrating in this case, as in our collection of drawings, mainly on artists working in France. Our fascination with the possibilities of paper as a medium, whether as a support for a print or a drawing, meant that a superb impression of Dürer's 1504 engraving

Albert Gleizes 1881–1953
Composition [cat.93]

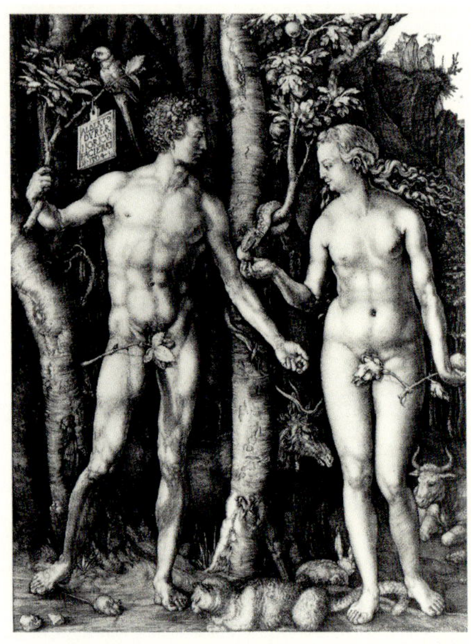

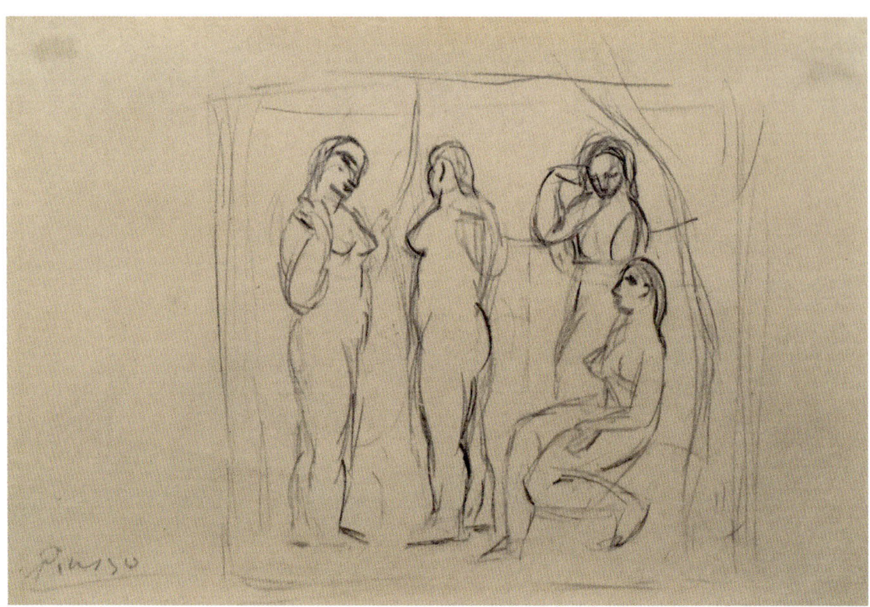

of Adam and Eve [fig.1] could sit comfortably alongside a sketch of nude figures drawn four centuries later by Pablo Picasso in 1906–7 as a study for his iconic *Demoiselles d'Avignon* [fig.2 and cat.57]. Similarly, we found fascinating points of connection – as well as noted profound differences – between a haunting self-portrait etched by Rembrandt in 1633 [fig.3] and Edgar Degas' equally revealing drawn self-portrait of *c.*1865 [fig.4 and cat.36]. Such unexpected but always thought-provoking juxtapositions have confirmed our consciously eclectic approach to collecting, and enhanced our appreciation of both prints and drawings as equally intimate and expressive modes of artistic creativity.

Although our collection of prints, drawings and, in smaller numbers, paintings and sculpture is in large part the result of fortunate circumstances – and sometimes even of outright luck – the ensemble nevertheless manages to cohere. This is largely thanks to the common cultural and aesthetic environment in which both native and foreign-born artists were immersed while studying, living and working in France from the late eighteenth century onwards. The works in our collection by artists as diverse as Eugène Delacroix and Édouard Manet, Jacques-Louis David and Paul Cézanne, Honoré Daumier and Fernand Léger, Mary Cassatt and Picasso provide evidence of great differences in individual techniques and styles, as well as of changing artistic and social preoccupations. Yet at the same time they testify to profound affinities, the result of their makers' shared cultural experiences while working in the French capital.

We too were affected by the culture of Paris during the decade we spent in the Latin Quarter close to the Jardin du Luxembourg, just a few blocks from the church of Saint-Sulpice and the Sorbonne [fig.5]. In this period, in contrast to the decades that followed, artistic and literary Paris was still a very small world in which just about everyone knew just about everyone else. It was not unusual to discuss philosophy after a seminar with Merleau-Ponty, hear Juliette Gréco singing in her bedroom through an open window across the street from our kitchen, or have lunch at the restaurant *Chez Denis* with Daniel Kahnweiler, the early champion of Picasso, Braque and the Cubists. On other days one

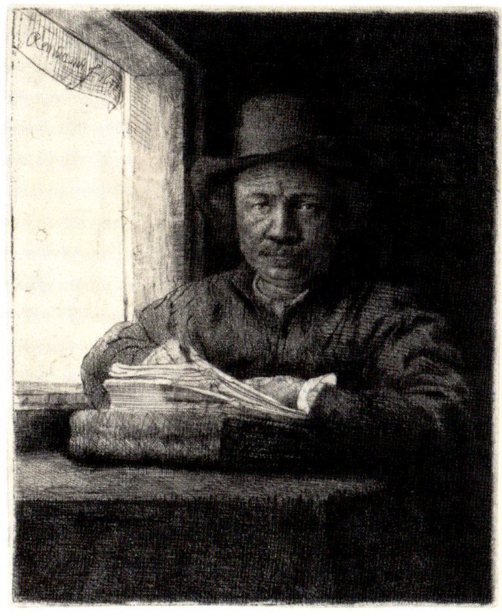

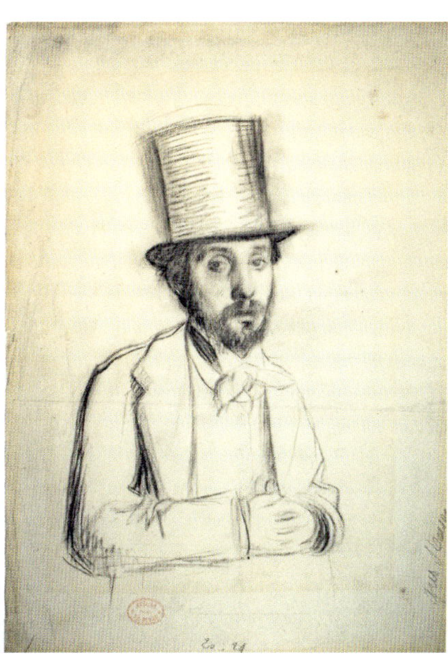

Fig.1 | Albrecht Dürer (1471–1528) *Adam and Eve*, engraving, 1504.

Fig.2 | Pablo Picasso (1881–1973) *Study of Four Nudes*, black crayon on laid paper [cat.57], 1906–7

Fig.3 | Rembrandt Harmensz van Rijn (1606–1669) *Self-Portrait Drawing at a Window,* etching, drypoint and burin, 1648.

Fig.4 | Edgar Degas (1834–1917) *Self Portrait in a Top Hat*, charcoal on tracing paper [cat.36], *c.*1865

might visit Mme Metzinger and her 22 cats on the rue Delambre, or share a glass of wine in the early evening with André and Simone Lhote or Marcel Gromaire in their respective Montparnasse studios. A particularly memorable afternoon in 1961 was spent having tea with Jean Cocteau after we had simply looked up his number in the phone book – such was the ease of contacting even the most well-known artists and writers in Paris at that time. Likewise Stanley remembers the intense conversations he had with Giorgio di Chirico over an unforgettable weekend in the late 1950s. Throughout our time in Paris we benefited from close friendships and passionate discussions about art with many other artists – both those from an older generation, such as the Fauve Béla Czóbel [fig.6] (whom we often visited in his native Hungary as well as saw regularly in Paris) and the Post-Impressionist Louis Neillot, and younger

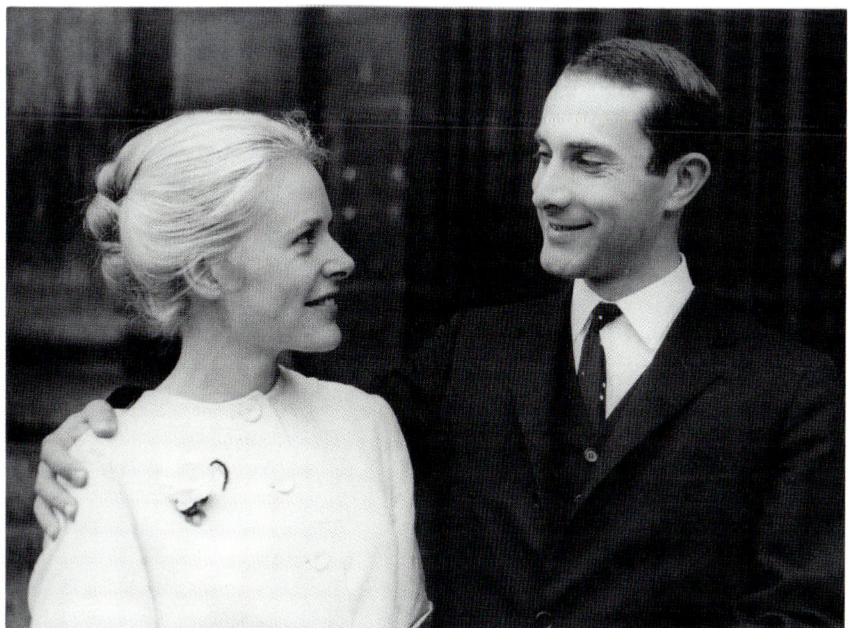

Fig.5 | Ursula and R. Stanley Johnson in Paris in 1960 on their wedding day.

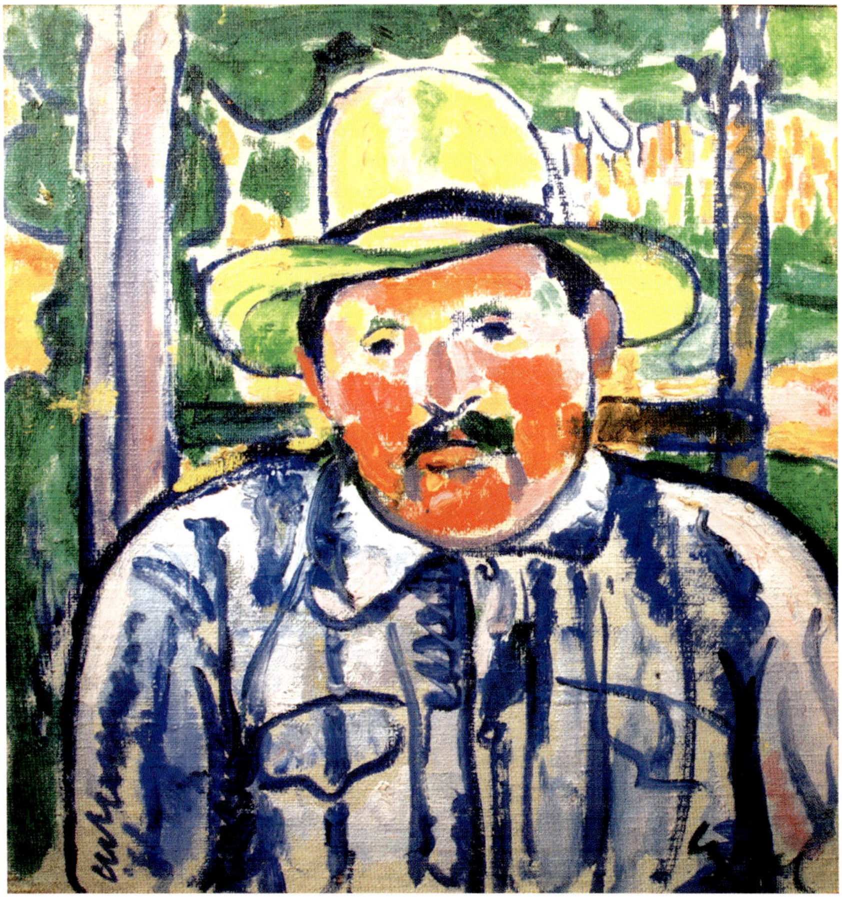

Fig.6 | Béla Czóbel, *Man with a Straw Hat*, oil on canvas, 1906–7.

painters, for example the colourists Paul Guiramand and Albert Zavaro or Duilio Barnabé, who had been Morandi's student in Bologna.

After we became parents we realised that our initial student apartment, a sixth-floor walk-up on the rue des Feuillantines in the *5ième arrondissement*, was too impractical. So we scraped together just enough funds to move across the Jardin du Luxembourg to a small but gracious apartment on the rue Huysmans in the *6ième arrondissement*, only two blocks from Gertrude Stein's former residence. As we settled into the neighbourhood we found ourselves by chance frequenting many of the same haunts that Ernest Hemingway and other leading artists, writers and expatriates had in earlier decades. Only years later could we fully appreciate the rich significance of Hemingway's famous description of life in Paris in the 1920s as a veritable 'moveable feast' of artistic, literary and intellectual offerings. Like Hemingway and others before us, as well as many of our contemporaries, our experiences in Paris fundamentally shaped our lifelong aesthetic preoccupations and, more broadly, our cultural and philosophical outlook.

Europe is not only France, however, and the years in Paris were complemented by postgraduate studies in Vienna, Innsbruck and Perugia, not to mention earlier research undertaken by Ursula in Bonn and Stanley in Mexico City and Lima. To detail the latter's Latin American escapades, not to mention Cold War espionage in circumstances reminiscent of Graham Greene's *The Third Man*, however, would require a separate essay. More relevant to our growing passion for the visual arts was a formative period of several months spent by Stanley in Florence, where he virtually lived in the Uffizi Galleries and Pitti Palace from dawn to dusk. Looking closely and at leisure at the works on display was an extraordinary experience; it provided a unique aesthetic education. But listening to what the visitors, in their various languages, had to say about the paintings proved to be almost as illuminating. Especially fascinating was the gradual realisation that European visitors' opinions tended to conform to the deep-seated cultural attitudes associated with their individual countries of origin. In contrast, visitors from the New World and beyond seemed to be much less predictable in their comments. While the latter may have been more superficial in their analyses in comparison to the more sophisticated Europeans, nevertheless the non-European visitors' sense of spontaneity and open-mindedness often provided refreshing new insights about the old masters. Combining the best of both approaches has remained a constant goal throughout our careers as scholars and collectors.

In bringing together our collection over the decades, we have had some unforgettable experiences. There was, for instance, a memorable afternoon in about 1970 spent with Daniel-Henry Kahnweiler, Picasso's art dealer. He told Stanley that the very next day he was planning to offer 120 Picasso drawings to nine of the most influential art dealers of the day, with each allowed to select five drawings at a time in each round of the proceedings. Stanley told Kahnweiler that it was an enormous privilege to be allowed to choose from such a splendid group of works alongside art dealers such as Eleanore Saidenberg from New York, Ernst Beyeler from Basel, Heinz Berggruen from Paris and Siegfried Rosengart from Lucerne. But as the ninth, youngest and definitely most junior of the group, by the time he, Stanley, was able to select his first set of five drawings the 'best' 40 would have already been taken; he would be left with 'only' the remaining 80 drawings from which to choose. With youthful enthusiasm Stanley pointed out to Kahnweiler how amazing it would be to be able to have first choice of just one work to keep for his own collection. Kahnweiler replied: 'Young man, take any one of the Picasso drawings, but do not tell the other dealers. Take it out of the room and put it behind my desk. But you must promise me two things: first, you will never sell that drawing and secondly, every time you look at it you will tell yourself (and here he broke into English) "What a great guy Kahnweiler was!"' The drawing is still in our collection today and, keeping our promise, we are happy to confirm that, at least in this instance, Kahnweiler was indeed a 'great guy' [cat.111].

Soon after we had moved to our first proper apartment on the rue Huysmans, we discovered the Galerie Bourdon on the nearby boulevard Raspail. This became the source of many wonderful acquisitions by artists such as Léger. As we became not just clients but close friends of the owner, Marcelle Bourdon, we gradually came to realise that she, together with Heinz Berggruen, had the most discerning 'eye' of all the art dealers in the Latin Quarter. Besides art, Mme Bourdon and her husband also loved animals, and there were always half a dozen cats and three or four dogs lounging around the rather ramshackle gallery. We often joined Mme Bourdon and her family for tea on Thursday afternoons. Among the guests there were usually three or four of her nieces and nephews who ungraciously ridiculed the gallery's feline and canine smells, as well as its general disorder. Several decades later the Bourdon collection was sold by the charismatic but famously corrupt auctioneer Guy

Loudmer at the Hôtel Drouot auction house in Paris. The final total of 509 million francs (at the time equivalent to more than $107 million) established a new French auction sale record. But these millions did not end up in the pockets of the discourteous nieces and nephews, since the Bourdons had arranged for the proceeds to be donated to France's animal anti-cruelty society, the Société Protectrice des Animaux (SPA).

One of our most remarkable works by Léger, *The Three Musicians* of 1932, was acquired not from Mme Bourdon, but from Louis Clayeux, one of the great art-dealing personalities of post-war Paris [cat.99]. Clayeux had been director of the Galerie Louis Carré and then of the Galerie Aimé Maeght. Between the two gallery owners it was Carré who had the better eye, but was completely impossible to deal with, whereas Maeght, although a great (if rather arrogant) businessman, seemed totally uninterested in the art itself. Clayeux once told us that he had gone with Maeght to Majorca to visit Joan Miró's *atelier*. Clayeux pointed out to Maeght half a dozen paintings that he thought might be good buys for the gallery. Maeght then asked Clayeux a single question: 'Is Miró important?' 'Very important!' Clayeux replied. Maeght then told Clayeux: 'I am going to take an hour's walk on the beach. When I return, I want you to tell me how much I owe Miró in order to buy his entire studio.' Such relationships were common in the Parisian art world in the post-war period: sensitive, intelligent, knowledgeable figures such as Clayeux, with little financial acumen, paired with ruthless businessmen like Maeght. The latter often failed to appreciate the significance of the art that passed through their hands, but they knew how to succeed in the rough and tumble of the art trade.

A constant worry for both aesthetes and entrepreneurs is the question of authenticity. In 1960 we were inadvertently introduced to the world of fakes and forgeries while spending our honeymoon in Ibiza, at that time a simple and sleepy island bereft of glamour or glitz. There, at a small café, we met the French art dealer Fernand Legros, the Hungarian painter Elmyr de Hory and the American writer Clifford Irving. Unbeknown to us de Hory, one of the greatest art forgers of the twentieth century, was in the process of producing over 1,000 fakes that were then sold by Legros to reputable galleries and private collectors the world over. After the fraud was uncovered in the mid-1960s Irving wrote a biography of de Hory, appropriately titled *Fake,* only to become notorious himself a few years later for publishing the forged autobiography of the reclusive multi-millionaire Howard Hughes. All three men – Legros, de Hory and Irving – spent time in prison. But just two years after our first encounter with the trio, and well before any of them had been unmasked, Legros invited us to visit his luxurious apartment on the avenue Henri Martin in Neuilly on the outskirts of Paris, a property that had previously belonged to the king of Morocco. The walls of the apartment were covered with works that at first glance appeared to be by modern masters such as Henri Matisse, Picasso, Raoul Dufy and Amadeo Modigliani – but when seen one beside the other it was clear that all been executed by the same hand and were thus obviously fakes. While de Hory's artistic skills were clearly crucial to the long-running scam, it was the utterly charming but extremely shrewd Legros' idea to produce fake authentication certificates, fake academic references and even entire fake books with colour reproductions depicting the fake art works he was offering for sale to unwitting dupes. Needless to say, while we enjoyed Legros' cordial hospitality, we were never tempted to fall into his trap.

Sourcing beautiful, important and, of course, authentic works for our own collection as well as for the family gallery in Stanley's native Chicago – an enterprise that was essentially a means of financing our art collecting habit – was an ongoing challenge, especially after we relocated to the US in the momentous year of 1968 with our two young children. Although the move was supposed to be temporary, family responsibilities eventually meant that Paris could no longer be our principal home. However, we spent many happy months each year visiting friends and relatives throughout Europe, as well as making shorter trips across the Atlantic specifically to acquire works of art.

One memorable example of the latter occurred in 1972. While planning a gallery exhibition of Matisse's prints, we decided that the group of nearly 40 works we had assembled was missing one final piece, the famous lithograph of 1925 known as the *Grande odalisque à la culotte bayadère* (*Large Odalisque with Striped Pantaloons*). Unbeknown to us, a certain Isidore 'Izzy' Cohen, who had made his fortune in New York's garment district, had just opened a gallery and was also planning a show of Matisse's prints. By chance an impression of the *Grande odalisque* came up for sale at the Hôtel Drouot, with an estimate of $5,000–$10,000. Both Stanley and Cohen flew to Paris to bid on the lithograph and, as luck would have it, each decided to stay at the Hôtel du Pont Royal. They ended up sharing a taxi to the Hôtel Drouot. In the taxi, Cohen demanded: 'Johnson, what are you going to buy in this auction?' Stanley replied: 'With people as rich as you, Mr Cohen, at the auction, I don't think I will be able to buy anything at all.' Cohen then announced that he had come to buy what he called 'The Pants' by Matisse, the same work that Stanley wanted to acquire. At the auction, Cohen sat in the first row and Stanley in the last. In between was Klaus Perls, the great Matisse specialist from Los Angeles. The bidding between Perls and Cohen went to $20,000, twice the upper estimate. The crowd gasped when the bidding stopped in favour of Cohen. At that moment, Stanley suddenly raised his hand and bid $21,000. After the gavel had banged three times in rapid succession, the print was his. Cohen stood up and turned around to see who had outfoxed him in the final crucial seconds. Realising it was Stanley, his erstwhile taxi companion, he turned purple with rage. Perls likewise lost control and began shouting in French: 'Johnson est fou! Tout le monde de Chicago est fou!'[2] For the rest of his life Cohen never spoke another word to us, and for the following five years neither did Perls. Although we kept the print in our own collection for many decades, we eventually decided to sell it to fund other, even more enticing acquisitions. Suffice it to say that the return on our initial outlay confirmed that the price we had paid had not been 'fou' at all. But as this incident demonstrates, emotions in the apparently genteel world of French art collecting can sometimes run very high indeed.

A much less fraught post-auction encounter took place just over a decade later in 1984 at Sotheby's in London, at the sale of the collection of Kenneth Clark, the famous art historian, National Gallery director and author-narrator of the landmark television series *Civilisation*. One of the drawings we bought from Lord Clark's collection was Cézanne's *In the Countryside* of about 1870 [cat.49], a work undoubtedly inspired by Manet's iconic painting *Le déjeuner sur l'herbe*. Just as noteworthy, however, is Jean-François Millet's *Shepherdess Seated on a Rock* of 1856, an outstanding example of the artist's shimmering drawing technique applied to one of his favoured rural subjects [cat.21]. The work's significance – as well as its enticing aesthetic appeal – was confirmed for us by the fact that immediately after the auction Lord Clark's son came over to tell us that his father had always been 'a Millet man', and that this particular Millet was the greatest work by the artist that his father had been able to acquire over a lifetime of collecting.

Another one of our favourite drawings likewise has a prestigious British provenance. In the late 1970s our friend Juliet Wilson-Bareau, the well-known Goya and Manet expert, was working on the *catalogue raisonné* of Henry Moore's drawings. Given her close access to Moore, she arranged for Stanley to visit the sculptor at his home in Much Hadham in Hertfordshire. The first thing that struck him about Moore's living room was his collection of Inuit carvings on display, which had obviously had an enormous impact on his own sculpture. After a leisurely conversation with the amiable artist, the rather arthritic Moore asked Stanley to go upstairs and bring down the painting hanging over his bed. This turned out to be Cézanne's famous *Three Bathers*, a work inspired by Rubens that depicts a group of nude figures, one seen from the front and two from behind. Moore then announced that he wanted to show his visitor 'something special' in his studio: the *maquette* for his own bronze entitled *Three Bathers after Cézanne*. The *maquette* was exhibited on a turntable, which Moore slowly spun, exclaiming: 'Now we can finally see what Cézanne's bathers look like from the front.'

While navigating his way around Moore's bedroom, Stanley had spotted a small but extraordinary drawing of 1822–3 by David, *An Old Man and A Young Woman* [cat.6]. He brought this work down to discuss with Moore as well. It was thus a singular pleasure for us to be able to acquire the drawing from Moore's estate after his death in 1986 and, like the sculptor, also to hang it in our bedroom. It was there that the drawing caught the eye of another friend, the eminent scholar and member of the *Académie Française* Marc Fumaroli. Inspired not only by the beauty of the drawing, but perhaps also by the fine champagne we shared while examining the image with him and two visiting curators, Ger Luijten from the Rijksmuseum and Martin Royalton-Kisch from the British Museum, Fumaroli decided to devote an entire lecture at the Art Institute of Chicago to this one sheet.

Another visitor to our home some years earlier was Françoise Viatte, curator of drawings at the Louvre. She was accompanied by Harold Joachim, curator of prints and drawings at the Art Institute, who knew our collection well and had become a kind of mentor to us as a fellow aficionado of works on paper. The lunch we enjoyed together was a pleasant gathering of like minds until the moment when Viatte, curious to see our entire collection, walked into our young daughter's bedroom. When the normally composed Viatte spotted a charcoal drawing by Roger de La Fresnaye, *Le cuirassier* of 1910–11 [cat.60], she literally shouted: 'You have no right to have that drawing in your daughter's bedroom!' 'Why not?' we asked. To which she replied: 'Because de La Fresnaye is one of France's greatest Cubists, his greatest painting is undoubtedly *Le cuirassier* in the Musée d'Art Moderne, and this is the greatest study for that painting. This drawing should be in the Louvre, not in your child's room!'

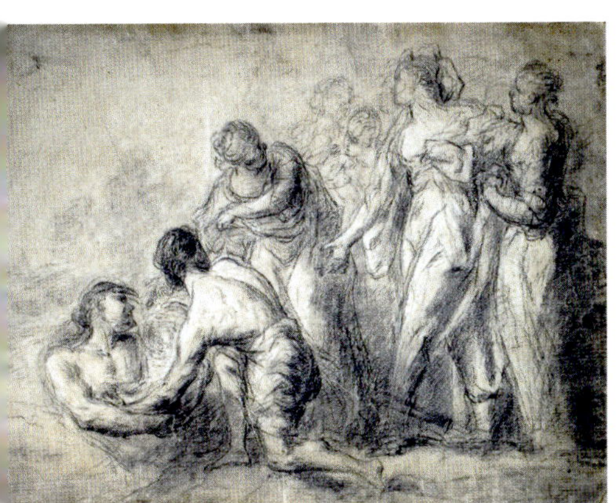

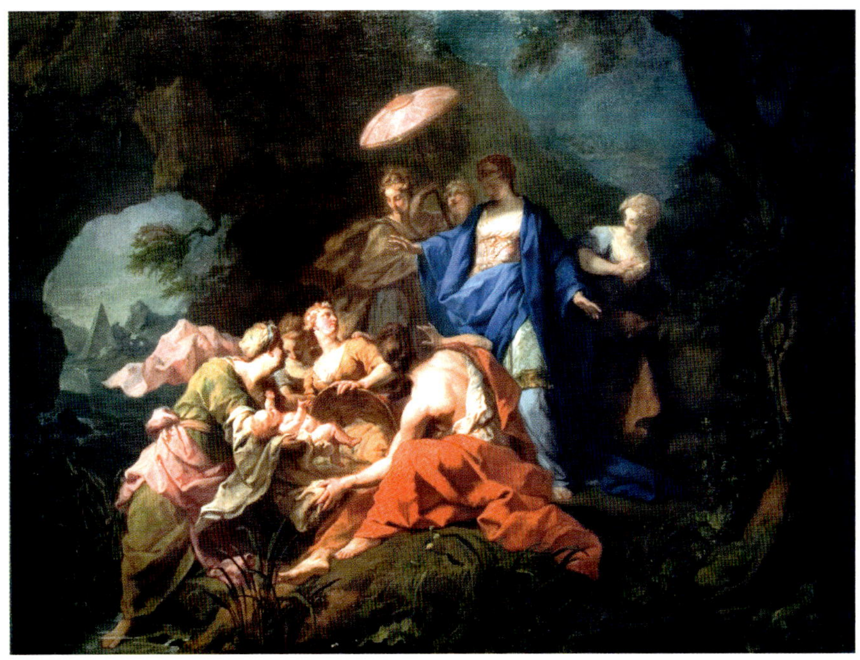

Fig.7 | Jean Restout the younger, *Study for The Discovery of the Infant Moses*, charcoal drawing with white bodycolour on darkened off-white paper, *c.*1730

Fig.8 | Jean Restout the younger, *The Discovery of the Infant Moses*, oil on canvas, 1730.

We told her that the Louvre had had the opportunity some decades earlier to acquire the drawing for itself at the same auction at which we had bought it, as young students still living in Paris. Viatte was somewhat placated by our offer to lend the work to the Louvre for several months, but we made it very clear that the drawing's home for the foreseeable future would remain our daughter's bedroom.

A bedroom was also the site for an unexpected attribution made during a visit to Chicago by an old friend and fellow student from our days in Paris, Pierre Rosenberg, who by then had become director of the Louvre. The painting in question was hanging in the main bedroom of our home, an imposing canvas depicting the Old Testament story of the discovery of the infant Moses in a basket made of reeds [fig.8]. Unable to afford paintings by established old masters, the canvas had come into our possession after Stanley had spotted it in about 1965 at the back of a second-hand frame shop in Paris on the rue du Cherche-Midi, unloved, unattributed and completely overlooked by the Parisian art establishment. Stanley, however, was convinced that it was the work of an eighteenth-century painter from the Rouen School and bought it for a song. Imagine our delight when Rosenberg confidently confirmed that its author was none other than Jean Restout the younger, a painter from Rouen who had been the subject of his own doctoral thesis. Even more unexpectedly, a few years later, we stumbled across a drawing that was clearly a study for the painting [fig.7], thus enabling us to reunite preparatory sketch and finished canvas for the first time in nearly three centuries. Without an element of luck and a good 'eye,' however, it was almost impossible to acquire high-quality paintings by pre-modern masters even in the 1960s, let alone in more recent decades.

Luck – or rather, perhaps, coincidence – also played a role in a much more recent acquisition, Manet's exquisite drawing of a mirabelle plum [cat.27]. The work was accompanied by a punning dedication to a fashionable Parisian beauty, Isabelle Lemonnier: 'à mademoiselle Isabelle cette prune de mirabelle

belle.'[3] In 2011 Ursula had spotted a very similar drawing, evidently from the same series and also dedicated to the same Isabelle, in a major Manet exhibition at the Musée d'Orsay. Enthralled by the sketch and amused by the fact that the dedicatee's first name was the same as that of one of her young granddaughters, Ursula bought a postcard of the drawing and sent it off. Then, just one week later and completely out of the blue, the drawing now in our collection was suddenly offered to us for sale. Clearly we must have been fated to become its happy owners.

Both as students in Paris and, later, returning visitors, the city's bookshops were often as much of a lure for us as its museums and galleries. One of our favourite *librairies* was *La Hune*, founded by the enlightened editor and art collector Bernard Gheerbrandt. It was located for many decades on the boulevard Saint-Germain, where it stayed open until midnight to satisfy the cravings of the most ardent bibliophiles. So it was particularly meaningful for us to acquire one of only two proof impressions of Jacques Villon's etched portrait of his brother Marcel Duchamp from the sale of Gheerbrandt's collection [cat.56]. The print had been made in 1904 when Marcel had joined his older brother (born Émile Duchamp before changing his name to Jacques Villon) in Paris to attend art school at the *Académie Julian*. Villon eventually donated one proof to the Bibliothèque nationale, while Mme Duchamp sold the proof given to Marcel to the owner of *La Hune* before it came, in time, to us.

Our collecting has not only been a way of maintaining contact with old acquaintances, but also of forging new friendships. In 2005, for instance, we were asked to lend a number of our Degas drawings, including two splendid pastels, to the Milwaukee Art Museum to complement an exhibition of all 73 of the artist's bronzes [cat.44 and cat.45]. At the opening we met the co-author of the *catalogue raisonné* of Degas's bronzes, the delightful Anne Pingeot, at the time curator of sculpture at the Musée d'Orsay and previously at the Louvre. We formed an immediate bond and invited her to see our own small collection of French bronzes during her stay in the US. What was initially planned as a brief visit to our home turned into a full day perusing our collection of French art. This was followed by a walk through Chicago's Lincoln Park, during which she provided us with expert commentary about the French foundries that had cast many of the late nineteenth-century bronzes of famous historical figures dotted around the park. On subsequent visits to Europe, in our ongoing quest to acquire art by both old and more modern masters, having dinner with Pingeot and other friends, both old and new, has helped us to stay in touch with the Parisian world of arts and letters that continues to beguile us.

In building our collection over many decades, we have prided ourselves on assessing potential acquisitions in a cool, calm and reasoned manner. Art historical considerations are always at the forefront: the significance of the artist in question, the importance of a particular work within his or her *oeuvre*, and the technical, formal, iconographic and socio-historical characteristics of a specific object, alongside its condition and provenance. A work's rarity – and thus the likelihood (or not) of being able to acquire something similar in the future – also has to be considered, and then cross-checked with what is possible given our means. As our collection has grown, the desirability – one could even say the apparent necessity – of each new acquisition seems increasingly influenced by the sense of particular lacunae lurking within the ensemble of works we already own. An expanding collection such as ours thus gradually takes on a life of its own, appearing over time to determine from within itself decisions about new acquisitions, with the inevitably futile aim of trying to achieve 'completeness.'

Even as we have strived to develop an 'objective' set of criteria for deciding which works to acquire, like many other collectors we have also been subject to sudden, passionate and sometimes almost irrational attractions to individual works of art. This is especially true for objects that strike us as exceptionally beautiful or, in other cases, magnificently sublime – although what exactly makes a work 'beautiful' or 'sublime' is something that even the most astute philosophers and eminent psychologists have been unable to define objectively. As the epigraph by Antoine de Saint-Exupéry at the beginning of this essay suggests, the most deeply felt reactions to works of art are often led by the heart, not the head – 'On ne voit bien qu'avec le coeur'.[4] This has certainly been true in our case.

The role played by the heart is also evident in the formation of truly private collections such as ours when compared to those developed by public institutions. Museums often strive to be encyclopedic, while private collections, even if sometimes very extensive in one area or another, are not so constrained – nor are they usually capable of achieving such a lofty objective. The holdings of a typical museum, formed by a combination of private donations, public initiatives and individual curatorial decisions, are ultimately intended to be constituted for the edification of the general public. Private collections such as ours, in contrast, can be assembled for purely individual pleasure and even idiosyncratically, normally with no external obligations or constraints beyond those of space and financial limitations. Ideally such collections need not be concerned with changing tastes and fashions, which is not necessarily the case for museums accountable to the public of the day either through their charters and organisational structures or through direct governmental support and management. In contrast, a private collection such as ours can be driven by the heart as much as by the head.

The legendary Dutch collector and art historian Frits Lugt once wrote that 'a collector is a constructor'. True enough! Once a building has been completed, however, the construction phase comes to an end. In the case of even a modest collection such as ours, there is no end to the building work: there are always new and exciting additions to be made, carefully and with due consideration, but also with genuine passion. To be able to share the results of our scholarly interest in, and heartfelt passion for, the visual arts with the wider public by exhibiting that part of our collection devoted to art created in France will undoubtedly provide us and, we hope, those who view the works we have gathered together with new and unexpected pleasures and sources of inspiration.

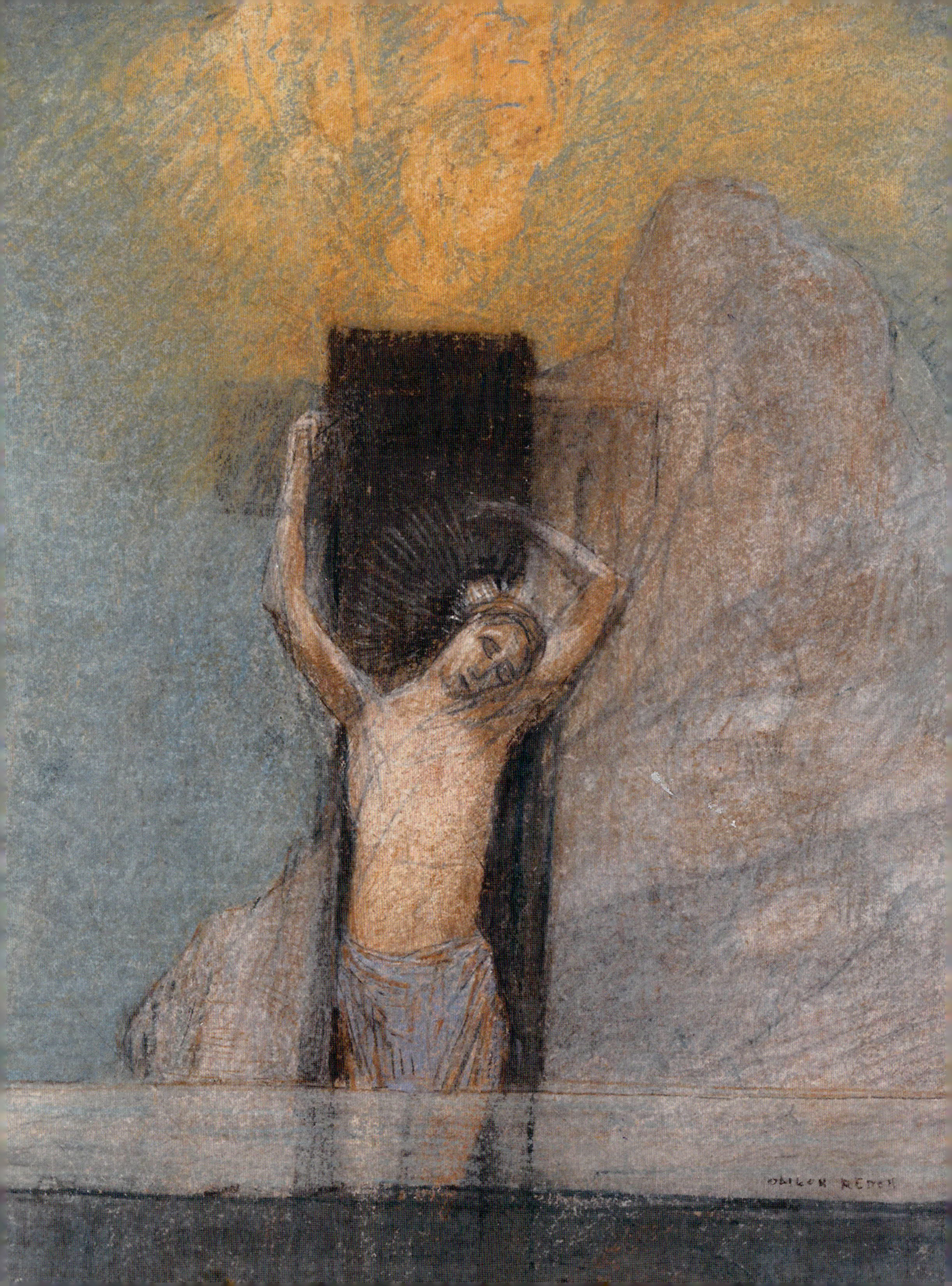
ODILON REDON

THE ART OF DRAWING IN FRANCE: FROM NEO-CLASSICISM TO CUBISM

Jon Whiteley

The French nineteenth century was a heroic age in the history of drawing. An unprecedented demand for images that depended on the art of drawing, from popular prints to large public murals, generated drawings in incalculable quantities. As anyone who has spent time browsing through portfolios of drawings will know, this demand produced a great deal of mediocrity, but it also inspired thousands of drawings of wonderful quality – not only by artists who are now famous, but also by many who have fallen into oblivion. Many of the best draughtsmen of the period have been written out of the history of nineteenth-century art because their work does do not conform to the idea of the century as the age of the avant-garde. The world of nineteenth-century French drawing, despite much recent work, is still, to a large extent, a *terra incognita*.

The diversity of nineteenth-century French drawing makes it difficult to say much of value about its character except to note that most of the artists of any interest in this period had received at least a brief training in a well-established tradition of preparatory drawing. Artists were instructed to prepare their paintings through a series of studies in pen, chalk or pencil, beginning with a number of rough compositional drafts [fig.9] and progressing through life drawings [cats 13 and 14] and drapery studies [fig.10] to a finished composition. Those who, like Gustave Courbet, worked directly on canvas without making preliminary studies were rare, at least before the emergence of Impressionism. Even then, traditional preparatory drawing remained the basis of most of the figurative art produced in France until the 1930s.

Although the age of Impressionism is associated with the triumph of colour, it was widely believed at the time that drawing was more important. 'If I had to put a sign above my door,' Jean-Auguste-Dominique Ingres declared, 'I would write "School of Drawing" and I am sure that I would produce painters.' This belief, originating in the studios of the Florentine Renaissance and reasserted by the followers of Nicolas Poussin at the end of the seventeenth century, was revived in a wave of Poussinism at the end of the eighteenth century and remained in force in some influential quarters throughout much of the nineteenth century. It was, however, a tiresome argument because it set up a false distinction between drawing and painting, and it only survived because, in practice, most artists based their paintings on preliminary drawings and most students had to acquire thorough drawing skills in pen or chalk before they were allowed to touch a brush. In an age that liked to divide politicians into left and right and artists into Romantics and Classicists (with a large 'Juste Milieu' to deal with the majority in between), artists had to be either draughtsmen or colourists. In reality, most artists were both. In a review of Marie-Elisabeth Cavé's drawing manual (see cat.10), Eugène Delacroix cited with approval her statement that an education in drawing was as essential to an artist as an education in grammar was to a writer. Ingres, the champion of drawing, would not have disagreed. Ideas about the relative merits of drawing and painting differed, but the fundamental importance of drawing was widely accepted by painters in all camps.

Detail of cat.48:
Odilon Redon 1840–1916
Christ on the Cross (Christ en Croix)

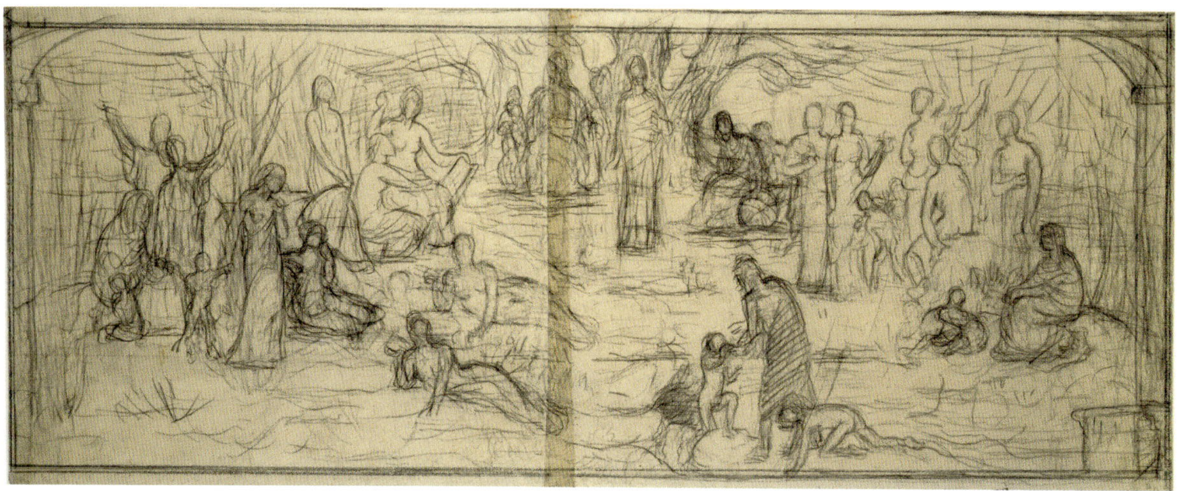

Fig.9 | Pierre-Cécile Puvis de Chavannes (1824–98) *Allegory of the Sorbonne: L'Eloquence et la Poésie*

Black chalk on two sheets of tracing paper, joined vertically, laid down on card, WA1942.106

DRAWING IN THE ART SCHOOL

For the great majority of art students, instruction was based on the study of the nude model, posed under the strong, steady light of a studio lamp. This allowed young figure painters to acquire the necessary skills in modelling the human form that they needed in their future careers. In many cases, particularly in the early years of the century, the contrast of light and shadow caused by the use of the academic lamp predisposed them to search for themes that involved striking effects of chiaroscuro. A full moon or a bolt of lightning provided a convenient excuse as well as a touch of fashionable sensationalism.

Drawings from the nude model, known as 'academies' because they were so closely associated with an academic education, represented the final stage in a training that began with copying prints, followed by drawing from the plaster cast and ending with the live model. Artists at an advanced stage were permitted to paint from the life, although the practice of making academies was based fundamentally on drawing. Until 1863 the Paris School of Fine Arts was little more than a drawing school based on a life class supervised by a rota of Academicians. This was balanced by the existence of private studios where techniques of painting were taught after instruction in drawing had been completed. Some private studios gave more instruction in painting than others. Ingres's pupils received notoriously little, whereas Thomas Couture's pupils were given extensive instruction in handling paint. Both artists, however, believed that drawing was the foundation of art, and pupils in both studios had to master the art of life drawing before moving to the painting class.

Academic life studies, made as exercises, were generally drawn in black chalk, laboriously hatched to create a sense of solid form. From the 1860s the use of charcoal became increasingly common in drawings of this kind and, because a stick of charcoal is a much softer and more friable implement than chalk, rubbing with the finger or with a stump became the normal means of modelling. These exercises were quite different from the life studies made in preparation for a composition, which were usually drawn more rapidly in pencil or black chalk with strong contours and, as a rule, less shading [cats 13 and 14]. Details such as draperies, finely modelled in chalk or ink, hands and heads, expressing a gesture or an emotion in keeping with the theme, were studied separately and added to the figures at a later stage [cat.3].

Nineteenth-century artists owed a large debt to the artists of the preceding century. This has been partly concealed by the contrast that is often made between the bravura of Jean-Honoré Fragonard [cat.1] and the clarity of drawing practised by his successors in the 1790s. In terms of drawing, the disappearance of red chalk, extensively used by figure painters and landscapists in the eighteenth century, marks a greater watershed. Artificial graphite, patented by the artist Nicolas Conté in 1795, provided an alternative that was quickly taken up. It did not have the warmth and painterly touch that had made red chalk so attractive to earlier generations, but it had qualities of its own that appealed to the artists of the 1790s. The graphite pencil is an inexpensive, portable and flexible instrument; it can be sharpened to a point and is ideal for drawing contours as well as the small details that are less legible when drawn with chalk or pen. Black chalk remained the favourite implement for life drawing in the Paris School of Fine Arts, but graphite became the tool of choice in many private studios. It suited a late eighteenth-century taste for outline and was used extensively for portrait drawings. Together with pen and ink, the graphite pencil became a standard implement for landscape artists.

The new rigour in late eighteenth-century drawing has often been linked to the influence of Jacques-Louis David. Both friends and enemies made much of his role in overturning the principles and techniques of the immediate past, although he inherited his manner of drawing and the purposes to which it was put from his master, Joseph Vien, and, more remotely, from Vien's master, Charles Natoire, both of whom worked within a well-entrenched academic tradition. David was moreover, contrary to what was often said by hostile critics, a liberal teacher who encouraged students to build upon their strengths. As a result, while several of his students took their cue from his manner of drawing, his studio produced a remarkable diversity of drawing styles. David was himself an insatiable draughtsman, but he rarely drew for the sake of drawing. His many notebooks and numerous figure studies were

Fig.10 | Henri Lehmann (1814–1882) *Costume Study with two separate Studies of the Sleeves and one of the lower Drapery*
Black crayon on off-white paper, WA1985.199

Fig.11 | Jacques-Louis David (1748–1825) *Youth standing by a Woman playing a Lyre and a Separate Study of an Embracing Couple (after the Antique)*
Black chalk and grey wash on white paper, laid down on a sheet of stiff greenish paper, WA1995.225

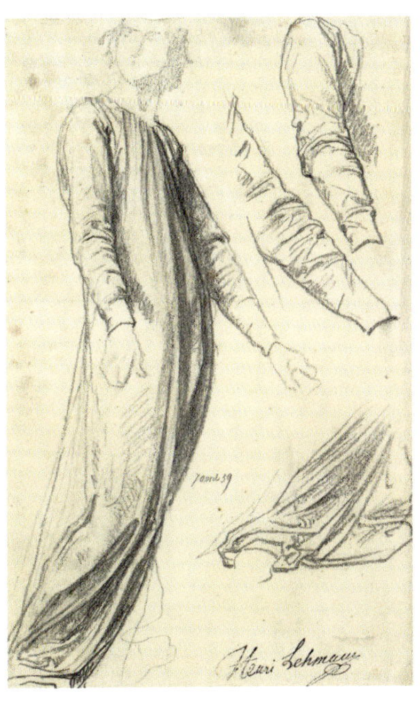

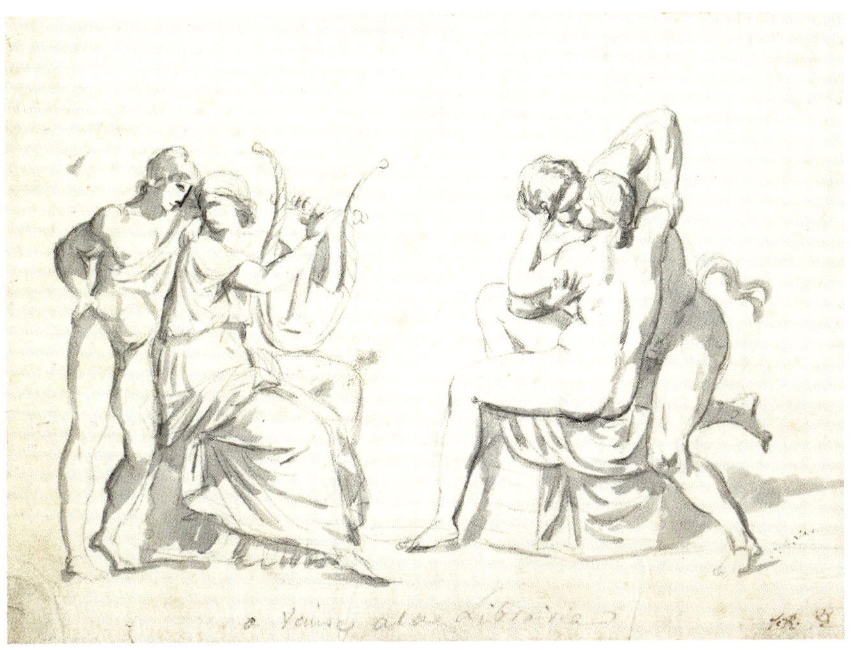

made for a practical purpose, to record and to document the material that he needed for his compositions [fig.11]. In this respect David's work was limited by comparison with the abundant and varied work of François-André Vincent, his greatest rival, or of his pupil Anne-Louis Girodet [cat.3]. It was only from 1816 to 1825, in his last years in Brussels, with more time on his hands, that David took up drawing as an independent form of art, employing his skill as a painter of *têtes d'expression* to create a series of heads in dense black chalk, drawn from his imagination and sometimes bizarrely and arbitrarily combined. These odd *capriccios*, touched with the melancholy of exile, may not be David's most attractive drawings, but they are among his most deeply felt [cat.6].

The demand for drawings among collectors was well established in the eighteenth century and many drawings were made specifically for this market. The disappearance of wealthy collectors in the French Revolution might have led to a falling away in the production of drawings for sale, but in the event the opposite occurred, as painters who could not sell their paintings as easily as before turned to drawings as an alternative. The aging Vien, having lost his patrons, began to specialise in drawings while a number of talented younger artists, including Fragonard's son, Alexandre-Evariste, earned a livelihood by designing for the decorative arts.

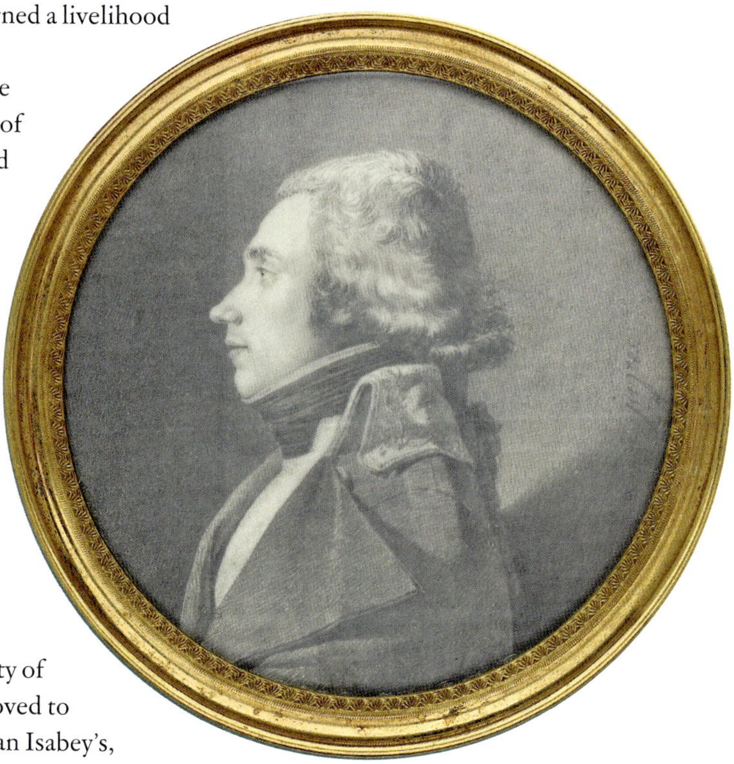

Fig.12 | Jean-Auguste-Dominique Ingres (1780–1867) *Portrait Head of a Man in Profile*

Graphite on smooth, thin white paper, WA1986.43

Portraits, both full-length and head and shoulders, were among the commonest of commissioned drawings. Many of those made between the 1790s and *c.*1815 are characterised by the use of dense black chalk or wash, stumped, stippled and heightened with added white. This fashion was linked at the time to the popularity of mezzotints or prints in the 'English manner', as they were known in France. The taste for these portraits, led by the miniaturist Jean-Baptiste Isabey [cat.2], was shared by Isabey's colleagues at David's studio, Pierre Révoil [cat.5], Fleury François Richard and Ingres, and by many others outside the studio whose work, unless signed, is often difficult to attribute.

Portraits of this type had gone out of fashion by the beginning of the Restoration. By 1806 Ingres had already abandoned the dense manner found in several of his early portrait drawings [fig.12] for a greater lightness and rapidity of touch. The portrait drawings made by him after he had moved to Rome were less time-consuming and more economical than Isabey's, and were much imitated by his pupils. Unlike his painted portraits where heads, costume and accessories are painted with equal care, Ingres' portrait drawings concentrate upon the head, using a soft graphite to mark the darker notes and finer details, while the costume is more summary and the background, if there is one, is lightly indicated [fig.13].

The use of pen, brush, wash and white body colour, extensively used in the studios of David and his rivals in the late eighteenth and early nineteenth centuries, continued in academic circles during the Restoration, but was applied with a freer and more painterly touch. It was a technique favoured by Jean Alaux, Léon Cogniet, Victor Schnetz, Théodore Géricault [cat.7], Antoine Thomas and others, a group of young artists in Rome who exploited its expressive possibilities. It was also well suited to the tonal qualities of lithography and continued in use, in a less dramatic manner, in the drawings that Emile Wattier, Eugène Devéria and Tony Johannot prepared for the print market in the 1830s and 40s.

The drawings made by Géricault for *The Raft of the Medusa*, beginning with a series of dramatic compositions in dark wash and white gouache and continuing through dozens of individual figure studies drawn in black chalk and in pen and ink, are the clearest evidence of his debt to the tradition of drawing in which he was instructed by Pierre-Narcisse Guérin: not that one could easily mistake one of Géricault's energetic figures for one by Guérin, but the underlying principles are identical. The admiration felt for these drawings by Delacroix, who posed for one of the studies and copied several, was shared by a number of artists in his circle. Ary Scheffer, Paul Delaroche and Horace Vernet, for a time, drew in the lively manner with pen and wash [fig.14] practised by Géricault and his contemporaries before they abandoned it for a neater, more linear and less emphatic style in the 1830s. The development towards a less expressive manner corresponded to a change that is also visible in contemporary painting. The change, at the time, was attributed to the example of Ingres, although he was only one of several influences that contributed to this shift. Contact with the German Nazarenes in Rome was certainly a factor. By the late 1830s only Delacroix had resisted the tendency among this group of painters towards a neater and more descriptive type of drawing.

The qualities of preparatory drawings anticipate the finished work. An artist such as Ingres, who emphasised contours in drawings, did the same when

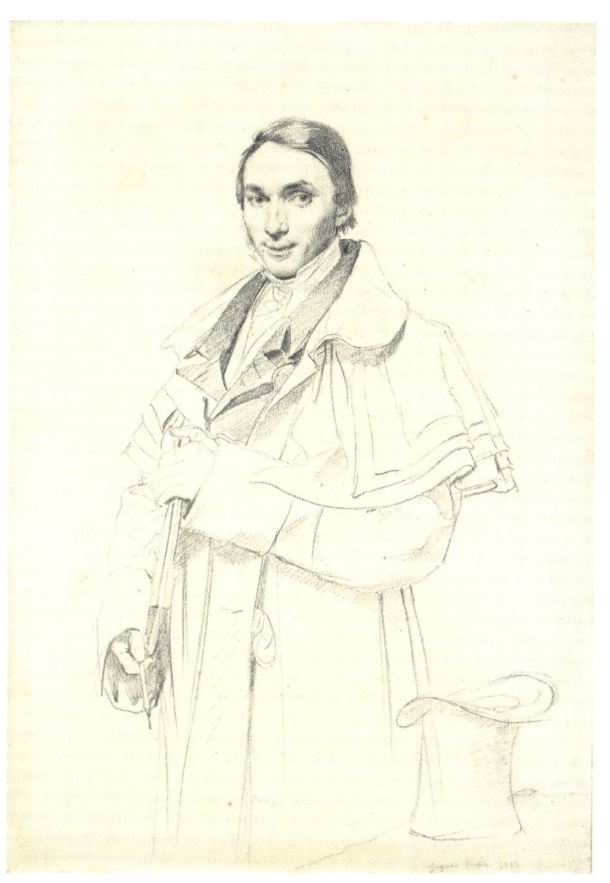

Fig.13 | Jean-Auguste-Dominique Ingres (1780–1867) *Three-quarter-length Portrait of Jean-François-Antoine Forest*
Graphite on medium weight, slightly discoloured, fine-textured white wove paper, WA1936.223

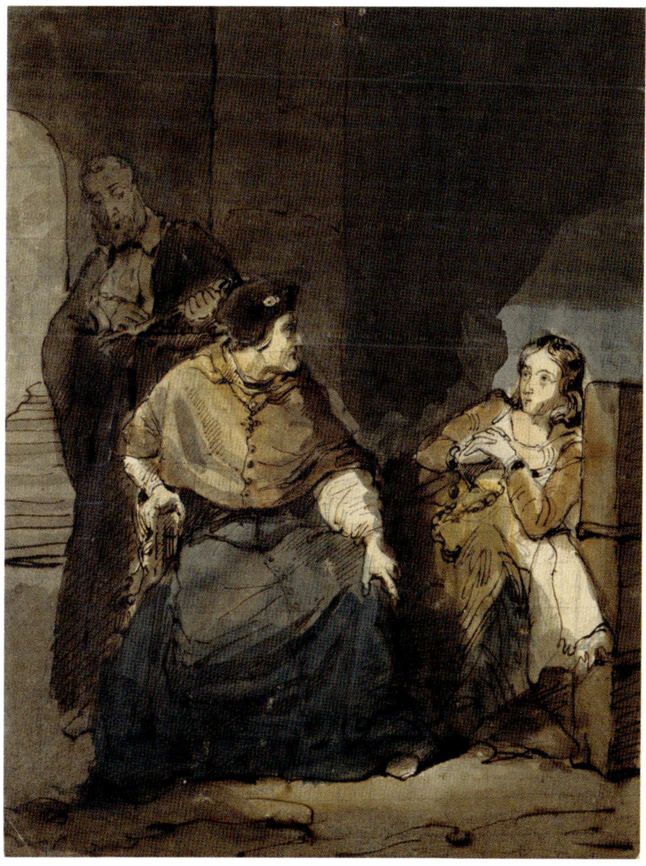

Fig.14 | Paul (Hippolyte) Delaroche (1797–1856) *Joan of Arc interrogated in Prison by Henry Beaufort, Cardinal Bishop of Winchester*
Watercolour with pen and black ink over graphite, squared in graphite, WA2001.165

using paint. Delaroche and his father-in-law Horace Vernet, who relinquished the relative freedom of their earliest paintings for greater polish, did likewise in their drawings, whereas Delacroix, who painted with a greater breadth, drew with a corresponding freedom. From the distance of over a century, the differences between these groups seem less extreme than they appeared at the time. In a revival of the old quarrel between the *Poussinistes* and the *Rubénistes,* Ingres and Delacroix were cast in opposing roles, despite the fact that, apart from obvious differences, both artists were working in variations of the same tradition. The artist with whom Delacroix was most at odds was not Ingres but Courbet - who, like Caravaggio, painted directly from the life with little or no preparatory drawing and with a crudity that mocked the cultivated effects of contemporary art. It was not, however, Courbet's direct manner of painting that shocked Delacroix, but rather the lack of '*disegno*', in Giorgio Vasari's sense of the word - the idea born in the imagination of the artist and given life in a series of preparatory drawings.

Delacroix, unlike Delaroche, had few pupils and, while his paintings became a model for many Salon painters, his influence on the course of French drawing was limited. Théodore Chassériau, an early convert, turned from Ingres to Delacroix in the 1840s, painting with a fluency that was in part inspired by Delacroix [cat.16]. His drawings also have a nervous vitality, particularly evident in his lithographs, that owes something to Delacroix's example. The influence of Ingres, however, is never far from the surface [cat.15], particularly in his portrait drawings [fig.15].

The study of nature and the rejection of convention that guided Ingres' approach to teaching drawing were identical to David's, although Ingres was a

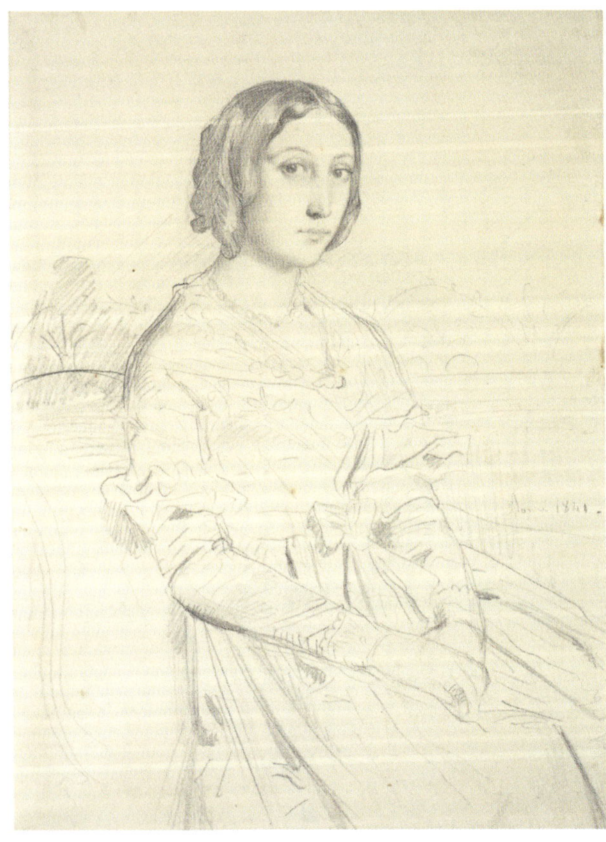

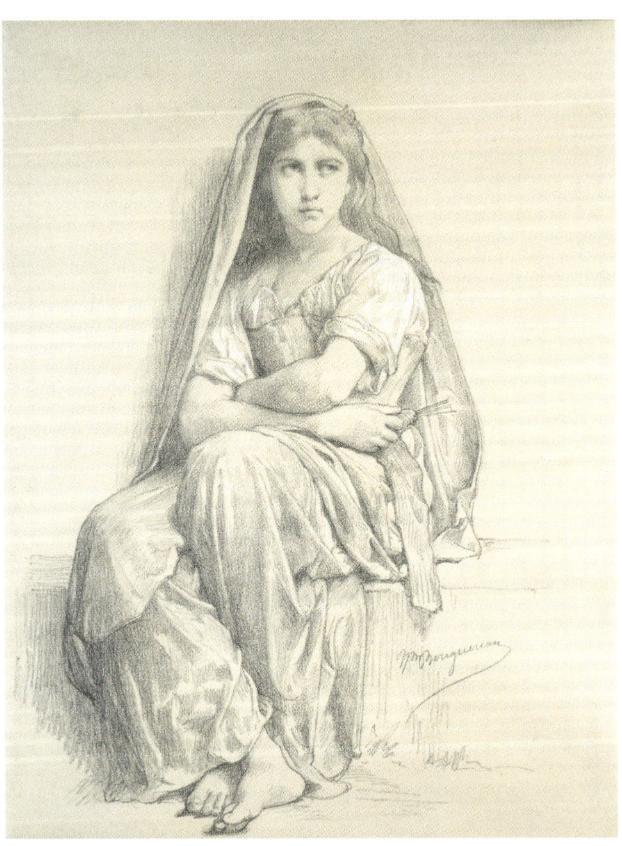

far less liberal teacher than his master. While it is difficult to identify a type of drawing that can be described as particularly 'Davidian', the impact of Ingres in forming the character of drawings by his pupils and followers is inescapable. A strong sense of line, extending from his immediate pupils to Degas and Art Nouveau, formed a major strand in the evolution of French drawing through the second half of the century.

The large part given to Ingres and Delacroix in standard accounts of French drawing tends to diminish the importance of the mainstream that was dominated by pupils from the larger teaching studios, chiefly those of Antoine-Jean Gros, Michel Martin Drolling, Léon Cogniet and François Picot – all of whom trained several generations of outstanding draughtsmen. Their record in producing Rome Prize winners indicates the importance placed in these studios on an academic programme of preparatory drawing that accurately targeted the qualities that guaranteed success. By way of contrast Couture's pupils, instructed in their master's individual manner, failed to gain a single prize. The more conventional instruction offered at the other studios explains a tendency among the students to produce neatly outlined figure drawings, carefully modelled from the live model, sometimes lightly idealised, in preparation for paintings that ranged across subjects of daily life, history, religion, mythology and allegory. This was particularly evident among the students of Picot who, following the death of Gros in 1835, became more successful than all others in securing the prize. William-Adolphe Bouguereau's immaculately finished pencil drawings, so closely linked to the related painting that it is sometimes difficult to distinguish between a preparatory study and an autograph repetition, represent the *nec plus ultra* of this type of drawing [fig.16].

Fig.15 | Théodore Chassériau (1819–56) *Portrait of a Young Woman, seated three-quarters to left*
Graphite on white wove paper, laid down on blue card within a line of black ink, a strip of gold ink, two lines of black ink, and an outer band of grey wash, WA1941.154

Fig.16 | William-Adophe Bouguereau (1825–1905) *Girl in Peasant Costume, seated, Arms folded, holding a Ball of Wool and Knitting Needles in her right Hand*
Graphite on fine-textured cream paper, WA1966.72.2

DRAWING LANDSCAPE

Because landscape formed the setting for many biblical and historical compositions, academic masters from Natoire to Charles Gleyre encouraged their students to study in the open air. Landscape painters, however, did not always feel the need to study in an academic studio. Jean-Baptiste Deperthes put the case in his influential *Theory of Landscape*, published in 1818:

> *It is not in the confines of a room, by the uncertain light of a lamp or semi-daylight, in front of an inanimate plaster or motionless model, that the landscapist seeks initiation into the deepest secrets of his art. His studio has no limits but the horizon, its dome is the vault of heaven, and its light comes from the rays of the sun.*

The expansion in the number of artists in the nineteenth century who specialised in landscape created a tradition of study that ran alongside but differed from the work of the figure painters. Unlike their academic colleagues, students of landscape were encouraged to work in oil from an early stage, sketching rapidly in the open air in order to master the effects of light and weather that they were required to recreate when painting landscapes in the studio. The generation of Théodore Caruelle d'Aligny and Jean-Baptiste-Camille Corot used graphite pencil or pen and ink when recording the outlines of a view or the details of leaves and rocks. From the 1850s the use of charcoal became increasingly common, in part because improvements in fixatives reduced its tendency to smudge, but chiefly because it allowed artists to catch a rapid impression of weather and atmosphere better than the graphite pencil.

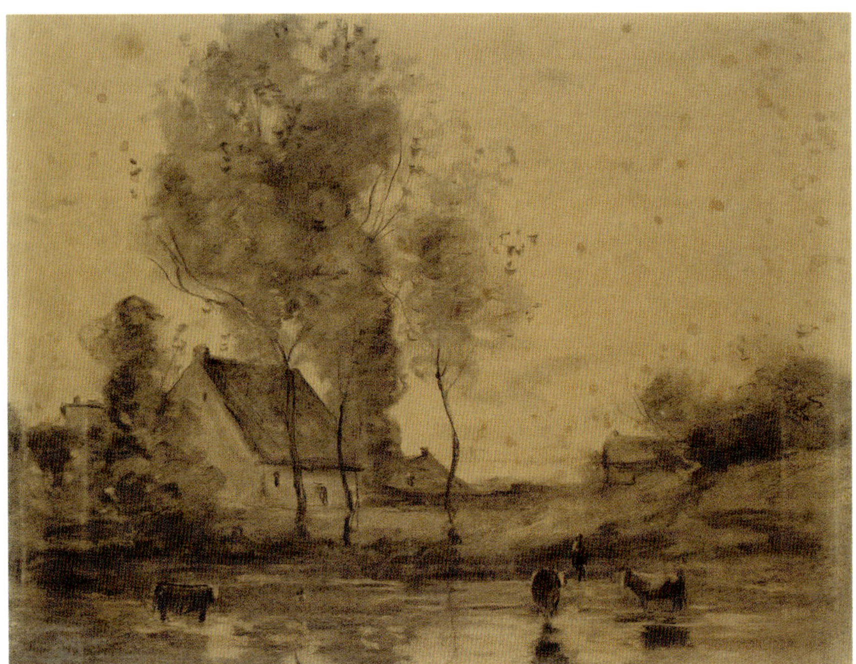

Fig.17 | Camille Corot (1796–1875)
Landscape with Pond, Trees, and Cottages
Charcoal, partly stumped, with rubbing out, on wove paper, discoloured brown, WA1937.19

This new breadth in landscape drawing followed changes in landscape painting towards an appearance of greater spontaneity in the finished work. Corot, anticipating the trend, used charcoal extensively in his late drawings [fig.17].

The rise in the fashion for pure landscapes lessened the need for tuition in figure painting, while a tendency to work directly from the motif led to a reduction in preparatory work. Among the Impressionists Auguste Renoir, Camille Pissarro and Edgar Degas, all deeply committed figure painters, never abandoned the practise of extensive drawing; in contrast Claude Monet [cat.29], who increasingly eliminated human presence from his work, felt less need to draw. It would be wrong, however, to conclude from the case of Monet that artists in general drew less than they did in earlier decades. The habits of most figure painters were unchanged and, while preparatory studies may have declined in importance among the landscapists, artists continued to draw and paint with watercolour in the open air.

Whether or not watercolour should be included in an account of drawing brings home the difficulty in deciding what constitutes drawing and what does not. Watercolours were always classified as drawings in the Salon exhibitions although, like the pastels and works in gouache with which they were exhibited, they included many highly finished works which had more in common with the oils shown in the section of paintings than with they had with preparatory studies. The works made in watercolour, too, were as varied as paintings in oil. Genre painters at the beginning of the century used it to tint their drawings [cat.4]. Richard Parkes Bonington and the artists in his circle painted marines, landscapes and historical compositions in watercolour from the 1820s onwards in response to the example of the British watercolourists. Ingres and his followers used the medium to add thin colour to outline compositions. Watercolour was also used by artists to record the colours and costumes of popular life in the countries that they visited: Delacroix in Morocco, Guillaume Bodinier in Italy, Louis Dupré in Greece and Turkey [fig.18],

Théodore Valerio in Hungary and the Balkans, Charles Gleyre in the Eastern Mediterranean – the list is long and includes a number of artists, such as Dupré and Valerio, who made their watercolours for publication. By 1879 the inadequate space set aside for watercolours at the annual Salon led to the foundation of The Society of French Watercolourists. The Society's membership included many specialists in watercolour alongside dozens of the most successful artists of the day: Henri Harpignies, Léon Bonnat, Guillaume Dubufe, Gustave Doré [cat.22], Eugène Isabey, Eugène Lami, Charles Cazin, Jean-Paul Laurens, James Tissot, Édouard Detaille and many others.

BOOKS AND PRINTS

No group of patrons had such a direct impact on the choice of subjects drawn by artists and on the manner in which they drew them as publishers of books and prints. Books of picturesque travel were by definition pictorial and depended heavily on the contribution of draughtsmen and watercolourists. Editions of poetry and fiction, illustrated by specialist illustrators and established painters, introduced new themes into the restricted field of the literary sources traditionally favoured by painters. These editions ranged from the deluxe volumes of Virgil and Racine, published by Pierre Didot in 1798 and 1801 and illustrated by David's friends and pupils, to more popular books of contemporary poetry and fiction issued in small formats. The drawings made for the popular editions anticipated the subjects from modern literature that became high fashion among painters from the 1820s onwards. Images based on the works of Marmontel, Gessner, Voltaire and Jean-Jacques Rousseau appeared at the Salon for the first time in book illustrations. Goethe, one of the most popular sources of subjects in nineteenth-century French art, made his debut at the Salon in 1808 with a drawing by Moreau le Jeune (Jean-Michel Moreau) for Didot's edition of the *Sorrows of Young Werther*. The sudden popularity of lithography in 1816–7, as explosive in its effect as the discovery of the daguerreotype in 1839, did not alter this tendency; it rather opened up a vast new field for those who drew subjects taken from popular literature and modern life.

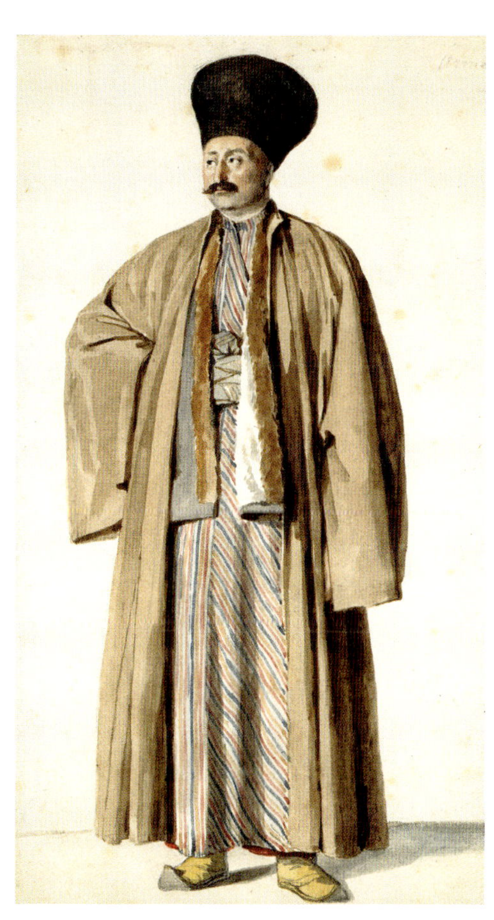

Fig.18 | Louis Dupré (1789–1837)
An Armenian, standing, turned somewhat to left
Graphite with watercolour on white paper laid down on white card backing, WA1942.65

LITHOGRAPHY

Lithography, the art of making prints from an image drawn on a limestone block, discovered by the Bavarian printer Alois Senefelder in 1798, belongs as much to the art of drawing as it does to printmaking. After a brief moment when early lithographers outlined their compositions on the stone with a lithographic pen, artists quickly discovered its potential for creating tonal effects with chalk or pen and chalk combined. Because of this, compositions with contrasts of light and shadow by Girodet and Pierre-Paul Prud'hon were at first much favoured by lithographic publishers who promoted the new art by exhibiting prints after both artists at the Salon. Despite the existence of a lithograph by Ingres after his own *Grande odalisque*, the nuanced contours and delicate shading of his drawings did not, it seems, suit lithography and it remains his only known work in the medium [cat.12].

It was not, however, in the Salon, but in the shops of the print-sellers and booksellers that the link between drawing and lithography was strongly established. It is not always easy to guess whether or not a lithograph after Girodet or Prud'hon is based on a painting or drawing, but there is no such doubt when looking at one of the many lithographs made by Carle Vernet, his son Horace, his friend and follower Géricault, the Rome prize winner Léon Cogniet, Géricault's friend Nicolas-Toussaint Charlet and many others who flooded the print shops after 1816 with their work. Géricault's lithographs [cat.8] with their grainy chalk lines, thick velvety blacks and delicately graduated tone, imitating the effect of wash, are works of pure graphic art, nurtured by the same academic habit of figure drawing that underpinned his masterpiece *The Raft of the Medusa*, exhibited in 1819.

Many lithographers including Géricault, Delacroix, Chassériau, Édouard Manet [cats 25 and 26] and Henri Fantin-Latour were draughtsmen and painters who came to the medium with ready-made drawing skills. The demand for these works, however, soon produced a generation of specialist lithographers who developed their technique while working on the stone. When Doré and Honoré Daumier attempted to escape from what many regarded as a lowly profession into the higher reaches of art, they brought with them working habits formed in the print market. Doré transferred the fluent, tonal, monochromatic effects of his drawings into his paintings and exhibited the results with popular success. Daumier's path from lithography to high art was less smooth. What we know of his manner of drawing in his early years is based almost entirely on the evidence of his prints, no doubt because he improvised his images directly on the stone without models or preparatory work [cat.17]. His earliest known drawings, mostly dating from the late 1840s and early 1850s, indicate a mix of sources that included Géricault and Paul Gavarni, two printmakers who appealed to Daumier's desire to be accepted as a history painter on the one hand and to his sense of humour and his interest in human character on the other [cats 18 and 19]. His finished watercolours, dating mostly from the 1860s, are more consistent and more confidently executed than the earlier works. Most are reworked variants of ideas that had already appeared in his lithographs. They employ a rich mixture of pen, wash, chalk and watercolour that equates to the fluency of line and the manipulation of chiaroscuro that Daumier used to magnificent effect when making prints.

FROM MILLET TO CÉZANNE

Both Jean-François Millet and Edgar Degas were trained in a tradition of fine drawing. It is easier in the case of Degas to trace his art to its origins, but both artists remained profoundly attached to the principles in which they were educated. Many of their earliest drawings were conventionally explorative, but, as their art progressed, drawing became increasingly important to both artists as an art form in its own right.

The work of Millet is difficult to fit into any of the terms that are normally applied to him: Realist, Naturalist, Idealist. He never lost the habit, acquired from his time as a pupil of Delaroche, of preparing his paintings through preliminary drawings, but none of his many drawings of this type, mostly in black crayon, show any sign of Delaroche's influence. Prud'hon is often cited, probably rightly, as one source of a soft, tonal quality in his earliest pastoral and erotic drawings, as well as a certain rococo element that he probably acquired from the popular landscapist Narcisse Diaz. There are hints of Daumier's fluent, lithographic contours in the drawings of the 1850s, along with some

Detail of cat.21: Jean-François Millet 1814–75 *Shepherdess Seated on a Rock (Une bergère assisse sur un rocher)*

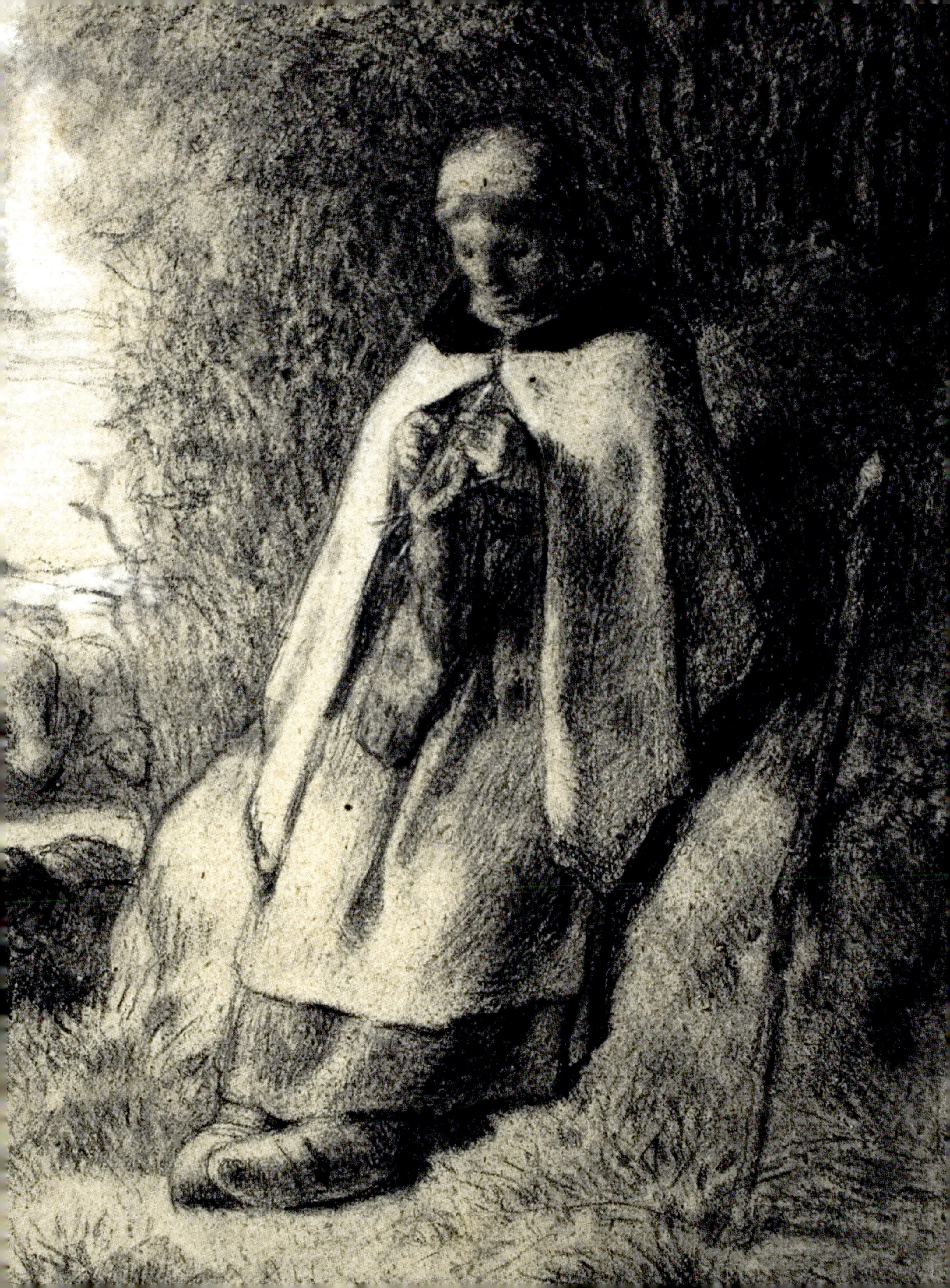

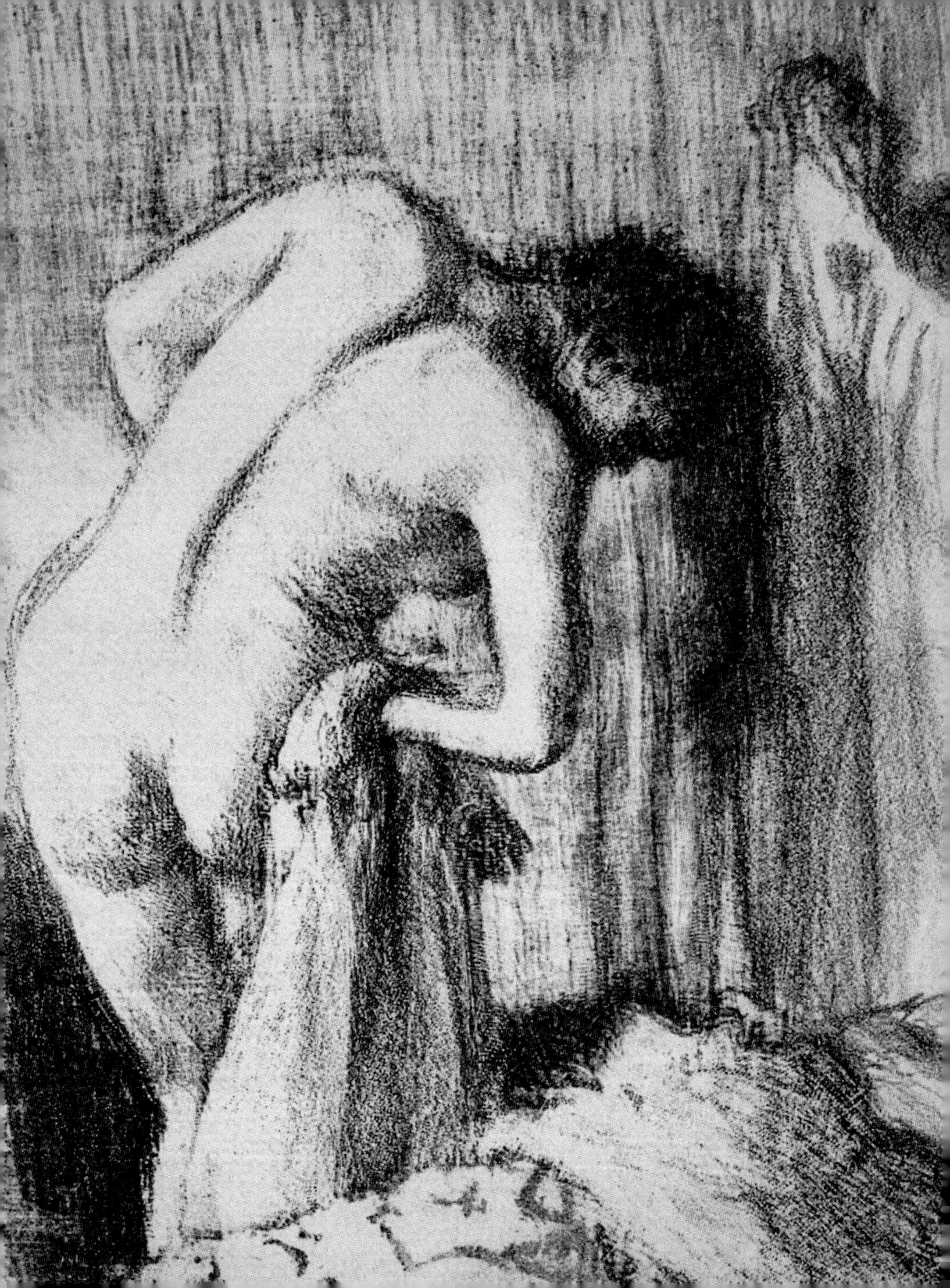

sfumato effects reminiscent of Rembrandt in his interior scenes, but Millet's manner of drawing becomes so strongly his own that influences are not always obvious. In the course of the 1850s, the dense shading with black crayon, sometimes rubbed to suggest the half tones [cat.20], diminished as he increasingly modelled his figures with short, straw-like strokes and shaded the background with long, thin, compacted lines, sometimes lightly cross-hatched. In several compositions the dense application of small strokes creates a tonal effect similar to the technique of blurred charcoal, black chalk or Conté crayon used by Jean-Jacques Henner, Charles-Albert Lebourg, Charles Sellier and Georges Seurat in their chiaroscuro drawings [cat.47].

Millet's use of lines inscribed with a sharp, soft crayon developed in tandem with his discovery of etching, which he took up seriously in the mid-1850s. At a time when his paintings sold with difficulty, prints and drawings offered a better livelihood. Scenes of seamstresses and shepherdesses, related to but not necessarily made for his paintings, appealed to collectors of modest means [cat.21]. The link, in any case, between Millet's preparatory drawings and those done for their own sake was always a fluid one. He clearly valued his more finished drawings of peasant life as independent works of art whether or not they were made as studies and, on occasion, took the composition of a drawing from a finished painting, particularly in his large pastels of the 1860s that became almost as important in his last years as his oils.

It is generally agreed that Degas' manner of drawing descended to him from Ingres by way of his master Louis Lamothe, who had been trained by Ingres, and by Ingres's pupil Hippolyte Flandrin. His earliest drawings are pale and deliberate, more like Flandrin's than Ingres', and delicately hatched with thin parallel lines imitated from the fifteenth-century silverpoint drawings that he had studied in Italy. Several of Degas' early portrait drawings, essentially head studies, belong to a type that originated with Ingres and became standard in the studios of his pupils [cats 35 and 36]. The fine manner of these drawings was still evident in the early 1870s [cat.37], but gradually disappeared in the course of the decade as his lines thickened, his instruments diversified, his touch became more spirited and he took up pastel, reflecting the dominant technique of his last years. As he turned away from the historical and biblical subjects that had attracted him in the 1850s [cat.34] and began to take his themes from modern life, the role of drawing in preparing his compositions remained for a time unaffected. Degas' first paintings of the theatre began with life studies drawn in the studio, progressing through the addition of costume and a process of transfer to the finished canvas. This traditional sequence, however, was modified in the later 1870s and through the 1880s as his preparatory work evolved into a complex interplay of life drawing, monotypes, sculptures, copies, counterproofs, photographs and tracings.

What originated as an academic technique for developing an idea from a rough sketch to a finished image became a means of reduction, replication and simplification that follows no clear path from a first idea to a final composition. The exploration of an image through copies and reversed copies produced prints, drawings and pastels, many of which exist as works of art in their own right [cats 41, 42 and 43]. The groups and single figures that were the building blocks of Degas's compositions through the 1870s became the main focus of his work in the 1880s. Many nineteenth-century artists, including Ingres and

Detail of cat.43: Edgar Degas 1834–1917 *After the Bath (small plate) / La sortie du bain (petite planche)*

Renoir [cat.46], had developed a genre of single nudes based upon the production of painted 'academies', but none pursued this development so exclusively as Degas. His pastels of women at their toilette relate in type to the bathers of Ingres, but the differences are more significant than the similarities. While the frank, urban modernity of the subjects cannot be matched in the work of Ingres and his followers, the free application of sometimes strident colour over rough charcoal that typified much of Degas' work in the 1890s and early 1900s marks a far greater gulf [cats 44 and 45].

Had Degas' career ended in the 1860s, when he was in his late 20s, he would still be remembered as one of the finest draughtsmen of the age. Had Paul Cézanne, Vincent Van Gogh [cat.54] or Paul Gauguin disappeared at the same age, their names would have made no mark on the history of French art. Their early works became admired as the prelude to their later achievements, although there are many who find that they have qualities of their own. They belonged to a generation in which amateurs and self-taught artists became figures of importance – not in spite of their limitations in traditional drawing skills, but largely because of them. It was an age when virtuosity became suspect in certain quarters and originality, even clumsiness, was preferred to traditional skills and accepted aesthetic standards. All three artists, however, drew extensively. Cézanne, in particular, has left a large body of drawings that chart his attempts to master life drawing and to draw lessons from the art of the past by making many copies. In 1863 he attended life-drawing classes each day from 7.00 to 1.00 in the morning and again from 7.00 until 10.00 in the evening. In the process his contours became more fluent and he developed a distinctive style of modelling, with small summary patches of hatched lines [cats 50, 51 and 52]. Cézanne had no real master, although his friendship with Pissarro in the 1870s had a moderating influence on his approach to painting. The relationship left its mark on the many sketchbook pages filled with thumbnail studies in black crayon of things seen in passing: portrait heads, domestic articles, old masters, classic statuary and landscapes. He also learned from Pissarro the value of watercolour and, from the 1870s onwards, developed a synthesis of drawing and watercolour in which the chalk or pencil marks became increasingly rudimentary and modelling and composition were reduced to patches of translucent colour [cat.53]. 'Drawing and colour,' he observed, 'are not at all distinct; as you paint, so you draw.' This belief did not imply an inferior role for drawing. Cézanne's example fed into the development of Cubism which, in its classic form, was not an art of painterly effects at all, but of structured drawing with a limited range of added colour. Cubist drawing could exist without colour [cat.70]. Cubist painting could not exist without drawing.

FROM ART NOUVEAU TO CUBISM

The early 1900s were marked by a nostalgia for drawing, perhaps in reaction to the colour of the Fauves, and a revival of interest in the art of Ingres among certain artists of the avant-garde. This was not so much a revival, but rather a resumption of a tendency that had never gone away. Admiration for Ingres is evident in the drawings of many diverse artists of the late nineteenth and early twentieth centuries from Pierre Puvis de Chavannes to Maurice Denis, as well as in the drawings of more conventional artists. The cult of line that became a

Detail of cat.53:
Paul Cézanne 1839–1906
Study of Pine Trees (Étude de pins)

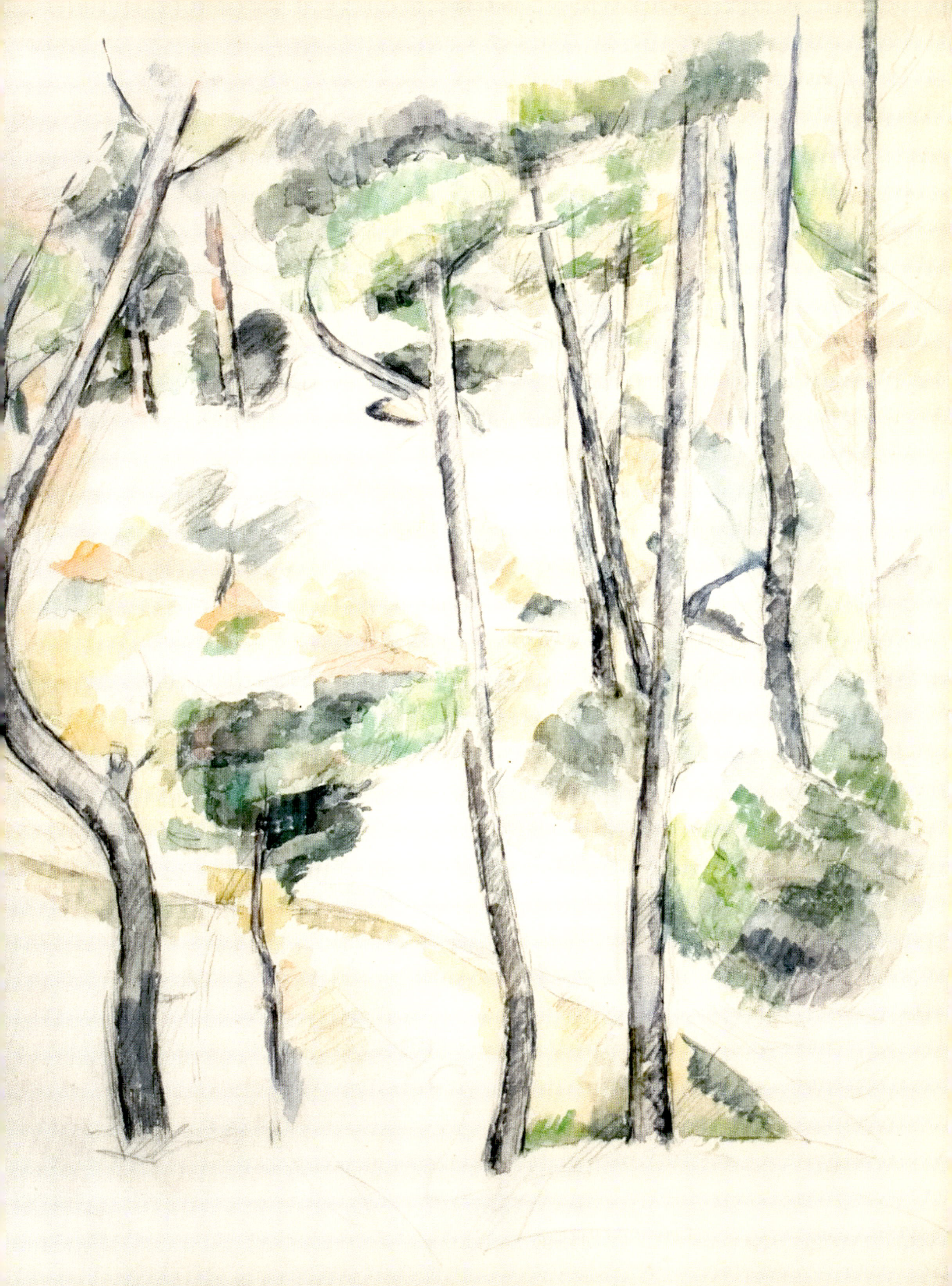

feature of much European art in the closing decades of the century was, rightly or wrongly, associated with Ingres. As Proust's Duchesse de Guermantes, always a reliable weathervane to current views, admitted: 'without complicating matters by speaking about David, about whom she knew little, in her early youth she had believed that Ingres was the most boring of academics, then, abruptly, discovered that he was the most delightful of the masters of Art Nouveau.'

Pablo Picasso went through a similar conversion when he saw the work of Ingres at the Salon d'Automne in 1905. The sight of Ingres' *The Turkish Bath* reinforced a lingering debt to Art Nouveau in his paintings and drawings that continued throughout his life [cats 109 and 111], although it was only in the 1920s that the linearity and the debt to Ingres became explicit in his etchings and drawings.

Although Picasso's career was punctuated by periods of change and experimentation, his commitment to line drawing remained constant. His conventional training at the School of Fine Arts in Barcelona gave his pen and chalk an easy fluency and taught him the value of making preparatory studies. When he first visited Paris in 1900 and when he finally settled there in 1904, he had the basic drawing skills that enabled him to respond easily to the work of a number of older artists: Henri Toulouse-Lautrec, from whom he acquired an edge of caricature [cat.55]; Puvis de Chavannes who gave him a taste for simplified classicising form; Ingres, whose immaculate sense of line became a recurrent model. But it was Cézanne, whose work he saw at the retrospective exhibition of 1907, who had the greatest impact, contributing to the flattening of space and the fragmenting of form that developed into Cubism in 1907–8.

In its early years Cubism depended more on drawing than it did on colour. Colour was a distraction from the structured character of Cubism, and Georges Braque and Picasso almost eliminated it altogether from their first Cubist works. The breaking up of form and the elimination of space required sharply defined edges, while the residual references to the natural world that are found in most Cubist art are clearly demarcated. The same reaction against colour is found in the early Cubist works of Albert Gleizes and Jean Metzinger, founders of the Section d'Or movement in 1911 which included many of the best known Cubist painters: Jacques Villon [cats 78, 79 and 84], František Kupka [cat.74], Fernand Léger [cats 75, 89, 91, 94, 95, 99 and 107], Henri Le Fauconnier, Roger de La Fresnaye [cats 60 and 88], Auguste Herbin [cat.62], Louis Marcoussis [cat.69], André Lhote [cat.67], Juan Gris [cats 61, 70 and 71] and others. Unlike Braque and Picasso, who were more instinctive artists, the members of the Section d'Or tended to find a rationale for their art in science, mathematics and philosophy. They imposed a diagrammatic and geometric character on their work that was intended to evoke mathematical relationships and philosophical arguments about the nature of Reality. Such an approach to art was more suited to drawing than it was to painting. The traditional value of the brushstroke counted for very little in their work. Structure is everything. Drawings by Cubist artists are, therefore, not only common, but reflect an essential aspect of their art.

By defining Cubist drawing in terms of line and form, there is a danger of falling into the ancient tendency to divide artists into colourists and draftsmen. This would exclude many drawings by Cubist artists, including works by Gleizes [cats 80, 81, 82, 83 and 93], as well as many drawings by near contemporary artists such as Odilon Redon [cat.48] which are heavily dependent on colour.

What is the essential difference between a late coloured drawing by Léger [cat.107] and a painting by him of the same period? Dictionaries are not of much help: drawing is defined as an art of lines, but it can be purely tonal; it is monochromatic, but it also uses colour; it is preparatory, but it can also exist in an independent work of art; and it can only be confined to media other than oil paint by excluding a large number of oil studies and sketches that are functionally little different from preparatory drawings.

The problem in defining what we mean by a drawing lies in its relationship to painting. It is easy to distinguish between an architect's preparatory drawing and a finished building. A building is not a drawing. But the differences between a drawing and a painting are more elusive. Traditionally, drawing and painting have been seen as partners working together, sometimes as sisters, collaborating amicably, or more commonly as husband and wife, or master and servant, with one in charge. The argument is as venerable as it is arid. Painting, as Cézanne noted, does not exist in partnership with drawing because it is itself a kind of drawing. Prints and painting are habitually separated from drawings for practical reasons, but in the mind of the artist there are no fundamental differences.

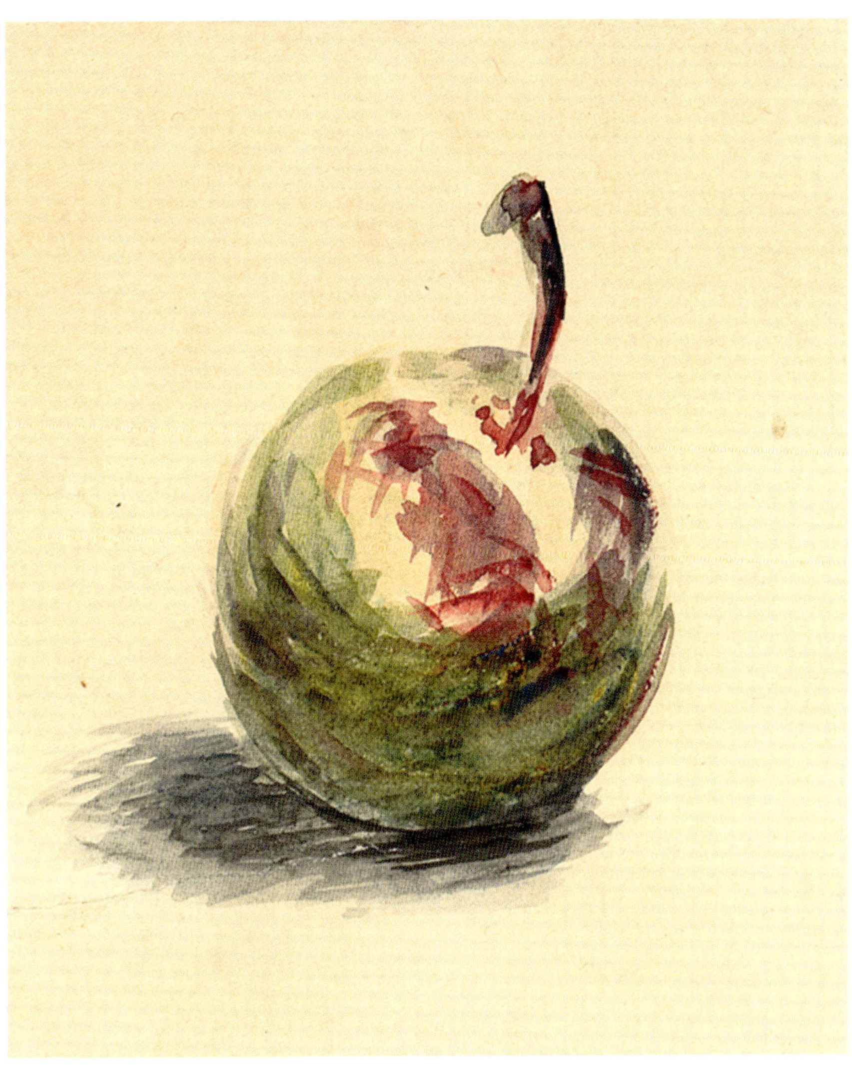

Detail of cat.27:
Édouard Manet 1832–1883
Mirabelle Plum (Prune de Mirabelle)

1

JEAN-HONORÉ FRAGONARD 1732–1806

Bireno leaving the Island, mid-1780s

Black chalk with brown and grey wash on paper, 39.5 × 26.8 cm

PROVENANCE: Hippolye Walferdin; his sale, Paris, 12–16 April 1880, lot 228; Louis Roederer, Rheims; Dr A. S. W. Rosenbach, Philadelphia, 1923; British Rail Pension Fund; Agnew's; Sotheby's, 2 July 1990, lot 101

LITERATURE: Seznec and Mongan (1945), no.52; Dupuy-Vachey (2003), no.78

According to Fragonard's younger son, Théophile, 'David and his school gave so different an impetus to the tastes of artists and *amateurs* that the vogue for Fragonard's work ceased before he reached the age of fifty'.[1] Although this judgement can be slightly modified,[2] it remains true that Fragonard gradually adapted his style to the new taste, though his subject matter remained predominantly the erotic scenes he had inherited from his master, François Boucher.

During the 1780s Fragonard worked on two major series of illustrations to the classics, Cervantes' *Don Quixote* and Ludovico Ariosto's *Orlando Furioso.* The latter group includes 137 sheets which were probably acquired by the great Fragonard enthusiast Hippolyte Walferdin directly from the artist's heirs, and some 40 others, mostly initial studies. The function of these drawings is not known, but it seems likely that they were intended to be bound in volumes with the accompanying text, perhaps handwritten, in the manner of the luxurious manuscripts commissioned by Louis XIV. Of Fragonard's other projects for illustrated books, the drawings for Cervantes were reproduced in miserable etchings by their first owner, Dominique Vivant Denon, and the later drawings to La Fontaine's *Contes* were published in more conventional fashion by Pierre Didot the Elder in 1795.

Ariosto's epic poem tells the story of Charlemagne's knight, Roland, and his tribulations in both love and war. It had been a favourite with French artists since Baskerville's edition illustrated by the leading French artists of the day – Moreau le Jeune, Charles-Dominique-Joseph Eisen, Charles Monnet, Greuze and Giovanni Battista Cipriani, published in 1773. The publication of the French translations by Louis d'Ussieux (1775–83), with many of the same illustrations, and the comte de Tressan (1780) may have stimulated Fragonard to produce his own suite of drawings. Only the first third of the poem is illustrated in a consecutive manner, the remainder more sporadically; and only one drawing was engraved, as a 'gravure imitant le dessin' by the marquis de Paroy, and shown at the Salon of 1787.

The episode illustrated here comes from canto X, line 19 of Ariosto's poem: Bireno, with his clothes rolled up under his arm, steals away from his lover Olympia to rejoin his earlier lover, the daughter of Cimosque. He has awoken his companions and, without making a sound, has ordered them to raise anchor and sail away. The drawing is one of the most brilliant of the series. Its bravura technique of fluid chalk strokes complemented by the very free use of wash in both grey and brown is brilliantly used to evoke the hasty departure of the ship, whose pennant flutters in the breeze. No other works in Fragonard's life, indeed no drawings in French art before the 1820s, so resoundingly demonstrate such virtuosity.

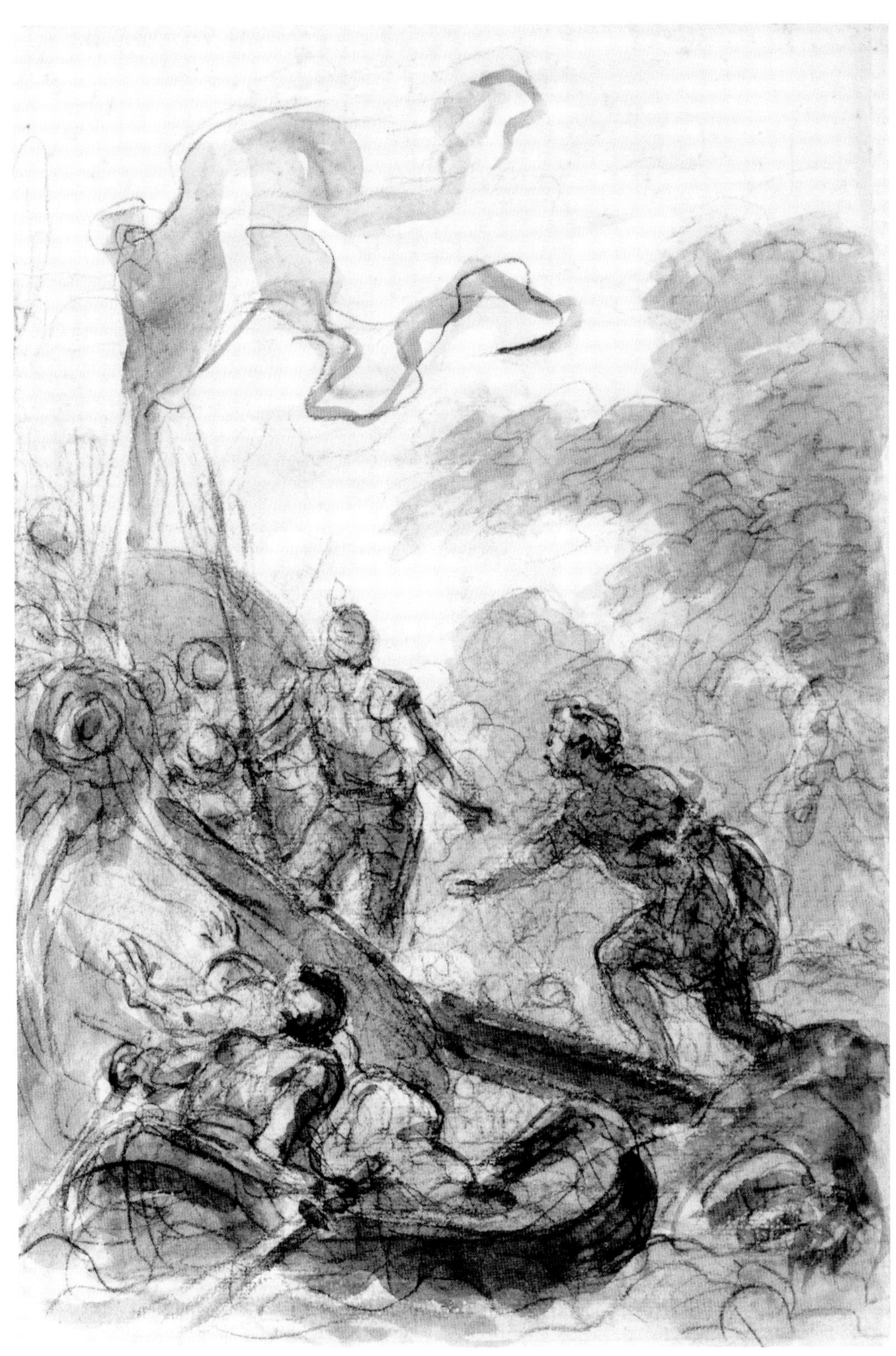

2

JEAN-BAPTISTE ISABEY 1767–1855

Portrait of François Gérard, 1789–90

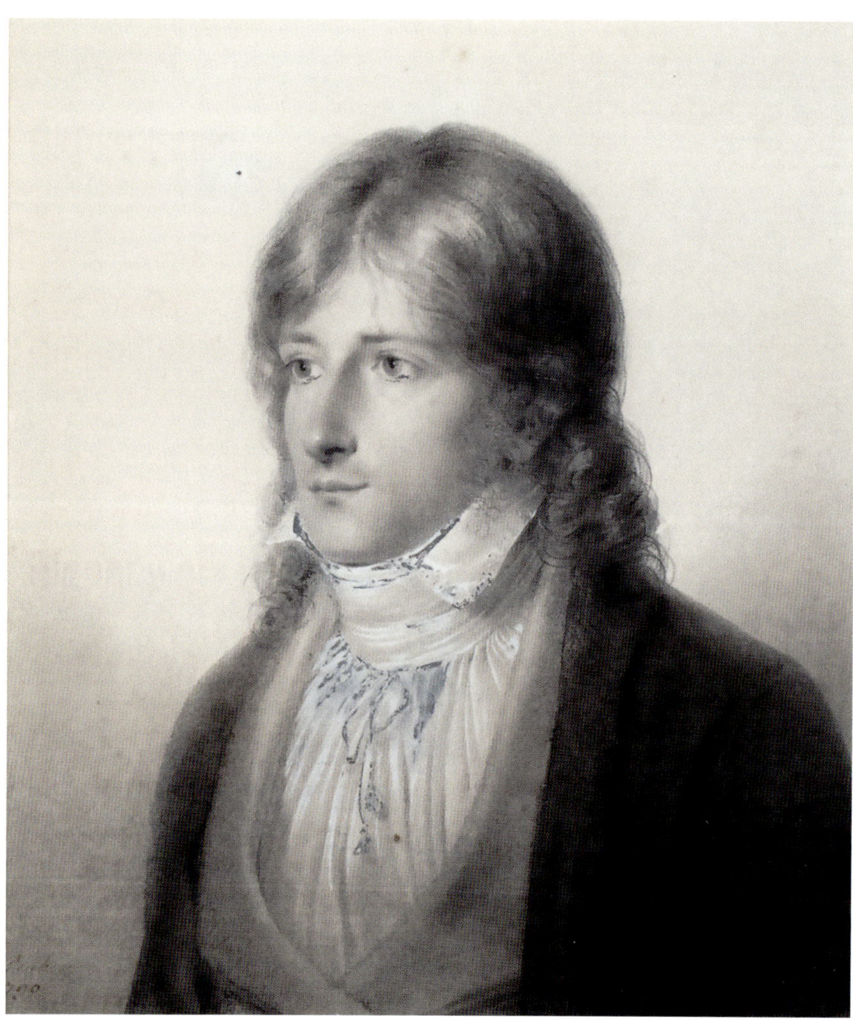

Black crayon and stump on paper, 19 × 16.5 cm

PROVENANCE: by descent from the artist through his niece, Countess Foy; sale Kapandji Morhange, Paris, 18 December 2015, lot 50

LITERATURE: Basily-Callimaki (1909), p.24; Lécosse (2006), pp.106, 108

In 1806 David wrote to Isabey giving the names of the pupils he most admired: François-Xavier Fabre, Girodet, Antoine-Jean Gros, Gérard and Isabey himself.[1] After a period in his native Nancy, studying to be a history painter with Jean-Baptiste Claudot, Isabey had entered David's studio in Paris in 1786. He won a second prize for history painting in 1788, but decided to specialise in portrait drawings and miniatures in watercolour on ivory. These quickly progressed from a severe outline manner towards a highly original style inspired by the contemporary popularity of the mezzotint. As Étienne Delécluze, a fellow pupil in David's studio, noted, 'Isabey, inspired by the sight of some English prints in the "manière anglaise" after Reynolds, decided to employ and promote this style in our country'.[2] Ironically, the French never mastered the art of mezzotint, and the new emphasis on the soft focus of chiaroscuro in drawing and painting was translated by printmakers using an immensely sophisticated technique of stipple engraving. Indeed, several of Isabey's most famous compositions, notably *The Boat* (1798) and the portrait of Jean-Luc Barbier, *The Smoker (Le fumeur)* (1804), were reproduced in this manner.

Isabey's fellow student in David's studio, Gérard, competed for the Rome Prize in 1789; he was placed only second, yet nevertheless arrived at the French Academy in Rome on 30 May 1790. Before leaving Paris Gérard and Isabey exchanged portraits. This small drawing is one of the most exquisite of Isabey's early drawings, and until its recent reappearance on the art market was only known from reproductions.

When Gérard returned to Paris in 1791 Isabey's friendship deepened and as a now successful portraitist, he was well placed to offer financial assistance to Gérard. So, when the latter's first great success at the Salon of 1795, *Belisarius*, on which his master had painted a celebrated picture exhibited in 1781 (Lille), remained unsold, Isabey apparently bought it for 4,000 francs. He sold it on to Caspar Meyer, the Batavian ambassador in Paris, for 10,000 francs, insisting that Gérard should keep the difference. In gratitude Gérard painted a magnificent full-length portrait of *Isabey and his Daughter* (Louvre), shown to great acclaim at the Salon of 1796 – when Isabey, for his part, exhibited his portrait of Mme Gérard (lost).

3

ANNE-LOUIS GIRODET-TRIOSON 1767–1824

Study of the Head of General Desaix, 1801

Graphite on off-white paper, 15.2 × 11.4 cm

PROVENANCE: Nikos Dhikeos (L.3529); Galerie Alfa, Paris, 2005

Another of David's favourite pupils, Girodet won the Rome Prize in 1789, at his fourth attempt, with a hard-edged, Neo-Classical *Joseph Recognised by his Brothers* (The École nationale supérieure des beaux-arts, Paris). However, on arriving in Rome, he immediately turned his back on David and academic convention, and made his reputation with the astonishing *Sleep of Endymion* (1791, Louvre), sent back to Paris and exhibited at the Salon in 1793. This painting, in which the goddess Diana appears as a moonbeam illuminating the body of Endymion, exudes eroticism and imagination, its light effects painted in the *sfumato* of Leonardo da Vinci and Correggio.

In spite of the mannered eccentricity of his later exhibits and his rejection of David, Girodet won the important commission in 1800 for one of two paintings to decorate the Salon Doré of Napoleon's country residence at Malmaison. The architects Charles Percier and Pierre-François Fontaine ordered pendants from Gérard and Girodet. Girodet's *Apotheosis of French Heroes Who Died for their Country during the War of Liberty* (Malmaison) was eventually exhibited at the Salon in 1802, where it met with incomprehension and ridicule; David saw it as further evidence of his pupil's insanity. The crowded composition depicts the mythical Gaelic poet Ossian, whose poetry had been popularised throughout Europe by James Macpherson in a controversial edition he described as a translation from the original texts, but which was eventually discovered to be his own invention. No fewer than 40 identifiable figures are shown being received into heaven by the blind Ossian, accompanied by his family, together with allegorical figures representing the warring nations and the Peace of Lunéville.

Girodet worked for 15 months on this picture, and the preparatory process was immensely elaborate. This drawing is a study for one of the principal figures in the picture, Louis Charles Antoine Des Aix, called Desaix (1768–1800), who won distinction during the campaigns in Germany and Egypt and whose exploits were greatly admired by Napoleon. He was killed shortly before the French victory in the battle of Marengo on 13 June 1800. In his *Apotheosis* Girodet made Desaix the focus of interest, the general who is being embraced by Ossian himself. It has been suggested that this very lively drawing may have been inspired by the posthumous portrait of Desaix by Andrea Appiani (1754–1817), based on a death mask. In spite of being at several removes from the subject, Girodet has made a remarkably speaking likeness.

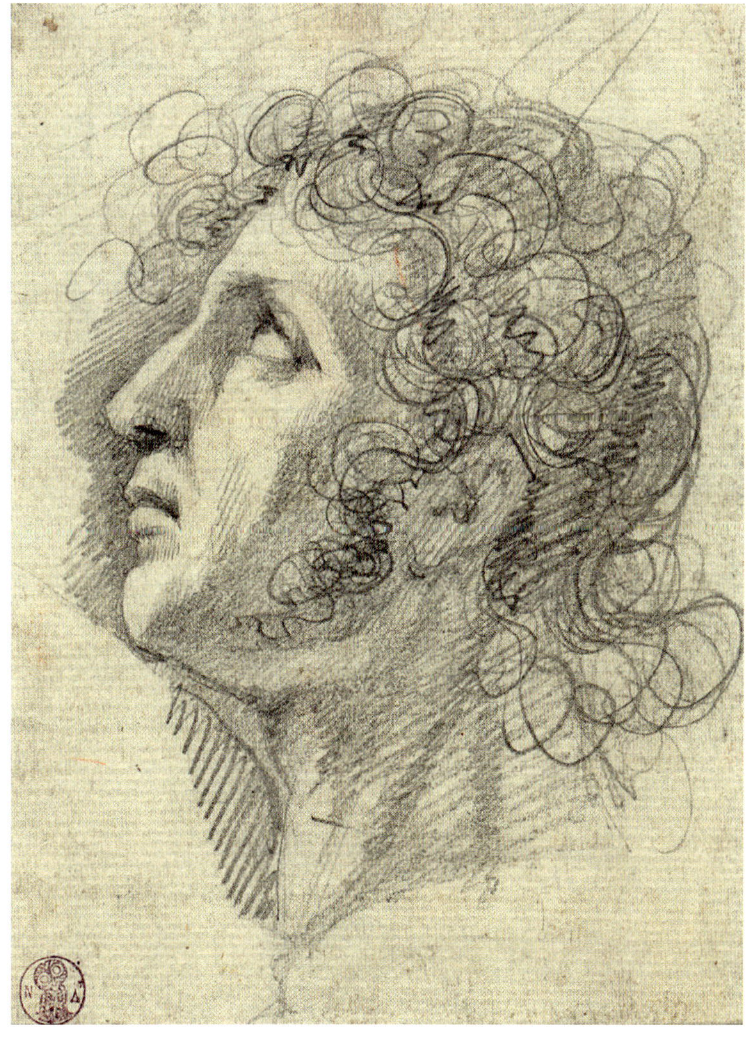

4

LOUIS-LÉOPOLD BOILLY 1761–1845

Pay and Cross or The Shower, ca.1805

Pen and black ink with wash and watercolour, 32 × 40 cm

PROVENANCE: Edmond de Goncourt; his sale, 17 February 1897, lot 18, where acquired by Henri-Julius Stettiner; Georges Dormeuil (L.1146a); sale Ader-Picard-Tajan, Paris, 13 June 1978, lot 2

LITERATURE: Harrisse (1898), no.1121; Launay (1991), no.17; Siegfried (1995), pp.87–90

During the 1790s Boilly preferred mildly erotic subjects in the vein of his predecessors Fragonard and Jean-Baptiste Greuze, but after the turn of the century he began to specialise in scenes from popular life. They were often deliberately moralising, in the manner of the seventeenth-century Dutch pictures he admired and collected.

In this watercolour, a bourgeois family crosses one of the makeshift moveable planks that were necessary for pedestrians in Paris. The streets of the city were generally unpaved, with poor drainage and few sewers, and were susceptible to flooding, as happened frequently in the first decade of the nineteenth century. The father is preceded by his son with a spaniel, and holds his daughter by the hand. Behind him follows his wife, protected from the rain by a large umbrella held by a nursemaid, who also struggles with the baby of the family. To their left a man stretches his arm out towards the father, who responds dismissively. By contrast a humble servant woman standing in front of the workman is seen putting a coin into his hand, the light shining on her generosity.

This was one of Boilly's most popular compositions. It seems to have developed from an earlier watercolour where the father holds the hands of both his elder children, making his refusal to pay his way less overt.[1] The present drawing is more closely related to the oil painting in the Louvre. To emphasise the moral, the pendant *The Little Chapel*, known only from the preliminary drawing,[2] shows a different family willingly giving alms to two young girls, while the young son drops a coin into the hat of a bald beggar.

Like his paintings, Boilly's finished drawings are very neatly executed and highly polished. They were intended for display rather than study in a library portfolio.

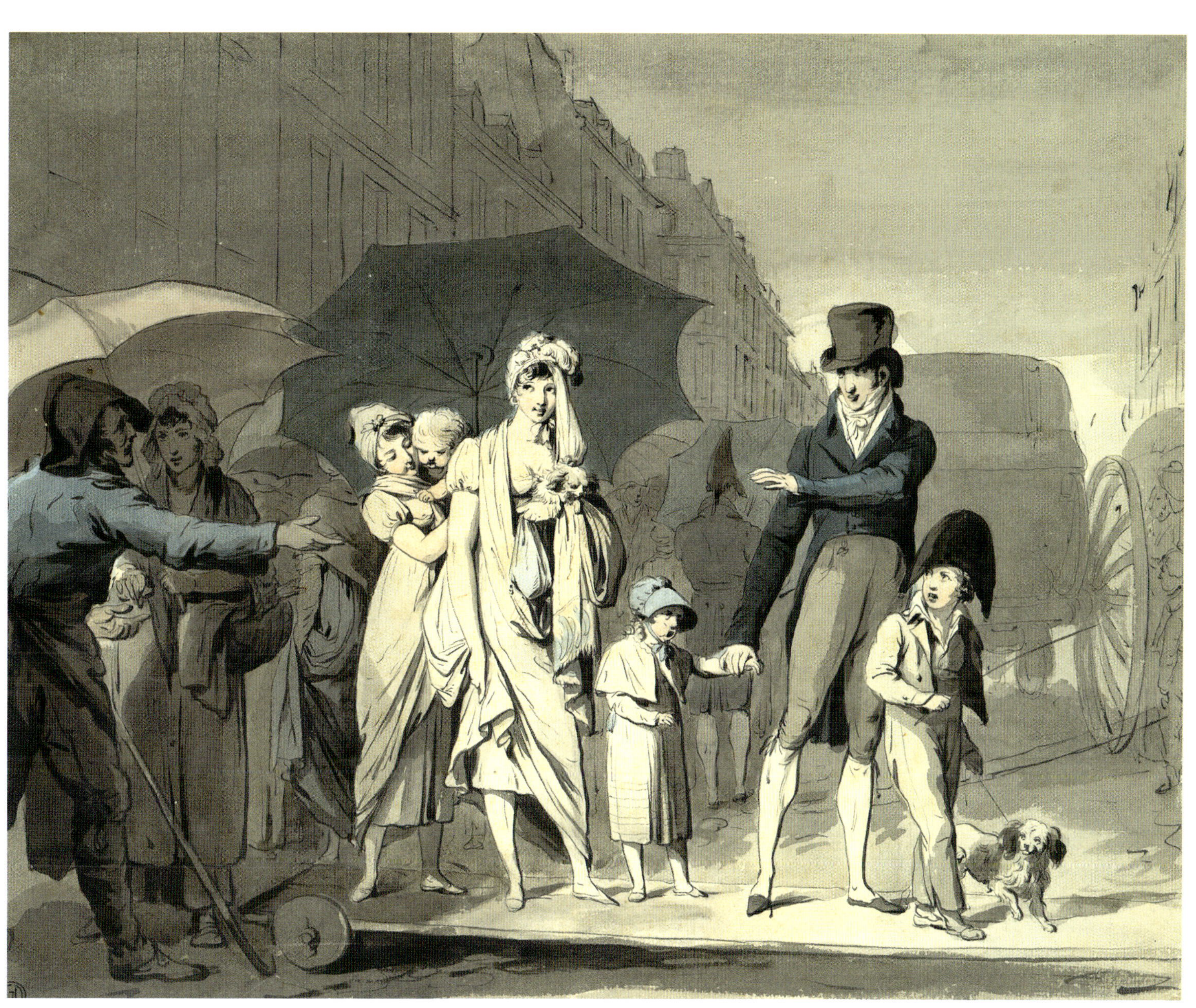

5

PIERRE-HENRI RÉVOIL 1776–1842

Portrait of a Woman, 1815

Pen and brush in watercolour and bodycolour on blue paper, 31.9 × 23.3 cm

Signed in monogram and dated: *PR 1815*

PROVENANCE: by descent from the artist; Galerie Bruno de Bayser, Paris

LITERATURE: Chaudonneret (1980), no.83

Of all the provincial drawing schools established in France in the eighteenth century, that at Lyons was the most distinguished; it was also the only one to develop a distinctive style of painting. Révoil studied there from 1791, and later in the studio of Jacques-Louis David in Paris. He achieved his first success in 1800 when he commemorated Napoleon's visit to Lyons to lay the foundation stone of the place Bellecour in the *Allegory of the Reconstruction of Lyons* (which he later destroyed).[1] In 1807 Révoil was appointed the first professor at the newly founded Academy of Fine Arts in Lyons, but later had a chequered relationship with that institution because of his royalist sympathies. From about 1810 he became one of the principal proponents of the Troubadour style, which depicted in meticulous detail scenes from French history. Even before the Restoration of the monarchy in 1815, the subjects were generally taken from the lives of the French kings. As an antiquary Révoil collected antiquities and manuscripts, his so-called 'cabinet de gothicités', which he mined for appropriate costumes and architectural features.

Portraits are uncommon in Révoil's output, and highly finished watercolours such as this example extremely rare. Among the oils is a self-portrait dated 1804 and another of his fellow painter, Pierre-Paul Prud'hon, of 1824. The sophisticated chalk drawings include a portrait of Révoil and his contemporary Robert Fleury Richard of 1798, and another of his fellow professor at the Lyons Academy, Claude Cochet (1760–1835) of 1813.[2]

According to family tradition, this remarkable drawing is a portrait of the artist's mother-in-law Anne Henriette Le Blanc de Servannes, the wife of Henri Antoine Révoil, director of mails at Aix-en-Provence. A companion drawing depicts her daughter Joséphine Révoil (b. 1797), who married her cousin Pierre Révoil on 6 February 1816.[3] In spite of their being first cousins, Révoil's marriage was happy. His portrait of his mother-in-law shows her to be somewhat severe in expression, but dressed in the highest fashion; the ruffles in her head-dress, round her neck and at her sleeve softening the effect of the very high waist of her dress. In her right hand she holds the pendant hanging from her neck, no doubt to emphasise its sentimental importance, presumably as a gift from her husband.

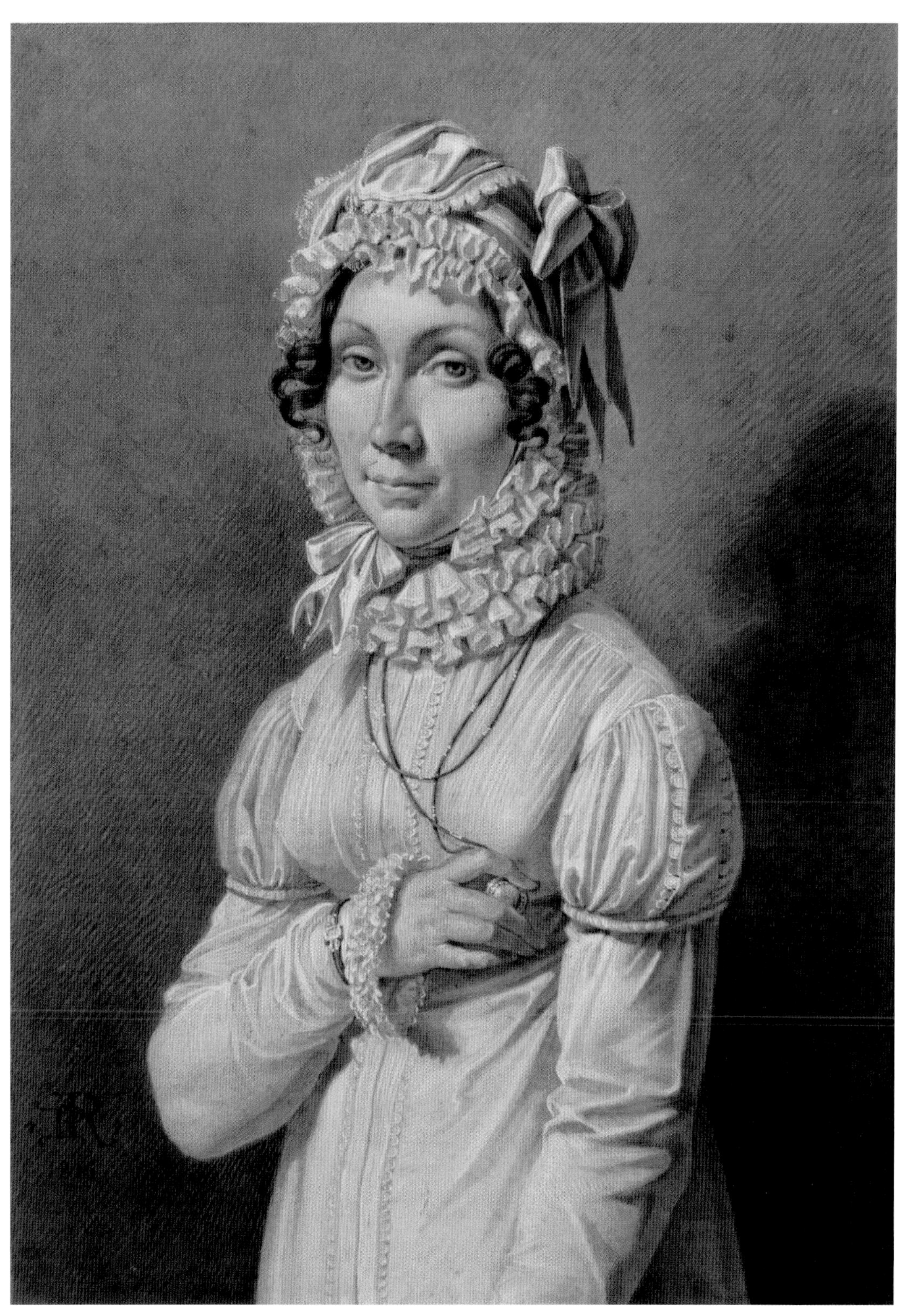

6

JACQUES-LOUIS DAVID 1748–1825

An Old Man and A Young Woman, ca.1822–23

Black chalk on paper, 18 × 12.8 cm

Signed: *L. David*

PROVENANCE: M. Delahaye, 1880; Wildenstein & Co., London; Gallery Arnoldie-Livie, Munich; Henry Moore, Much Hadham, Herts; Mary Moore; Sotheby's, 13–14 May 1997, lot 301

LITERATURE: Rosenberg and Prat (2002), no.335

From relatively modest beginnings, David quickly rose to be the most prominent artist of the Revolutionary period. He won the Rome Prize in 1774 and exhibited what is widely regarded as the first great Neo-Classical painting in France, *Belisarius Receiving Alms* (Lille), in 1781. There followed a succession of history paintings which effected a revolution in taste and set the standard for students in the Academy until the reform of the 1860s. David was the most influential painter of his day, running a studio that included many prominent artists. He was also active in revolutionary politics, being elected a deputy in 1792, voting for the death of the king in the following year and spending some months in prison in 1794–5 after the execution of Robespierre.

David was the artist most closely identified with Napoleon Bonaparte, whom he immortalised in a succession of grand portraits as soldier, conqueror and emperor. The most notable are *Napoleon Crossing the Alps* (1800–1; Malmaison), the *Coronation of Napoleon in Notre Dame* (1805–7; Louvre) and *Napoleon in his Study* (1812; National Gallery of Art, Washington).

Following the Restoration of the Bourbon monarchy in 1814, David felt obliged to go into exile in Brussels. He spent the remaining ten years of his life painting portraits and a succession of strange and mannered mythological scenes, often on amorous subjects, of which the best known is *Mars disarmed by Venus and the Graces* of 1824 (Brussels). He also began to make drawings for their own sake – his earlier drawings had been essentially functional and sketchy, copies after antique sculpture or the old masters, or studies for paintings. His grandson described how, on the days when the theatre was closed, David stayed at home, 'in the large room which served as drawing and dining room, decorated with the *Mont Saint Bernard* and the portrait of *Napoleon in his Study*, to invent and execute drawings in black chalk, of which some had been commissioned by publishers'.[1] Together these sheets, mostly showing figures from antiquity at head and shoulders or half-length, constitute something of a textbook of human expression. They are far more highly finished than almost anything else in David's earlier work and many are signed. Most passed to the artist's family on his death.

The subjects are generally mysterious, and this one has not been conclusively identified. It has been suggested that it may represent Caecina Paetus, who was found guilty of treason by the emperor Claudius in AD 42 and given the choice of killing himself. When he could not bring himself to do so, his wife Arria stabbed herself to show that it did not hurt. The figures are far removed from the idealised forms of David's earlier work, and the insistent shading gives these works a sculptural quality that no doubt appealed to an earlier owner of this drawing, the sculptor Henry Moore.

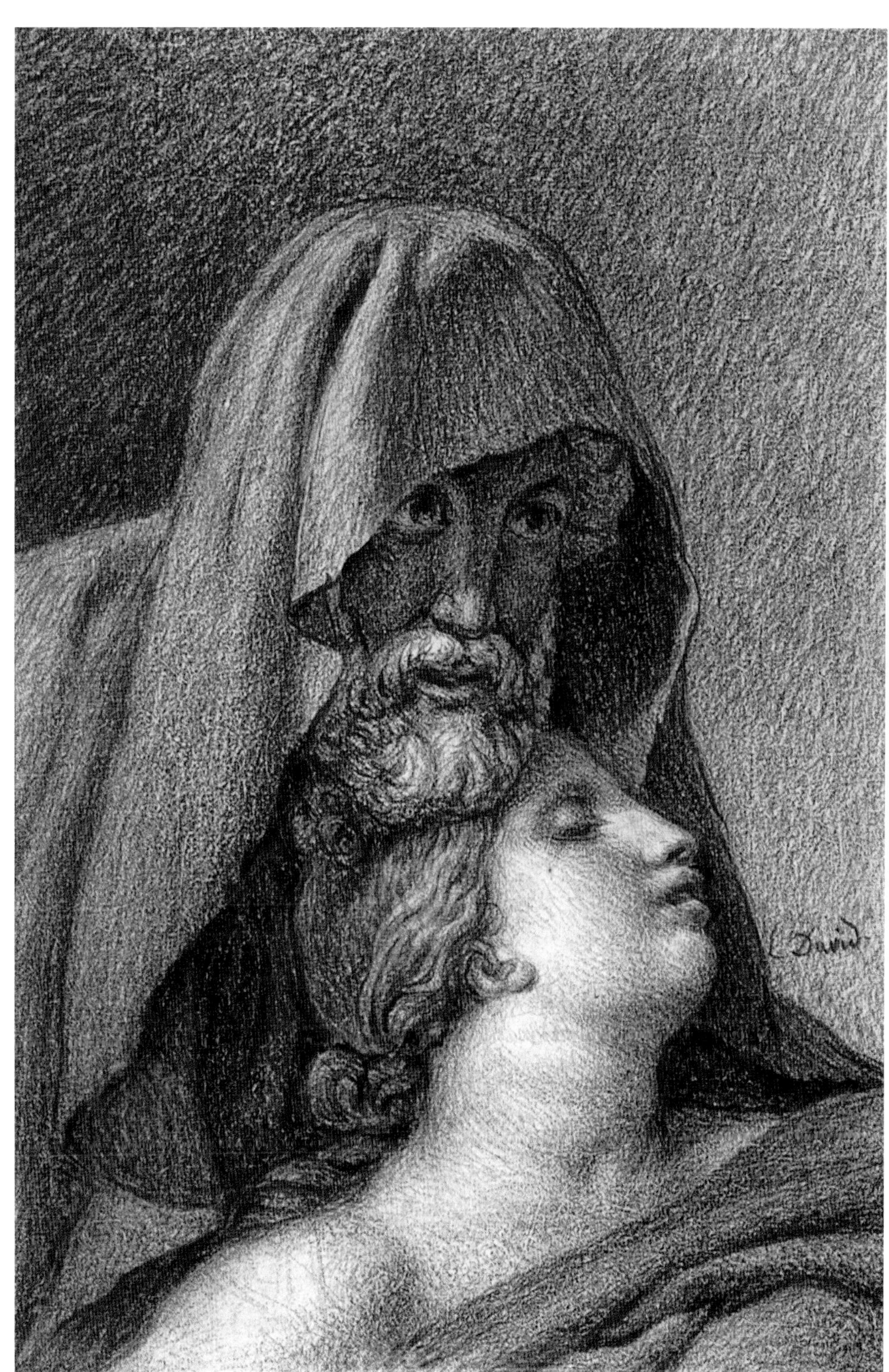
L David

7

JEAN-LOUIS-ANDRÉ-THÉODORE GÉRICAULT 1791–1824

Charging Polish Lancer, ca.1817–18

Pen and brown ink and wash, heightened with white bodycolour, over graphite on brownish paper, 25.8 × 21.4 cm

Signed, verso: *Géricault*

PROVENANCE: Antoine Madeyski

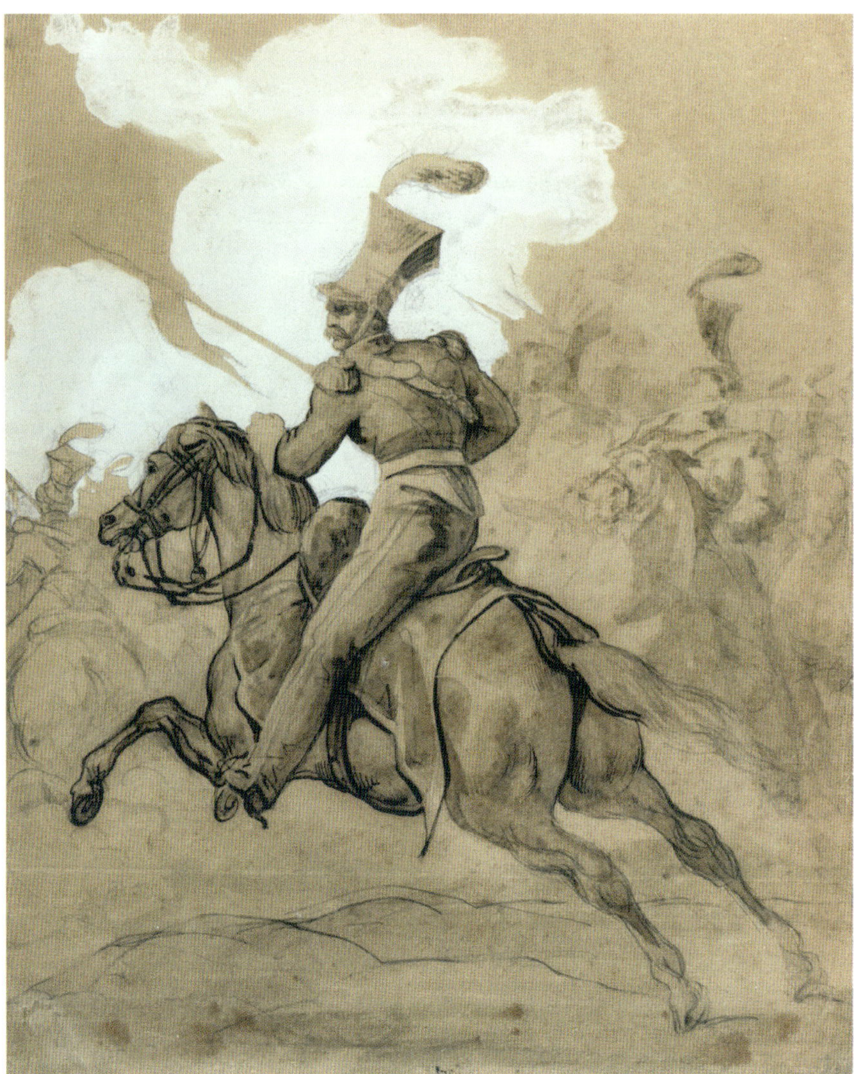

A pupil of Pierre-Narcisse Guérin (1774–1833), who was one of David's many followers, Géricault seems to have learned as much from his friendship with the celebrated horse painter Carle Vernet, and even more from the study of old and modern masters displayed in the Louvre and at Versailles. He first made his mark at the Salon of 1812 with the monumental *Charging Cuirassier* (Louvre), which earned him a gold medal. It was followed two years later by its extraordinarily emotional pendant, the *Wounded Cuirassier Leaving the Field of Battle* (Louvre), which was seen as a symbol of the defeat of Napoleon's forces in successive battles, leading to the Restoration of the monarchy in April 1814. After the ultimate defeat of Napoleon at the battle of Waterloo, Géricault temporarily abandoned military subjects and, although he failed to win the Rome Prize, spent a year studying in Italy, impressed equally by the sublimity of Michelangelo and the refinement of Raphael.

Géricault returned to Paris in late November 1817 and settled with his father into a rented house at 23 rue des Martyrs. His landlord was Colonel Louis Bro, a veteran of Napoleon's Grande Armée; next door lived the artist Horace Vernet. Géricault seems to have become reconciled to the new regime, but remained nostalgic for the heroism of earlier struggles. He made numerous drawings of Napoleonic subjects, based not on observation from the battlefield, but on inspiration found in the picture galleries of Europe. Some were intended as illustrations of specific soldiers, others were more generalised. This unpublished drawing was made in the technique characteristic of the years 1817–18, pen and brown ink with white bodycolour highlights. The charging horse is ridden by an officer wearing the distinctive plumed headgear of one of the regiments of *chevaux-légers*, who reappears in several other drawings by Géricault.[1] The penwork is bold and confident, over preliminary drawing in black chalk, and the complex perspective achieved without effort. In the background the battle rages, its confusion and din evoked in an almost breathless composition of mounted soldiers seen from a variety of angles and in different poses, as if to emphasise the courage and determination of the charging lancer.

8

JEAN-LOUIS-ANDRÉ-THÉODORE GÉRICAULT 1791–1824

The Return from Russia (Le Retour de Russie) 3rd state, 1818

Lithograph with tint stone on paper, 44.4 × 36.3 cm

Signed in the stone: *Géricault*

PROVENANCE: Collection Amédée Faure (1801–78); private collection, Nancy; Kornfield & Klipstein, Bern, June 1983, lot 225

LITERATURE: Delteil (1924), no.13, I/II; Delteil, Hyman and Joachim (2010), no.13, III/IV; Bazin (1987–97) no.1461; Michel (1991) no.66

After his return to Paris in 1817, Géricault began to experiment with lithography. The technique was ideally suited to a confident draughtsman: a drawing was made with a greasy crayon on a prepared lithographic stone and the printing achieved through the antipathy of grease and water. Although it had been invented in Munich in the late 1790s by Alois Senefelder, lithography did not become popular in France until Godefroy Engelmann (1788–1839) moved his press from Mulhouse to Paris in 1816. It was enthusiastically taken up as a means of propaganda, and a large number of shops sold prints depicting the consequences of Napoleon's defeat by artists specialising in such imagery, notably Nicolas-Toussaint Charlet (1792–1845) and Auguste Raffet (1804–60). Napoleon's army had been disbanded on 16 July 1815, and the French capital was flooded with officers on half pay and soldiers in a wretched state. The propaganda from the printmakers was blatant: 'the Bonapartists have only lithography on their side, but they are using it beautifully. The walls are covered with prints of six sous representing the Old Guard under all its guises'.[1]

Géricault was probably introduced to lithography by Vernet. His first lithograph was based on a drawing made in Rome, but he quickly turned to Napoleonic subjects. *The Return from Russia* depicts one of the most ignominious episodes in the war, following the retreat from Moscow in 1812 and the deaths of nearly half a million French soldiers of the Grande Armée. On a frozen plain, a one-armed grenadier leads a horse carrying a blind and wounded cuirassier. An exhausted and starving dog walks by their side while, behind, an infantryman carries his comrade. The preparatory drawing includes four main figures,[2] but Géricault understood that reducing their number to two increased the pathos of the scene. In a remarkable new departure, Géricault used for the first time in the history of lithography a second stone to give light and shade to the scene, in particular to emphasise the chill of snow and sky.

Géricault made nearly 100 lithographs in the five years before his death, but this has long been recognised as his masterpiece. His first biographer, Charles Clément, wrote in 1879 that 'It is the same inspiration as in the *Wounded Cuirassier,* but the execution is more sophisticated and the impression grander and even more affecting'.[3]

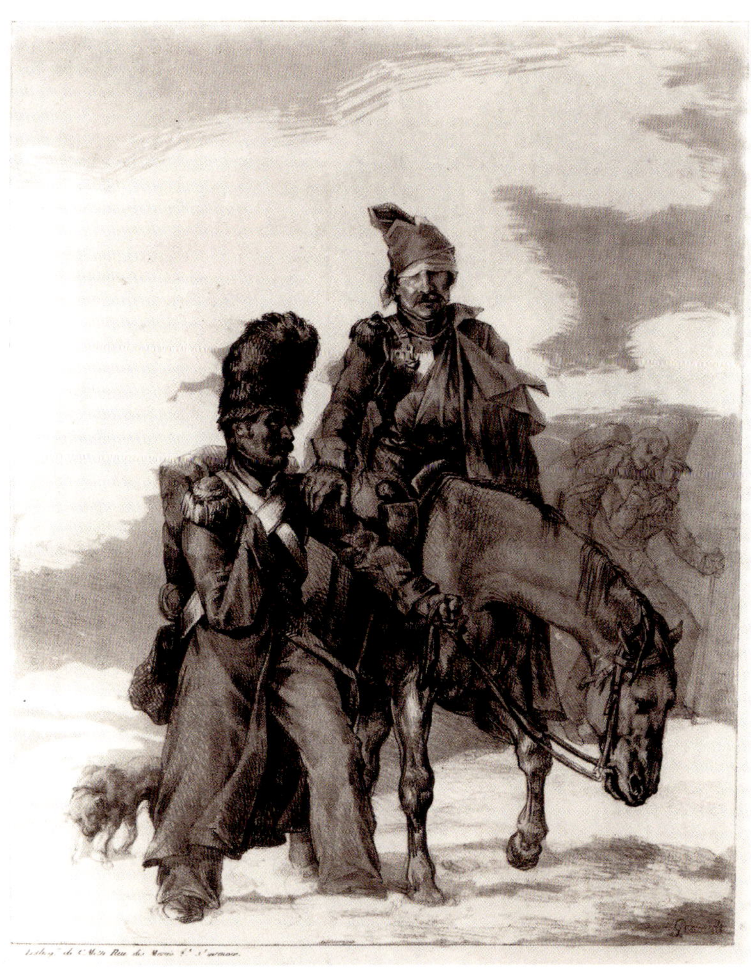

9

JEAN-LOUIS-ANDRÉ-THÉODORE GÉRICAULT 1791–1824

Combat of a Lion and a Tiger, Three Studies of the Head of a Lion, and a Study of a Paw, ca.1822

Watercolour and graphite on off-white paper, 24.5 × 30.5 cm

PROVENANCE: Maurice Gobin (L.1124a); private collection, Paris

LITERATURE: Bazin (1987–97), no.2,351

In 1820 Géricault travelled to London to organise an exhibition of his masterpiece shown to sensational effect at the Salon in the previous year, the *Raft of the Medusa* (Louvre). He remained in England for 20 months, socialising with his compatriots, especially Charlet, and meeting distinguished contemporaries such as Sir David Wilkie and Sir Thomas Lawrence. He was persuaded to revise his estimate of the English School, and was especially admiring of Sir David Wilkie's *Chelsea Pensioners*, which he described as achieving 'the last degree of pathos, like nature itself'.[1] Although he completed only one major oil painting, *The Epsom Downs Derby* (Louvre), Géricault worked very hard. His 12 lithographs, published in spring 1821 as *Various Subjects Drawn from Life and On Stone by J. Gericault,* demonstrate a new enthusiasm for everyday life. Nine of the prints have the horse as their main subject, while the other three are compassionate evocations of a bagpipe player, a beggar and a paralysed woman. His watercolours also concentrate on daily life in the streets, the stables and the docks.

According to Clément, Géricault also visited the zoological gardens where he made studies of lions and tigers. Although he has generally been assumed to be referring to the Zoological Society in Regents Park, this did not in fact open until 1828; it is more likely that Géricault made his studies at the royal menagerie in the Tower of London, which had housed lions and other wild animals since the late Middle Ages. This dramatic watercolour is generally believed to have been made shortly after Géricault's return to Paris in December 1821.[2] The inspiration, however, is English: Géricault would certainly have known at least one of the many versions of George Stubbs composition of a *Horse Attacked by a Lion*. Indeed, he had considered as early as 1814 the subject of the horses of Xerxes being attacked by lions, and, shortly before his visit to London, had made a lithograph of a *Lion Devouring a Horse*.[3] If these studies of a *Combat of a Lion and a Tiger* were made from life, as the subsidiary drawings of the lion's roaring head, of the lion reclining and of a hind leg would suggest, they may have been executed in the Jardin des Plantes in Paris. The rapid drawing and boldly applied watercolour of the principal scene demonstrate Géricault's consummate mastery of a technique he had only recently adopted, in an evocation of almost primeval violence.

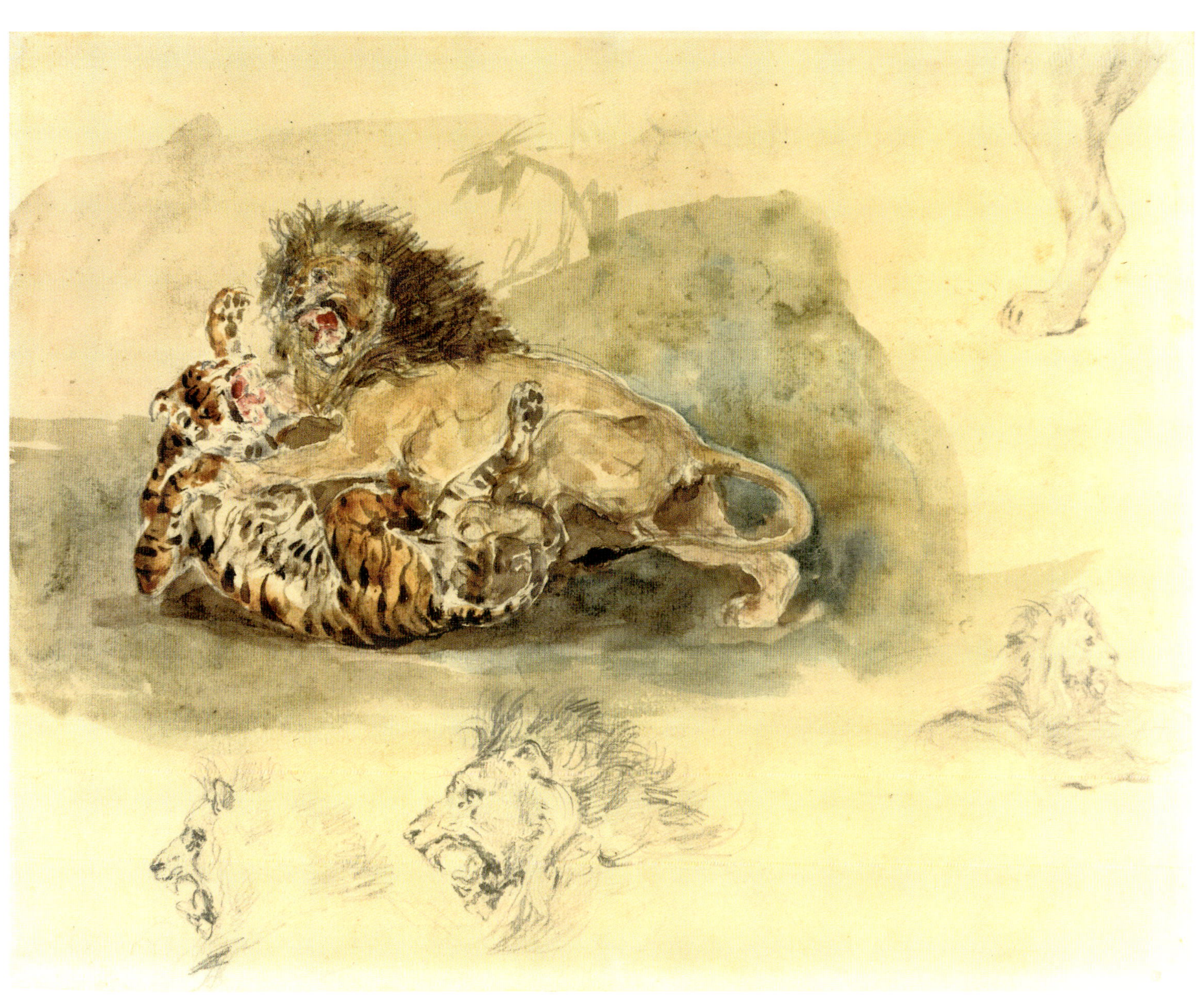

10

FERDINAND-VICTOR-EUGÈNE DELACROIX 1798–1863

Madame Cavé, ca.1836–46

Pastel on paper, 30 × 23 cm

PROVENANCE: Jenny Le Guillou, the artist's housekeeper; given to Constant Dutilleux; Henri Rouart; 16–18 December 1912, lot 95; Louis Rouart; Galerie Charpentier, Paris, 3 December 1957; F. & P. Nathan, Zurich; Walter Franz; sale, Lempertz, Cologne, June 1984; Christie's, London, 4 December 1984, lot 137a; Christie's, London, 27 June 1989, lot 102

LITERATURE: Robaut (1885), no.983; Johnson, L. (1995), no.15

Although Delacroix's early work includes a preponderance of portraits, his ambitions as a history painter soon left little time for portraits in oil, and, unlike Ingres and many of his contemporaries, he rarely undertook commissions. Indeed, his mature portraits all depict close friends, such as Louis-Auguste Schwiter and the lovers Frédéric François Chopin and George Sand. He also painted himself three times.

Even in the much less demanding medium of pastel, Delacroix made few portraits. He worked in pastel from the 1820s onwards, sometimes making studies from nature or from life for larger compositions in oils, sometimes creating independent works of art. He may have been stimulated to explore its properties by his friend, the sculptor Jules-Robert Auguste (1789–1850), by whom he eventually owned nine pastels. Another friend who used pastels was Schwiter. Delacroix would certainly have quickly become aware of what Diderot and D'Alembert's *Encyclopédie* described as the medium's special attraction, that 'of all manners of painting it passes for the easiest and most convenient, in that it can be left, resumed, retouched, and finished at will'.[1] Moreover, he would have been aware of the great series of pastel portraits by earlier French artists such as Maurice-Quentin de La Tour. Indeed, Delacroix's earliest dated pastel is a copy after an eighteenth-century portrait of a *Young Man in a Wig* that, in its unfinished state, resembles some of La Tour's preparations.[2]

The sitter in this striking portrait has always been identified as Marie-Elisabeth Blavot (1809–83). Herself an artist, she married a pupil of Ingres, Clément Boulanger (1805–42), and, after his premature death, became the wife of Edmond Cavé, head of the Department of Fine Arts in the Ministry of the Interior. She exhibited regularly at the Salon and wrote numerous drawing manuals. Delacroix had certainly become friendly with her by 1833, when they exchanged pastels. Later the pair were sufficiently intimate to travel together (without her husband) to the Low Countries in 1839. He later read and commented on her treatise *La Couleur… ouvrage approuvé par M. Eugène Delacroix* (1863). Although the portrait has traditionally been dated (on no evidence) to 1846, Lee Johnson suggests it may be compared with a drawing dated 1836 which apparently depicts the same person. In the pastel, the unflinching gaze, the rapid delineation of the features and the free handling, especially in the flesh and hair, suggest a warmth between artist and sitter that is rare in Delacroix's work.

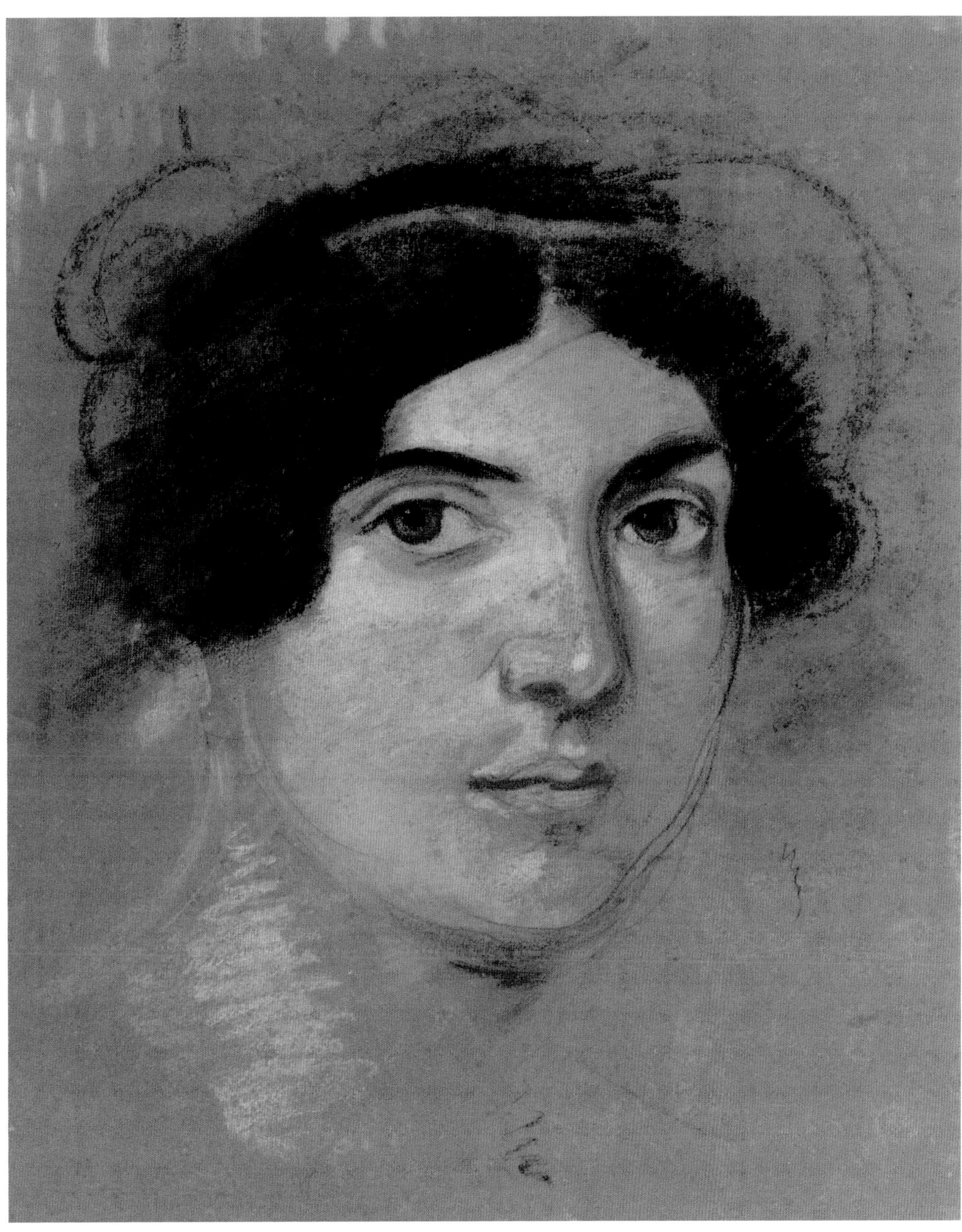

11

FERDINAND-VICTOR-EUGÈNE DELACROIX 1798–1863

Encounter of Moorish Horsemen (Rencontre de cavaliers maures), 1834

Etching and drypoint on paper, 18.1 × 24.9 cm

Signed in the plate: *Eug. Delacroix / f. 1834.*

LITERATURE: Delteil and Strauber (1997), no.23; Stuffmann (1987), no.H23; Alaoui (1994–5), no.68

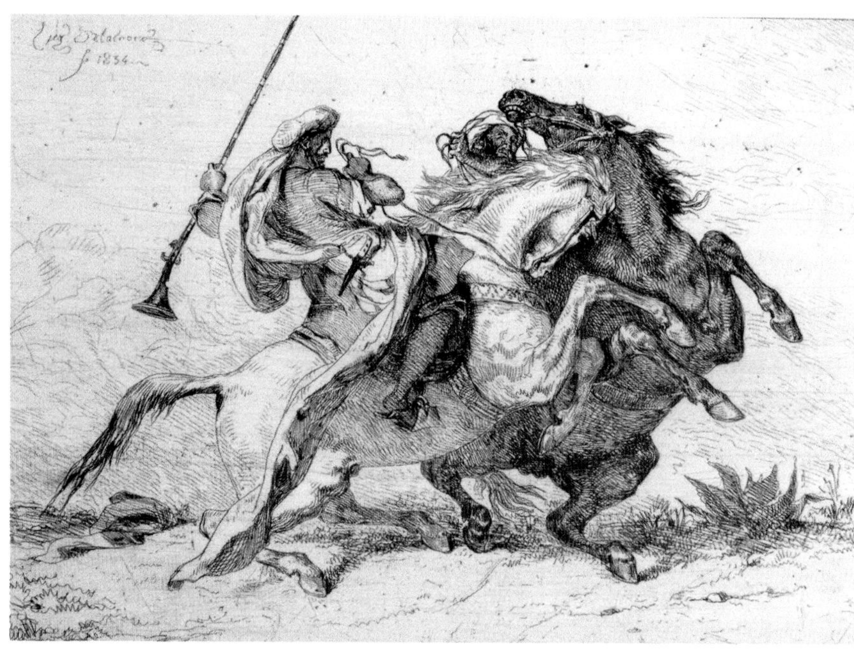

Delacroix's journey to North Africa in 1832 was fundamental to his future development as an artist. He believed that, for the first time, he would experience the costumes and habits of true antiquity, rather than the false 'antique' values promoted by the Academy. The authenticity of his experience made him feel that he had hitherto been living and seeing second-hand, through the eyes of others. Moreover, the brilliance of the colours in dazzling sunlight encouraged him to adopt an even more daring palette. From the three months he spent in Morocco, Delacroix brought back seven albums and sketchbooks, providing him with material which he used for the rest of his life.

Delacroix accompanied the comte de Mornay on a diplomatic mission, made delicate after the French occupation of Algeria in 1830. They disembarked at Tangiers on 24 January 1832 and were received by the Emperor at Meknes on 22 March. On the way, the men several times witnessed the military exercises of the Moroccan troops known as the '*course de poudre*', for example on 6 March. 'This consisted of horsemen charging at the highest speed and suddenly reining in their mounts, having fired their muskets. It often happens that the horses run out of control and fight with each other when they meet'.[1] Mornay noted that 'this exercise was undertaken in great solemnness, and in front of personages deserving of the highest marks of respect. Moreover, this honour is not without danger for the Christians who are accorded them, because the Moors like to shoot in their faces to see if they allow themselves to appear frightened'.[2] These episodes inspired several oil paintings, notably the *Collision of Arab Horsemen*. The work was one of Delacroix's principal submissions to the Salon of 1834, where it was rejected, together with *Les Femmes d'Alger* (Louvre), which was accepted.[3]

This rare etching, of which only six impressions are known to exist, was made to accompany the deluxe edition of Alexandre Decamps' *Le Musée, Revue du Salon de 1834*; the reproductions in the ordinary edition were lithographs. It is traditionally attributed to Delacroix, although Lee Johnson and others now attribute it to Célestin Nanteuil (1813–73).[4] This prolific printmaker did indeed contribute several etchings to this publication, including the *Femmes d'Alger* and the *Portrait of Rabelais* after Delacroix.[5] There were three impressions of the print in Delacroix's posthumous sale, but Decamps noted in *Le Musée* that Delacroix had provided a drawing after his painting. However, the signature in the etching is quite categorically that of Delacroix, and would surely not have been inscribed thus by Nanteuil.

12

JEAN-AUGUSTE-DOMINIQUE INGRES 1780–1867

Odalisque, 1825

Lithograph on wove paper, 13.2 × 21 cm

Lettered: *Ingres 1825. I. lith. de Delpech ODALISQUE.*

LITERATURE: Delteil (1908), no.9; Salmon (2006), pp.37–40

After studying with Jacques-Louis David and winning the Rome Prize in 1801, Ingres travelled to Italy in 1806. He remained in the peninsula for nearly 20 years, not returning to Paris until 1824. During this period Ingres completed his education at the French Academy, received several prestigious commissions and made a number of influential friends. Among the most powerful was Joachim Murat, King of Naples, who was married to Napoleon's youngest sister, Caroline Bonaparte. In 1809 they acquired Ingres' *Sleeping Woman* (the *Dormeuse de Naples*; destroyed), painted in the previous year, the first of the full-frontal nudes which culminated in the *Odalisque with a Slave* (1839; Fogg Art Museum, Cambridge). The Murats later became important patrons: in 1814 Ingres painted two Troubadour pictures for them, as well as a group portrait of their family and a single, full-length portrait of the queen (Louvre). In addition, he executed a pendant to the *Sleeping Woman*, the *Grande odalisque* (Louvre), intended as a mirror image to its pendant. The figure is here seen from behind rather than from the front, looking forwards rather than back, with her arms down rather than up, and is altogether far less lascivious. Ingres was paid 1,200 francs for the painting in 1813, and completed it in his studio in Rome in the summer of 1814. It was apparently delivered to Naples, but the fall of Napoleon's regime and the departure of the Murats deprived Ingres of his most important collectors and, in his own words, 'ruined him'.[1] The *Grande odalisque* was exhibited at the Salon of 1819, where it attracted almost universal derision. Nevertheless it became popular with collectors, and at least six replicas were executed by Ingres or under his supervision.

In 1825 Ingres made this lithograph after the painting. It was his only work in this medium – and only a very small number of impressions were printed – but reveals a consummate mastery of the technique. Only the fact that he made the drawing on the stone in the same direction as the painting, so that it printed in reverse, may betray his inexperience. It shows two main differences from the painting: the fly swat is of horse hair, rather than peacock feathers, and the censer is a different shape. Otherwise Ingres remained remarkably faithful to his original. However, of all the prints after this painting, which became the most reproduced in the whole of Ingres' career, it is only his own lithograph that is more than a translation. It was published by François Delpech in his *Album lithographique* in 1825.

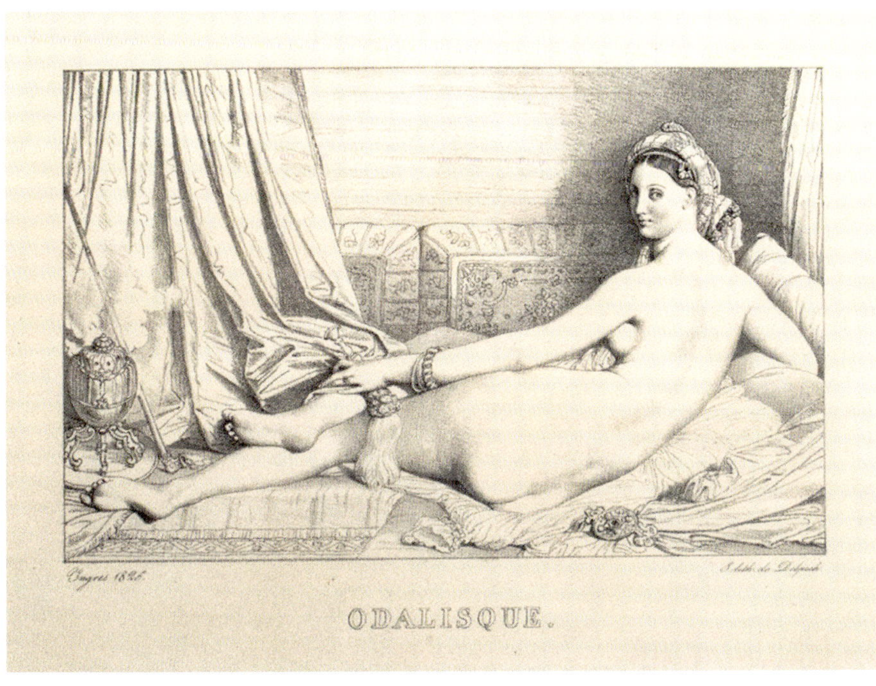

13 & 14

JEAN-AUGUSTE-DOMINIQUE INGRES 1780–1867

Study for Sainte Geneviève, Patron Saint of Paris, 1844
Study for Saint Germain, Bishop of Paris, 1844

13: *Study for Sainte Geneviève, Patron Saint of Paris*
Graphite on tracing paper, 36.2 × 15.2 cm

PROVENANCE: Jacques Édouard Gatteaux (L.852); Étienne Moreau-Nélaton; sale, Paris, 5 December 1879, lot 15; Bromberg collection, Paris; Sotheby's, Monaco, 3 December 1989, lot 526; galerie Perreau-Saussine, Paris, 1990; Christie's, London, 10 July 2001, lot 136; Arturo Cuellar

LITERATURE: Foucart (2002), under no.18

14: *Study for Saint Germain, Bishop of Paris*
Graphite on tracing paper, 36.2 × 15.2 cm

PROVENANCE: Jacques Édouard Gatteaux (L.852); Degas (L.657); his sale, 26–7 March 1918, lot 194; sale, Bayeux, 17 September 1995, lot 21; Sotheby's, New York, 24 May 1996, lot 454

LITERATURE: Foucart (2002), under no.22

After the death of his eldest son and heir Ferdinand, duc d'Orléans, in 1842, it was natural that King Louis-Philippe should turn to Ingres to design two sets of memorial stained-glass windows, since he had recently painted the prince's portrait. Ingres undertook the commission willingly, since he had become deeply attached to the prince; he wrote to a friend that 'All I do is cry and I shall cry for a long time. The only thing that consoles me is that I am fortunate to have painted his portrait'.[1] The first design, in 1842, was for 17 cartoons of individual saints for the chapel of St Ferdinand, newly constructed near the spot where the prince had died; and the second, in the following year, was for eight cartoons for the royal chapel at Dreux. This was the burial chamber of the Orléans family, which had been built in 1816 and extended in neo-Gothic style from 1839. Ingres was commissioned in July 1843, but seems not to have begun work on the project until early the following year. The north transept was decorated with figures of the following saints: Geneviève, Denis, Clotilde, Ferdinand, Amélie and Philip, while opposite appear saints Louis, Isabelle, Germain, Radegonde, Rémi and Bathilde. Each window included a male and a female saint in pairs. The borders and crosses at the tops of the windows were designed by Eugène Viollet-le-Duc.

Ingres prepared the windows in the traditional academic manner, making studies from nude models to determine the pose of each figure, then working from the clothed models to establish the fall of the draperies. He then moved on to the full-scale cartoons, each some two metres in height. These in turn were painted in the royal porcelain factory at Sèvres. When installed, the windows gave the interior a newly medieval emphasis, the richness of the colouring emphasised by the hieratic poses of the saints. These two studies represent the earliest phase of work on the figures. Saint Geneviève of Nanterre (*c.*AD420–*c.*500) is the patron saint of Paris. She is seen holding the medallion given her when she was a child by Saint Germain l'Auxerrois. Saint Germain (d.576) founded the abbey of Saint-Germain-des-Prés in Paris. Ingres shows him holding a bishop's crozier, but without the traditional attributes of chains and flames.

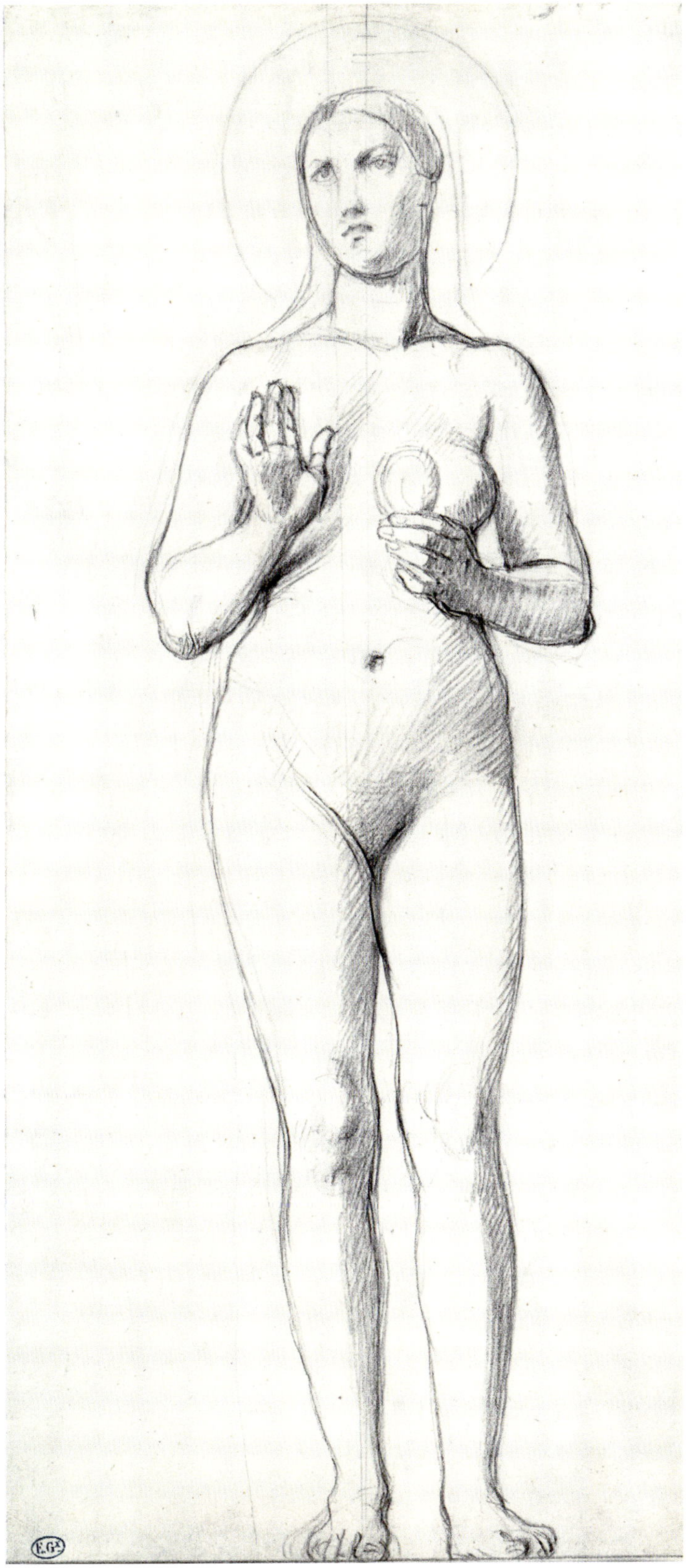

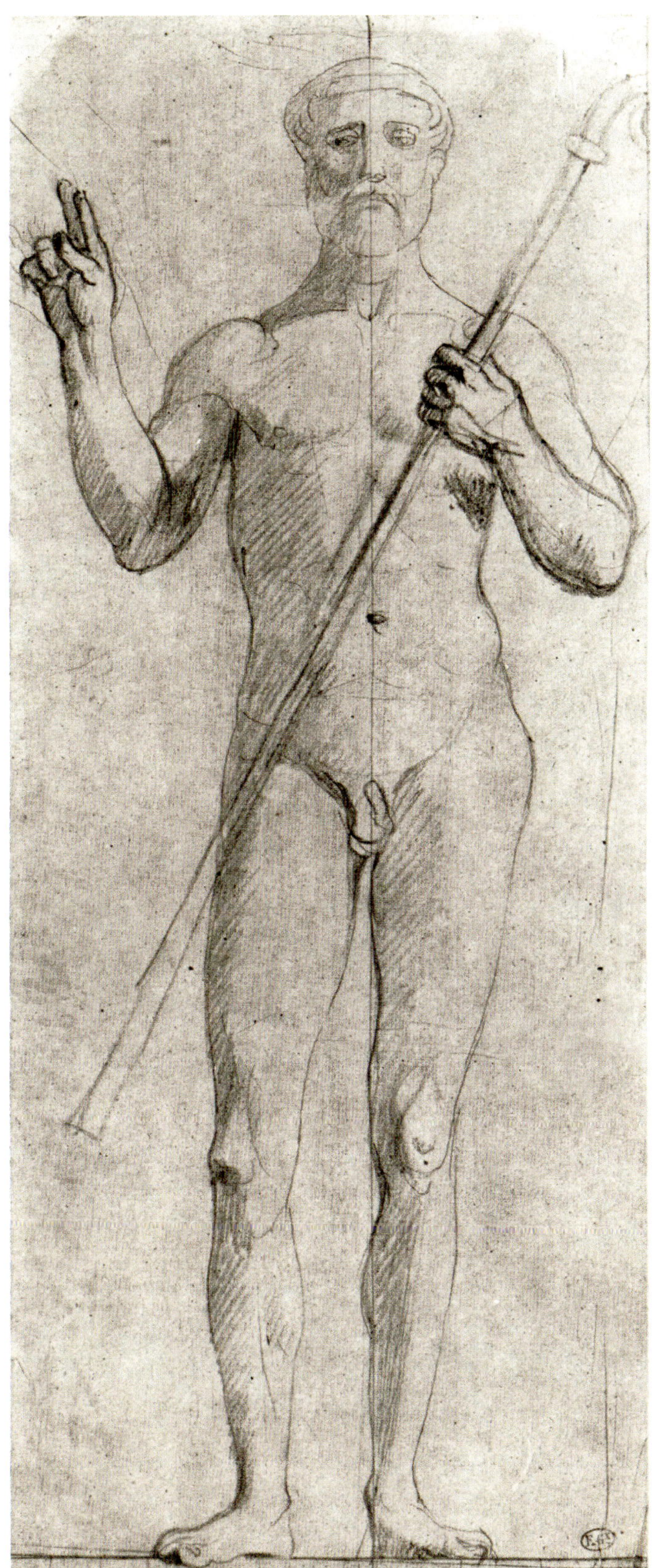

15

THÉODORE CHASSÉRIAU 1819–1856

Venus Anadyomene 1st state, ca.1841–42

Lithograph on wove paper, 32 × 26.6 cm

Lettered: *Th. Chasseriau 1839. Lith. D'Auguste Bry.* APHROGENEIA *Paris, Goupil et Vibert, editeurs, boulevard Montmartre, 15*

LITERATURE: Sandoz (1974), no.266; Fisher (1979), no.3 I/II

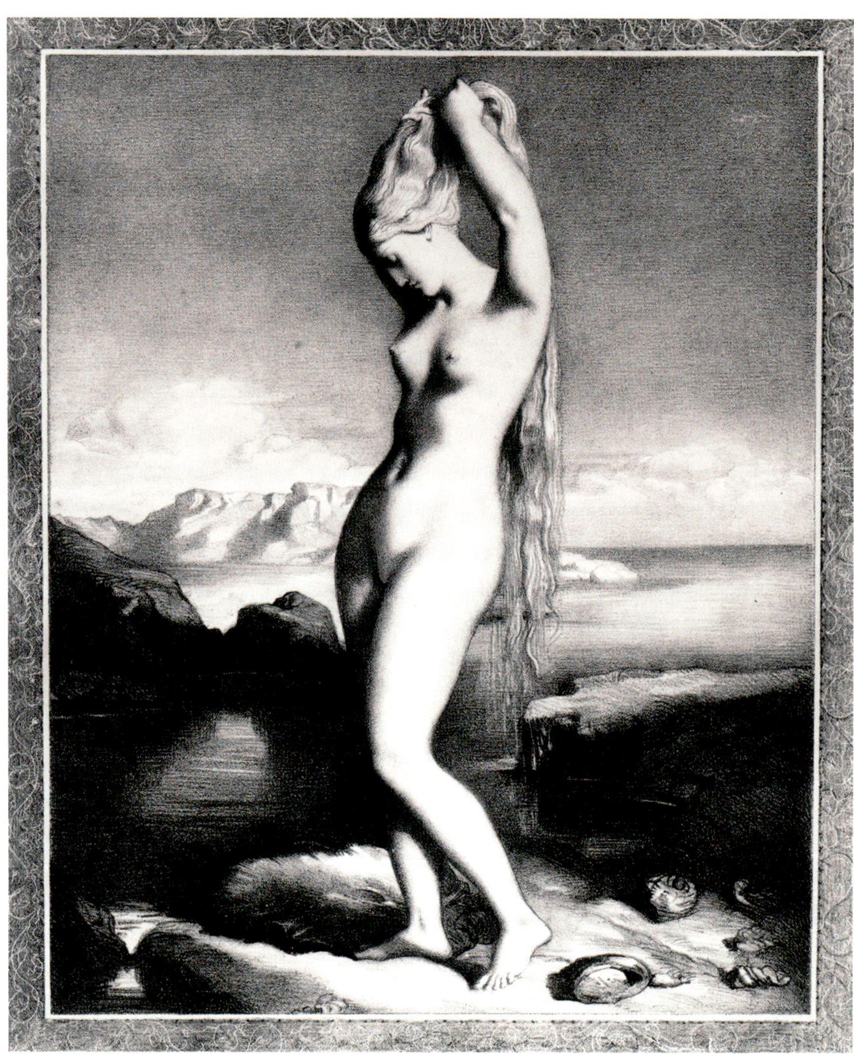

Chassériau was precociously gifted. At the age of 11 he entered Ingres' studio, where he remained until his master's departure for Rome to take up the directorship of the French Academy in December 1834. His first notable success came at the Salon of 1839, where he showed two contrasting nudes, one sacred and one secular: the huge *Susanna at her Bath* and the tiny *Marine Venus* (both Louvre), the one as imposing and decorative as the other is intimate and refined. The birth of Venus is related in Hesiod's *Theogony*: Time had hacked off the genitals of his father the Sky, which, after being transported by the waves of the sea, produced a white foam. From this a daughter was born, emerging from the sea on the coast of Cyprus. Since the Renaissance the subject had been popular, and Ingres had been working on his own version since 1807 (completed in 1847; Chantilly). Chassériau's painting was much admired by the writer Théophile Gautier, who translated its charms into words, describing the antique beauty of the goddess, still moist from the kisses of the sea, who twists the pearls of her hair into tears and develops through the gracious arch of her stance the form of a divine beauty and of youthfulness.[1]

Some time later – it was not recorded in the official registers until June 1842 –Chassériau made a lithograph after his painting. Although it was his first essay in this medium, he succeeded in producing one of the masterpieces of Romantic lithography, the subtlety of draughtsmanship and shading quite different from Ingres' *Odalisque* [cat.12]. The print was based on a preparatory drawing in red chalk.[2] In the rare first state, of which only six impressions are known to exist, including the present example, the composition is surrounded by an elegant and subtly classical border. For the commercial publication by Bertauts, however, the artist removed the border.

Although Chassériau made a suite of 15 etchings illustrating *Othello* in 1843–4, and several other single plates, he produced only three lithographs. The others were *Apollo and Daphne*, published in *L'Artiste* in 1844 and taken from his own painting, and the *Betrayal of Iago*, copied from an etching of 1844 but not published.

16

THÉODORE CHASSÉRIAU 1819–1856

Two Women in a Forest, ca.1840–41

Graphite heightened with white bodycolour on blue-grey paper, 23.3 × 15.8 cm

PROVENANCE: Comtesse de Prailly, Rome; Germain Seligman, New York (L.3863); Galerie Krugier, Geneva

LITERATURE: Sandoz (1974), p.27; Sandoz (1986), no.161; Prat (1988), under no.1414; Prat (1988 b), no.72

After many frustrating delays, Chassériau was eventually able to travel to Rome in July 1840. He remained in Italy until January 1841, making an extended visit to Naples in the summer, where he studied in the museum and at Pompeii. Unfortunately he showed some of his studies to Ingres, which led to a break in their relations, as Chassériau described:

In a long conversation with M. Ingres, I saw that in many ways we will never understand each other. He has already passed his prime, and has no understanding of the ideas and of the changes that have been wrought in the arts in recent times.[1]

While in Italy, Chassériau's main project was the portrait of the Dominican monk Dominique Lacordaire (1840, Louvre), which was generally well received when shown at the Salon of 1841. However, as he wrote to his brother in September 1840, he was 'horribly pressed from all sides', but would return to France with many compositions for the future and 'loaded with studies of all sorts',[2] after the antique or in the open air, in the time-honoured fashion of pupils at the French Academy since the middle of the eighteenth century. Among these studies is a group of distinctive drawings in graphite, heightened with white bodycolour on blue paper. Most seem to have been made in Rome or the surrounding Campagna, for example a composition of two lovers inscribed and dated at the Villa d'Este at Tivoli in 1841.[3] The subjects are probably imaginary. Here two women gracefully draped in flowing robes stand on a wooded river bank, their forms subtly reflected in the calm water.

The general composition was later resumed in Chassériau's gently affectionate portrait of his two sisters, the *Portrait of Mlles C.,* shown at the Salon of 1843 (Louvre).

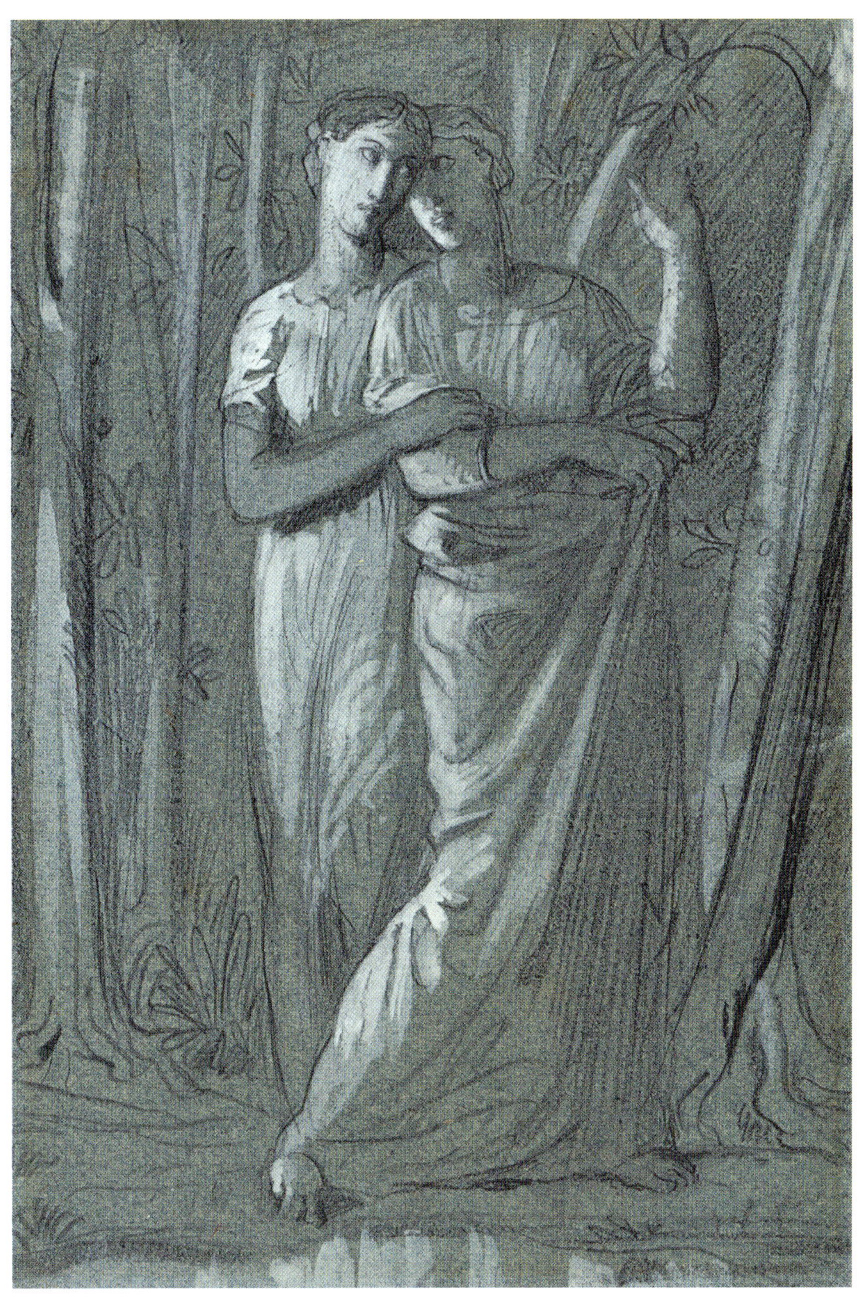

17

HONORÉ DAUMIER 1808–1879

The Legislative Stomach (Le ventre législatif. Aspect des bancs ministeriels de la chambre improstituée de 1834), 1834

Lithograph on wove paper, 32.5 × 43.5 cm
Signed in the stone: *h. Daumier*
LITERATURE: Delteil (1925–30) 131; Loyrette (1999), no.55

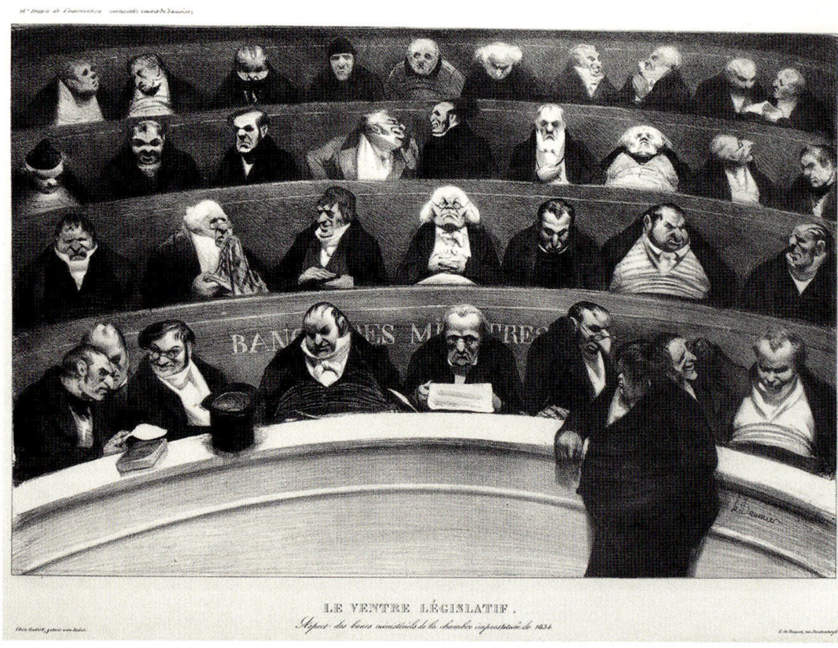

Following the revolution in July 1830 which brought about the constitutional monarchy of Louis-Philippe, Charles Philipon and his father-in-law Gabriel Aubert launched the anti-monarchist weekly *La Caricature* and it was followed on 1 December 1832 by the first daily newspaper illustrated by lithography, *Le Charivari*. Daumier was the principal contributor of caricatures to both journals. So successful were his attacks on Louis-Philippe that he was sent to prison for six months for portraying the king as *Gargantua*. In order to pay the fines levied on his newspapers, Philipon launched in 1832 a new periodical, *L'Association mensuelle lithographique*, which was offered to subscribers to *La Caricature* on payment of an extra franc, for which they received a large lithograph. Five of Daumier's most powerful satires were published in this way, notably his first contribution, *Le ventre législatif* (January 1834), and the last issued by *L'Association mensuelle*, the harrowing *Rue Transnonain, le 15 avril 1834* (July 1834).

Le ventre législatif marks the culmination of a concerted campaign by Daumier to make portraits of the 'celebrities' of the *juste milieu*, as Louis-Philippe described the policies of his government, 'equally distanced from the excesses of the power of the people, and from the abuses of royal power'. Early in 1832, at Philipon's behest, Daumier began a series of clay busts, probably from memory, of members of the government. They served as models for lithographs of each figure which appeared in *La Caricature* and *Le Charivari* in 1833–4. Finally 35 caricatures were combined in this group portrait in the chamber of deputies itself. Each member is individually characterised and identifiable. On the far left of the front row, the 'Banc des ministres', are such celebrated men as François Guizot, Adolphe Thiers, sitting behind his top hat, and Marshal Soult, glumly reading a document. Several members are portrayed in characteristic actions: Jean-Marie Harlé, seen second from the left on the second row, holds his handkerchief to his runny nose, having earlier been described in *La Caricature* as 'gouty, doddery, asthmatic, rheumatic, a magistrate, snotty-nosed'.[1]

Ever since its publication, *Le Ventre législatif* has been acclaimed as one of the greatest of all lithographs, both in subject matter and execution. It represents the ultimate condemnation of the pretensions of those who pretend to govern. As Edmond Duranty, the critic and friend of the Impressionists, wrote in 1878: 'The deputies read, chat, laugh, think, take snuff, or blow their noses; a few have that sagging, stupefied look of old men in their dotage.' Of Daumier's technique, he noted that 'the bold, transparent, velvety blacks, and the delicate clear halftones, modulated over a range of varying intensities, preserve the warm, limpid, creamy whites that this disciple of Rubens and the Venetians was so skilful at deploying'.[2]

18

HONORÉ DAUMIER 1808–1879

Accusation (The Prosecutor's Charges), ca.1860s

Pen and ink and wash, 19.4 × 27.1 cm

Signed: *h. Daumier*

PROVENANCE: M. Villemot 1878; Joseph Hessel, Paris; Robert von Hirsch, Basel; Sotheby's, London, 20–27 June 1978, lot 810

LITERATURE: Maison (1968), no.665

Daumier was familiar with lawyers and the legal process all his life. When he was a boy he ran errands for a bailiff, and for most of his adult life, he lived near the Palais de Justice on the Ile Saint Louis. For several years after his release from prison following the court case of 1832, he often made caricatures from life in the courts. Lawyers became frequent subjects in his work, notably the set of 39 lithographs that enjoyed great success when published as *Les gens de justice* between 1845 and 1848. In this gallery of portraits he depicted lawyers and judicial authorities as essentially rapacious and unscrupulous; self-important in their long black gowns and caps, they appear interested only in the means, not the ends, and their clients are seen as victims. Daumier also painted a number of oils of courtroom scenes in the late 1840s and 1850s.

After *Le Charivari* terminated his contract to supply lithographic caricatures in 1860, Daumier turned increasingly to drawing, finding a ready market for his gentle satires on modern life. This sheet and another, almost identical,[1] show the moment of highest drama in a trial, when counsel accuses the prisoner at the bar. Like a bird of prey, he stands and points with menace, while the accused is seen in profile, his head hanging low. The scene probably took place in the old *cour d'assizes*, with three judges on the bench. The rapid, almost frenetic penwork and skilfully applied wash are generally seen to characterise the artist's late works, though there is evidence that he had already employed this style in the late 1840s.

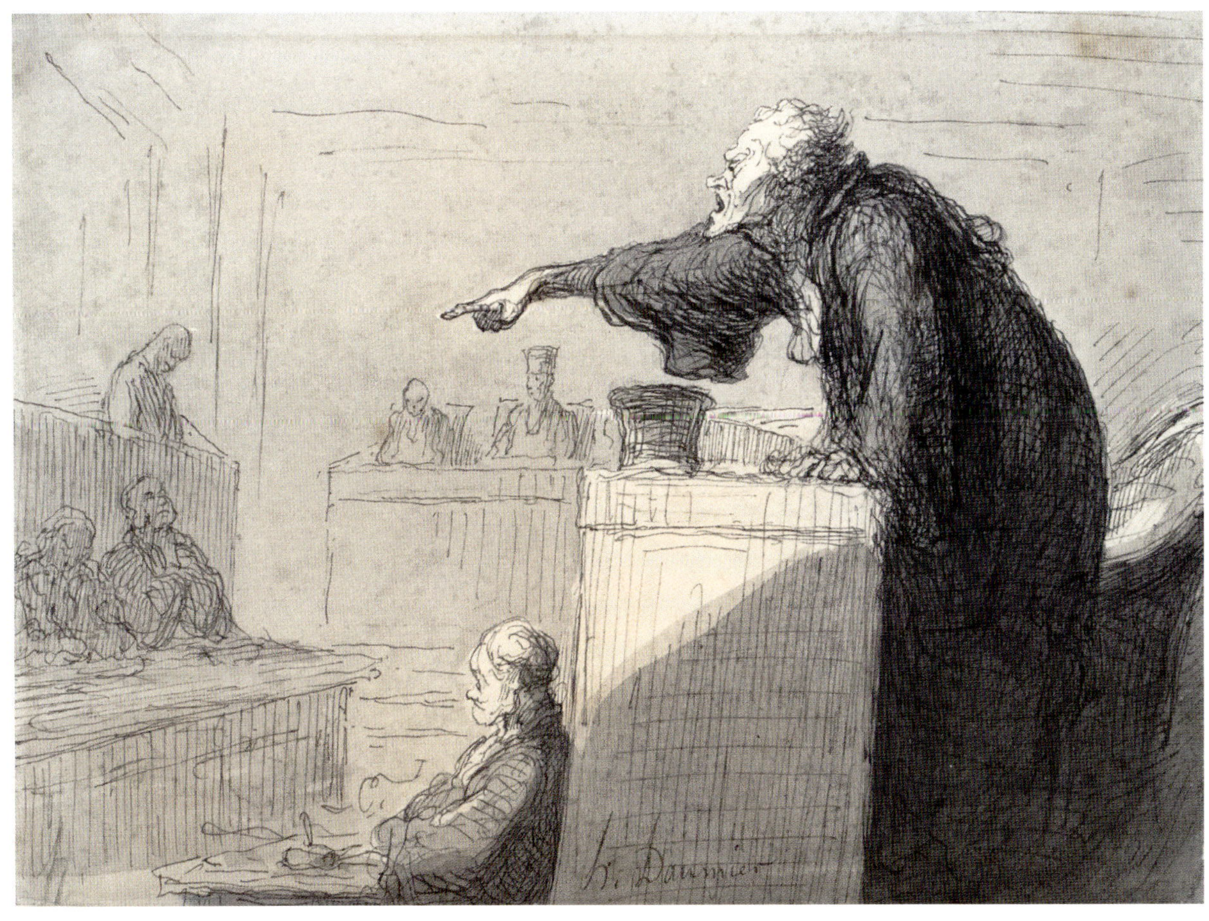

19

HONORÉ DAUMIER 1808–1879

Politics, mid-1860s

Pen and brush in black ink with grey wash and charcoal, 39.3 × 32 cm

Signed: *h. Daumier*

PROVENANCE: Galerie Camentron, Paris; Paul Aubry, Paris; his sale, Galerie Georges Petit, 10 May 1897, lot 41; Galerie Durand-Ruel; Galerie Moline; Otto Gerstenberg, Berlin; Margarethe Scharf, Berlin, 1935; Galerie Matthiessen Berlin; Albert C. Nussbaumer, Lugano, 1942–1961; Matthiessen Ltd, London; Sotheby's, 28 June 1999, lot 2; acquired at Sotheby's by Achim Moeller Fine Art on behalf of John C. Whitehead; his sale, Christie's, New York, 14 May 2015, lot 23

LITERATURE: Maison (1968), no.325

Daumier's portrayal of the everyday life of the bourgeois Parisian was most systematic in his series of 82 lithographs entitled *Les bons bourgeois*, published in *Le Charivari* between 1846 and 1849. Many depict the pastoral pleasures of Sunday outings in the countryside (which began just outside the ramparts of the city), drinking at the inn and dancing in the open-air café. During the 1860s Daumier took up such subject matter in his drawings too, and in 1865 he took a lease on a house in the commune of Valmondois, north-west of Paris. This enabled Daumier to live in both town and country – he retained his apartment in the boulevard de Clichy until shortly before his death.

In this characteristic drawing of the mid-1860s, three men are portrayed round a table in the garden of an inn. On the right, one stands with his back arched to light his cigar with an air of immense self-importance, the smoke billowing up into the foliage. Seated is a second figure wearing a contrasting bowler hat and nonchalantly reading a newspaper, while beside him a third, his top hat carelessly placed on the table, urgently gestures towards his friend. The restrained palette and clear outlines of the figures and the dappled effects of light coming through the leaves, are found in a number of other works of this period, notably the oil painting of *The Drinkers*, the watercolour of *The Good Friends* and two watercolours of *The Reader*.[1] These last have traditionally been supposed, on no evidence, to represent Daumier's friend Corot in the garden of his house at Ville d'Avray.

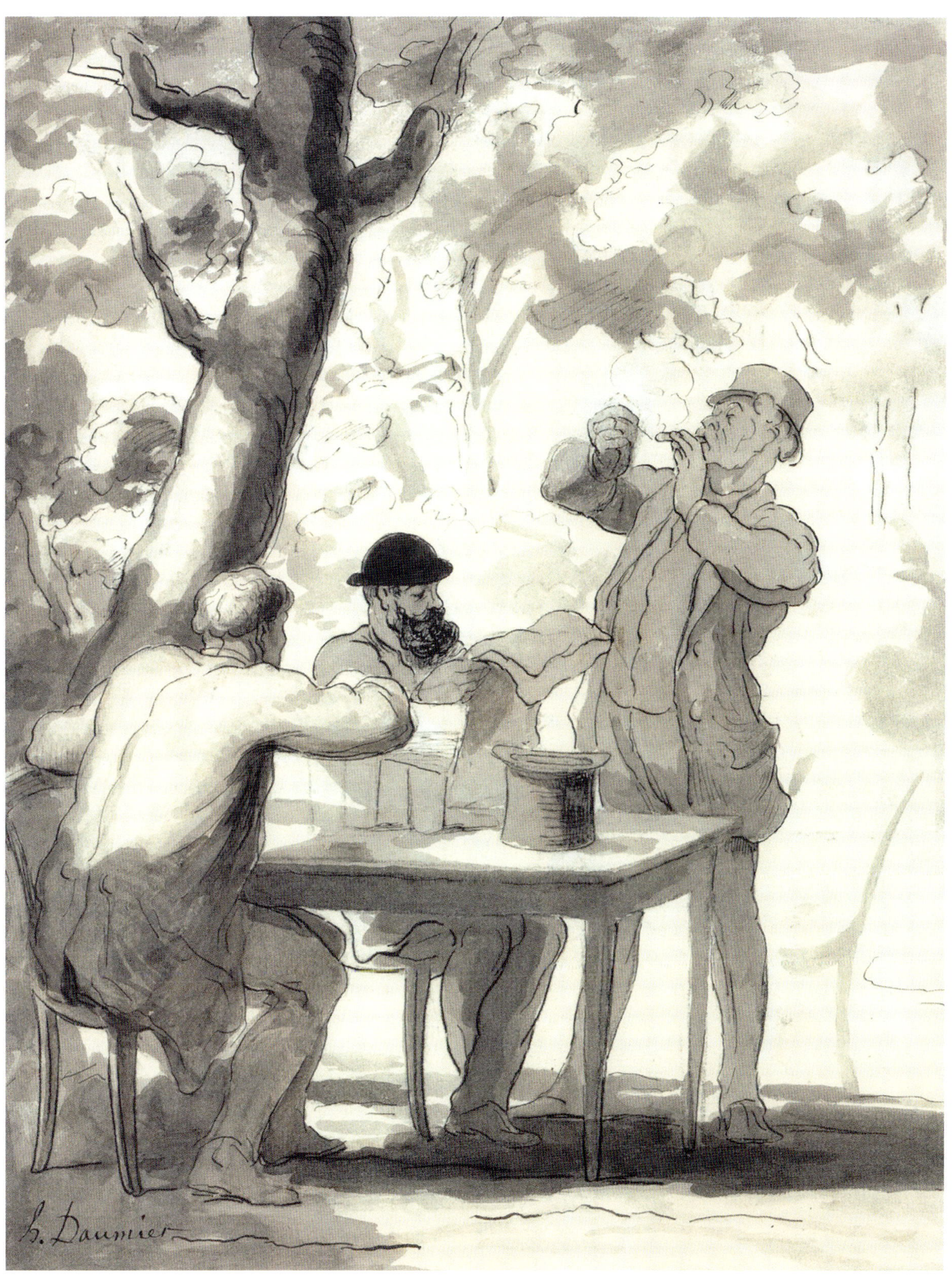
h. Daumier

20

JEAN-FRANÇOIS MILLET 1814–1875

The Seaweed Gatherers, 1854

Charcoal and white bodycolour on buff paper, 20 × 32 cm

Signed: *J. F. Millet*

PROVENANCE: Galerie Georges Petit, 1881; James Staats Forbes

LITERATURE: Sensier (1881), pp.9–10; Bénédite (1906), pl. 50; Moreau-Nélaton (1921), II, p.14

Millet was born and brought up in the hamlet of Gruchy, some ten miles east of Cherbourg. After the death of his wife in 1844, he seems not to have returned to Gruchy until the death of his mother in 1853. In the following summer he spent four months in Normandy, making a comprehensive survey of his family's possessions prior to their sale and depicting the house, garden, meadows and surrounding area in a series of about 20 drawings and 14 paintings.

In a note now lost, but translated by the American visitor Henry Naegely, Millet described the scene featured in this striking drawing:

Although the villagers did not fish, they do not neglect to gather the seaweed which the sea brings on shore in great abundance when the wind has been blowing hard from the north, and you may be sure that they do not miss the time of the tide when it floats in. The task of dragging it out of the raging sea is rough and perilous, as it is almost always driven into nearly inaccessible creeks. On these occasions the whole population is at work, for this wrack is deemed a most valuable manure for the fields. Such as have no land dry it and burn it to make kelp. A person unacquainted with the value of this seaweed would be astonished to see the trouble that the people take to get it, for in many places the men have to carry it up on their backs from the bottom of the creeks to the top of the cliffs. These cliffs, too, are often without a path, and with but just a foothold here and there along their almost perpendicular sides.[1]

Millet went on to describe the danger involved in harvesting this valuable commodity – the overloaded carts, the precarious footholds in the narrow paths. Overhead wheel great flights of seagulls, their piercing cries heard above the noise of the storm and adding to the sense of desolation. In spite of the vigorous immediacy of the handling of this drawing, it is likely that it was worked up from memory indoors. A related study in black crayon was presumably made in the open air.[2]

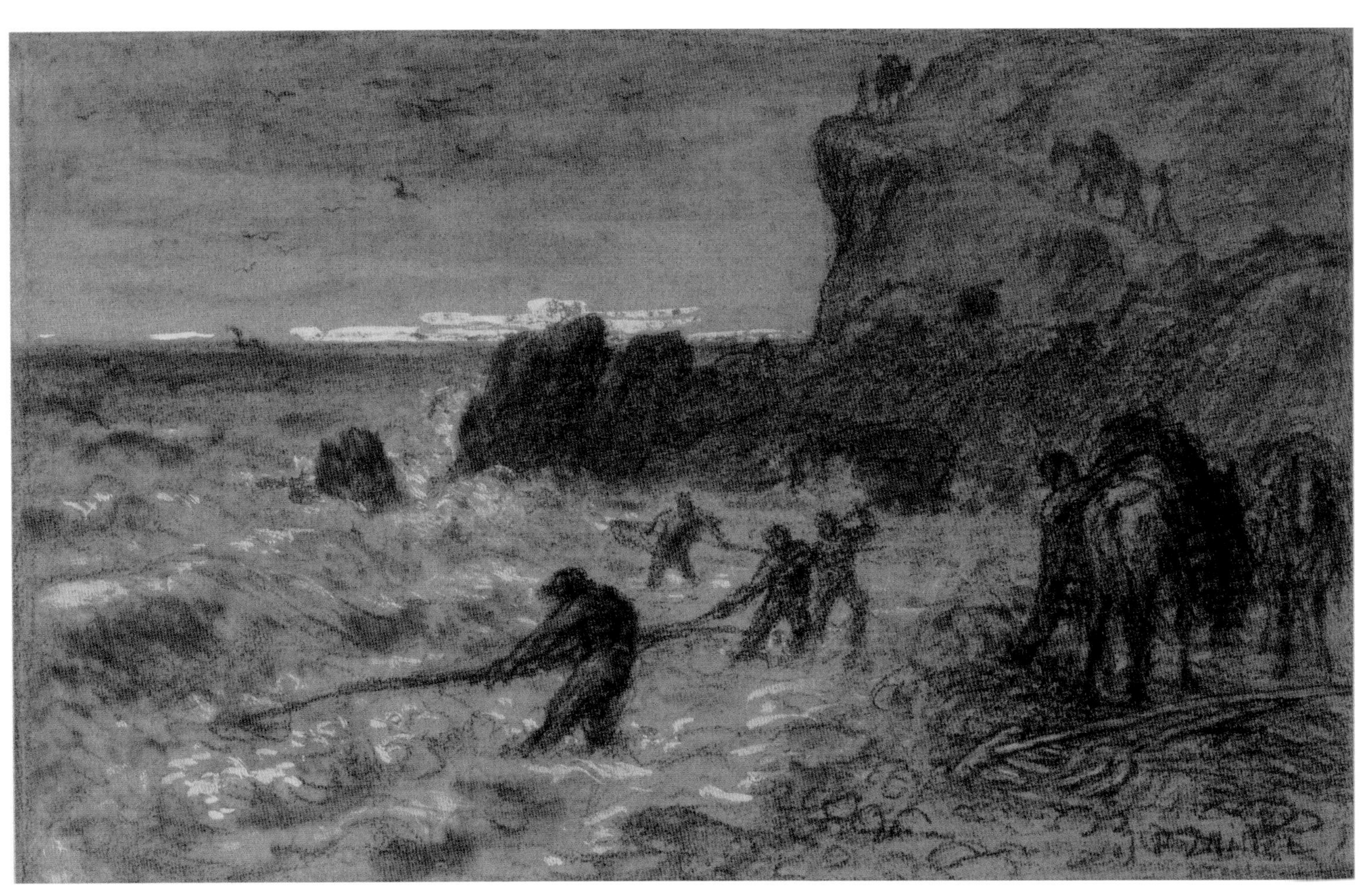

21

JEAN-FRANÇOIS MILLET 1814–1875

Shepherdess Seated on a Rock, 1855–56

Charcoal heightened with white chalk on buff paper, 37 × 28 cm

Signed: *J. F. Millet*

PROVENANCE: H. A. Budgett; Sotheby's, 20 January 1947, lot 167; Kenneth Clark; Sotheby's, 27 June 1984, lot 24

LITERATURE: Herbert (1975), no.56

In the *Atlantic Monthly* of September 1876, the American collector Edward Wheelwright gave an account of his visit over 20 years earlier to the village of Barbizon, where Millet had settled in 1849. Wheelwright stayed at Barbizon from 29 Oct 1855 to 23 June 1856. He described seeing the artist at work on a picture for Charles Tillot of 'a peasant girl, wearing the distinctive white cloak peculiar to Barbison (*sic*), reclining against a rock overshadowed by trees, and engaged in knitting, while a flock of sheep under her charge was feeding around her. In the distance was a glimpse of the Plain and men at work in the fields'. Wheelwright commissioned a replica of the composition, which Millet completed in a fortnight. He gave the collector the choice of the original or the replica, without telling him which was which; and Wheelwright chose the original.[1] As was his usual practice, Millet made at least two preparatory drawings for the composition. The first was quickly drawn in black chalk, describing not only the shepherdess but also the background, with the distant view of the plain.[2] The second drawing, seen here, is much more elaborate. Indeed, it is an independent work of art in its own right, which the artist has carefully signed – at this stage he found a market more readily for drawings than paintings.

Millet's first painting of a single agricultural labourer was *The Winnower*, exhibited at the momentous Salon of 1848, to considerable controversy.[3] He developed the genre, which Herbert has described as 'epic naturalism', in the following decade. It began with the showing of his first great success, *The Sower*, at the Salon of 1850–1 and culminated in his two most celebrated works, *The Gleaners* and *The Angelus* of 1857.[4] The figure of the shepherdess knitting was one of a sequence of scenes with peasant girls resting, ultimately derived from the *Abandoned Girl* of the mid-1840s.[5] The composition remained a favourite throughout the 1850s, and Millet returned to it in the early 1860s. The peasant girl in the etching of *La grande bergère* of 1862 is a close cousin, and she also appears in a contemporary pastel.[6]

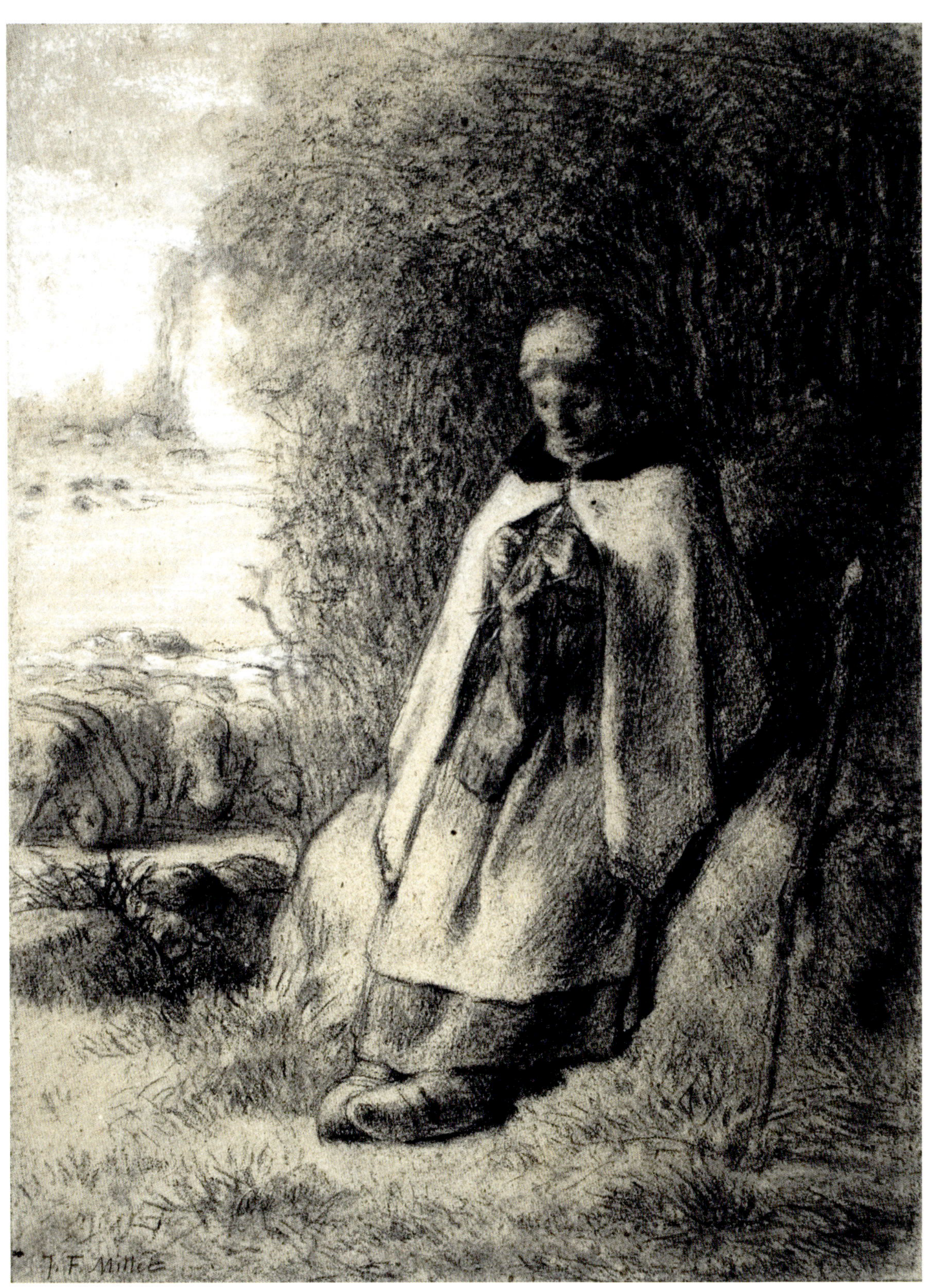

22

LOUIS-AUGUSTE-GUSTAVE DORÉ 1832–1883

Mountainous Landscape, 1879

Watercolour on off-white paper,
47 × 31.2 cm
Signed and dated: *G. Doré 1879*
LITERATURE: Zafran (2007), p.121

As a draughtsman, Doré was precocious and extraordinarily prolific. From the age of four, he worked with astonishing rapidity. Soon after his arrival in Paris from his native Strasbourg in 1847, when he was 15, he began providing publishers with drawings – initially caricatures, but later illustrations to the great classics of French and European literature. His first success came in 1854 with an illustrated edition of Rabelais' works, followed in later years by Dante's *Divine Comedy*, the Bible, Cervantes' *Don Quixote* and Ariosto's *Orlando Furioso*. He also illustrated plays and poetry by English authors such as Shakespeare and Tennyson and, most evocatively, Coleridge's *Rime of the Ancient Mariner* (1875). Almost single-handedly Doré perpetuated the taste for fantastic and Romantic imagery, not just in France, but all over the world: the publishers Cassell and Galpin had offices throughout the British Empire and Dominions. He also frequently exhibited drawings and paintings in Paris and London, with considerable success. An estimated two and a half million visitors paid a shilling each to see the Doré Gallery in Bond Street in London between 1868 and the artist's death in 1883.[1]

Although he had used watercolour in his drawings from at least 1849, it was not until 1873 that Doré began to paint in 'pure' watercolour. He had become familiar with English practitioners during his first visit to London in 1868, but it was a visit to Scotland with Sir Christopher Teesdale, Master of Ceremonies to the Prince of Wales, that marked the turning point in his technique. They travelled from Aberdeen up the River Dee to Braemar, and Doré wrote to his mother that 'I shall have my memory pretty well filled with an ample number of landscapes, which seem to me more suitable to my London exhibition than Swiss Alpine scenes'.[2] The power of the Highland scenery on Doré's imagination moved him to claim to the critic and traveller Amelia Edwards that 'Henceforth, when I paint landscapes I believe that five out of every six will be reminiscences of the Highlands, of Aberdeenshire, Braemar, Balmoral, Ballater, etc. I took a good many notes and jottings in watercolour – the first time I have tried that medium. I have employed it solely in obtaining qualities of intention or impression'.[3] Such was the artist's reputation that he was invited to join the newly founded Société des Aquarellistes Français (Society of French Watercolourists) in 1879, and showed with them annually. In spite of this success, Doré is reported to have attached relatively little importance to his watercolours, commenting that 'watercolour is only a form of handwriting with which one takes notes' – an 'artistic stenography of a special kind'.[4]

Notwithstanding his fondness for Scottish scenery, it is likely that the magnificent *Mountainous Landscape* was made during Dore's eleventh visit to the Swiss Alps with his mother and friends in 1879. The composition of strong vertical tree trunks in the foreground of a panoramic view was a favourite of the artist in the late 1870s.[5] The fluency in technique and evocative atmosphere are typical of his best works at this date.

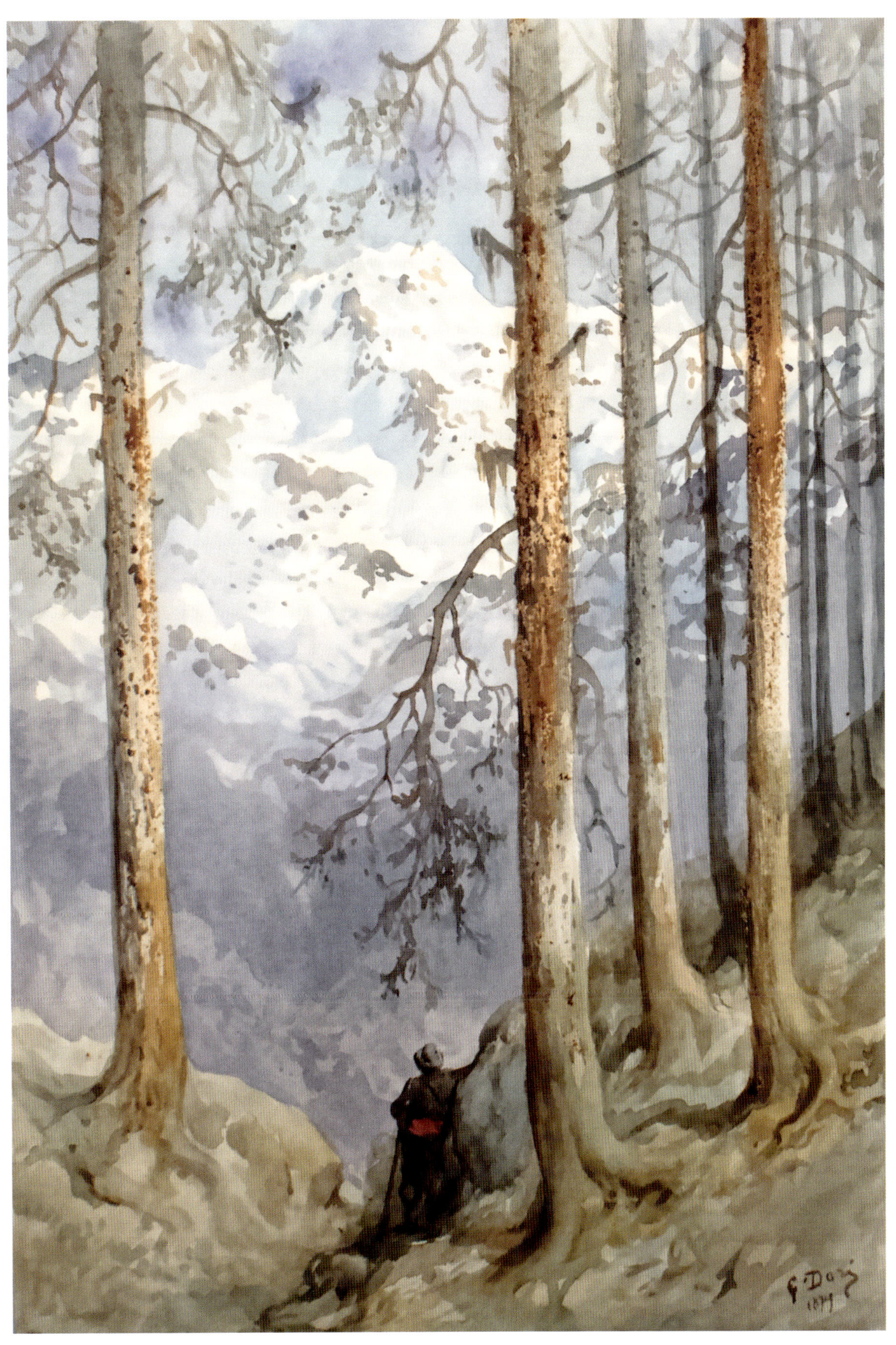

23

ÉDOUARD MANET 1832–1883

La toilette 1st state, 1862

Etching on off-white paper, 28.7 × 22.5 cm

PROVENANCE: Loys Delteil; his sale, Hôtel Drouot, 13–15 June 1928, lot 302; Otto Gerstenberg

LITERATURE: Guérin (1944), no.26; Harris (1970), no.10; Wilson Bareau (1977), no.8 I/III; Wilson Bareau (1978), no.37 I/III; Cachin, Moffett, Wilson Bareau (1983), no.25

Perhaps as a reaction to the large number of academic nudes exhibited at the Salon of 1859, Manet began working on three major compositions incorporating a naked female figure. Two were eventually exhibited to great scandal: the *Déjeuner sur l'herbe* at the Salon des Refusés in 1863, and *Olympia* at the Salon itself in 1865 (both in the Musée d'Orsay, Paris). The third, however, survives only in a summary compositional sketch and a finished fragment. Originally, Manet had intended to make a very large painting of *The Finding of Moses*, in which Pharaoh's daughter is seen drying herself with the help of an attendant after bathing in the Nile, while in the background one of her handmaidens discovers the infant Moses on the river bank. Dissatisfied with the narrative element, Manet transformed the composition into a *Nymph and Satyr*. He later apparently removed the satyr, and the painting was shown with its current title, *The Surprised Nymph*, in 1867 (Museo Nacional de Bellas Artes, Buenos Aires). While it owes much to mythological subjects such as *Diana at the Bath* by Boucher (Louvre, Paris), the figure is resolutely modern, her solid flesh and self-conscious modesty covering her breasts provocatively.

Following the establishment of the Société des Aquafortistes (Society of Etchers) in May 1862, the publishers Alfred Cadart and Félix Chevalier announced in the following September the publication of a suite of *8 Gravures à l'eau-forte* by Édouard Manet. The opportunity was taken by Manet to make etched copies or versions of some of his most important paintings. He had begun etching in 1861 under the instruction of Alphonse Legros (1837–1911), and quickly achieved a distinctive mastery of the medium. *La toilette* is a variation on the painted *Surprised Nymph*. Here the scene takes place indoors, with the bather seated on a bed, her servant behind and a large vessel in the foreground. The details suggest that Manet may have had the toilet of Bathsheba in mind. The print was prepared in a number of drawings for which the model was the artist's mistress, Suzanne Leenhoff. Notable among them is a sheet in red chalk, which stands as a remarkable demonstration of Thomas Couture's instruction.[1] The first state is known in only two, very different proofs: in the present example the plate was wiped clean, whereas the other was printed with a thick film of ink in the lower part, giving a quite different effect.

Manet went on to make a number of other etchings after his major paintings. Among them were two plates after *Olympia* (1867) and another, his largest plate, after *The Dead Christ and the Angels* (1866–7). The projected print of *Le Déjeuner sur l'herbe* survives only in the preparatory watercolour in the Ashmolean Museum.[2]

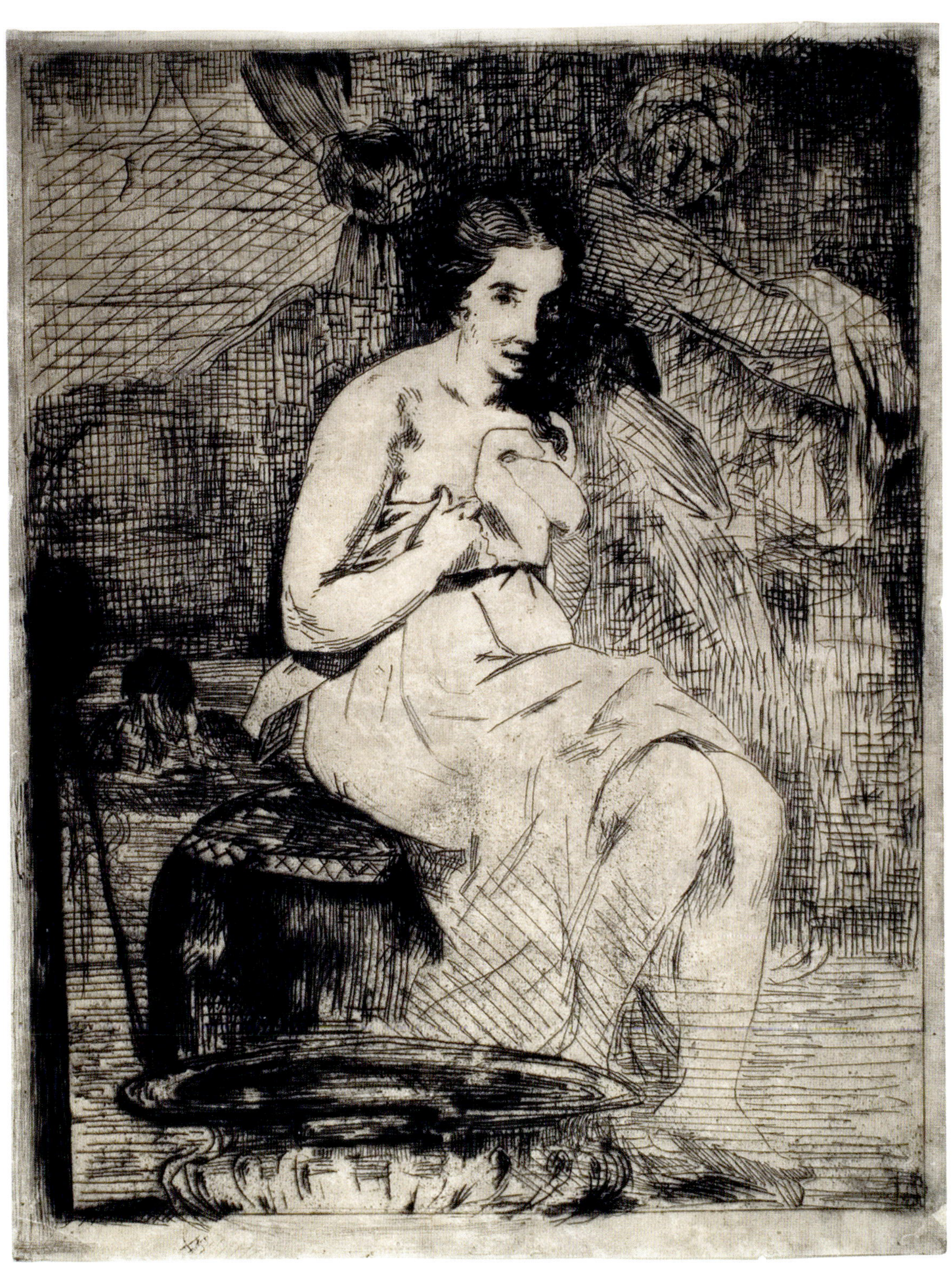

24

ÉDOUARD MANET 1832–1883

Bullfight, 1863–64

Brush in ink and watercolour with graphite, 30 × 59 cm

Inscribed (? by Mme Manet): *E. Manet*

Inscribed in graphite: *Eventail / Cristal*

PROVENANCE: Manet studio sale, 4–5 February 1884, lot 134; Auguste Pellerin; sale, Bernheim-Jeune, Paris 1910; Durand-Ruel; Jacques Rouché; Sotheby's, London, 23 October 1963, lot 19; Zdenko Bruck, Buenos Aires; E. B. Kornfeld, 1995

LITERATURE: Tabarant (1947), no.565; Bodelsen (1968), no.134; Rouart and Wildenstein (1975), no.529

Long before he wrote to Baudelaire from Spain on 4 September 1865 that 'I hope when I return [to Paris] to put on canvas the brilliant, shimmering, and at once dramatic aspects of the *corrida* I attended', Manet had painted scenes from the bullfight – described in the same letter as 'one of the finest, strangest, and most fearful spectacles to be seen'.[1] Early in 1862 he had painted the ambitious portrait of *Mlle V... in the Costume of an Espada* (Metropolitan Museum, New York); her costume was probably part of the artist's collection. Later Manet showed an *Episode from a Bullfight* at the Salon of 1864, subsequently cutting it up and reworking two parts as *The Dead Toreador* (National Gallery of Art, Washington) and *The Bullfight* (Frick Collection, New York). His fascination with the bullfight reached its climax in the *Bullfight* of 1865–6, known in two versions (Musée d'Orsay, Paris, and the Art Institute of Chicago).

According to his friend Antonin Proust, one of the paintings that most interested Manet was Alfred Dehodencq's *Bullfight*. The work was shown at the Salon of 1850–1 and acquired for the Musée de Luxembourg (now at Pau). Naturally he was also familiar with Goya's etchings of the *Tauromaquia*. The present watercolour is generally dated to the same period as the *Episode from a Bullfight*, both from the winter of 1863–4. It is one of only four fan-shaped designs, inspired not by Japanese models, as the Impressionists later were, but by examples that Manet would have seen carried by Lola de Valence and the dance troupe from the Royal Theatre in Madrid, who performed in Paris in 1862.[2]

As a photograph taken by Fernand Lochard shortly after Manet's death shows, the sheet was originally a different shape; the curve at the bottom was less pronounced and had flat sides.[3] At some stage in its history the design was roughly cut vertically into three pieces which were then realigned, with additions on either side. In order to make the main composition more coherent, the small square of still life of the tambourine was moved from the top to the bottom; it has, however, been stuck upside down. The scene in its present state shows ladies in mantillas on the right, sitting behind a barrier and enjoying the spectacle, with gentlemen in dark costumes standing. On the left stands another spectator, while in the centre the picador sits proudly astride his grey horse and elegantly thrusts his pike into the neck of the bull.

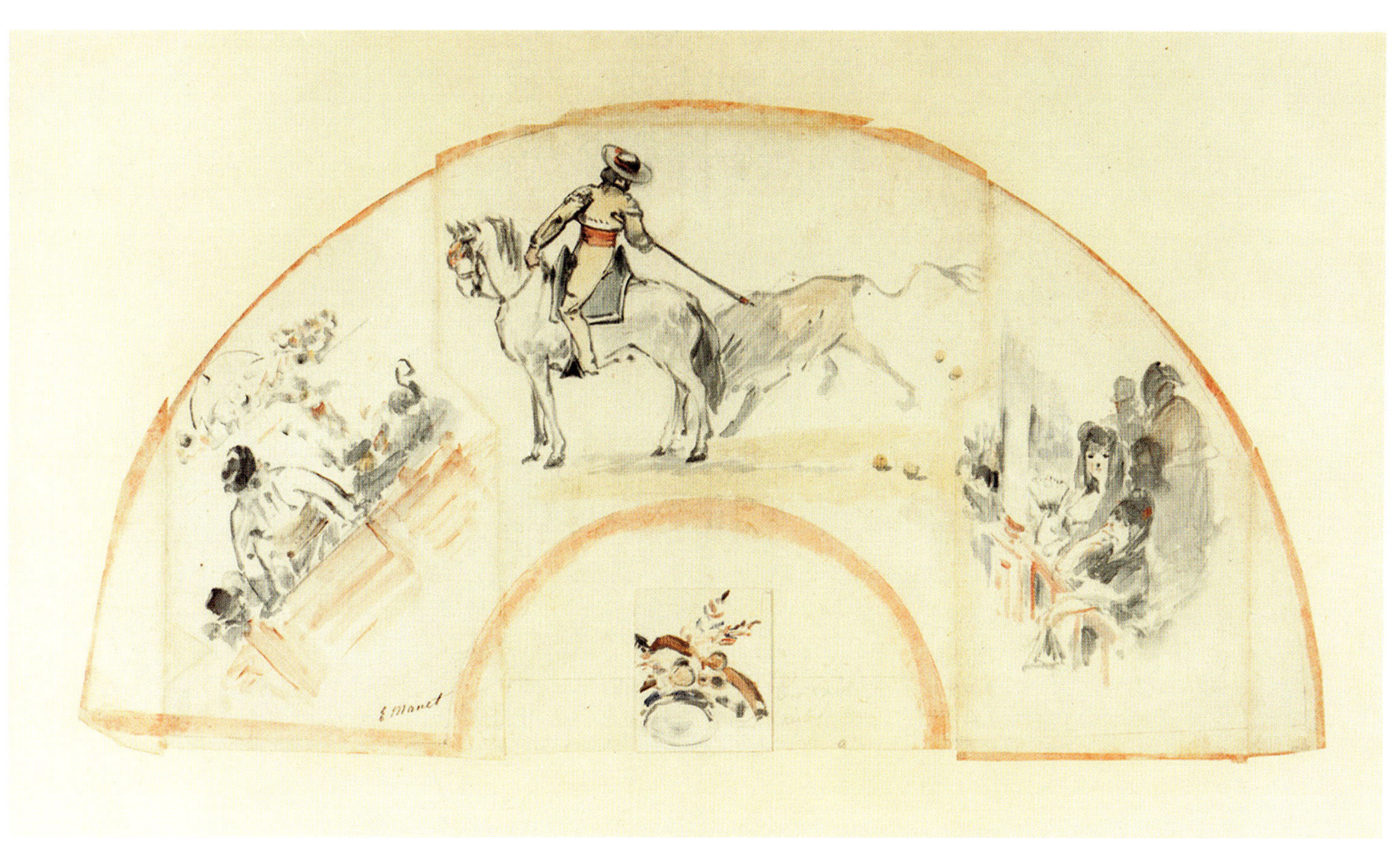
É Manet

25

ÉDOUARD MANET 1832–1883

The Execution of Maximilian (L'Exécution de Maximilien), 1867–68

Lithograph on chine collé, 33.5 × 43.5 cm

Signed in the stone: *Manet*

LITERATURE: Guérin (1944), no.73 II/II; Wilson Bareau (1977), no.54; Wilson Bareau (1978), no.77; Cachin, Moffett, Wilson Bareau (1983), no.25

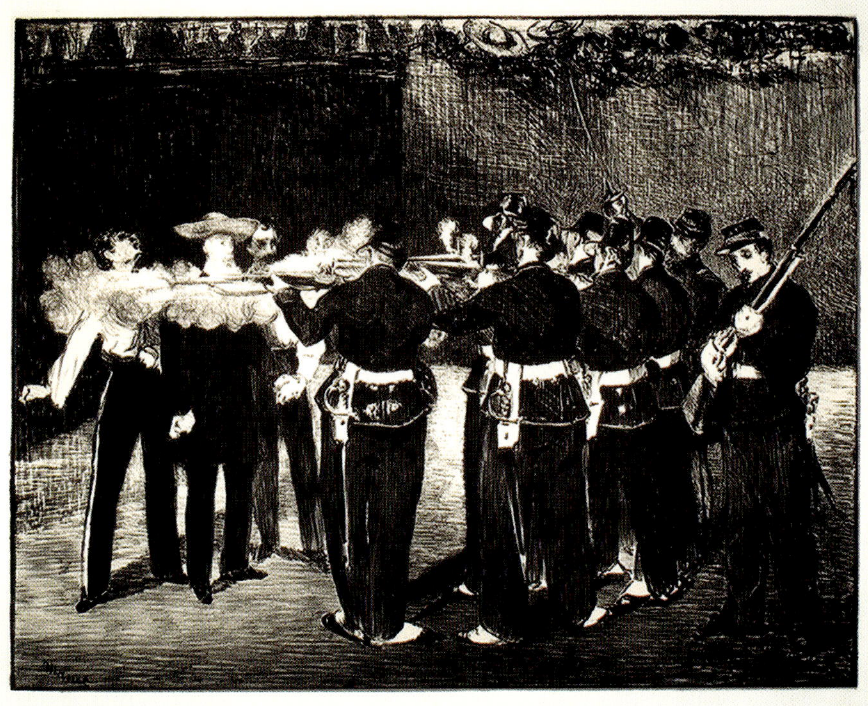

Until its inglorious end in the Prussian occupation of Paris in January 1871, the Second Empire, under Napoleon III, was the longest regime to survive in France after the Revolution. An earlier disaster in its foreign policy was the execution on 19 June 1867 of Maximilian of Austria, Emperor of Mexico, together with the Mexican generals Miramon and Mejia, by nationalist forces under Benito Juarez. The reaction in France was one of shock and outrage, both because Napoleon III had been instrumental in imposing Maximilian in 1864 and because he failed to support him with the necessary troops that would have enabled the Emperor to survive.

Manet's friend Ludovic Halévy noted on 2 July 1867: 'The melancholy news has been circulating in Paris since morning. The Emperor Maximilian shot by order of Juarez. What a tragic end to that ruinous, bloody farce, the war in Mexico!'[1] It is evident that Manet shared his feelings. From the summer of 1867 until the end of the following year he worked on four similar paintings on the subject of *The Execution of Maximilian*, intending to submit the last (Kunsthalle, Mannheim) to the Salon of 1869. The composition was intended as both political comment and history painting, inspired by Goya's *The Third of May, 1808* (Prado, Madrid) – in which, conversely, Spanish patriots are murdered by French imperial troops.

Largely on the basis of the second major oil, which he found unsatisfactory and cut into pieces of irregular size (three survive in the National Gallery, London), Manet worked on this lithograph. The frieze-like composition shows the Emperor wearing a straw hat, holding the hands of his generals – Mejia on the left, Miramon on the right – at the moment of execution. As in the final oil, the scene is set not in the open countryside, but in a walled courtyard, with the crowd eagerly watching from above. Apart from the three victims, the only identifiable person in the scene is the anonymous soldier on the right, nonchalantly reloading his rifle.

In January 1869 Manet was officially advised not to proceed with the printing of this lithograph, nor with the submission of the oil painting to the Salon. The print was eventually published in an edition of 50 by Lemercier in 1884.

26

ÉDOUARD MANET 1832–1883

Berthe Morisot 2nd state, 1872

Lithograph on chine collé, 20.4 × 14 cm

LITERATURE: Guérin (1944), no.77 II/II; Wilson Bareau (1977), no.75; Wilson Bareau (1978), no.81

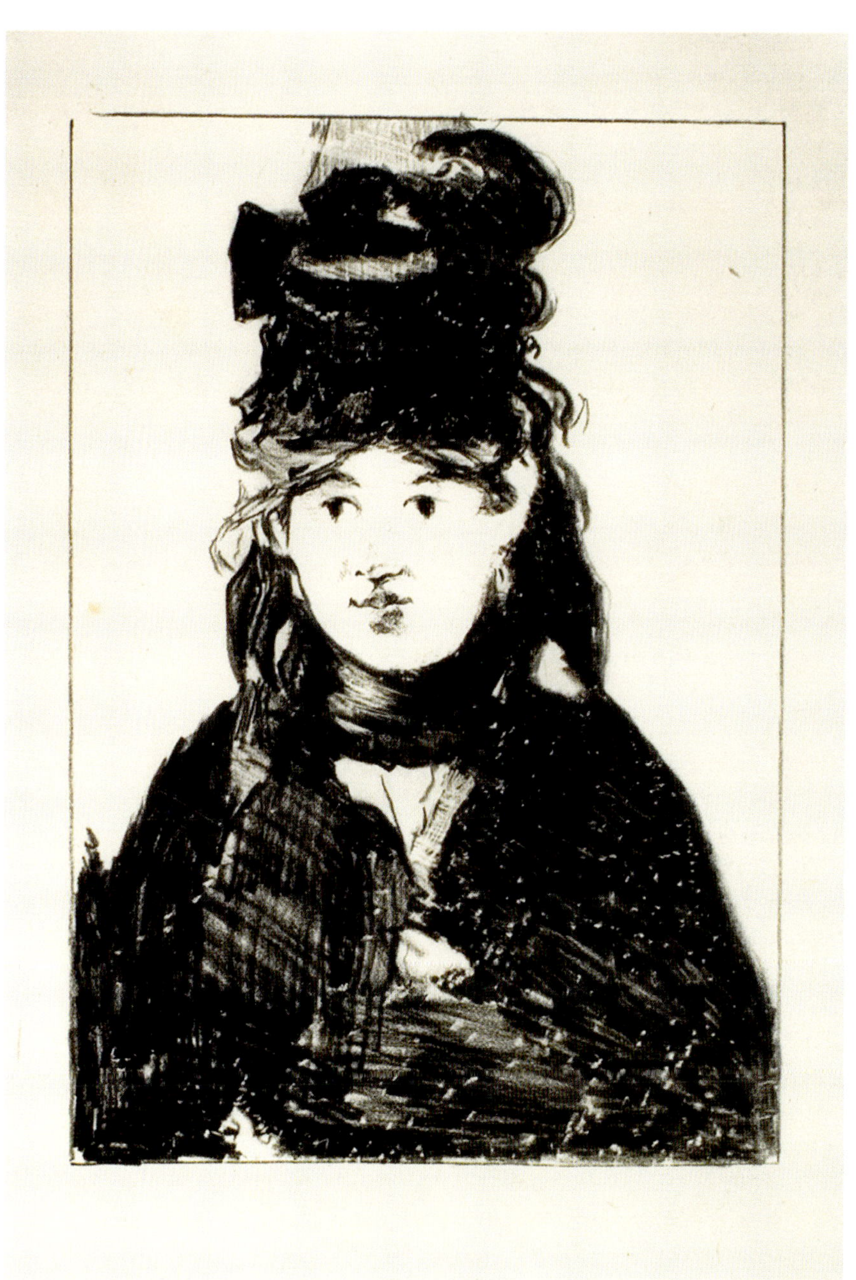

Berthe-Marie-Pauline Morisot (1841–95) and her sister Edma were introduced to Manet by their friend, Henri Fantin-Latour. In 1868 Manet wrote that 'the Misses Morisot are charming. It is a pity they are not men. Never mind, as women they will be able to serve the cause of painting by marrying a member of the Academy and sowing discord in that camp of spoil-sports'.[1] In fact neither sister married an artist, though Berthe married Manet's brother Eugène in 1874. Encouraged by their parents to take up drawing, the Morisot sisters studied with teachers in Paris and, from 1858, made copies in the Louvre. Having enjoyed some success at the Salon between 1864 and 1868, Berthe allied herself with the Impressionists, showing at seven of their eight exhibitions. Her brightly coloured and freely painted oils and watercolours were highly distinctive. The poet Stéphane Mallarmé described them as 'fairy-like' and their author as 'a magician'.[2]

Soon after their first meeting Manet included the figure of Berthe Morisot in his major exhibit at the Salon of 1869, *The Balcony* (Musée d'Orsay), where her dark beauty and lustrous curly hair dominate the composition. Later he painted a series of portraits, of which the most remarkable is *Berthe Morisot with a Bunch of Violets*, dated 1872.[3] Here she appears wearing mourning against a grey background, her elaborate black hat with ribbons tied under her chin and her black cape relieved only by the hair, flesh and white collar. Soon afterwards Manet made three prints of this painting, one etching and two lithographs. The second lithograph, seen here, has the appearance of being traced in outline from the first, which is one of the artist's most subtle exercises in black and white. In particular he has used a sharp tool to give the black of the costume a 'pock-marked' appearance to lighten the tone. Both lithographs were among the group printed in editions of 50 by Lemercier in 1884.

27

ÉDOUARD MANET 1832–1883

Mirabelle Plum, 1880

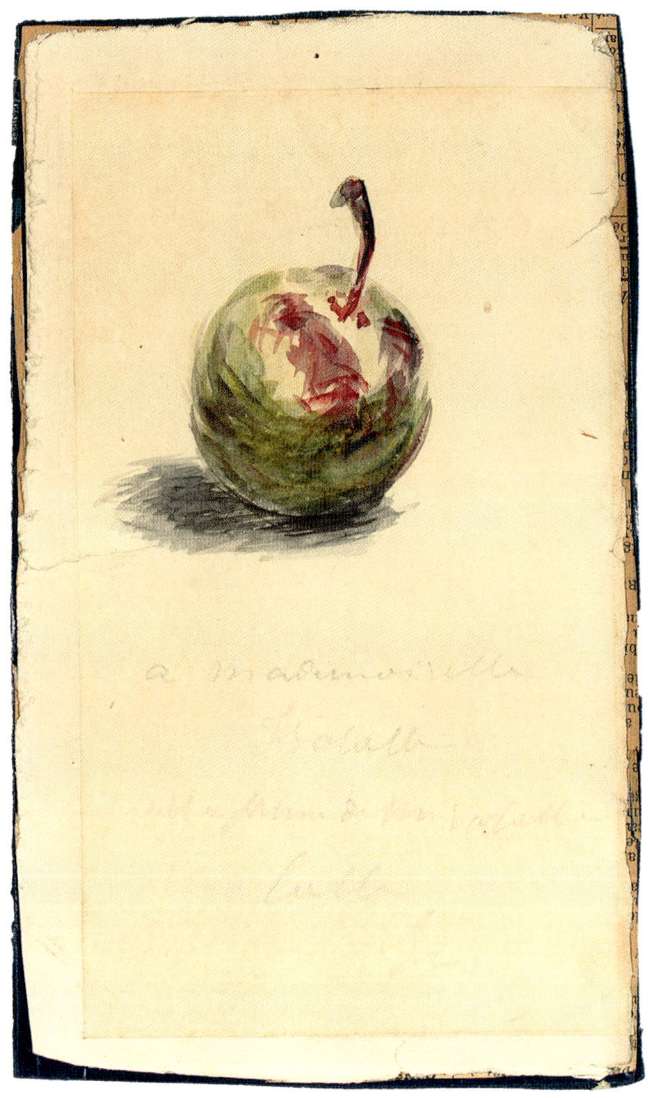

Watercolour on off-white paper, 16.7 × 9.8 cm

Inscribed and signed in graphite: *a mademoiselle Isabelle cette prune de Mirabelle belle* EM

PROVENANCE: Isabelle Lemonnier (married Albert Robida); by descent to Jeanne Robida

LITERATURE: Robida (1958), pl. XXVIII; Rouart and Wildenstein (1975), II, no.587

On the advice of his doctor Manet and his wife retreated to Bellevue, a suburb of Paris, where they rented a house at 4 route des Gardes between July and October 1880. During his convalescence the artist painted a number of portraits and landscapes, and amused himself by sending drawings and illustrated notes to a number of friends. The most fortunate recipient was Isabelle Lemonnier (1857–1926), the younger daughter of the jeweller to the imperial court, Alexandre-Gabriel Lemonnier (1808–84). His elder daughter, Marguerite, was the wife of the publisher Georges Charpentier (1846–1905), a notable patron and supporter of the Impressionists. Charpentier established a gallery, La Vie Moderne, in the passage des Princes off the boulevard des Italiens, where he held an exhibition of Manet's work in April 1880. Isabelle sat six times for Manet between 1879 and 1882; he was beguiled by her youth, her interest in the latest fashions and her lively opinions.

Étienne Moreau-Nélaton acquired from Isabelle Lemonnier 16 of the illustrated *billets doux* sent by Manet from Bellevue while she was on holiday in Normandy; these are now mounted in an album in the Louvre. Among the subjects are fruit and flowers, and several charming evocations of Isabelle at the seaside. These include a watercolour of a mirabelle that is characteristically inscribed in ink with four lines: *A Isabelle / cette mirabelle / et la plus belle / c'est Isabelle*.[1] Isabelle kept the previous version of this watercolour, seen here, which until recently remained with her descendants. It is less polished than the other, the plum more freely and brilliantly painted, and the verse inscribed in pencil. This work may have been intended as a first draft, either sent by Manet or given to Isabelle by his family after his death in 1883.

28

EUGÈNE BOUDIN 1824–1898

Beach Scene at Trouville, 1866

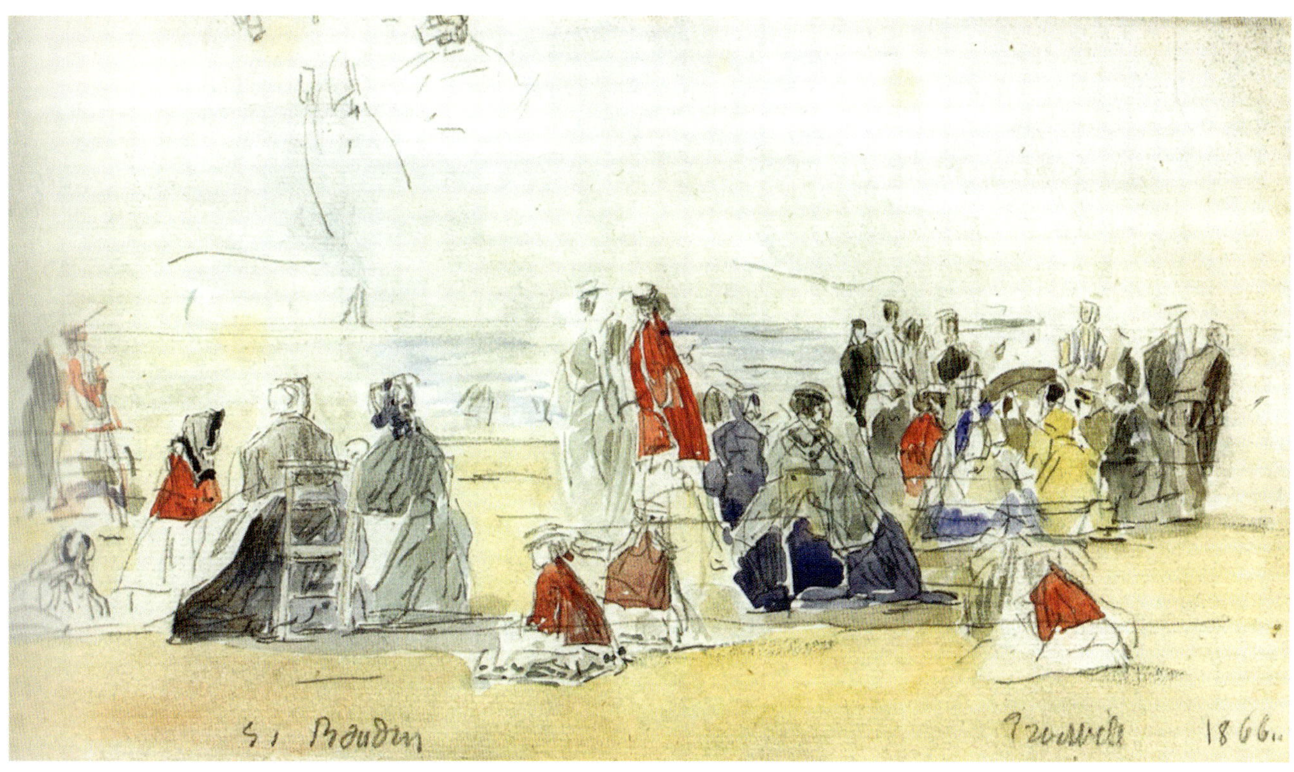

Watercolour and graphite on laid paper, 14.5 × 25.5 cm

Signed: *E Boudin* and inscribed and dated: *Trouville 1866*

PROVENANCE: Galerie Schmit, Paris

A native of Normandy, Boudin painted the sea coast all his life, and it was perhaps natural that he should have been attracted to the new resorts of Deauville and Trouville. He first visited Trouville in 1857, possibly on the advice of the marine painter Eugène Isabey and certainly with the encouragement of his dealer, Père Martin. From then until his death Boudin generally spent the summer on the coast and the winter in Paris. At the beach, he transferred the attention he had already given to the costumes of the Breton peasants to the colourful dresses of fashionable women up the coast, although in a letter to Martin he complained that by comparison he found Trouville 'a frightful masquerade'.[1] Among the earliest of the paintings of Trouville is *The Jetty at Trouville, Sunset*, dated 1862 (Ashmolean Museum); so successful was the genre with the picture-buying public and at the Salon that by 29 November 1865 Boudin could lament to his brother that 'I shall always be labelled as the painter of beaches'.[2] Ernest Chesneau's label in 1867 was 'a witty chronicler of ladies' fashions at the seaside resorts'.[3] Watercolours were ideally suited to capturing these scenes, but it was not until about 1862 that Boudin adopted the medium seriously. He made many rapid sketches from life, using pencil to define the composition and watercolours to add atmosphere. Boudin himself believed that 'what is painted directly and on the spot has a force, a power, a liveliness of touch that it is impossible to find in the studio'.[4] His watercolours were profitable, and he sold them to dealers such as Cadart and Luquet for between 10 and 40 francs each. However, a great many remained in his studio after his death, and the minority which were not then given to the State were dated in the studio sale in 1903.

Here the beach is crowded with women in crinolines standing, sitting and walking. On the right stands a large group of men, eagerly chatting to a smaller group of seated women. In the foreground, a young girl sits disconsolately by herself.

29

CLAUDE-OSCAR MONET 1840–1926

Sailing Boat Beached on the Shore at Sainte-Adresse, ca.1864–65

Charcoal on paper, 20.6 × 31.4 cm

Signed: *Cl. Monet*

PROVENANCE: Michel Monet, Giverny; private collection, Switzerland; sale, Kornfeld, Bern, 6 June 2008, no.24

LITERATURE: Wildenstein (1974–91), v, no.D418

In his earliest sketchbooks of 1856–7 Monet was already fascinated by the motif of a beached sailing boat, which had earlier been treated in lithographs and paintings by Eugène Isabey and others.[1] However, he rarely made drawings for their own sake, and the sequence of six finished drawings exploring the gradual disintegration of a fishing boat on the beach at Sainte-Adresse, near Le Havre, is unique in his output.[2] The drawings are generally dated to 1864–5, when the artist is recorded as painting in the vicinity. As has recently been discussed, the drawings owe most to the example not of Boudin, who had first encouraged Monet to paint in the open air, but to that of Johan Barthold Jongkind (1819–91), whom he had met in 1862.[3] The composition of most of Monet's drawings of this period shows the coast as a plunging diagonal, a device much used by Jongkind and others. The six drawings of the beached fishing boat were made, presumably over a fairly extended period of weeks, at the foot of the cliffs of the cap de Hève. The first shows the boat intact. The present drawing is the second in the sequence: the main mast has collapsed on to the beach, causing the boat to tilt dangerously, but the mizzen mast is still nearly upright. In the next drawing the boat is in a similar state, but seen from a different angle. The following two drawings show further depredations, with the rigging almost entirely lost. The final drawing in the sequence shows the boat almost completely wrecked, its fate poignantly emphasised by the inclusion of a steam ship and sailing boat in the background.

The function of these drawings is not known. Clearly they stand as works of art in their own right, in which the thick, greasy crayon is manipulated with great skill. It is unlikely, however, that Monet intended them for sale. He may have had in mind a suite of lithographs, having seen how easy the technique was when he saw Théophile Gautier using it in 1859. Alternatively he may have wished to experiment with etching – Jongkind had published his *Cahier de six eaux-fortes* in 1862, and the foundation of the Société des Aquafortistes (Society of Etchers) had encouraged an explosion of interest in the medium.

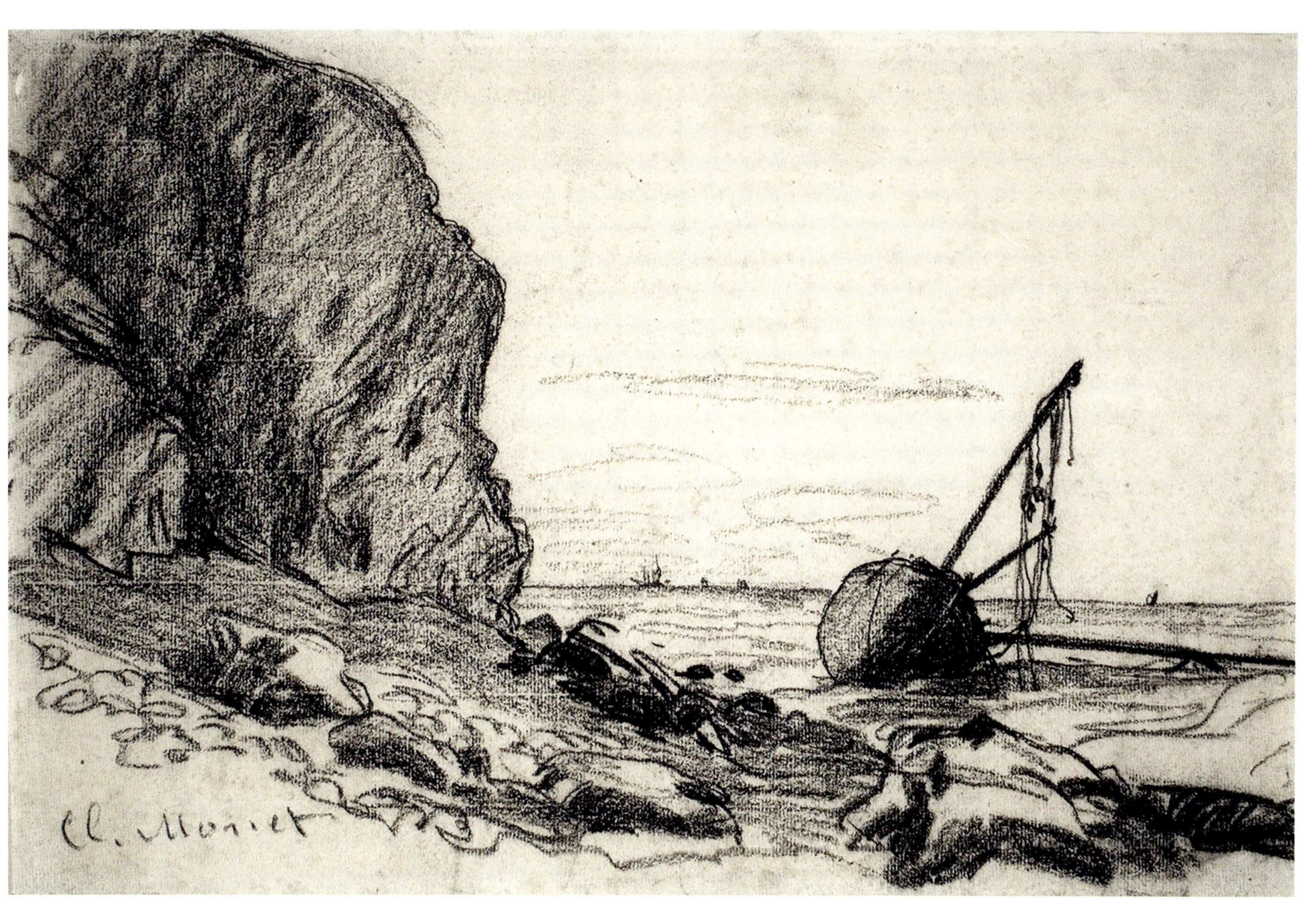
Cl. Monet

30

CAMILLE PISSARRO 1830–1903

Portrait of Lucien Pissarro, ca.1868–70

Pastel on grey-blue paper, 34.6 × 26.7 cm

Signed with initials in brush and ink: *C.P.*

PROVENANCE: by descent from the sitter to Orovida Pissarro

LITERATURE: Pissarro and Venturi (1939), no.1520; Johnson (2015), no.1, ill. p.7

Unlike some of his fellow Impressionists, notably Renoir, Pissarro never painted portraits on commission; instead, those he made are of members of his family and close friends. His most frequent subjects were his wife, Julie Vellay, and their eight children – either portrayed as reluctant sitters or engaged in characteristic activities such as sewing, drawing or reading. The portraits range from the tiny oil of Julie sewing (*c.*1860; Ashmolean Museum) to the last of four painted self-portraits, completed shortly before the artist's death on 13 November 1903 (Tate, London).

The most monumental of Pissarro's portraits is the allusive icon of Paul Cézanne (on loan to the National Gallery, London). It was painted during the winter of 1873–4, while Pissarro was living at Pontoise and Cézanne at Auvers-sur-Oise nearby. In 1874 Pissarro made a lithograph of his eldest child Lucien (1863–1944). Lucien occupied a special place in his father's affections because, from a very young age, and much to the despair of his mother, he showed a determination to be an artist. He was a frequent subject for his father, especially when young. The earliest drawings were made when he was still a baby, in 1864.[1] Later Pissarro seems to have been fascinated by the roundness of Lucien's head, with close-cropped hair – much as Cézanne was with his own son. The present pastel is closely related to an experimental drawing in brush and ink which has convincingly been dated *c.*1868–70, when Lucien was five or six years old.[2] In 1873–4, at about the time of the lithograph, Lucien and his sister Minette were painted in small and intimate watercolours, and in two oils.[3] Pissarro's use of pastel at this early date was unusual – it was not until after his return from London in 1871 that he began to use it more frequently, for both portraits and landscapes. So, for example, the mature Lucien was drawn in a magnificent pastel of 1883.[4] Such portraits were not intended for sale, but served as souvenirs of the members of his family, household and friends at various stages of their lives. The portraits of Lucien, in particular, suggest a father's pride in the studious concentration of his eldest son.

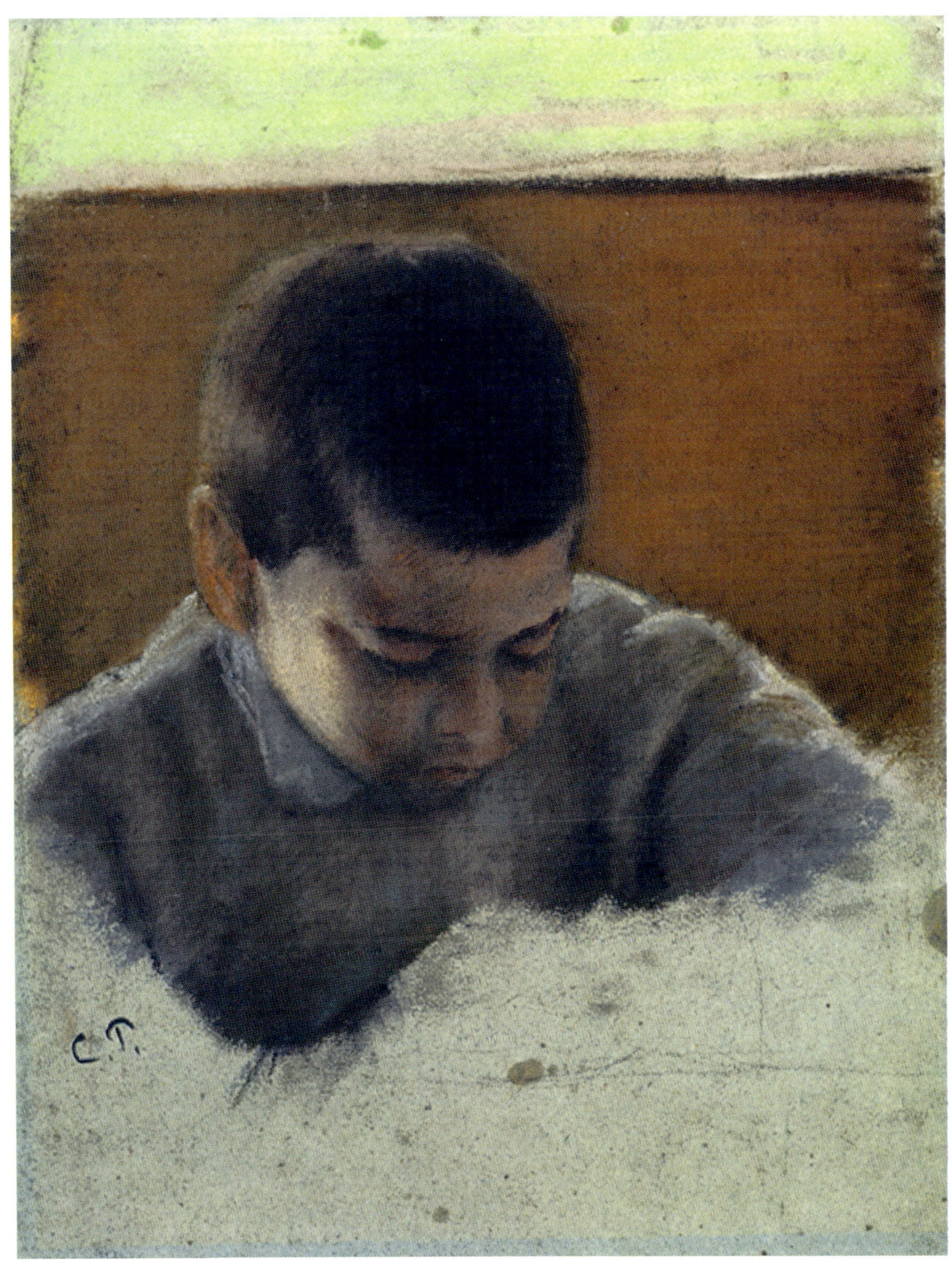
C.T.

31

CAMILLE PISSARRO 1830–1903

Workers in the Fields, early to mid-1890s

Watercolour and black chalk on off-white paper, 28.6 × 21.9 cm

Signed: *C. Pissarro*

PROVENANCE: Émile Strauss; his sale, Paris, 3–4 June 1929, no.21; sale, Paris, 10 June 1937, no.7; sale, 12 May 1939, no.33; Paul Ebstein, Galerie de l'Elysée, Paris; private collection; Christie's, New York, 7 November 2007, lot 309

LITERATURE: Pissarro and Venturi (1939), no.1486; Johnson (2015), no.2, ill. p.9

In December 1873, shortly before the first Impressionist Exhibition, Théodore Duret wrote to Pissarro that 'I continue to believe that what best suits your talent is the agricultural landscape, rustic scenes with animals. You have neither the decorative feeling of Sisley nor the eye for fantasy of Monet, but you have what they lack, a deep and profound feeling for nature and a powerful brush which means that a beautiful painting by you is something quite other.'[1] Pissarro responded that this exactly confirmed his own inclinations, but that, until that point, he had lacked models. Fortunately, for the remainder of his life he lived in small villages in the countryside near Paris, first at Pontoise, then at Éragny-sur-Epte, to which he moved in spring 1884. From 1874 the figure of the peasant played an increasingly important role in Pissarro's landscapes as, following Millet's example, he explored the reality of rural life in the fields and marketplaces.

Pissarro used watercolours most intensively in the last two decades of his life. During his stay in London in 1870–1 he had greatly admired the display of Turner's watercolours at the National Gallery. On his return to France Pissarro employed the medium for making studies during his early Impressionist phase. During the late 1880s, as the artist struggled with the laborious technique of Neo-Impressionism, watercolour became in part a means of working more quickly. The establishment of the Société des Aquarellistes Français (Society of French Watercolourists) in Paris in 1879 encouraged collectors, and Pissarro's dealers increasingly found a market for his works on paper.

The present watercolour dates from the early or mid-1890s, when the round brushstrokes of Neo-Impressionism had given way to a more fluent and spontaneous style. In a field near Éragny a female peasant wearing wooden clogs awkwardly puts on her jacket; her male companion behind her stoops to harvest or plant. Both figures are found in other works of this period. In particular, the woman appears in one of the compositions for the *Travaux des champs*, a collaboration between Camille and his son Lucien illustrating the various activities associated with farming.[2]

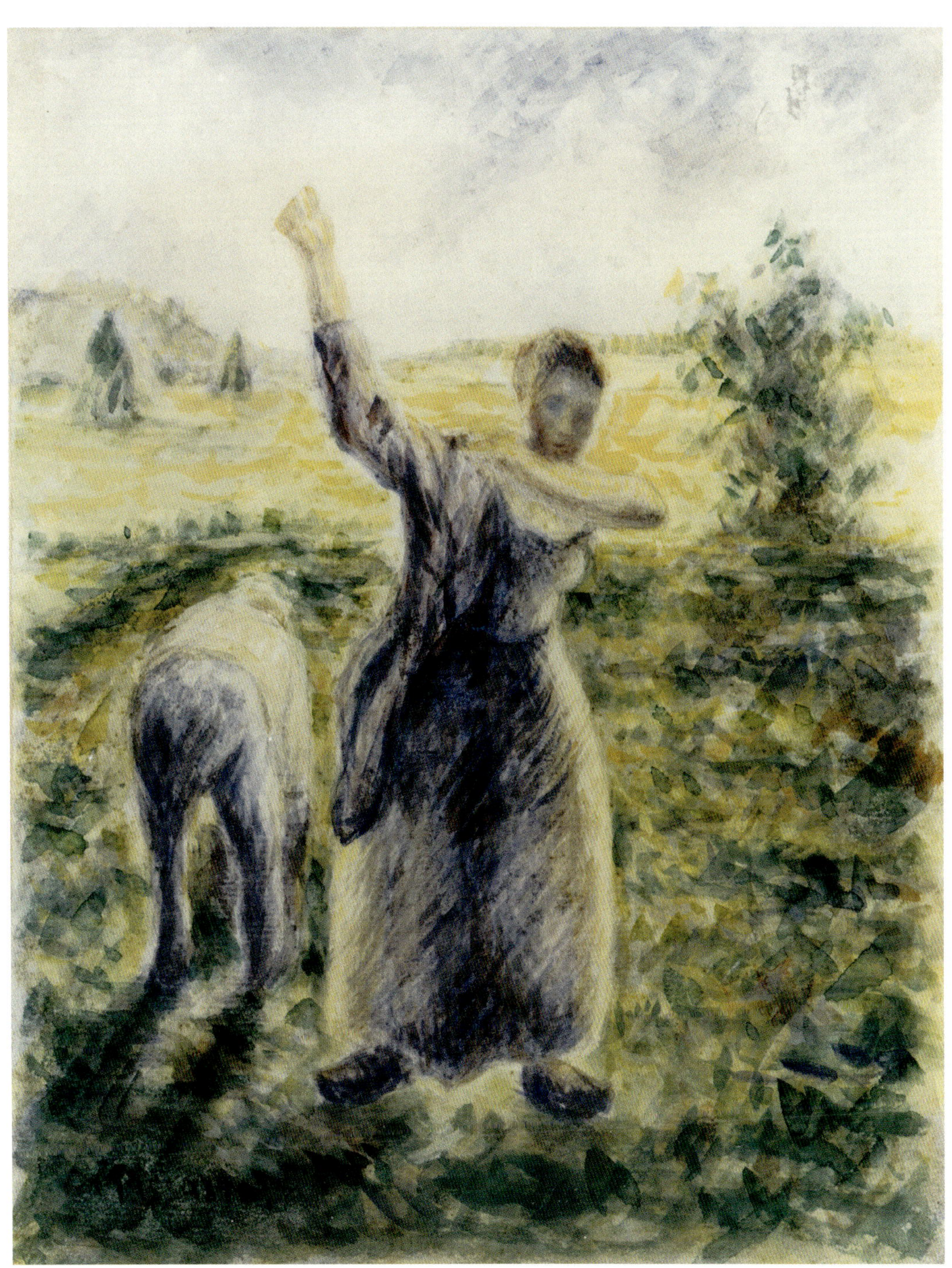

32

MARY CASSATT 1844–1926

Interior: On the Sofa, early 1880s

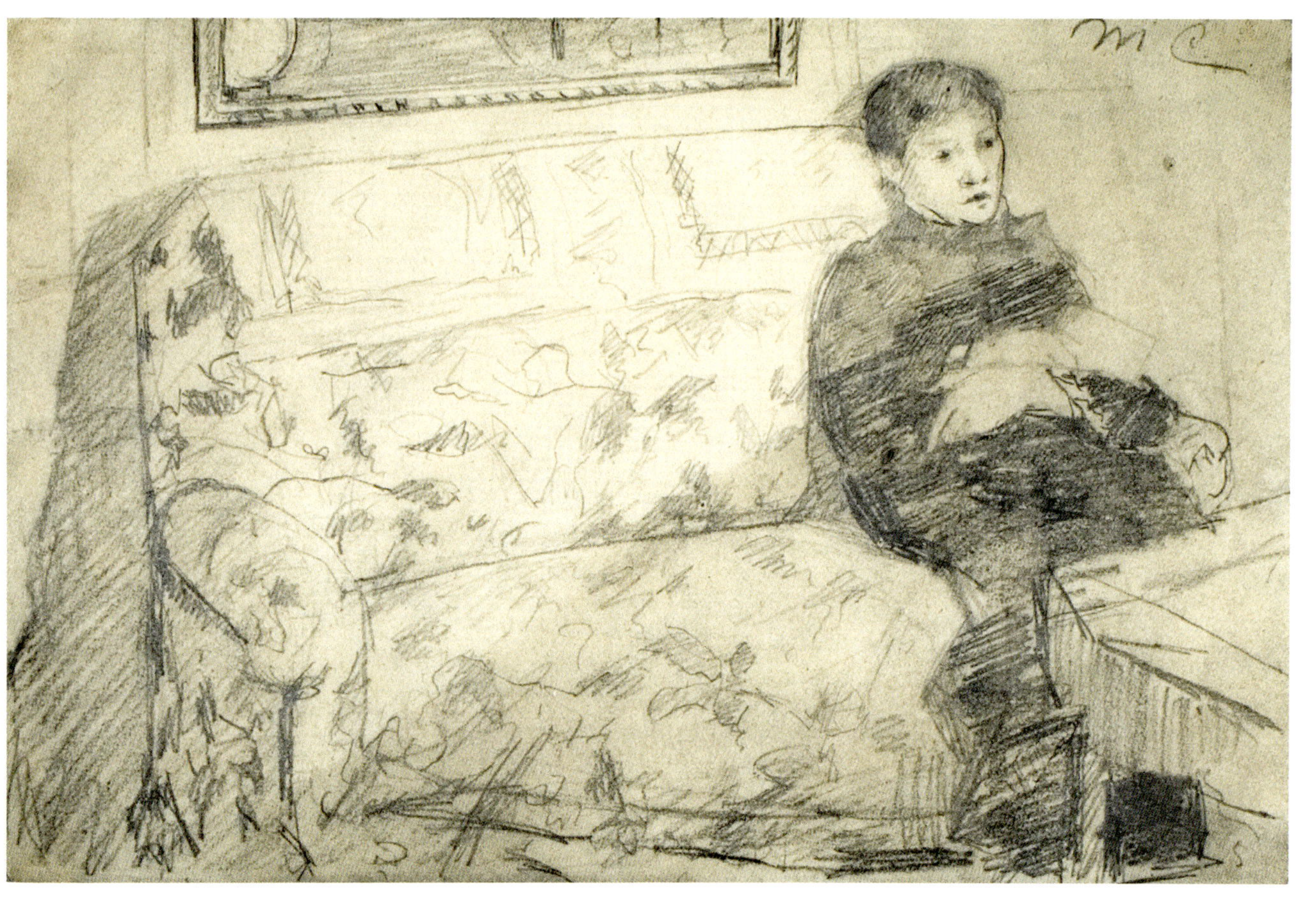

Graphite on paper, 14.2 × 21.8 cm

Signed: *MC*

PROVENANCE: M. Suzor, Paris; O. Wertheimer, Paris; International Galleries, Chicago

LITERATURE: Breeskin (1970), no.769; Breeskin (1979), no.76; Barter (1998), no.41

Cassatt had a conventional artistic education in her native Philadelphia, and also in France and Rome. She enjoyed some success when she exhibited at the Paris Salon between 1868 and 1876. Her friendship with Degas led to an invitation to show at the fourth Impressionist exhibition in 1879, which she accepted with enthusiasm: 'at last, I could work with absolute independence without considering the opinion of a jury. I had already recognized who were my true masters, I admired Manet, Courbet and Degas. I hated conventional art – I began to live.'[1]

Cassatt's first biographer, Achille Segard, recorded that the artist took up the technique of etching while studying for eight months with Carlo Raimondi in Parma in 1872–3. Her intention was deliberate and specific, as Segard noted: in order to 'impose on herself absolute precision in drawing after the living model [she] chose this means of excluding all trickery and inexactitude'.[2] Later Degas encouraged her to experiment with drypoint and aquatint, and she made some of her most impressive plates during the autumn and winter of 1879–80 for the abortive journal *Le Jour et la nuit*.

Both this drawing and the following one are studies for etchings. *Interior: On the Sofa* probably portrays Cassatt's elder sister Lydia (1837–82), in the sitting room of the family apartment in the rue Trudaine in Paris. Her parents and sister had settled in Paris in 1877, and were frequent models for Cassatt's paintings, pastels and prints. In spite of the relaxed pose of the sitter, the drawing was made with great energy and speed, the patterns of the chintz covering the wide expanse of sofa being especially suggestive rather than descriptive.

33

MARY CASSATT 1844–1926

Mathilde with her Dog, early 1880s

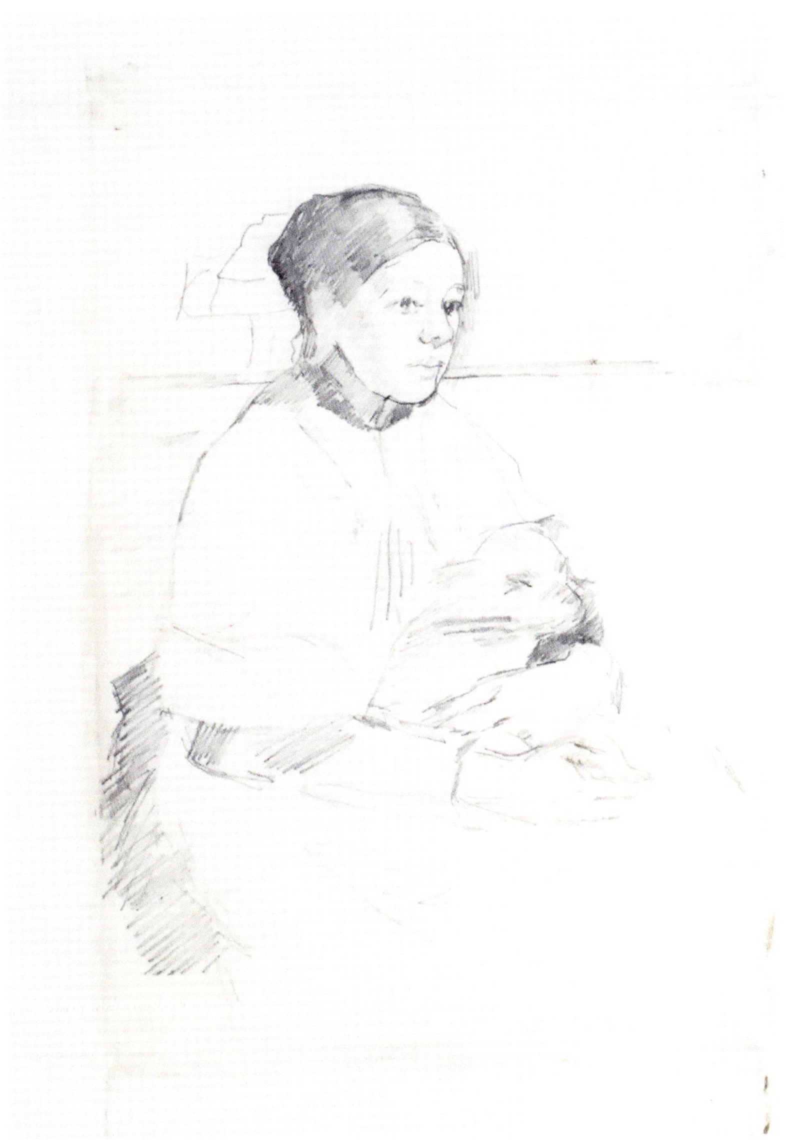

Graphite on paper, 17.5 × 12.5 cm

PROVENANCE: Mathilde Valet, and by descent

Mathilde with her Dog is a portrait of Mathilde Valet, Cassatt's devoted servant and companion. She was the subject of three etchings,[1] and here holds a Pekinese dog. Both this drawing and the one on the previous page were made in the early 1880s, when Cassatt preferred to work on a tiny scale. Her later prints, generally colourful variations on the theme of the mother and child, were more ambitious, but they lack the private intimacy of the earlier, distinctively Impressionist snapshots of family life.

34

EDGAR DEGAS 1834–1917

Saint John the Baptist and the Angel, 1857–58

Watercolour and graphite on paper, 20.5 × 15.5 cm

Sale stamp (L.658), lower left

Inscribed in graphite: *Rome*

PROVENANCE: the artist (L.658); his studio sale, fourth sale, 2–4 July 1919, lot 65 (part); collection Prat, Paris

LITERATURE: Lemoisne (1946–9), no.20; Nathanson and Olszewski (1980), p.250

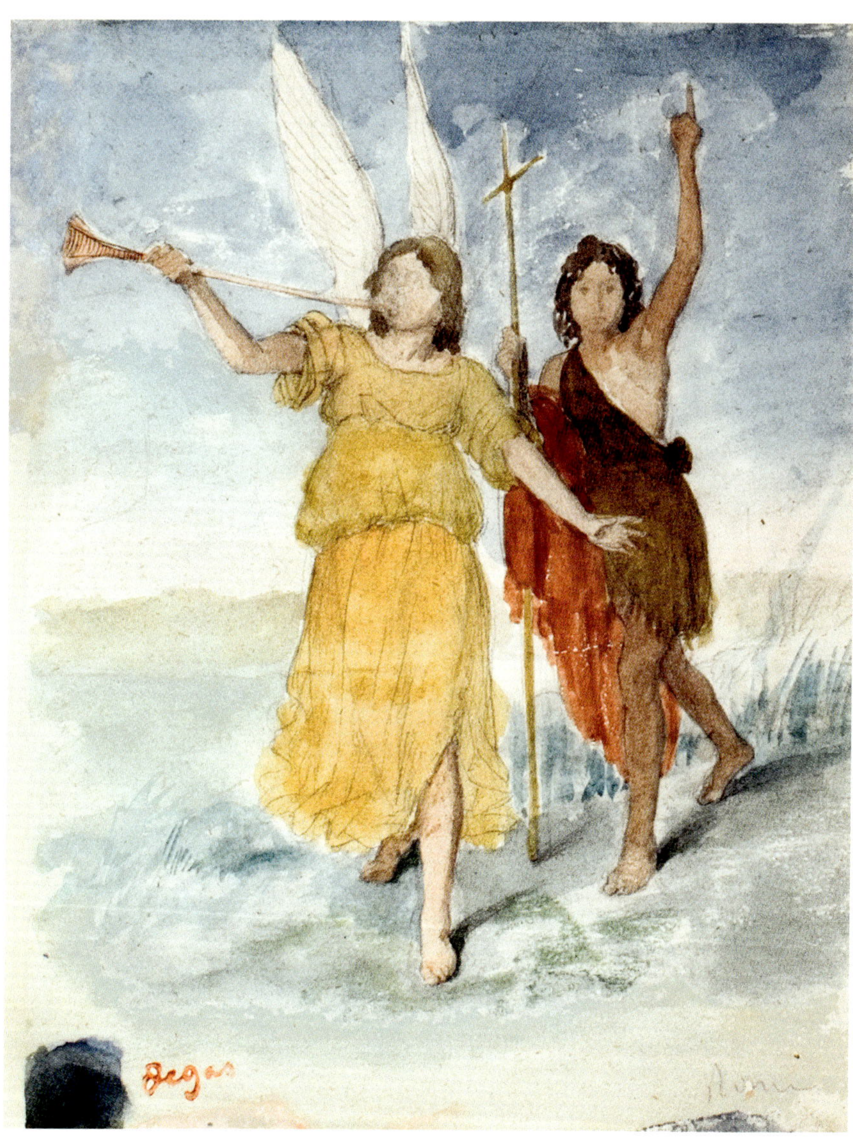

Degas was initially taught by Félix Barrias, who had won the Rome Prize in 1844. However, his most important master was Louis Lamothe (1822–69) who had studied with Hippolyte Flandrin, himself a pupil of Ingres. In the early stages of his career Degas' admiration for Ingres and Flandrin was so intense that he might have been expected to become a conventional academic history painter. Although he never competed for the Rome Prize, he made extensive studies in Italy between July 1856 and April 1859 – both in Rome, where he made drawings from the nude at the French Academy, and in Naples, where he continued his activity as a copyist.

Shortly before he left for Italy, Degas sketched an initial idea for a composition showing St John the Baptist walking in the desert, preceded by an angel and foretelling the coming of Christ, as described in the gospels. The gestation of the composition was to prove long and arduous, and Degas made many further studies while he was in Rome in 1857–8. Although the pose of the saint was established at an early stage, Degas had great difficulty with the angel and the relationship between the figures. He made many drawings and an oil sketch in pursuit of a satisfactory solution. Several studies show Degas experimenting with the angel to the right of St John before he decided on the arrangement shown in this remarkable watercolour. The work is generally agreed to represent the final stage in the preparatory process – Degas often used a watercolour as the final preparatory study for a history painting in his early years. Since this was his major history subject during this period, it is perhaps surprising that the artist abandoned it; he may have felt that the composition of only two figures was not sufficiently ambitious, although the first canvas that he sent back to his father in Paris was *Dante and Virgil*.[1]

35

EDGAR DEGAS 1834–1917

Portrait of Alfredo Morbilli, ca.1856–60

Graphite on paper, 24 × 16 cm

Sale stamp (L.658), lower left

PROVENANCE: the artist (L.658); his studio sale, 7–9 April 1919, lot 93B; Lucien Mellerio, Stresa; Hélène Mellerio, Paris; sale, Tajan, Paris, 10 June 2001, lot 18

LITERATURE: Boggs (1962), p.11; Boggs (1989), p.45, n.17; Loyrette (1991), p.85; Loyrette (2016), ill. p.18

Degas' father, Auguste De Gas (1807–74), was born in Naples to an Italian mother, and Degas had a large extended family divided between Naples and Florence. His father's sister Rosa-Adelaida had married Giuseppe Morbilli, Duca di San Angelo in Frosolone, and had three surviving sons, Alfredo, Adelchi and Edmondo. Another sister, Stefanina Primicile Carafa, had married the Marchese di Cicerale and Duca di Montejasi, and had had two baby daughters; while a third sister, Laura Baronessa Bellelli, lived in political exile in Florence with her two daughters. During his years in Italy Degas made portraits of them all, ranging from intimate drawings to the huge masterpiece of the artist's early years, the *Bellelli Family* (Musée d'Orsay, Paris).

In the letter of 11 November 1858 acknowledging receipt of a crate containing some of his paintings and drawings made in Italy, his father encouraged Degas to believe that 'portraiture will be the most beautiful jewel in your crown'.[1] Among the drawings he may have admired were several of the artist's cousins, the Morbilli brothers. Degas would have become friendly with them while staying with his grandfather in Naples in the summers of 1856 and 1857, and he briefly renewed his acquaintance on a day they spent together on 22 March 1860. The eldest brother Alfredo (1837–1907) worked as a civil engineer. This portrait was originally framed with two others of Adelchi Morelli; another frame in Degas' studio sale included full-length wash drawings of the brothers and their mother, Rosa-Adelaida.[2] The pencil portraits show Degas moving away from what his father called 'flaccid and trivial Flandrinian-Lamothian drawing'[3] towards a much more subtle yet incisive style, more akin to that of Ingres, with the painstakingly wrought details of the face offset by the rather spare description of the costume.

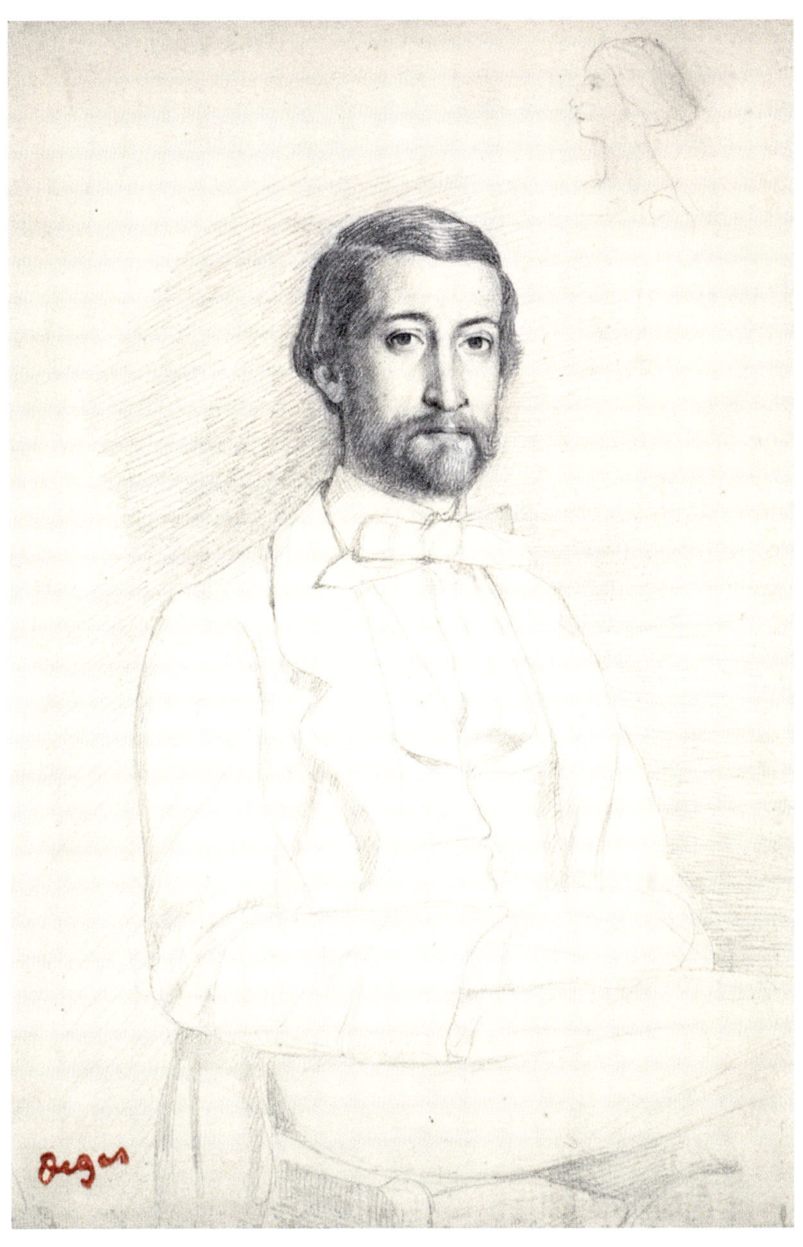

36

EDGAR DEGAS 1834–1917

Self Portrait in a Top Hat, ca.1865

Charcoal on tracing paper, 35.5 × 25 cm

Studio stamp (L.657)

PROVENANCE: Odette Degas and Roland Nepveu and by descent; sale, Ader Tajan, Paris, 19 December 1994, lot 17

LITERATURE: Valéry (1965), pl. 30 ; Russoli and Minervino (1970), p.83, ill.

Degas' *Self Portrait with Evariste de Valernes* of *c.*1865[1] marked the culmination of a protracted and intense examination of his own features; the only later self-portrait was a pastel of the late 1890s. Stimulated by the example of Rembrandt, Degas made many drawings, paintings and etchings, generally depicting himself at head and shoulders, between 1854 and 1858 – the period from just before he joined Lamothe's studio until the later stages of his time in Italy. The works derived partly from loneliness and partly from feelings of self-doubt: as he wrote to Gustave Moreau in 1858, 'Myself again. But what do you expect a man on his own and so abandoned to his own devices as I am to say? He has only himself in front of him, sees only himself, and thinks only of himself'.[2]

Following his return to Paris, Degas was no longer so preoccupied with his own identity. The double portrait rather records the intimacy between a rising star, still unsure of himself, and a perpetually unsuccessful older artist who always had the courage of his convictions. Evariste de Valernes (1816–96) came from a noble but impoverished family; in 1863 he was reported to be in a state approaching destitution. Degas probably met him in 1855, when both men were making copies in the Louvre. The artists shared a passion for Delacroix, and Valernes was sufficiently progressive in his views to support the aims of the Impressionists.

Thanks to an especially instructive x-ray, it is possible to trace the genesis of the painting. Degas originally portrayed himself in ordinary outdoor dress: a dark frock coat, white shirt, bow tie and top hat, with his hands lightly clasped in front of him. This is the preparatory drawing for the first version of this composition. Unlike the exquisitely moulded portrait drawings from the 1850s, however, it is roughly made and functional, in charcoal rather than pencil. Degas has concentrated on the pose, and on his expression, which appears almost resolute. Having completed the painting he changed his mind, removing his hat and putting his right hand up to his chin, giving himself an air of uncertainty as if thinking before speaking. He also studied this pose in a preliminary drawing.[3] Both studies were reversed when incorporated into the painting, which shows the artist on the right of the composition against a view of Rome.

Degas and Valernes remained lifelong friends, and Degas made a second portrait of him in 1868 (Musée d'Orsay, Paris). Towards the end of Valernes' life Degas remembered the painting of the double portrait in which the older artist was always the same, but Degas was constantly displeased with the world and with himself.

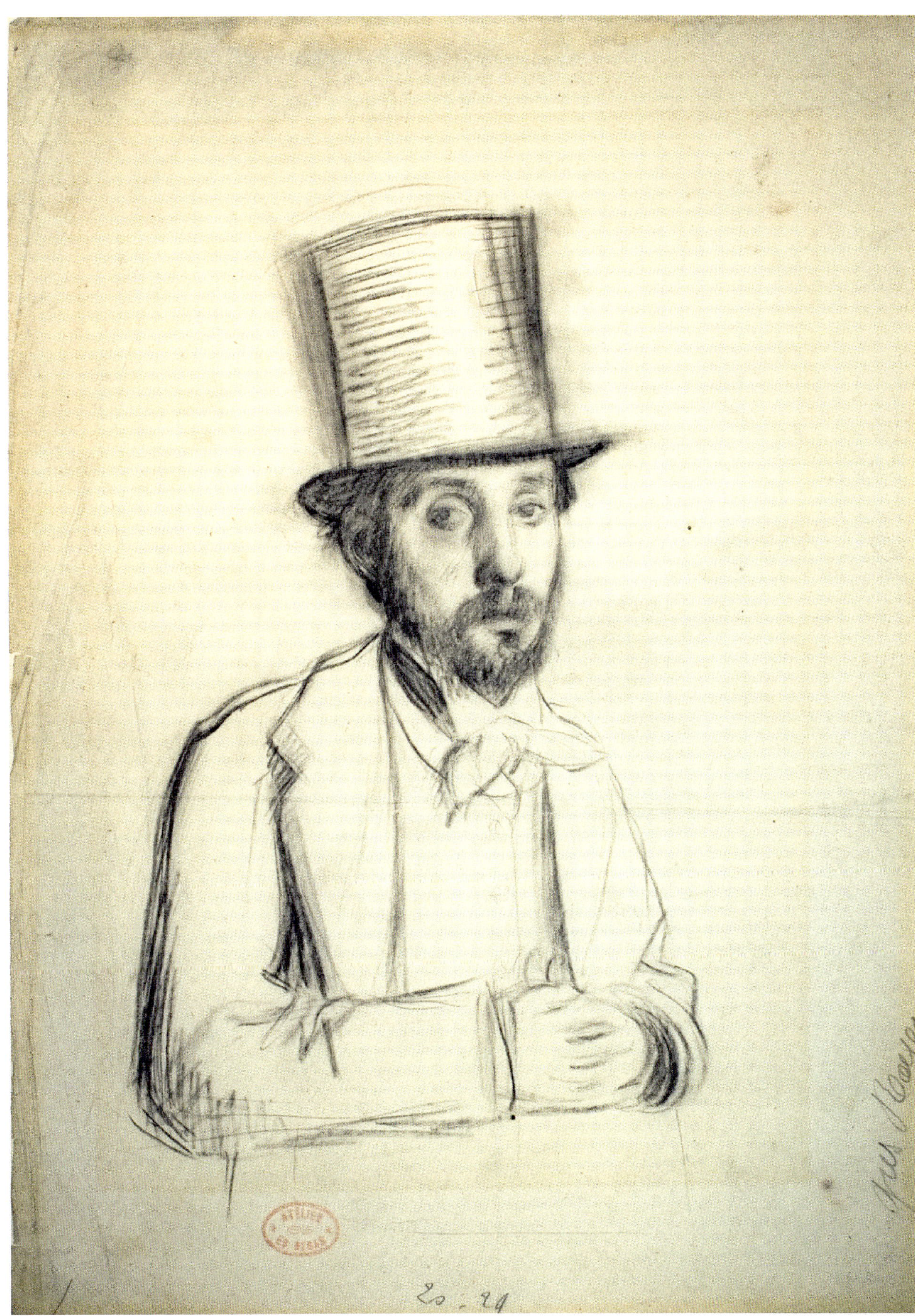

37

EDGAR DEGAS 1834–1917

Man on Horseback, early 1860s

38

EDGAR DEGAS 1834–1917

Study of a Horse, early 1860s

37: Graphite on wove paper, 41 × 26 cm

Sale stamp (L.658), lower right

PROVENANCE: Degas' fourth sale, 2–4 July 1917, lot 245a; Jean Cau and by descent; Beaussant and Lefèvre, Hôtel Drouot, 16 December 1993, lot 51

38: Graphite on wove paper, 28 × 17.5 cm

Nepveu-Degas stamp (L.4349), lower left; studio stamp verso (L.657)

PROVENANCE: Nepveu-Degas collection; sale, 6 May 1976, no.22

Like other children from prosperous families, Degas learned to ride at an early age and although he did not ride in later years, the horse was a source of continuing fascination. In the 1850s and early 1860s, while perfecting his art, he copied horses from plaster casts of the Parthenon frieze, from Italian old masters and from the work of his contemporaries. Like Géricault, he included at least one horse in most of his early paintings and when he eventually turned away from historical and literary themes in the early 1860s, he discovered a source of equestrian subjects in the contemporary race-course. Both these studies probably date from the early 1860s when he painted his first race-course pictures. Unlike the vast majority of Degas' many drawings of horses, however, neither of the two shown here represents a race-horse and the rider in cat.37 is not a jockey nor a 'gentleman rider', as amateurs were known, but a man of substance dressed in top hat and knee-length coat.

Despite the vivacity of Degas' pencil, cat.37 is not a fleeting image of a horse and rider seen in passing but a drawing that has been carefully composed. Degas drew the horse first in outline and added the rider before completing it with delicate strokes of graphite. The outline of a second horse suggests that Degas was thinking of a work with two mounted figures possibly in connection with a composition of a man and woman riding side by side that is known in an oil sketch (Lemoisne, supp. 38), a water-colour,[1] two drawings[2] and a pastel. The riders are seen from behind in the other studies, but the two studies of a horse's hindquarters that appear in the upper half of the drawing suggest that he may already have been considering this idea.

While it should be recalled that one horse seen from behind looks much like another, it is worth noting that these studies are not dissimilar to the hindquarters of the two horses as they appear in the oil sketch.

Degas must have valued no.37 as he framed it in his studio along with three other drawings of horses: a study for *The Fallen Horseman of 1866* (National Gallery of Art, Washington), a slight scribble of a shying thoroughbred and a copy of a detail from Géricault's *Race of the Riderless Horses*, based on a lithograph or preparatory drawing. Whether Degas saw any significance in this grouping other than the fact that all four drawings represent a horse is difficult to say.

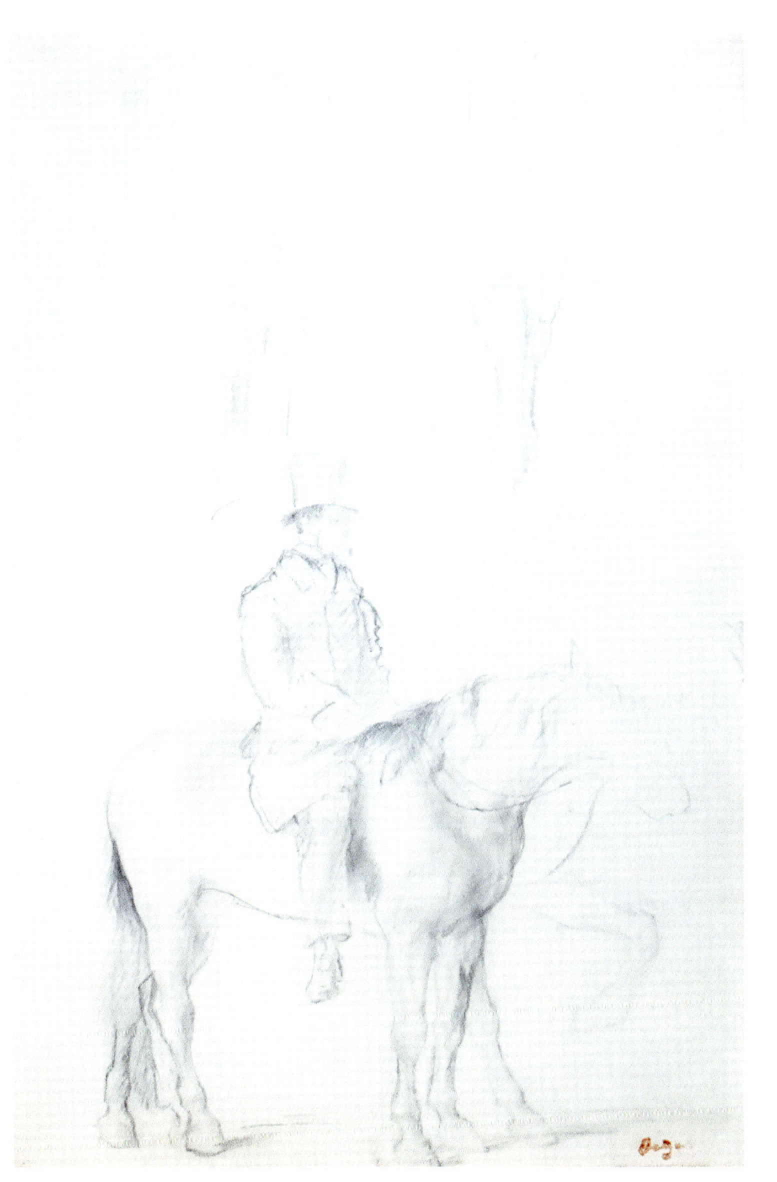

NEPVEU
DEGAS

39

EDGAR DEGAS 1834–1917

A Café-Concert Singer (Derrière le rideau de fer), 1877–78

Aquatint, drypoint and scraping on paper, 16 × 11.8 cm

LITERATURE: Delteil (1919), 21; Adhémar (1974), 29; Reed and Shapiro (1984), 32a; Hauptman (2016), p.63, fig.7

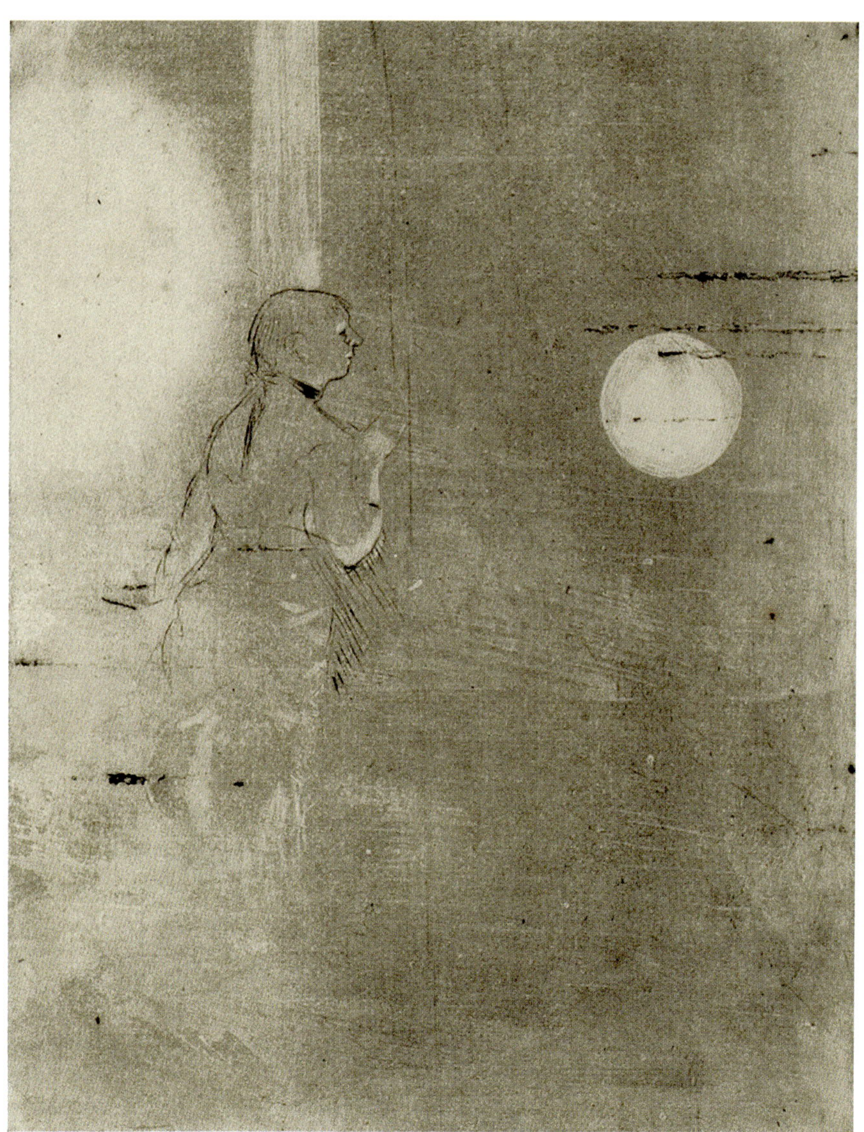

Although traditionally entitled *Behind the Safety Curtain (Derrière le rideau de fer)*, the subject of this print has been convincingly identified as a café-concert singer with a gaslight globe on the right and a mirror on the left.[1] It is difficult to make out these details here, but they can be seen clearly in a number of Degas' pastels and prints of the late 1870s which feature singers in a café in similar scenes.[2]

Degas printed this very rare image (only four impressions are known, including the present one) from a daguerreotype plate of electroplated copper. Like the plates used to print two of Degas' other etchings, *The Two Dancers*[3] and *The Laundresses*,[4] the plate for *A Café-Concert Singer* was stamped with the name of the maker of the plates, Fr. Schneider of Berlin. This stamp was inked along with the etched image and appears printed in reverse on the lower left.

Degas was keenly interested in the advances of science. Following the launch of photography in 1839, he would have known of the various attempts to perfect a system of printing from a daguerreotype. He was probably aware of Hippolyte-Louis Fizeau's experiments in the 1840s which used nitric acid lightly to bite out the darks and added a ground of rosin for the tone. Degas' use of drypoint and aquatint was somewhat similar, but more traditional and less complex than Fizeau's approach. He may simply have turned to the daguerreotype plates because they were to hand, and the highly polished surface provided an ideal basis for making prints

40

EDGAR DEGAS 1834–1917

Leaving the Bath (La sortie du bain) 1st state, ca.1879–80

Drypoint and aquatint on laid paper, 12.7 × 12.7 cm

Annotated in pencil: *Femme à sa toilette (Sortie de bain) 1 Etat nce*

LITERATURE: Delteil (1919), 39; Adhémar (1974), 49; Reed and Shapiro (1984), 42.1

In 1879 Degas set out a proposal for a journal of original prints, *Le Jour et la nuit* (*Day and Night*), involving his friends Mary Cassatt, Jean-François Raffaelli and Marcellin Desboutin and coinciding with a period of experimental etching by Degas himself. This print must date from the time of these discussions, but, judging by the rarity of the different states, it was probably not intended for publication. According to Degas' friend, the print collector Alexis Rouart, he first sketched it on to copper while stranded overnight in Rouart's house by the icy conditions. In an attempt to date this episode, assiduous scholars have discovered that there was a particularly cold spell in the winter of 1879 that began in October and continued for several weeks.[1]

In the present first state of the print (one of only three known impressionss of this state, the other two being at the Art Institute of Chicago and the Albertina in Vienna) the initial drawing in light, scribbled lines is clearly visible, especially in the body of the bather. Much of the rest has been heavily gone over with an incisive point, particularly evident in the dark, furry strokes that cover the floor. Behind the maid hangs a barely perceptible frame, probably enclosing a mirror. On the right is a small, fringed, button-back nursing chair and a mantel shelf with a fringed cover; on the latter is a garniture of two vases of an oriental type which in the later states contain tall plants. In the lower left is an upholstered armchair, with one arm visible. These details become clearer in the succeeding states, of which Reed and Shapiro have identified 22 – a surprising indication of how involved Degas became in achieving a final resolution to what seems to have begun as a *jeu d'esprit*. In the succeeding states Degas introduced more pattern on the walls, vases, carpet and armchair before finally erasing much of the added work, particularly on the body of the bather and on the towel, and then abandoning the print.

The somewhat caricatural, almost humorous character of the image links it to the monotypes that Degas had been making since *c.*1876. There is a close resemblance in theme with three monotypes, one printed in black (Adhémar, 133) and two others that Degas worked over with pastel.[2] The idea of the bather and her maid carrying a towel, appears elsewhere in the artist's work, notably in his last lithograph [cat.43]. In contrast to this print, however, that work has a monumental gravity, stripped of the distracting accessories that appear here and in the monotypes.

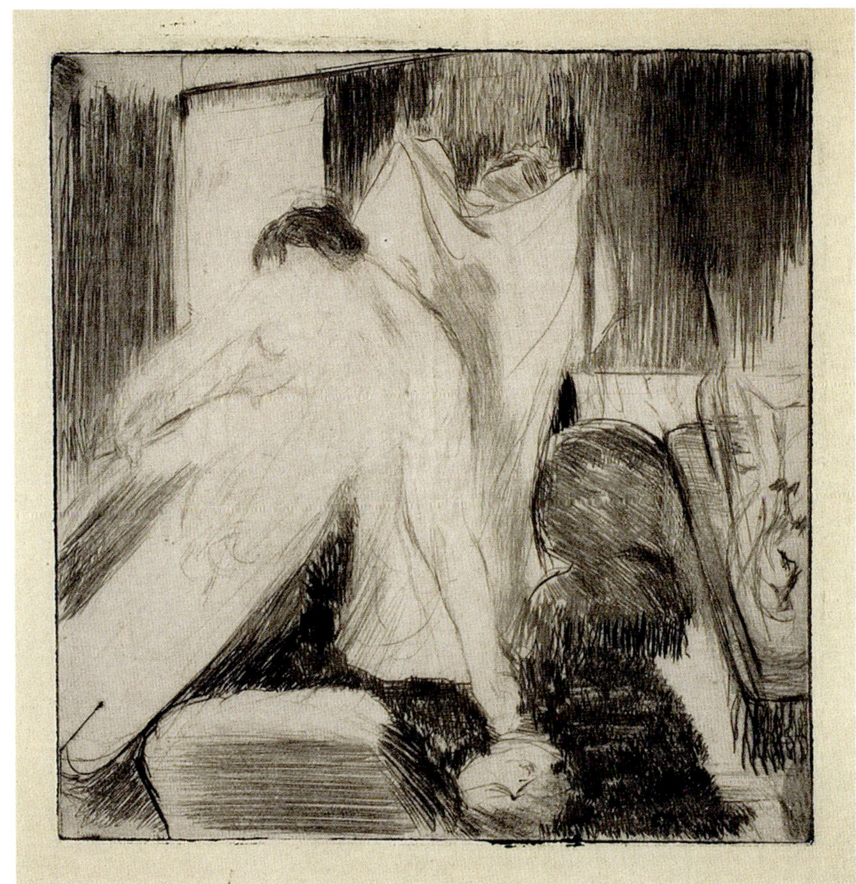

41

EDGAR DEGAS 1834–1917

Nude Woman Standing at her Toilette (Femme nue debout, à sa toilette) 4th state, 1891

In his later years, Degas obsessively repeated his favourite motifs in multiple variations. While other artists progressed from a life study through a series of copies to a finished work, Degas copied, traced and reversed his images in a process of reduction and rethinking that seems, at times, to have become an end in itself. The composition illustrated here first appeared in Degas' work in the early 1880s (for example Lemoisne III, 384) and reappeared in many subsequent drawings, prints and pastels. Degas seems to have begun work on the lithograph in 1891, refining and retouching it in a series of six states[1] and reproducing it in five further lithographs – cat. 41 is an example of the fourth state of the original lithograph and cat. 42 is an example of the sixth state.[2]

The lithograph seems to have been based on a drawing made with greasy ink on a celluloid plate that Degas transferred directly onto a lithographic stone. This would have resulted in a print facing in the same direction as the original image. As the figure in the lithograph is in reverse to the known drawings, however, it is probable that Degas had transferred an earlier drawing to the celluloid. The pallid image in the first state of the lithograph, perhaps four times removed

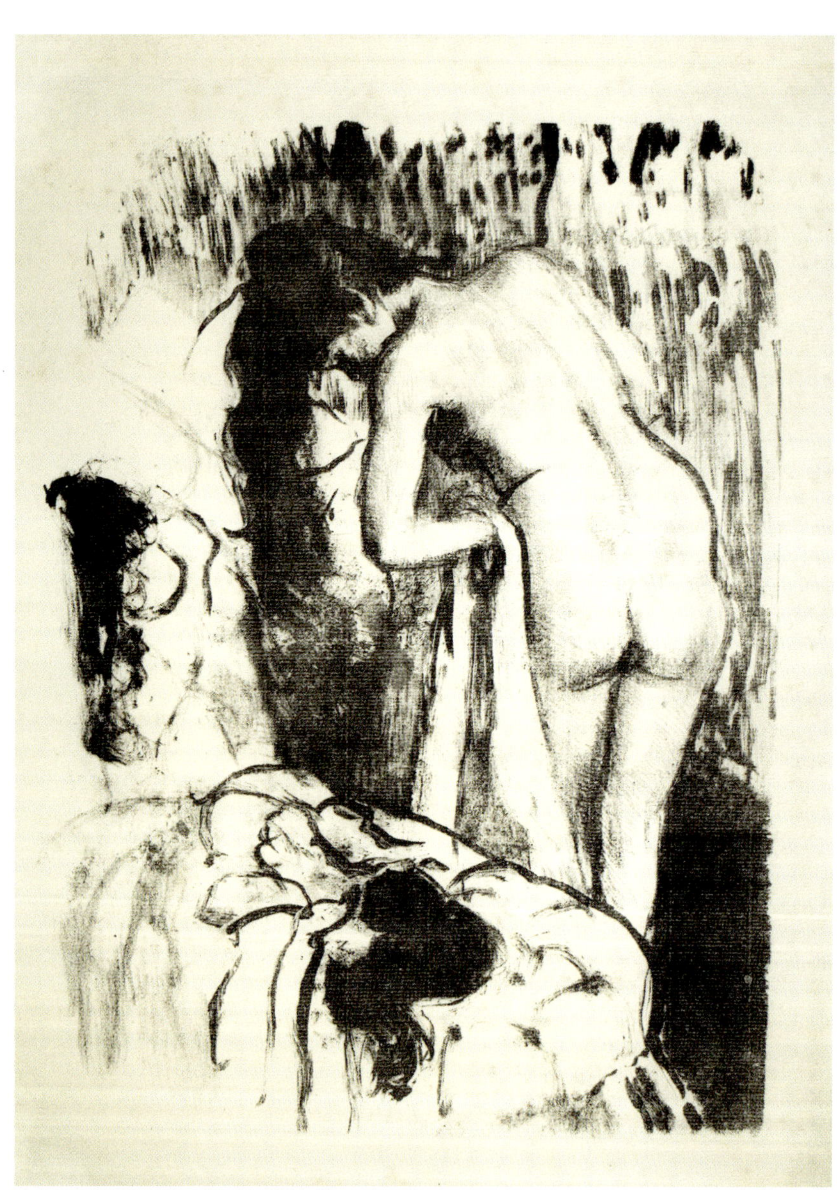

Lithograph, 33.5 × 24.5 cm

Signed in the plate

LITERATURE: Delteil (1919), 65.III; Adhémar (1974), 63 III; Reed and Shapiro (1984), no 61.IV

42

EDGAR DEGAS 1834–1917

Nude Woman Standing at her Toilette (Femme nue debout, à sa toilette) 6th state, 1891

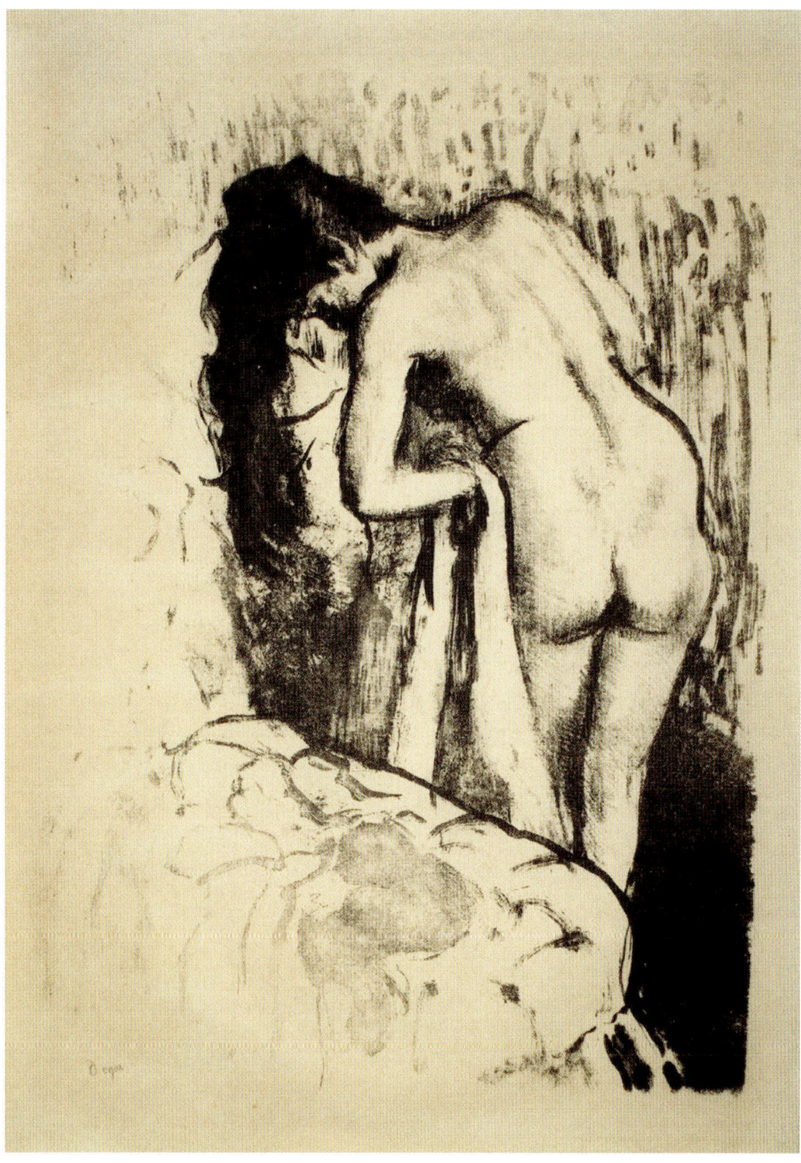

Lithograph, 33.5 × 24.5 cm

Signed in the plate

LITERATURE: Delteil (1919), 65.IV; Adhémar (1974), 63.IV; Reed and Shapiro (1984), no.61.VI

from the original drawing, was strengthened with crayon in a second state and with extensive reworking with brush, crayon and scraper in the third.[3] The fourth state, [cat. 41] does not differ from the third in detail; instead it is printed with a greater contrast of tone and fewer highlights. In the third state Degas added the cascade of hair that he used in several different images of bathers in this period. The motif appears for the first time in his *Scene of War in the Middle Ages*, painted in 1865 (Musée d'Orsay, Paris) – inspired, perhaps, by a similar figure in Delacroix's *Entry of the Crusaders into Constantinople* (Musée du Louvre, Paris).[4] By the 1890s, Degas had transformed his academic nude acting out a part in a historical drama into a modern bather seen in a moment of intimacy and insignificance.

By the time of the sixth and final state [cat.42], Degas had consolidated the effect of monumental form by eliminating much of the surrounding detail. The figure is given relief by the dark patch on the lower right, balancing the dark of the bather's hair – now even more conspicuous with the reduction of many of the inessentials.

43

EDGAR DEGAS 1834–1917

After the Bath (small plate) (La sortie du bain, petite planche) 1st state, ca.1891–92

Lithograph on wove paper, 24.5 × 22.1 cm
LITERATURE: Delteil (1919), 63; Adhémar (1974), 67.1; Reed and Shapiro (1984), no.65.1

From a close investigation of the prints, Reed and Shapiro have concluded that Degas made a series of three lithographs that originated in a single drawing made on celluloid with lithographic crayon[1]. This was transferred photographically from a counterproof to the stones used for the first and second prints. While this complex sequence seems to offer few practical advantages, the use of a counterproof, made on damp paper in a printing press, explains why these three prints are in the same direction as the related drawings but in the opposite direction to the earlier prints (for examples of the earlier prints see cats 41 and 42).

Reed and Shapiro conclude that the print illustrated here, a rare example of the first state, was transferred to a larger stone from an impression of the fifth (and last) impression of the second lithograph. This was then thoroughly revised in black crayon and a maid holding a towel was added. A maid does appear on occasion in the pastels and drawings of the bathers, but in general Degas seems to have preferred to concentrate on a single, isolated figure, self-absorbed and unaware of the presence of the artist and, even when a maid was included, indifferent to her presence. In the second state of this print, he wiped out the servant and the background and printed an unbalanced composition with a large blank area on the right. He may have intended to reintroduce the maid into this space, but set it aside and continued to work on the motif of the bather and her maid on a new stone.[2]

None of Degas' previous prints had involved such technical complexity nor such constant revision as this sequence of five prints in 19 states. Possibly they never achieved a result that satisfied the artist. Whatever the reason, Degas abandoned making prints once he had set aside the second state of the final version of *After the Bath*.

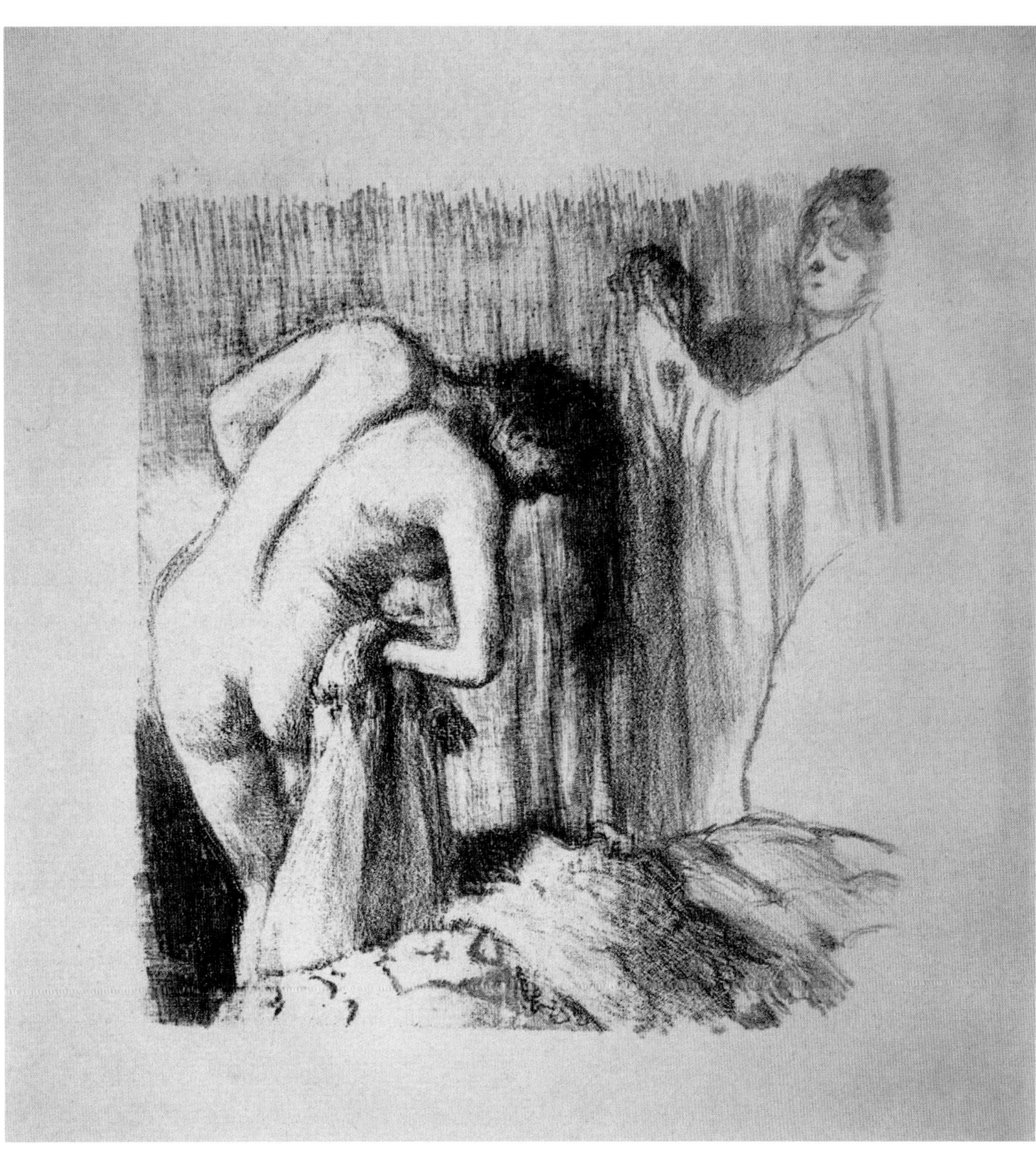

44

EDGAR DEGAS 1834–1917

Woman after her Bath, 1900–05

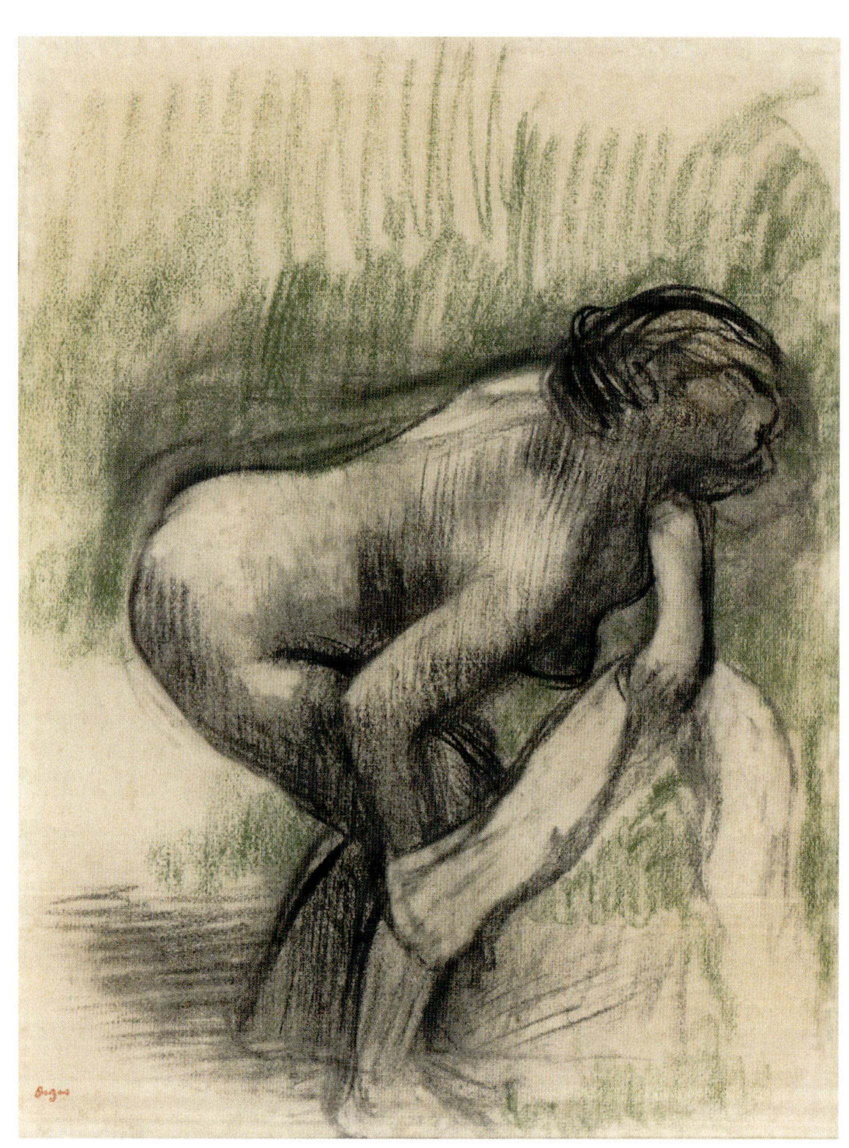

Charcoal and green pastel on buff paper, 61 × 47 cm

Sale stamp (L.658), lower left studio stamp (L.657), verso

PROVENANCE: Degas' second studio sale, 11–13 December 1918, lot 314, ill.; Ira Hotchkiss, Hollywood; private collection, USA; Parke Bernet, New York, 21 October 1976, lot 105; Sotheby's Parke Bernet, New York, 6 November 1981, lot 510

LITERATURE: Kendall (1996), p.156, fig.182

Beginning in about 1887 (Lemoisne, 917) and continuing on occasion over the following 18 years or so (see Lemoisne, 1138), Degas made a series of drawings and pastels of a woman drying her foot while seated on the edge of a tub. In about 1900–5 his interest in the theme quickened, and he studied it again in a series of charcoal drawings often coloured with a touch or two of pastel.[1] The present drawing, *Woman after her Bath*, belongs to this late group, but does not feature the tub that appears in the other drawings. The subject's crouching pose would have looked less awkward if Degas had included it.

Here the artist used a charcoal stick of a relatively hard quality. He applied it with rough, searching strokes along the back and round the head, and with lighter, vertical lines in the modelling of the figure. The result is compact and solid, resembling a small sculpture; it is enhanced by the strong light from upper left and by the dark green background which throws the bather's pale back into relief.

45

EDGAR DEGAS 1834–1917

After the Bath, Woman Drying her Leg, 1900–05

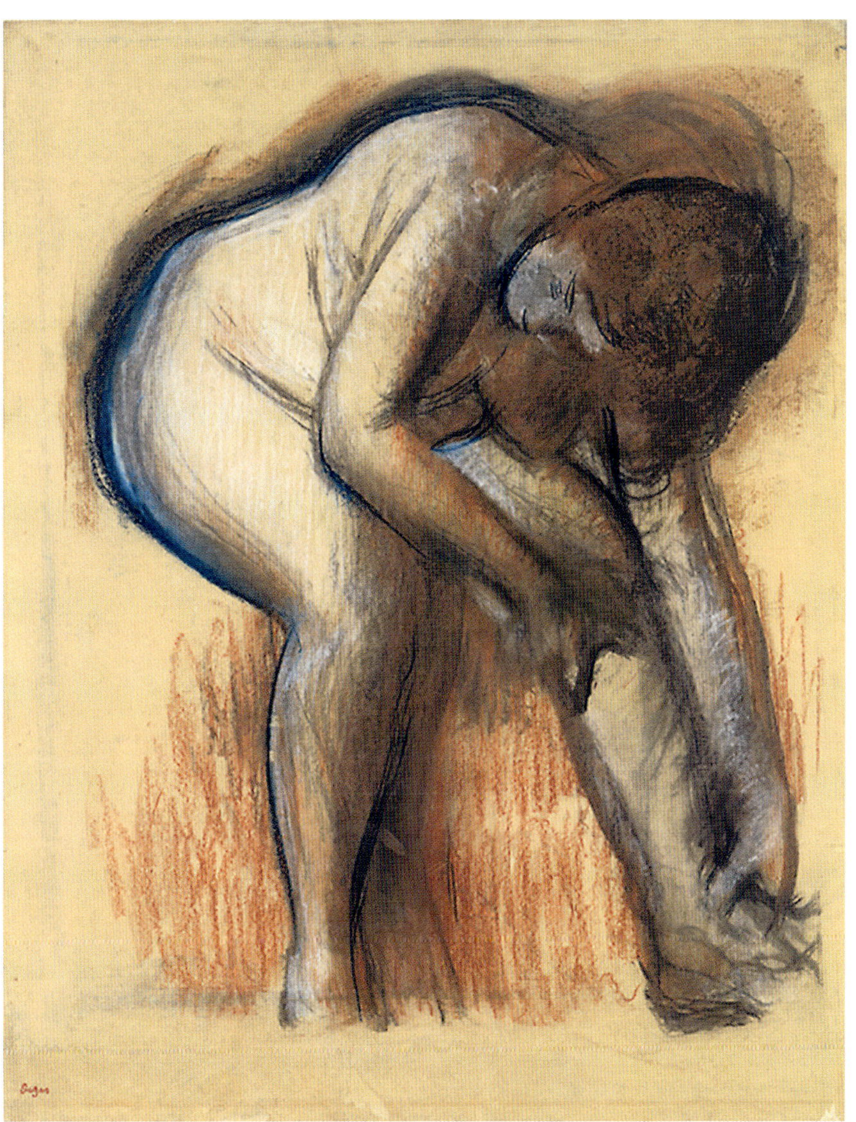

Charcoal, white chalk and pastel on tracing paper, 62.5 × 51.5 cm

Sale stamp lower left (L.658)

PROVENANCE: Degas' second studio sale, 11–13 December 1918, lot 187, ill.; Ambroise Vollard; sale of *collections provenant des châteaux* étrangers, Hôtel National, Lucerne, 8 September 1924, lot 40; Kornfeld, Bern, 26 June 1981, lot 175

LITERATURE: Lemoisne III, no.1436; Kendall (1996), p.146, fig.167, Loyrette (2016), p.161

Like cat.44, this drawing belongs to the series of studies of women drying a foot, drawn between 1900 and 1905. It differs from the others, however, in showing the subject from a more frontal position. This drawing also assumes the presence of a bath tub on which the bather is seated. Like other studies of bathers by Degas from this period, it is outlined with a bold, schematic freedom. The contours are drawn and redrawn with an exploratory charcoal, while the volume of the figure is emphasised by an outline in charcoal and blue chalk and by the extensive use of white chalk in the highlights. Degas often employed tracing paper in his late drawings, and the use of it here does not necessarily imply that the figure has been traced. The noticeable revisions, particularly in the right leg and head, suggest that the image was improvised on the paper.

Ambroise Vollard, the dealer who acquired many works from Degas in his lifetime, bought this study, along with much else from the sale of Degas' studio, in 1918–19. His purchases included an offset[1] taken from this drawing (Lemoisne, 1436 bis) by Degas who was in the habit of tracing, copying and reversing his compositions in his later years.

46

PIERRE-AUGUSTE RENOIR 1841–1919

Bather Drying Herself, 1912

Charcoal on pinkish-brown wove paper, 64 × 48.5 cm

PROVENANCE: Fritz Gurlitt, Berlin; Josef Haubrich, Cologne; Josef Jackel

LITERATURE: Rewald (1946), no.84

Renoir's visit to Italy in October–November 1881 heralded a turning point in his art. In the future he was to turn further away from the modernist tenets of Impressionism, as advocated in particular by Monet and Pissarro, towards a more personal style which owed as much to his admiration for the classical tradition as to the immediacy of the impression from nature. In Rome Renoir particularly admired Raphael's frescoes in the Villa Farnesina, including illustrations of the legend of Cupid and Psyche, and the *Triumph of Galatea*, which offered the greatest concentration of nudes anywhere by the Renaissance master. Renoir also travelled to Naples and Pompeii, as well as to Venice and Padua in the north of Italy. The effect of these journeys on his painting was gradual, but by the middle of the 1880s he had effectively fixed upon the female nude as his principal subject, with a subsidiary interest in the clothed female figure engaging in everyday activities. He made remarkably few depictions of men. As Renoir later told his friend, the Post-Impressionist painter Albert André, 'The simplest subjects are eternal. A nude woman getting out of the briny deep or out of her bed, whether she is called Venus or Nini, one can invent nothing better'.[1] During the 1890s Renoir's nudes in both paintings and drawings became increasingly monumental and, in the final decade of his life, sculptural. Indeed, in 1913 he was persuaded by the dealer Ambroise Vollard to experiment with sculpture, but his acute rheumatism prevented Renoir from executing the two bronzes exhibited in 1916; they were made by an assistant under his direction. He was, however, still able to manipulate paintbrushes and drawing materials. This majestic drawing is a preparatory study for a painting of 1912.[2] Like many nudes of this period, it illustrates Renoir's admiration, renewed on a visit to Munich in 1910, for the 'glorious fullness' of Rubens' nudes.[3] In the drawing, the folds of flesh in the stomach are emphatically described, as the seated figure dries her leg and balances herself with her left arm. She appears to be oblivious to the viewer, calmly concentrating on her task.

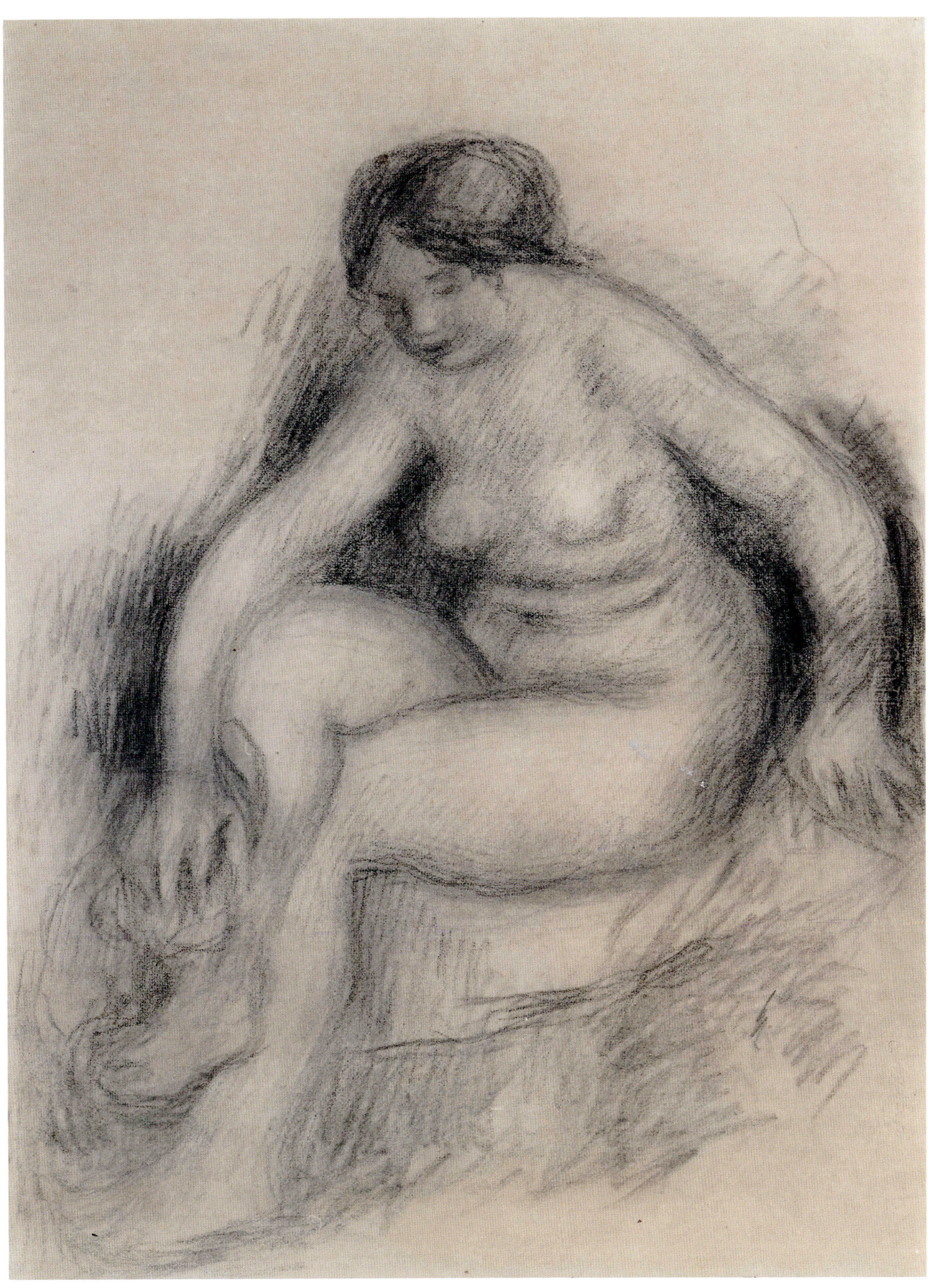

47

GEORGES SEURAT 1859–1891

Man Seen from Behind, early 1880s

Conté crayon on paper, 17.5 × 10 cm

PROVENANCE: studio sale, lot 265; Jacques Bonjean, Paris; Bruno de Bayser, Paris

LITERATURE: Hauke no.427

Drawing for Seurat, as for Degas, was central to his artistic practice. In 1878 he went to the École des Beaux-Arts where he studied with Henri Lehmann, a talented draughtsman who had trained with Ingres. Like Degas and Ingres, Seurat believed strongly in the primacy of drawing. The purity of line, emulation of which he had demonstrated in his student copies after Holbein and Ingres, soon gave way to what appears to be a diametrically opposed technique of tonal drawing. Such a style of drawing was not uncommon at the time in academic circles. It followed a shift in drawing practice at the École des Beaux-Arts which encouraged the use of charcoal and crayon in place of the traditional, harder chalks. Tonal drawing was also taken up by those associated with both the Barbizon School and with Realists such as Millet and Fantin-Latour. Essentially, though, a sense of form remained of central importance for Seurat.

In the period immediately following his military service at Brest, Seurat devoted himself to making studies of the passing scene. Degas' close friend Émile Duranty, in his extended pamphlet, *La Nouvelle Peinture* (1876), had stressed the importance of the contemporary world as a subject for the modern artist. So had Thomas Couture, Manet's master, who encouraged his pupils to seek out characters and types among the working people of Paris. During the early 1880s the subjects of many, if not most, of Seurat's drawings were nursemaids, beggars, elegant figures, workmen and clowns – the cosmopolitan cast of urban Paris. Most of these, including this drawing, are not related to any known composition.

In the case of this drawing, a comment made by Duranty in his *Nouvelle Peinture*, which Degas understood so well, seems apt: 'a back should reveal temperament, age and social position.'[1] This figure within its desolate and limitless setting – a place between town and country, the edge of Paris, haunt of rag-pickers (whom Seurat also drew) – fulfils Duranty's requirement to perfection. For all its urban and modern character, this drawing, like many of those of Degas, recalls the manner of Millet, the great draughtsman of the mid-century whom Seurat had also copied. Like Millet, Seurat used conté crayon on Michallet paper, a handmade, French laid paper with a heavy grain; it produced a close-knit texture of effects of dark and light while recording the varying degrees of pressure of the artist's hand. In addition, Seurat drew with a sureness of touch that perfectly expresses the condition of the subject, infusing it with a strong sense of the pathos of a figure on the margin of society. The theme was also explored by Degas' friend, Jean-François Raffaelli, in many drawings and paintings of workers and outcasts. Yet Raffaelli's peasants and rag-pickers are drawn with much circumstantial detail; Seurat's old man is, in contrast, miraculously economic.

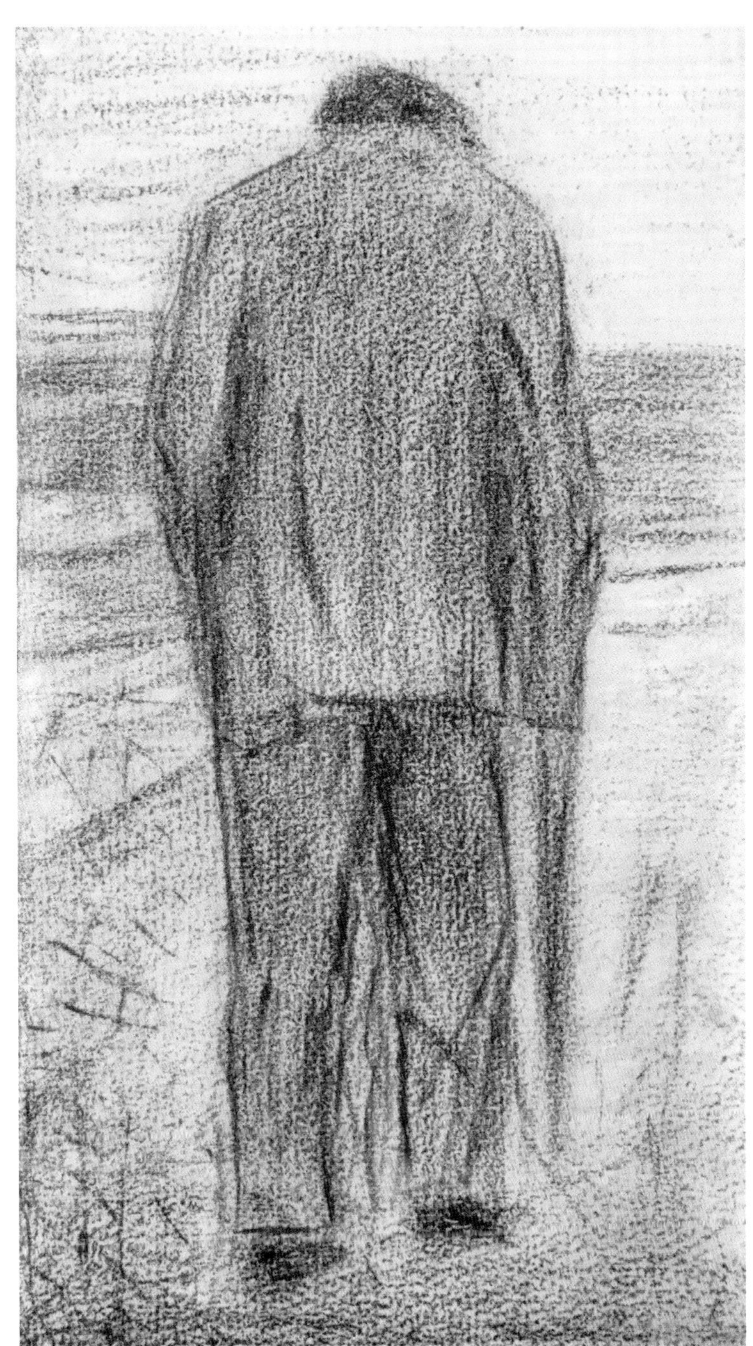

48

ODILON REDON 1840–1916

Christ on the Cross, ca.1910

Pastel with graphite on brown wove paper, 32.5 × 25.8 cm

Signed: *ODILON REDON*

PROVENANCE: Emmanuel Albert Lewensten; Paul Citröen, Wassenaar; W. Serra, Wassenaar; Sotheby's, London, 29 November, 1989, lot 427

LITERATURE: Wildenstein (1992), vol.1, no.523

This pastel originally represented the martyrdom of St Sebastian before Redon painted out the tree that was once behind the saint and turned the subject into a crucifixion. St Sebastian's martyrdom was a common theme in Redon's work. The subject appears for the first time in a thumbnail sketch in a notebook of 1864 (Wildenstein 2114) loosely based on Delacroix's painting of *St Sebastian tended by the Holy Women* (Church of St Michel, Nantua) that Redon would have seen in 1864 when it was exhibited in Paris. Most of Redon's images of Saint Sebastian show the more common subject of the saint tied upright to the tree. This pose was probably inspired by Corot's *Saint Sebastian,* painted in the early 1850s (Musée du Louvre, Paris), a work still in the artist's studio when Redon and Corot first met in 1864. The gouache illustrated here probably dates from about 1910 when he made a number of similar studies and paintings of St Sebastian, standing or hanging from the tree, notably a painting in Basel (Kunstmuseum) and a related gouache in Bordeaux (Musée des Beaux-Arts) in which the saint's arms are raised over his head and an oil painting in Washington (National Gallery of Art) in which the saint's hands are tied behind his back. In the present work, the saint was originally painted with both hands above his head before Redon changed the position of his left arm.

Redon made a copy of this gouache in its altered form (Wildenstein, 528) and seems to have had it in mind when drawing a highly coloured pastel of the crucifixion (Wildenstein, 522) that appeared on the London art market in 2016.[1] The ledge that runs across the lower part in the latter composition explains the white band that Redon painted over the legs of the saint in the gouache. This ledge, on which the artist has placed a vine and a column, emblems of Christ's ministry and suffering, appears below a frame or opening that encloses a vision of the crucifixion.

Redon had, at first, specialised in disturbing dream-like images drawn or printed in black and white. In the 1890s, he turned to colour and by 1900 had abandoned his 'blacks', as he called them, in favour of richly coloured oil and pastel. At the same time he became involved with artists and writers of the Catholic revival, notably with Maurice Denis, who introduced him to the Nabis in 1899. Through the influence of contemporary spiritualism, his art became infused with a mysticism that drew on Eastern and European sources. His themes are often commonplace, but the deeper significance of his work is generally elusive. One senses a layer of meaning in this image of martyrdom that touches on larger themes of spiritual experience, but it is difficult to pin this down. Redon's drawings, as he noted in his memoirs, 'inspire and cannot be defined. They resolve nothing. Like music, they transport us into the ambiguous world of the indeterminate'.[2]

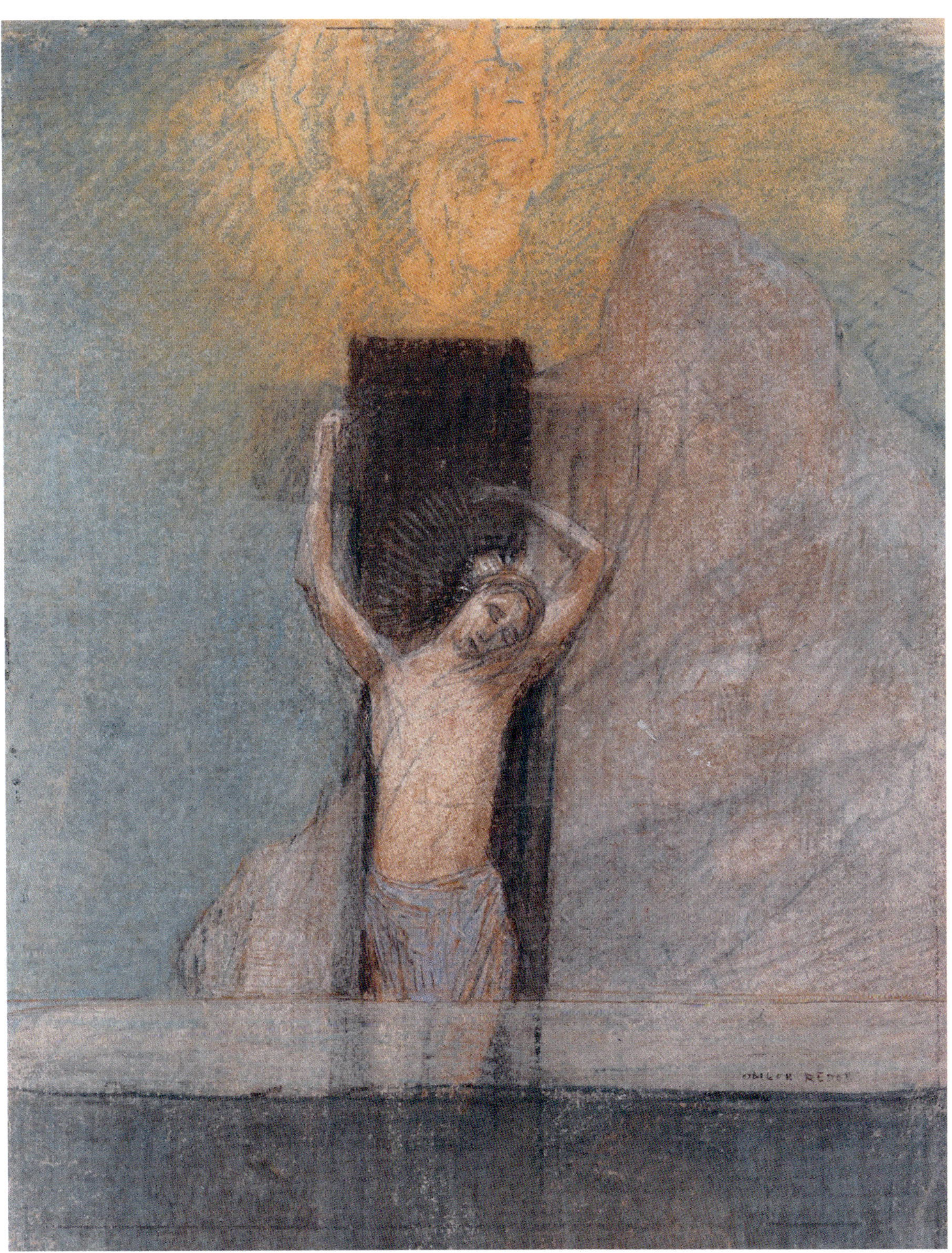

49

PAUL CÉZANNE 1839–1906

In the Countryside, ca.1870

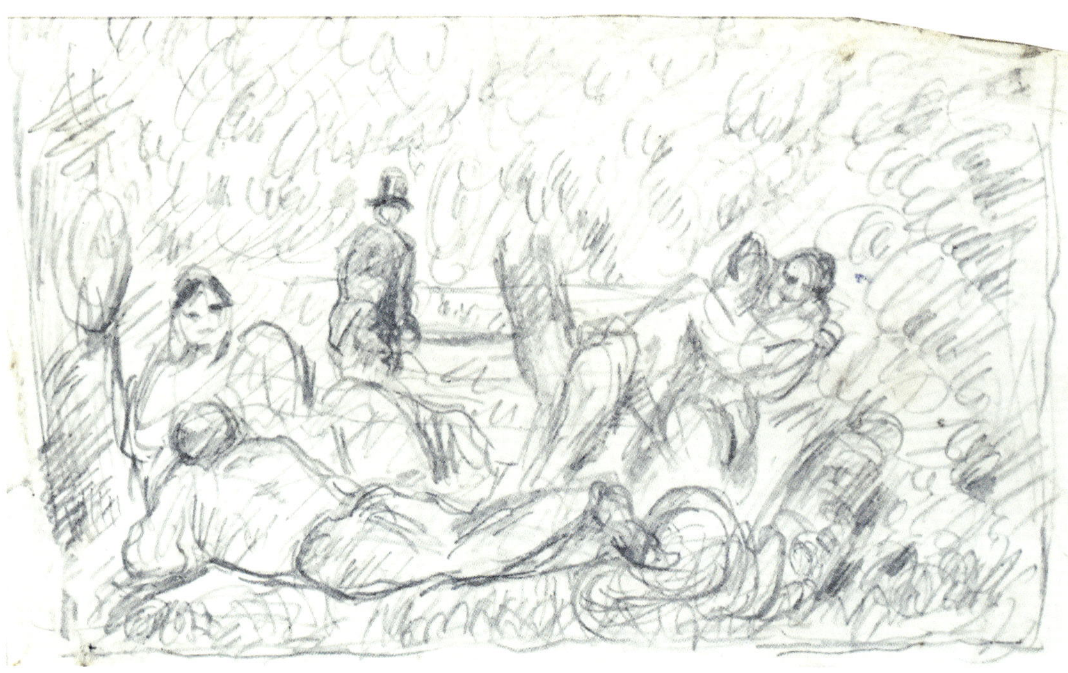

Graphite on paper, 9 × 14.6 cm

PROVENANCE: Ambroise Vollard; sale of collection of Kenneth Clark, Sotheby's, London, June–July 1984

LITERATURE: Vollard (1915), p.177; Meier-Graefe (1922), p.64; Chappuis (1973), no.318

Cézanne studied at the Académie Suisse in Paris from late 1862, and in the following year registered to make copies in the Louvre. He must have visited the Salon des Refusés many times after it opened in May 1863, and especially admired the most scandalous painting, Manet's *Déjeuner sur l'herbe*. He had a second opportunity to admire the work when Manet put on a personal exhibition in 1867; the event also included Manet's other very controversial painting, *Olympia*, already shown at the Salon of 1865. As his own paintings were repeatedly rejected by the Jury of the Salon, Cézanne no doubt identified both personally and artistically with Manet, with whom he was by this time on friendly terms.

In the early 1870s the artist worked on three compositions inspired by Manet: *Pastorale* (dated 1870) and *Le Déjeuner sur l'herbe*, both indebted to Manet's picture of the latter title; and *A Modern Olympia*, completed in 1873 and shown at the first Impressionist Exhibition in 1874.[1] The *Pastorale* includes clothed male figures and naked females, as Manet's painting had done, but, unlike Manet, Cézanne did not intend the scene to be taken literally. Rather it was an imaginary juxtaposition of figures in various poses, apparently quoted out of context and not integrated into a narrative whole.

This drawing, made on the back of a print, may have been an early idea for the *Pastorale*. It shows a man fully clothed and wearing a top hat in the middle distance, while in the foreground are two couples. On the left a nude reclining woman chats to an apparently clothed man with his back to the viewer, while on the right a couple energetically embrace. The airless atmosphere of a warm day in the woods is emphasised by the extraordinary rapidity of the drawing style, the loops and lines of pencil almost frenzied in their nervous energy.

50

PAUL CÉZANNE 1839–1906

Studies of Bathers and a Caryatid, 1876–78

Graphite on paper, 12.5 × 21.6 cm

PROVENANCE: Paul Cézanne, the artist's son; Paul Guillaume; Adrien Chappuis; by descent to Georges and Jean Barut, Chambéry; Christie's, London, 26 June 2003, lot 323

LITERATURE: Venturi (1936), no.1299; Reff (1962), p.181; Chappuis (1973), no.631

At the third Impressionist exhibition in 1877, Cézanne showed a painting of *Les baigneurs; étude, projet de tableau*. This work, generally identified as the monumental canvas *Bathers at Rest* in the Barnes collection, was more likely to be one of the two much smaller related studies.[1] In these compositions he combined male and female bathers in a studied variety of poses. At the same time Cézanne was exploring a composition of a single male bather, standing upright and seen from the front, with his arms stretched out. The related drawings and paintings have been dated from the late 1870s to the mid-1880s, but specialists still do not agree on the dating. However, a small sketch of the finished composition on a sheet which also includes portraits of the artist's son, born on 4 January 1872, at the age of five or six confirms the earlier dating.[2]

In all four small oils known as the *Bather with Outstretched Arms (Baigneur aux bras écartés)* are recorded, together with a number of related drawings.[3] All were presumably made in preparation for the largest of these oils, the statuesque *Baigneur aux bras écartés*.[4] The first work, painted in a broken Impressionist technique, depicts a nude boy standing beneath a tree. The others show a youth in underpants walking precariously on the edge of a cliff, steadying himself with his raised arms. All are traditionally, but perhaps wrongly, held to be part of a preparatory process which culminated in a quite different composition, the *Large Bather* (*Le grand baigneur*) of *c.*1885. This painting shows the young man still in his underpants but with his hands on his hips, as in the *Bathers at Rest*; there is no suggestion that he is about to go swimming.[5]

This sheet from a sketchbook has generally been dated to the mid-1880s. However, since it shows the finished composition of a *Bather with Outstretched Arms*, it was more probably drawn *c.*1876–8. This would accord with the date of the later 1870s for the drawing on the verso, a study of a mantel clock. Various fanciful interpretations of the bather have been proposed, both psychological and sexual. The inclusion on this sheet of a study after a caryatid by the Renaissance engraver Marcantonio Raimondi (1470/82–1527/34) would suggest that it might be seen as another attempt by Cézanne to pit himself against the Old Masters – a modern reinterpretation of a classical subject.

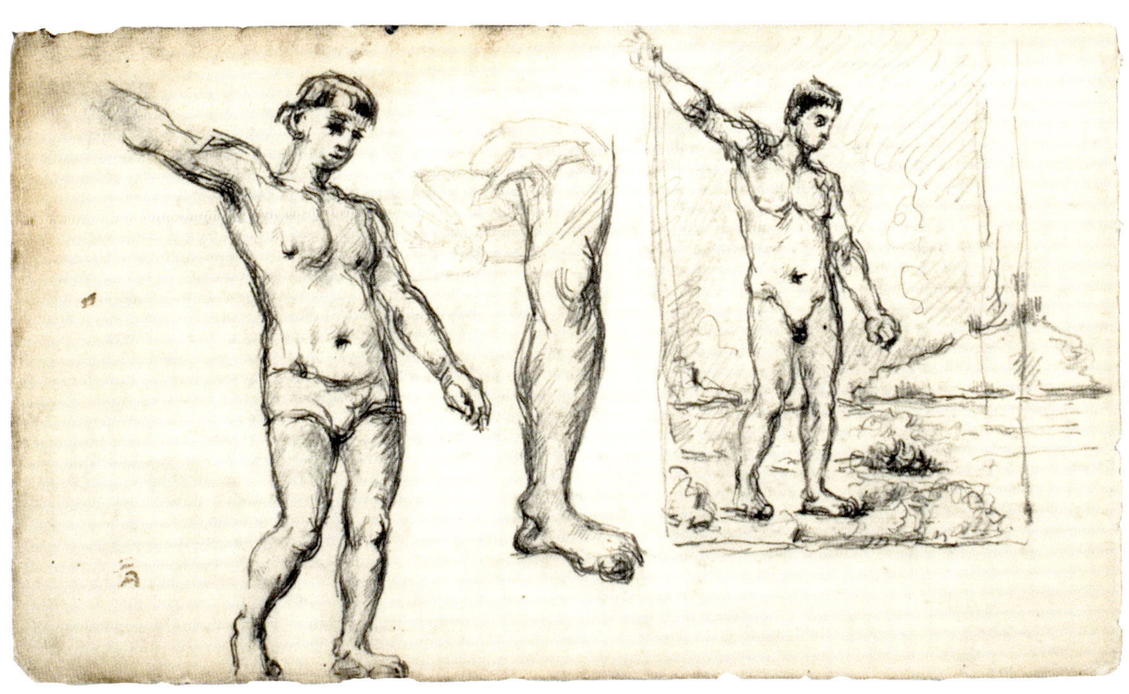

51 & 52

PAUL CÉZANNE 1839–1906

The Bathers, small plate (Les baigneurs, petite planche), 1896–97

51: Lithograph in black ink on chine volant, 23.2 × 28.8 cm

52: Lithograph in colour on chine collé, 21.8 × 26.6 cm

LITERATURE: Venturi (1936), no.1156; Cherpin (1972), no.6; Druick (1978), nos 3 I/IV and III/IV

Soon after reaching Paris from the remote French colony of La Réunion in the Indian Ocean, Ambroise Vollard (1866–1939) settled into a career as an art dealer and publisher:

I was hardly settled in the rue Laffite when I began to dream of publishing fine prints, but I felt they must be done by 'painter-printmakers'! My idea was to obtain works from artists who were not printmakers by profession.[1]

His first album was Pierre Bonnard's *Quelques aspects de la vie de Paris*, which appeared in 1895. Later in the same year Vollard mounted the first exhibition of the work of Cézanne. He pursued Cézanne's work in the following summer, travelling to Aix-en-Provence to buy more of his pictures and meeting the artist for the first time, having previously dealt with his son.

When Vollard invited Cézanne to participate in his album of prints by painter-printmakers in 1896, the artist had little experience of print-making – he had made only five etchings, all in 1873, largely owing to the encouragement of Dr Gachet (see cat.54). Vollard's *L'Album d'estampes originales de la Galerie Vollard,* published in 1897, was the second of the dealer's miscellaneous albums of prints; the first, the *Album des peintres-graveurs* of the previous year, had consisted of 22 prints, mostly lithographs. The new album comprised 32 prints, of which 30 were lithographs; 24 of them were in colour, suggesting that Vollard was capitalising on the new interest in this medium. Cézanne's *Bathers (small plate)* was based on a sequence of watercolours and oils with a similar, frieze-like composition. On the left is a seated figure under a tree, seen from behind; to his right are two standing figures, one seen from the rear, the other from the side; on the far side of the river is a fourth figure, apparently about to take the plunge, while below him is shown the head, shoulders and torso of a boy already in the water. On the far right is an enigmatic crouching figure.

Druick has convincingly established that Cézanne drew the composition in black and white directly on to the stone, and then, with the help of the great printer Auguste Clot (1858–1936), prepared the four separate stones for the colour impressions. He has further suggested that Cézanne's larger lithograph of bathers, which shows signs of having been prepared with a transfer drawing, was earlier than the smaller print, even though it was not published until 1897.[2] The monochrome lithograph of the smaller *Bathers* [cat.51] was printed in only ten proofs, while the colour impressions [cat.52] number at least 100.

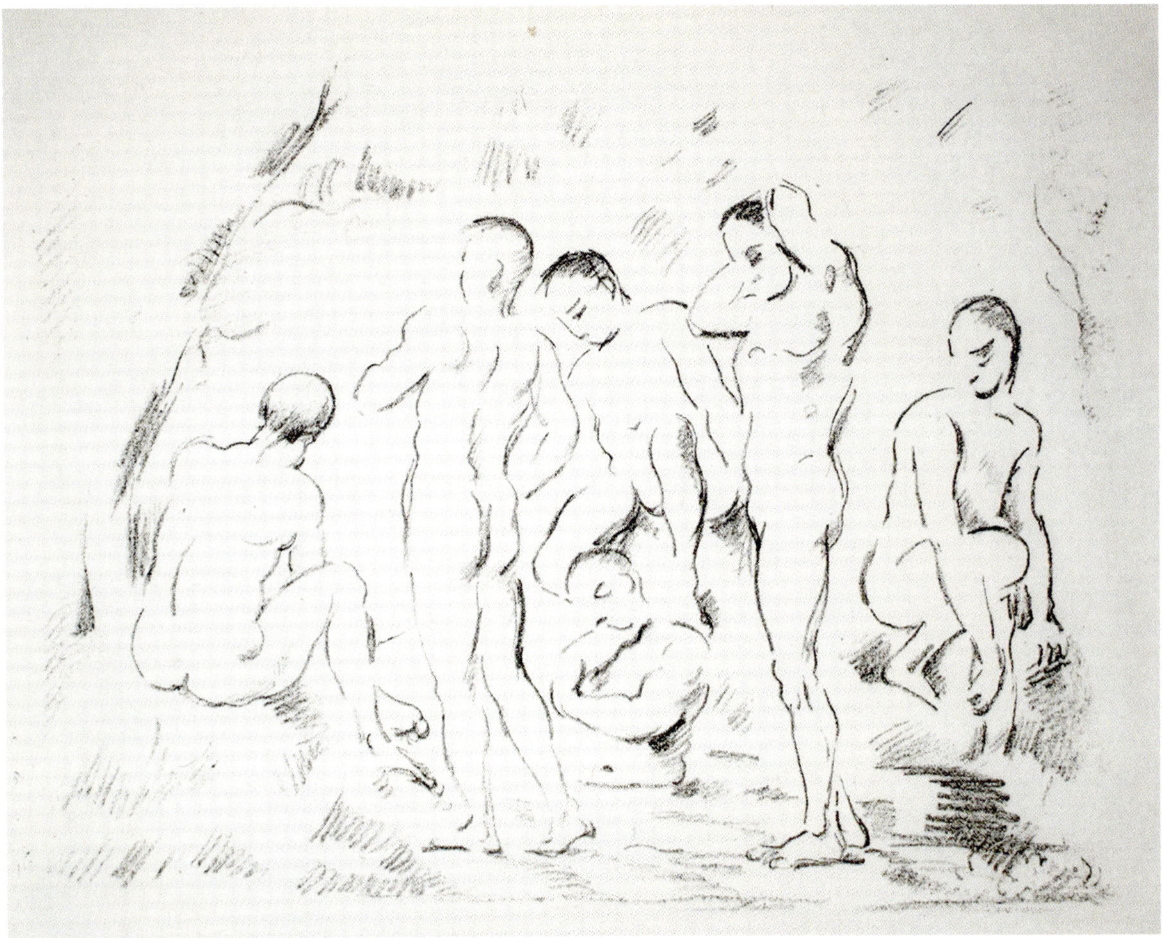

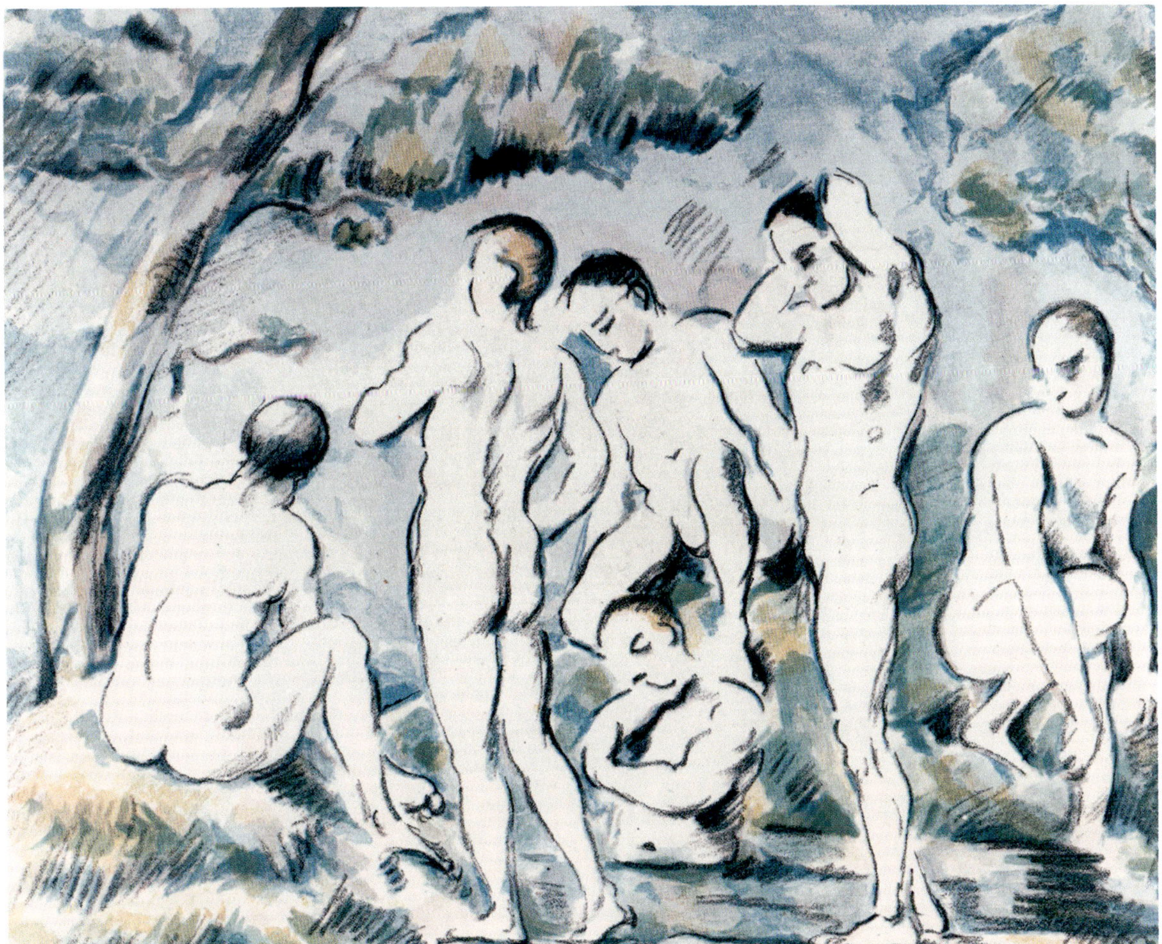

53

PAUL CÉZANNE 1839–1906

Study of Pine Trees, 1890–95

Pencil and watercolour, 55 × 43 cm

PROVENANCE: H. Silberberg, Breslau: his sale, Paris, Galerie Georges Petit, 9 June 1932, no.1; Friedrich Wolff, Vienna; Marlborough Fine Art, London; Fritz Nathan, St. Gallen; E. V. Thaw, New York; Sotheby's, London, 1 July 1981, lot 314

LITERATURE: Venturi (1936), no.982, ill.; Feist (1963), p.45, no.10

Cézanne's art was of central importance to Cubism, though in different ways and at different times for each of the painters associated with the movement. Both Metzinger and Gleizes were resolute in their view of the importance of the relationship, writing in 1912, in their account of the movement, that: 'To understand Cézanne is to foresee Cubism.'[1] The posthumous exhibition of the artist's watercolours at Bernheim-Jeune in June 1907, and the retrospective showing of his work at the Salon d'Automne of the same year, had allowed a reconsideration of Cézanne for a younger generation. Among them was Braque, upon whom the influence of works like the present watercolour is clearly visible in his own early landscapes. Apollinaire declared he had seen the 'rout of Impressionism' in works shown at the Salon des Indépendants in 1910,[2] but for the Cubist painters Cézanne had already effected this in his detachment, his purity and his apparently exclusively artistic concerns.

This watercolour, beautiful as such delicately minimal works by Cézanne almost invariably are, must be a view in Provence, Cézanne's own 'classic ground' and native earth to which he returned in the 1890s. Only the trunks of the trees have any literal indication of their form (and this in a manner always admired by Léger); patches of green and yellow, superimposed and translucent, clothe them sufficiently. The blank paper beneath, barely touched with colour, miraculously and unmistakeably evokes the shape of the hillside in which the pine trees are rooted.

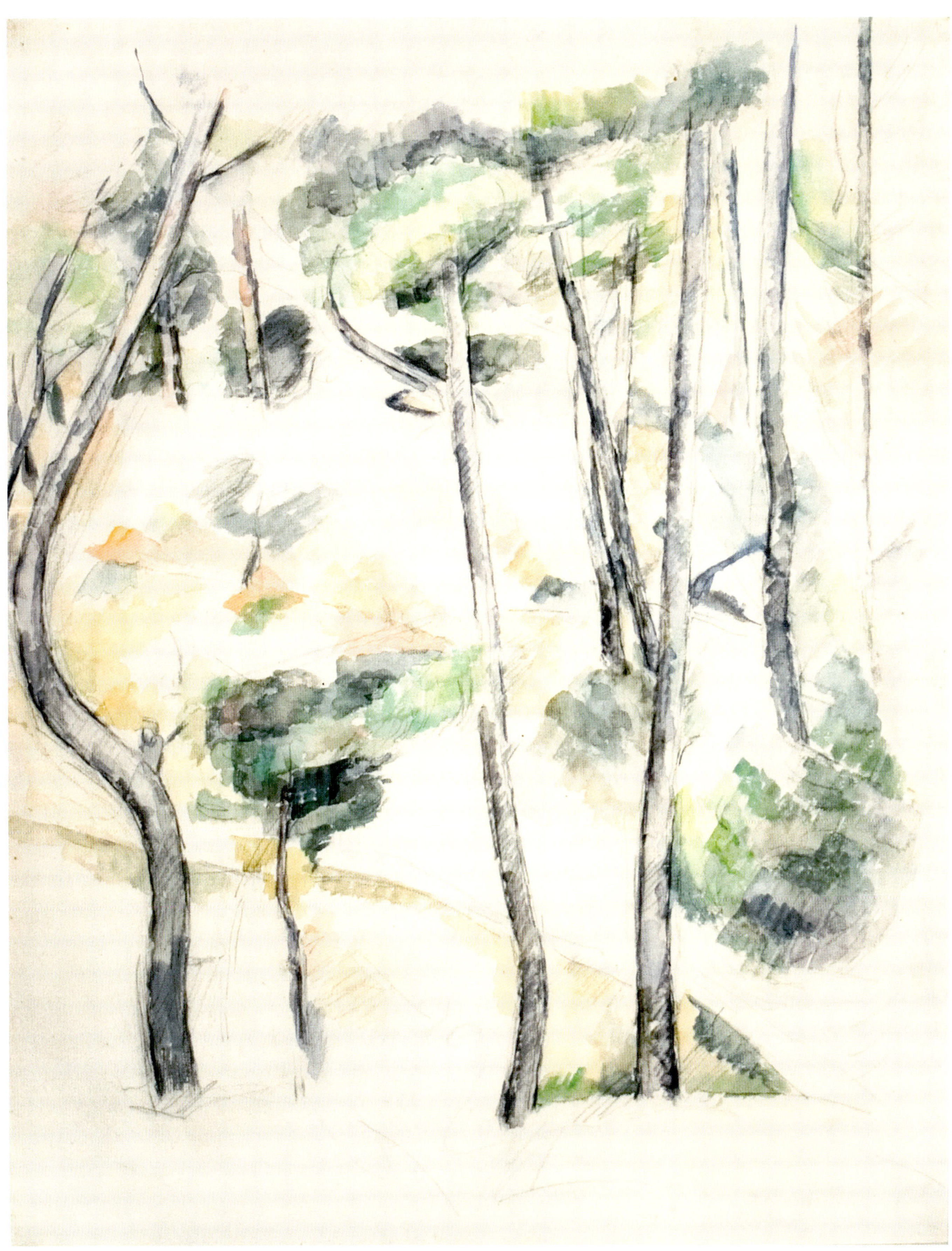

54

VINCENT VAN GOGH 1853–90

Portrait of Doctor Gachet (The Man with the Pipe) (Portrait du docteur Gachet [L'homme à la pipe]), 1890

Etching, 18 × 15 cm

PROVENANCE: Dr Gachet (L.1195b); bought by Julius Meier-Graefe, 1895; Sotheby's 15–16 November 1990, lot 225

LITERATURE: La Faille (1970), no.1664; Van Heugten and Pabst (1995), no.10.25

In May 1890, at the instigation of Camille Pissarro, Van Gogh moved from the asylum at Saint Rémy to Auvers-sur-Oise in order to consult Paul Gachet (1828–1909). Gachet was both a doctor specialising in mental illness and an amateur artist who signed himself 'Van Ryssel'. They immediately became firm friends, Van Gogh writing to his sister that 'I have found a true friend in Dr Gachet, something like another brother, so much do we resemble each other physically and also mentally'.[1] Once a week the pair ate together, and after lunch one day Gachet's son relates that 'once the men's pipes were lit, Vincent was handed an etching needle and a varnished copper; he enthusiastically took his new friend as his subject. As soon as it was sketched, the drawing was bitten – under the eye of Van Ryssel – just as Cézanne's had been 17 years earlier. Thus was born *The Man with a Pipe*, Van Gogh's only etching'.[2] Van Gogh immediately pulled several proofs, which were too dark because he had failed to wipe the plate; he later experimented with different colours of ink. In their census of surviving impressions Van Heugten and Pabst count perhaps 20 printed in the presence of the artist and with his collaboration, and a further 19 probably printed by Gachet alone. The plate was later entrusted to the master printer Auguste Delâtre.

Although the plate is inscribed '25 mai 1890' (or perhaps '15 mai 1890'), it is generally agreed that it was etched on 15 June 1890. Van Gogh sent impressions to his friend Paul Gauguin and to his brother Theo, who wrote to congratulate him on 23 June 1890: 'it is a true painter's etching. No refinement in the technique, but a drawing made on metal.'[3] Van Gogh was so delighted with the results that he planned a suite of etchings after his earlier paintings at Arles. He died on 29 July 1890, before he had time to begin work on them.

This impression, printed by Dr Gachet, was owned by the German art critic and novelist Julius Meier-Graefe (1867–1935). In his *Entwicklungsgeschichte der modernen Kunst* (1904), published in English as *Modern Art* in 1908, Meier-Graefe became one of the first to propose a history of modern art in terms of formalism. His biography of Van Gogh (1910), portraying the artist as a victim of social and artistic alienation, was enormously influential and has been frequently reprinted.

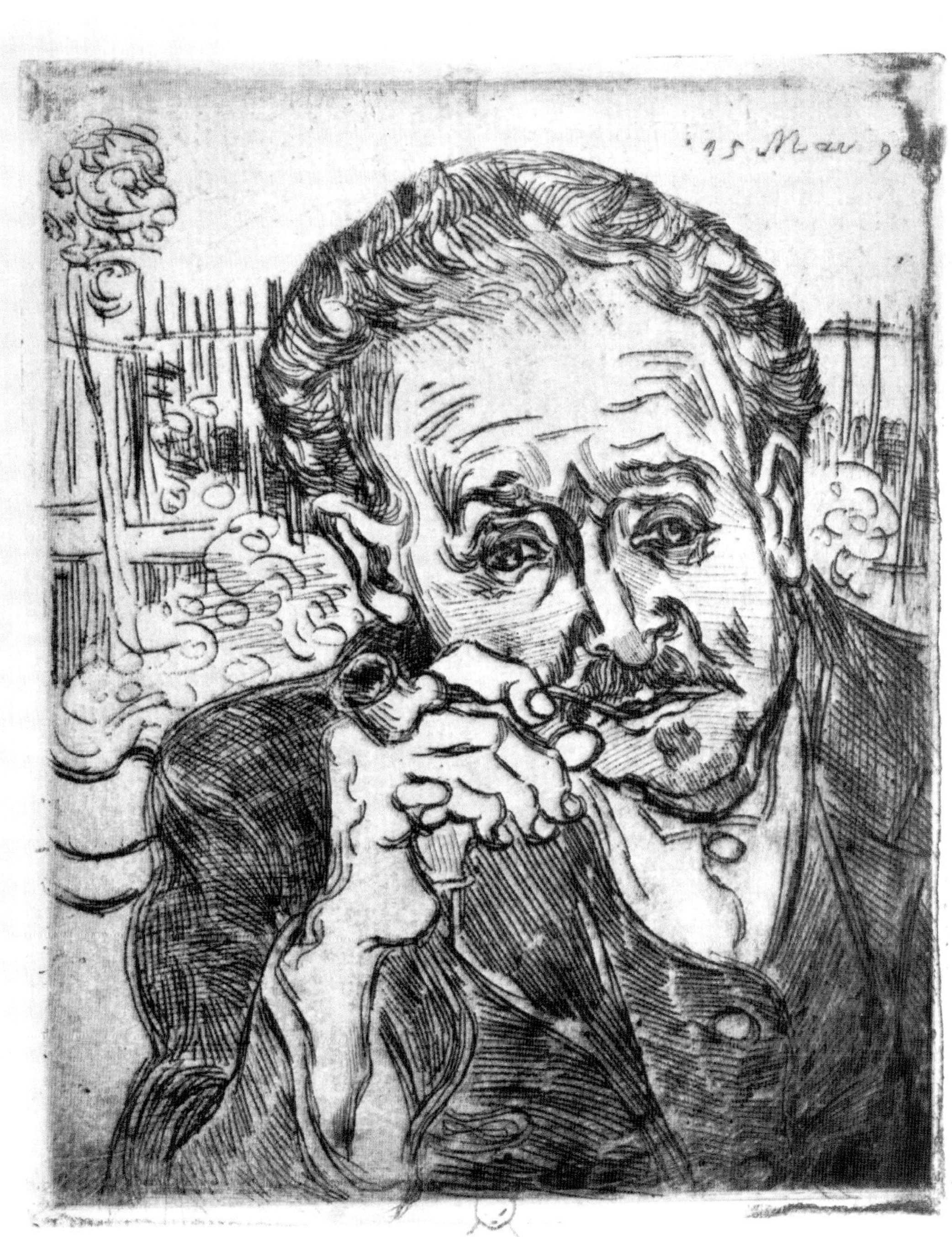

55

PABLO PICASSO 1881–1973

Three Heads with Christ on the Cross, 1901

Black crayon and blue pencil on wove paper, 15.3 × 23.3 cm

Signed: *Picasso* and inscribed and dated: *Malaga 9 enero 1901*

PROVENANCE: Galerie G.& L. Bollag, Zurich, until December 1919; Mme Hahnloser, Winterthur; Kornfeld, Bern

LITERATURE: Daix, Boudaille, Rosselet (1967), no.D.III.2; Palau i Fabre (1981), p.211

Picasso met Carlos Casagemas (1880–1901) in the spring of 1899, and for a period of 18 months they were inseparable. The friendship was not altogether suitable – Casagemas was the spoilt youngest child of a wealthy family, addicted to morphine and alcohol; he was also an anarchist. Together the young men visited Malaga in the summer of 1899, and then shared a studio in Barcelona, where they both exhibited at Els Quatre Gats. Casagemas accompanied Picasso to Paris in October 1900, but, after two months of intense work, they returned to Barcelona. On New Year's Day 1901 they arrived in Malaga, looking scruffy and dissolute. For a fortnight they spent their time in bars and brothels. Eventually Picasso lost patience with his friend and they separated, Casagemas returning to Barcelona and then going on to Paris, where he committed suicide on 17 February, and Picasso going back to Madrid.

Very little survives from Picasso's stay in Malaga, though he did make a few drawings in a sketchbook. This characteristic sheet was probably made in a café or bar. It includes two sketches of a female head from different angles, the head of a man wearing a Homburg and smoking a cigar, seen from behind, and a crucifix, probably worn on a necklace by one of the other customers. Among other drawings from this fortnight are miscellaneous studies of heads, a group in a café-concert and a double-sided pastel of a dancer.[1]

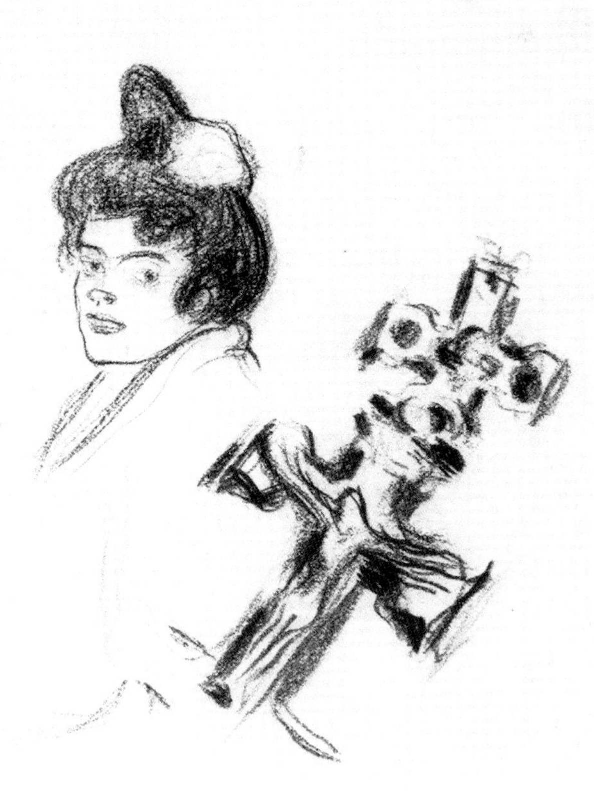
– Málaga – 9 Enero – 1901
– Picasso –

56

JACQUES VILLON 1875–1963

Marcel Duchamp, 1904

Etching, 39.2 × 30.1 cm

Signed and dated: *Jacques Villon 04*; and annotated in pencil: *1 ère épreuve*

PROVENANCE: Marcel Duchamp (the sitter and brother of the artist); Mme Marcel Duchamp (the sitter's wife); Bernard Gheerbrant, Paris.

LITERATURE: Auberty and Perussaux (1954), no.62; Ginestet and Pouillon (1979), E.90

Jacques Villon received his first training in art from his maternal grandfather, Émile-Frédéric Nicolle, who combined a career as a ship's broker with a serious talent in printmaking. After leaving the Lycée Corneille in Rouen Villon moved to Paris to study law, but was almost immediately drawn into the world of art, supplying images to the illustrated reviews and designing posters. He exhibited his first etchings in 1901 and by 1904, the date of this portrait, his reputation as a printmaker had been established.

Toulouse-Lautrec, who befriended Villon when he attended the studio of Fernand Cormon, was an early influence. By 1904 Villon had begun to imitate the work of Paul Helleu, a friend of the Impressionists, whose fluent portrait etchings were then much admired. The free, sweeping strokes of the etching needle in this portrait, the concentration on the densely worked head and the unfinished appearance of the rest recall Helleu's work, but have none of Helleu's elegant mannerisms.

In October 1904 Marcel Duchamp completed his schooling at Rouen and moved to Paris, where he lived with his brothers Gaston and Raymond at 71 rue de Caulaincourt. Gaston, who took the name Jacques Villon, became Marcel's artistic mentor. Villon shows his brother here on the brink of his career in art, palette in hand and painting with his right hand (reversed in the etching). This is the first of only two known impressions of the etching, the other belonging to the Bibliothèque nationale in Paris.

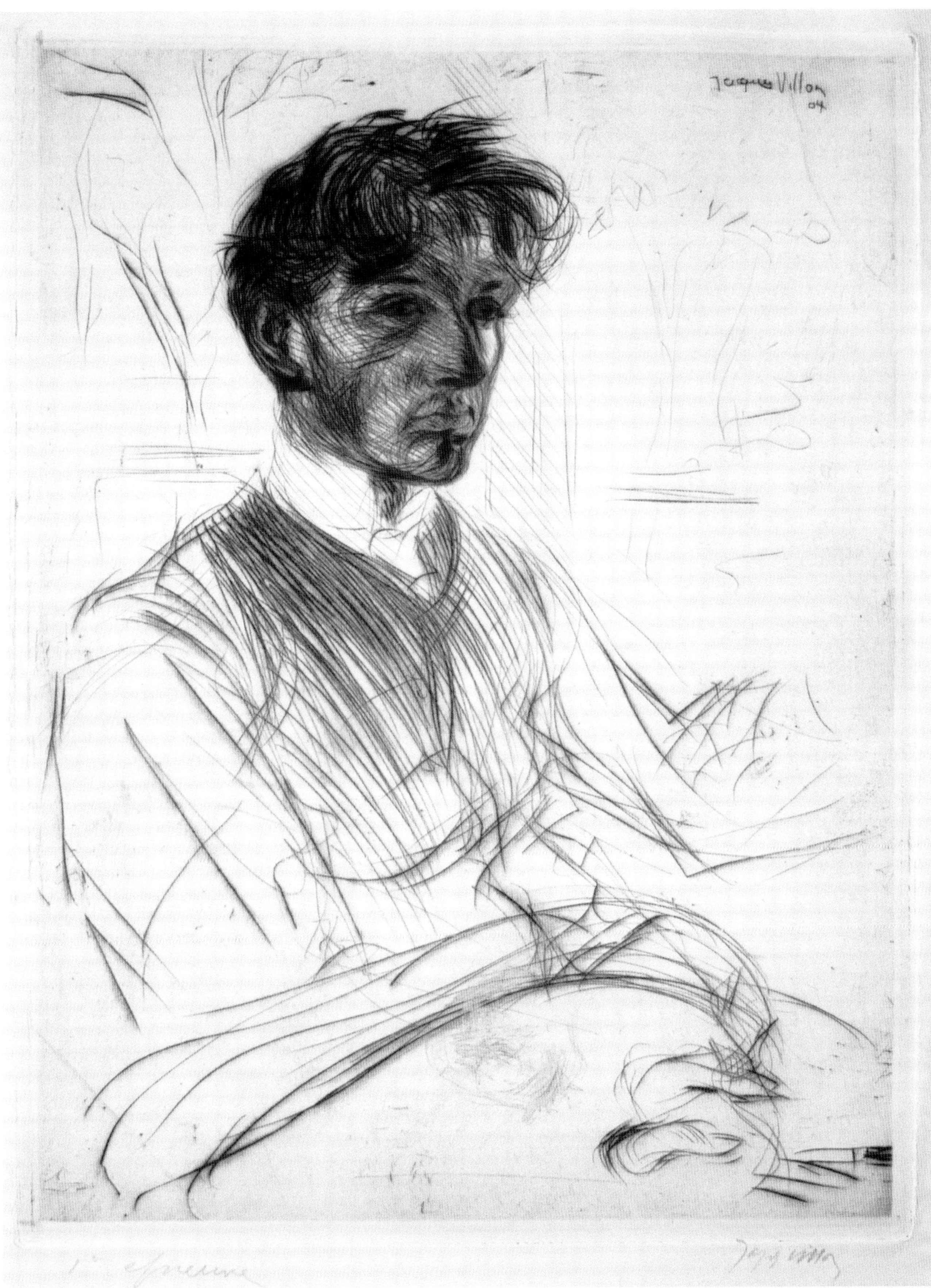

57

PABLO PICASSO 1881–1973

Study of Four Nudes, ca.1906

Black crayon on laid paper, 20 × 30 cm

Signed: *Picasso*

PROVENANCE: Heinz Berggruen, Paris; David H. Cogan Foundation

LITERATURE: Zervos XX (1970), no.461; Seckel (1988), III, no.18; Johnson (1991), no.31, ill. p. 91; D'Alessandro (2013), no.31

Picasso spent the summer of 1906, between 2 or 3 June and 15 August, in the isolated village of Gósol in the Pyrenees, in the company of Fernande Olivier, who frequently served as his model. He worked on a number of landscapes and still lifes, and a series of compositions on the theme of the female nude, of which the most ambitious and complex was *The Harem*.[1] On his return to Paris, Picasso completed the celebrated portrait of *Gertrude Stein*[2] and worked further on paintings of nudes. During this time he moved away from the elegant classicism, characteristic of the pictures made at Gósol, towards a new sculptural monumentality, reflecting his growing interest in the primitivism he found in Gauguin's wooden sculptures, African masks and ancient sculptures from Osuna, Andalusia. Picasso's research eventually led to the most radical experiment of his entire career, the *Demoiselles d'Avignon*, which depicts the interior of a brothel; the work was completed in July 1907.[3]

This sheet from a sketchbook was probably made in the autumn of 1906 as part of the long preparation for the *Demoiselles d'Avignon*. The two figures on the left were later extracted from this composition and developed in a sequence of drawings and a small oil related to the painting *Two Nudes* in the Museum of Modern Art in New York. Their massive forms are posed awkwardly with arms raised, one to open a curtain and the other to point. The two figures on the right of this study were not incorporated directly into a larger composition. However, the conjunction of a standing and a seated nude appears in a number of Picasso's works towards the end of 1906, notably the very polished drawing *Woman Seated and Woman Standing*.[4]

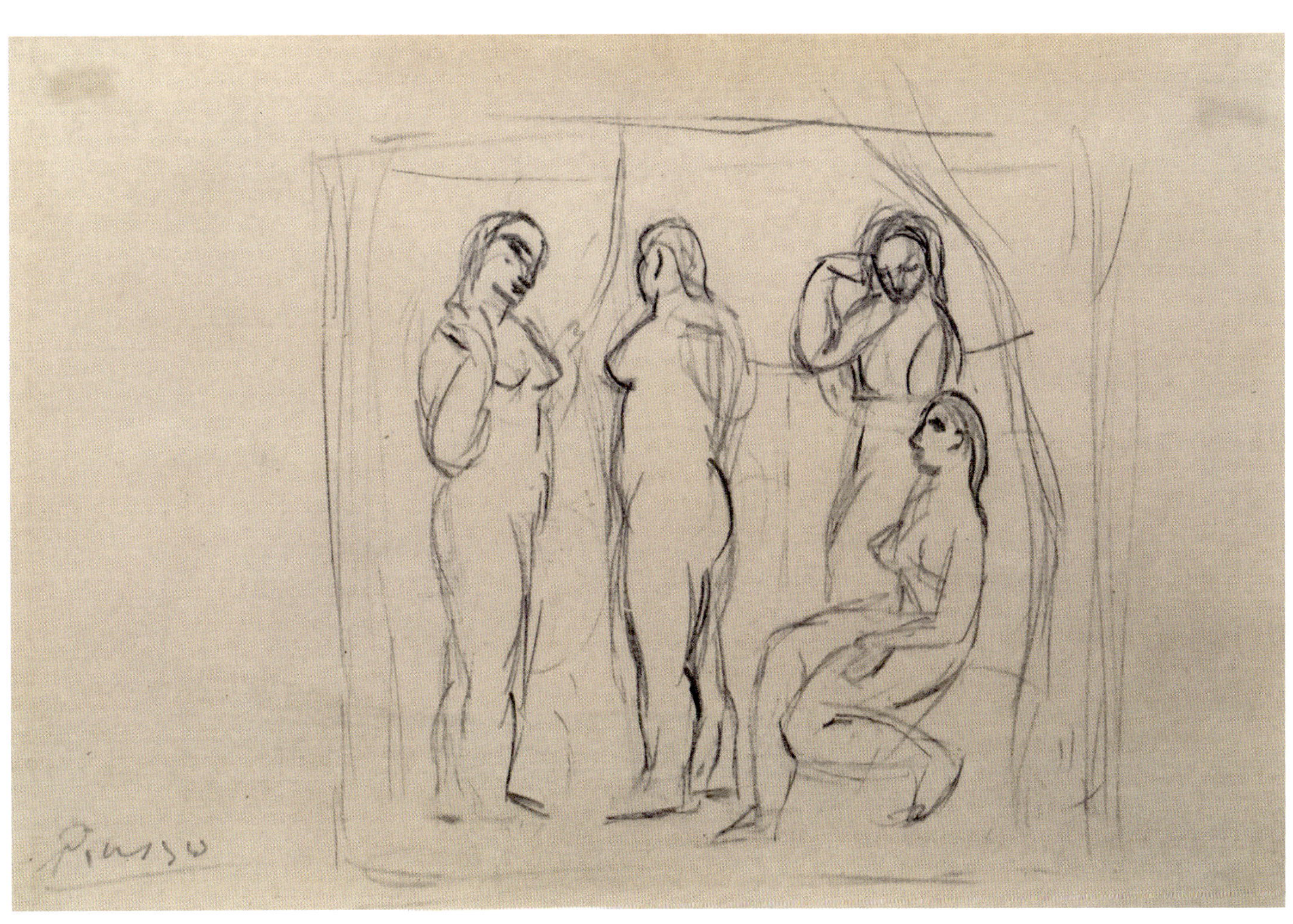
Picasso

58

HENRI MATISSE 1869–1954

Nude in Profile on a Chaise Longue (The Large Woodcut) (Nu de profil sur une chaise longue [Le grand bois]), 1905–06

Woodcut on paper, 41.3 × 48.2 cm
Signed and numbered: *Henri Matisse* 32/50
LITERATURE: Duthuit (1983), no.317

After his first unsuccessful solo exhibition, at Vollard's gallery in June 1904, Matisse's art developed quickly. He spent two successive summers painting in the dazzling light of the Mediterranean, first at St Tropez (1904) and then at Collioure (1905). The works he exhibited at the Salon d'Automne in October 1905 earned him the distinction of leader of the Fauves. During the winter of 1905–6 Matisse worked in his studio at 19 quai Saint Michel towards his second one-man exhibition, held at the Galerie Druet in March 1906. Among the exhibits were three woodcuts of nudes, of which this was the largest.

Matisse's interest in the medium was stimulated by Vollard, who had asked him to print from blocks sent by Gauguin from Tahiti in 1904. He was attracted by the crude primitivism and the unique expressive possibilities it offered. The preliminary drawing for the large woodcut matches the final print almost exactly; it has been suggested that the drawing was transferred to the block using a photomechanical process such as that invented by Auguste Clot.[1] Mme Matisse made the initial cuts, probably using carpenter's tools – knives and chisels – rather than the sophisticated equipment of the professional wood engraver. The resulting image is immensely arresting. The emaciated figure, her shoulder blades jutting out uncomfortably, sits with her eyes closed on a chaise longue, resting her head on her hands; she appears to be asleep. The swirling background, a reminder of Matisse's admiration for Van Gogh, contrasts starkly with the simple outline of the figure. Both subject and treatment suggest that Matisse may have had in mind a recent wood engraving by Aristide Maillol, *The Wave* (*La vague*), which similarly presents the nude as an almost unmodulated silhouette against a busy and mobile background.

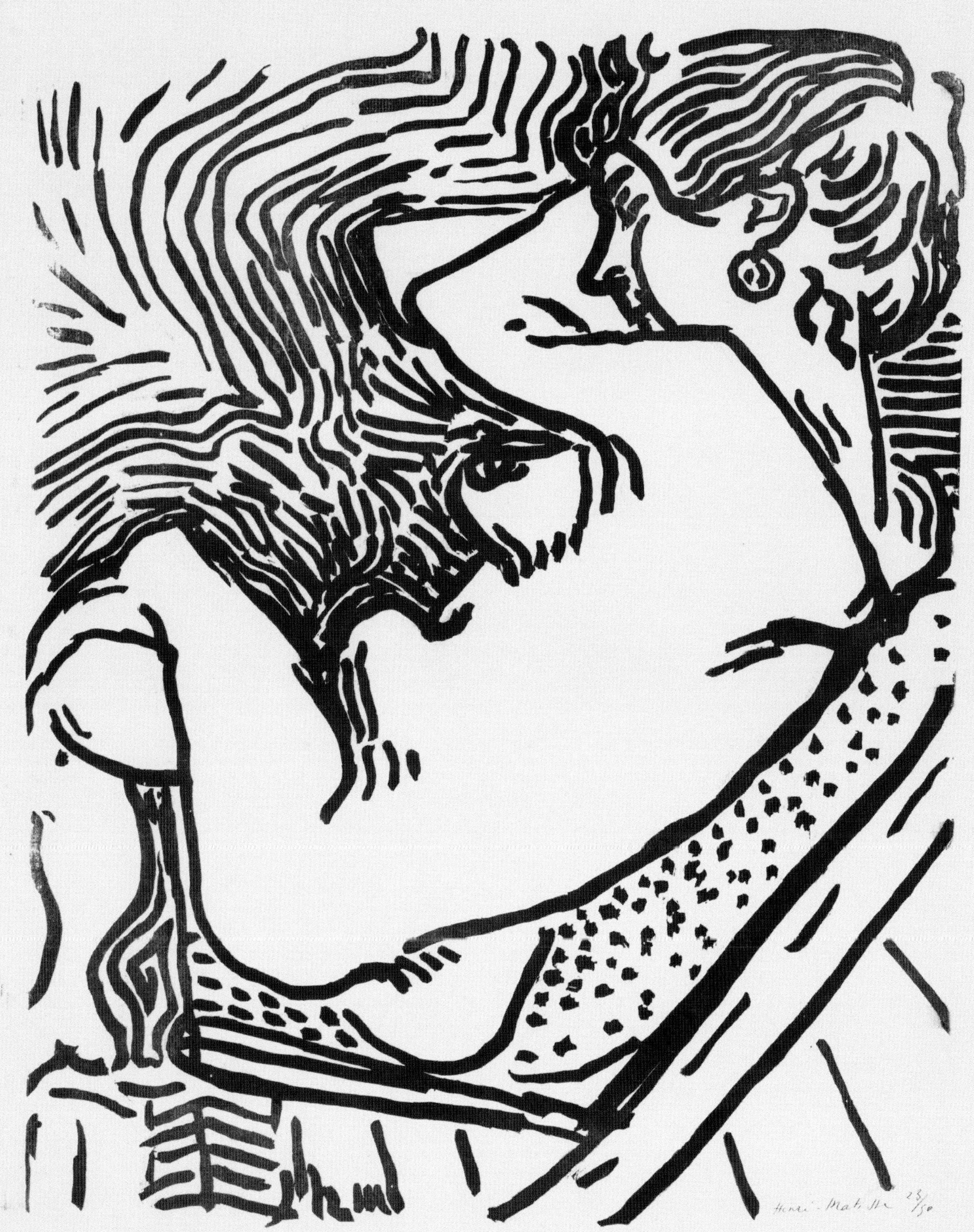

59

RAOUL DUFY 1877–1953

Palm Tree and Terrace at L'Estaque, 1908–09

Oil on canvas, 73.4 × 60 cm

Signed: *Raoul Dufy*

PROVENANCE: Marie Cuttoli Laugier, Paris; Chiu Gallery, London ; Christie's, New York, 7 May 2008, lot 362

Like several other artists of his generation, Dufy was deeply affected by the 1907 retrospective exhibition of Cézanne's work at the Salon d'Automne from 1 to 22 October. He had been briefly attracted by the Fauves, but now began to have doubts. Before the month had ended, Dufy had left for the port of Martigues on the coast of Provence; here he continued to paint with Fauve colour, but combined this with a new touch of angularity. In the spring of 1908 he moved to L'Estaque, a seaside town that had been one of Cézanne's favourite sites. In early summer Braque followed him to L'Estaque, where the two artists worked in partnership. At this point, encouraged by Braque, Dufy's forms became bolder and flatter, in keeping with the lessons of Cézanne, while his range of colours largely contracted to a contrast of yellowish-brown and deep green.

The view in this painting is taken from the approach to the terrace in front of the Hôtel de la Falaise, built as a manor house in the seventeenth century on a slope overlooking the sea. The terrace became one of Dufy's favourite motifs during his time in L'Estaque – seen either, as here, flanked with palm trees on the approach to the hotel, or in views from the terrace itself, looking the other way out to sea. On a previous visit to L'Estaque Braque had painted the terrace from the same spot[1] using similar colour and flattened forms but with a stronger formal structure. Dufy relished the effects of paint and colour too much to surrender either completely to the severe implications of Cubism.

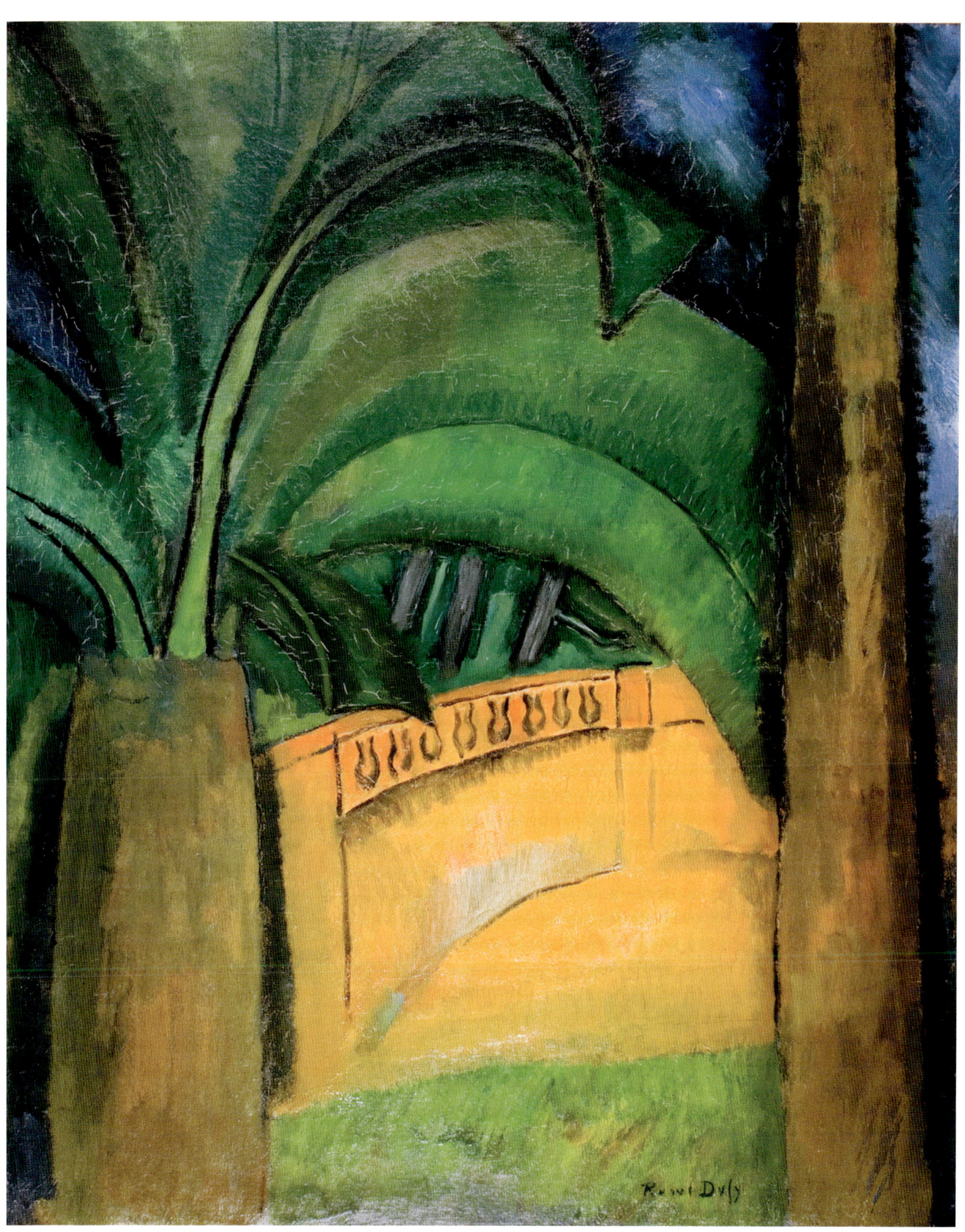
Raoul Dufy

60

ROGER DE LA FRESNAYE 1885–1925

The Cuirassier, 1910–11

Charcoal on paper, 51.5 × 50 cm

PROVENANCE: the artist until 1925; Mme Josette Gris (the artist's wife); Gonzales Gris (the artist's son); Galerie Louise Leiris (Kahnweiler), Paris

LITERATURE: Johnson (1991), no.18, ill. p.65

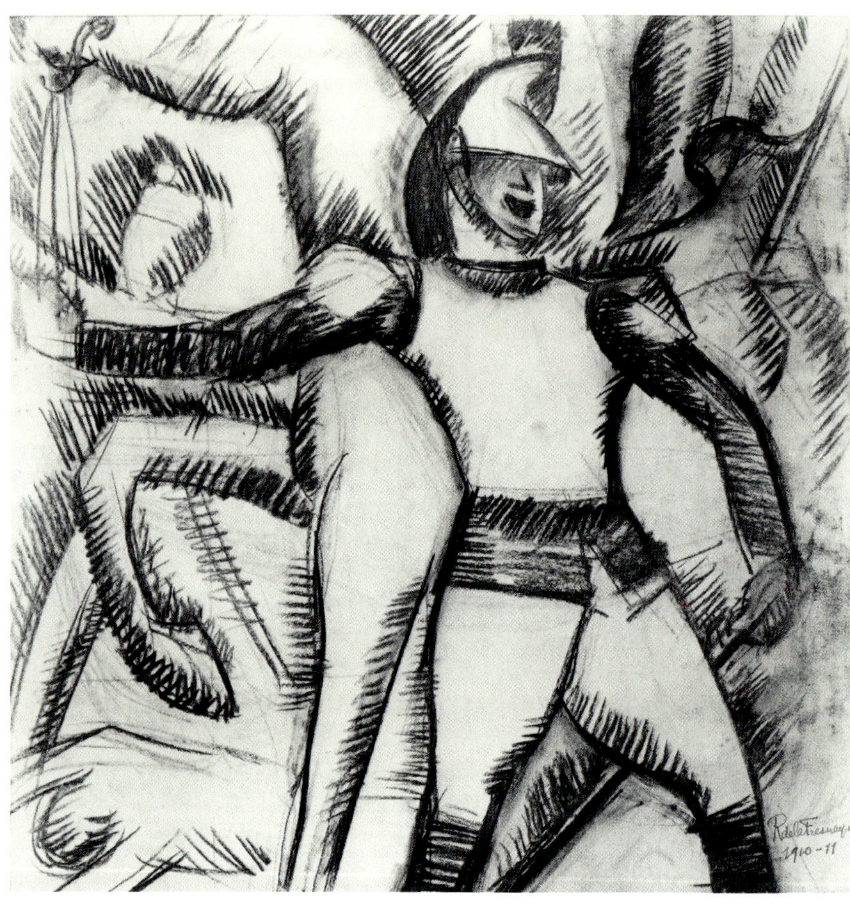

In 1911 La Fresnaye supplied 12 drawings to illustrate Paul Claudel's spiritualist drama *Tête d'Or*. One of them features a mounted cuirassier and is inscribed with a text from Claudel's play (Seligman, no.438): 'And I cry, march on! Rise up everyone, pull the carts and the cannons!'[1] Although the present drawing does not appear among the illustrations, the caption seems a perfect match for the episode it represents. In 1912 La Fresnaye exhibited a second military composition, *Artillery* (Metropolitan Museum of Art, New York), based directly on another of the illustrations for the *Tête d'Or*. The idea of the cuirassier in the drawing may also have begun life as an illustration for the Claudel play.

The drawing was used as a study for *The Cuirassier* (Musée Nationale d'Art Moderne, Paris), exhibited by La Fresnaye in 1911 at the Salon des Indépendants. The style of the study marks an important point in La Fresnaye's art as he evolved away from Maurice Denis and the Nabis, with whom he had worked since 1908, and moved towards Cubism. In comparison with his earlier drawings, the study is rough and expressive, in keeping with the subject matter, while angular, schematic details indicate his growing allegiance to the artists of the Section d'Or.

Although La Fresnaye is said to have used a cousin, Georges de Miré, as a model for the cuirassier, Géricault's *Wounded Cuirassier* (Musée du Louvre, Paris) was the immediate and obvious source. La Fresnaye, however, has eliminated all the pathos of Géricault's composition and produced a more conventional scene of action. The drawing includes the figure of a dead soldier, with a single foot-soldier charging to the left. In the painting the body has been removed and a second foot-soldier has been added. Both drawing and painting include a prominent tricolour in the upper right, a patriotic motif that reappears in La Fresnaye's most famous composition, *The Conquest of the Air*, 1913 (Museum of Modern Art, New York), in *Artillery* and in *The Fourteenth of July* (Museum of Fine Art, Houston). La Fresnaye, the loyal son of an army officer, would have welcomed the chance to celebrate the role of the military at a time of much tension between Germany and France.

61

JUAN GRIS 1887–1927

La rue Ravignan, 1906–10

Charcoal with white chalk on paper, 48 × 31 cm

PROVENANCE: with the artist until 1927; Josette Gris, the artist's wife; Gonzalez Gris (the artist's son); Galerie Louis Leiris (Kahnweiler), Paris

LITERATURE: Johnson (1991), no.15

Between 1902 and 1904, José Victoriano Gonzalez worked as an illustrator for periodicals in Madrid. In 1906, after changing his name to Juan Gris, he migrated to Paris and moved into an apartment in the building popularly known as the Bateau-Lavoir, located at 13 rue Ravignon. Gris continued to support himself by supplying magazines with illustrations until 1910, when he turned more exclusively to painting. His fellow Spaniard Picasso, who had lived at the Bateau-Lavoir since 1904, became a close friend and played a fundamental role in directing him towards Cubism.

Gris' surviving work consists largely of still-life subjects. Most of his earliest known drawings are compositions of bottles, bowls, drinking glasses and other simple objects from the kitchen, These are modelled with charcoal, carefully highlighted with touches of white bodycolour, In about 1910 his drawings begin to show intimations of the Cubist style that dominated his art from 1911 onwards. The subjects remain the same, but they are less shaded and lines begin to splinter. The loss of many of Gris' early drawings makes it difficult to be precise in dating those that survive, but the smooth finish and complete absence of any signs of Cubism in this composition suggest it was drawn in his early years at the Bateau-Lavoir. The window in the background opens onto a view that must represent the trees in the Place Émile Garreau, which faced the Bateau-Lavoir building half way along the rue Ravignan.

Like much of Gris' art, this is an exercise in effects of light, delicately suggested with soft rubbed charcoal and touches of white. The technique recalls the drawings of the minor Impressionist artist Charles-Albert Lebourg, but it was not uncommon among his contemporaries.

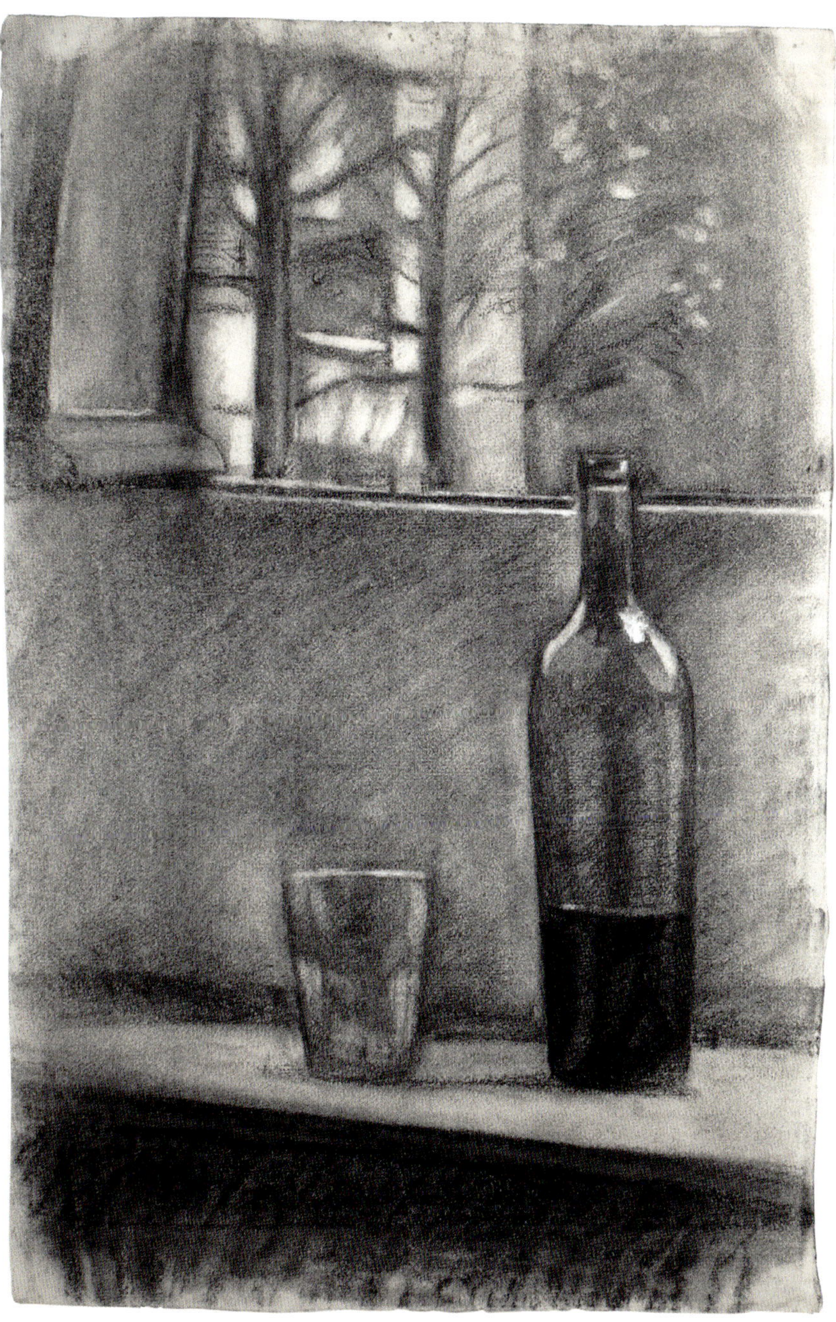

62

AUGUSTE HERBIN 1882–1960

Still Life, 1911

Watercolour, 55 × 29.5 cm

Signed twice lower right: *Herbin*

PROVENANCE: Michael Tachemin, London; Artcurial, Paris, 8 December 2015, lot 177

In 1911/12 the group formed by Metzinger, Gleizes, Le Fauconnier, Léger and Delaunay in Passy expanded with the arrival of La Fresnaye, and, most importantly, through contact with the Duchamp brothers. Shortly afterwards František Kupka, a neighbour of the Duchamps, became a member of the group. John Golding takes the formation of *Les Artistes de Passy* in October 1912 as an indication of the continuing importance of the sense of community existing among the 'Salon' Cubists.[1] At one of their meetings La Fresnaye read a paper on Cézanne, possibly taking up the trajectory described by Metzinger in his *Note sur la Peinture* of 1910. This is significant as it was at this time, in 1912, that Juan Gris joined the group – effectively taking over from Metzinger as an exponent of Cubist principles, which now emanated directly from Gris' friends Picasso and Braque.

Herbin exhibited in the same room as the original group at the Salon des Indépendants of 1910. In the previous year, however, he had moved to the Bateau-Lavoir studios, where he had approached Cubism directly through contact with Braque and Picasso. Both Gris and Herbin also exhibited with the Cubists at the Section d'Or of 1912. Although part of the original group's intention was to introduce a theoretical and mathematical basis absent from the work of Picasso and Braque, who did not exhibit with them, the presence of Gris and Herbin nevertheless gave an appearance of unity to the different Cubist groups after 1912. The inaugural lecture by Apollinaire, always a deeply appreciative admirer of Picasso, and the writings of a number of Apollinaire's friends, published to coincide with that exhibition, also contributed to such an impression.

However, the evidence of the present watercolour suggests that Herbin did not imitate the contemporary work of either Braque or Picasso; he rather found his own way towards abstraction (which he never then abandoned) out of the Fauve manner of his earlier work. This watercolour does indeed have something of the narrow vertical thrust of Braque's work, as well as a comparable recurrence of rectilinear forms. While tending towards a greyish-brown tonality, Herbin maintains the warmth of Cézanne's subdued tones; there is still a feeling of an identifiable space within which the overlapping forms exist, some approaching the literal while remaining elusive. The whole composition constantly resists any temptation to a closely-knit stasis; a dynamic flight from it, indeed, is heightened at the edges by the directional use of the parallel hatching.

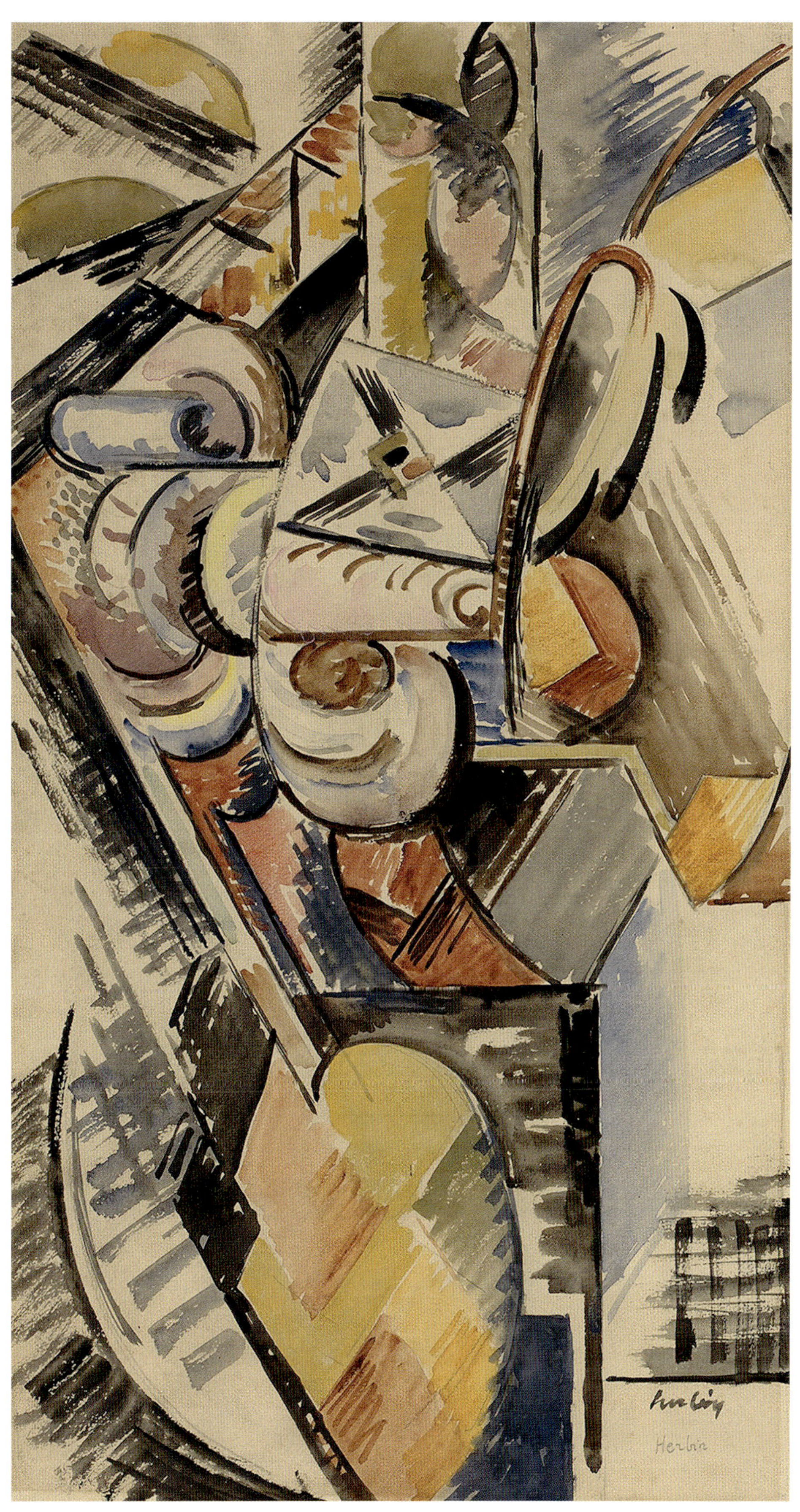
Herbin

63

PABLO PICASSO 1881–1973

The Fan, 1911

Ink and sepia wash on paper, 28.5 × 22.2 cm

Signed: *Picasso*

PROVENANCE: J. Leperrier, Paris; André Lefèvre, Paris; Thomas Agnew & Sons, Ltd., London; Alan Wilkinson, London and Toronto.

LITERATURE: Level (1928), p.33, ill.; Zervos (1932–78), vol.II, no.269; Daix and Rosselet (1979), no.406, ill.; London (1980), no.2, ill.; Palau i Fabre (1990), no.589; Johnson (1991), no.35; ill. p.99; D'Alessandro (2013), ill. p.53

The Fan was drawn in the summer of 1911 in Céret, a small town in the foothills of the French Pyrenees. Picasso arrived there in July, at the invitation of the Spanish sculptor Manolo Huguet. Georges Braque followed in August, and the two artists painted there in partnership until early September when Picasso, suspected of involvement in the theft of the *Mona Lisa*, left abruptly for Paris.[1]

During the weeks spent with Braque in Céret, Picasso worked on a series of still-life compositions painted in a restricted range of muted colours and inscribed with intersecting lines and simple rounded forms offering only basic clues to identify the objects represented. This drawing appears to be a study for a more elaborate composition, *Still Life with a Fan* (Metropolitan Museum of Art, New York, promised gift of the Leonard A. Lauder Cubist Collection), painted in Céret in 1911. The short, straight lines and scumbled touches of sepia anticipate the stabbed brushwork in the painting of the fan, a common feature of the works painted by Picasso at this time.

In addition to the fan, the painting contains a drinking glass, a small flower and a copy of the local newspaper. Only the fan, however, is included in the drawing. It is easily identified by the guard-stick that cuts across the image, and by the folds of the half-opened leaf that make a serrated pattern along the top. Like the flat sound board and simple curves of the guitar, the faceted shape and shallow relief of the fan were well adapted to the purposes of Cubism. Both the guitar and the fan, with their Spanish associations, would also have had a particular personal appeal to Picasso – particularly in Céret, which lies very close to the Spanish border.

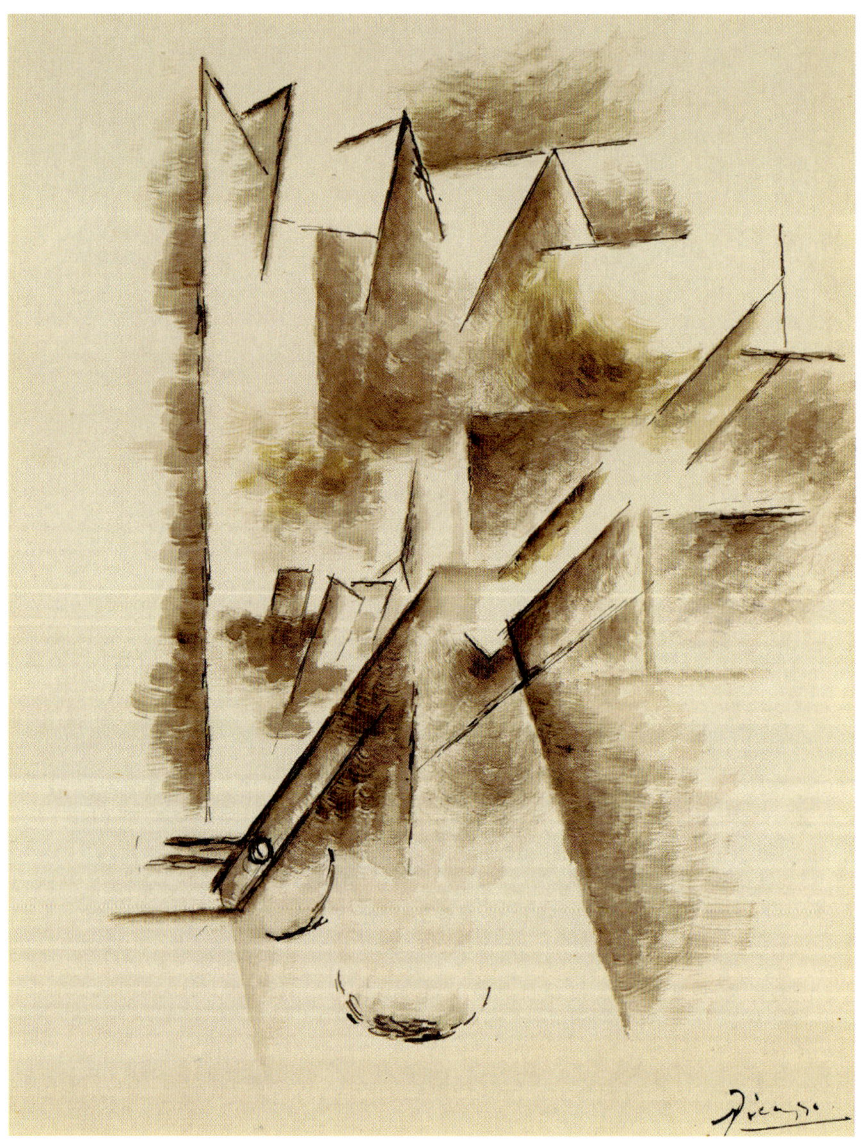

64

GEORGES BRAQUE 1882–1963

Fox, 1911

Drypoint on paper, 54.5 × 37.5 cm
Signed in pencil: *G Braque*
LITERATURE: Vallier (1988), no.6; Johnson (1991), no.4

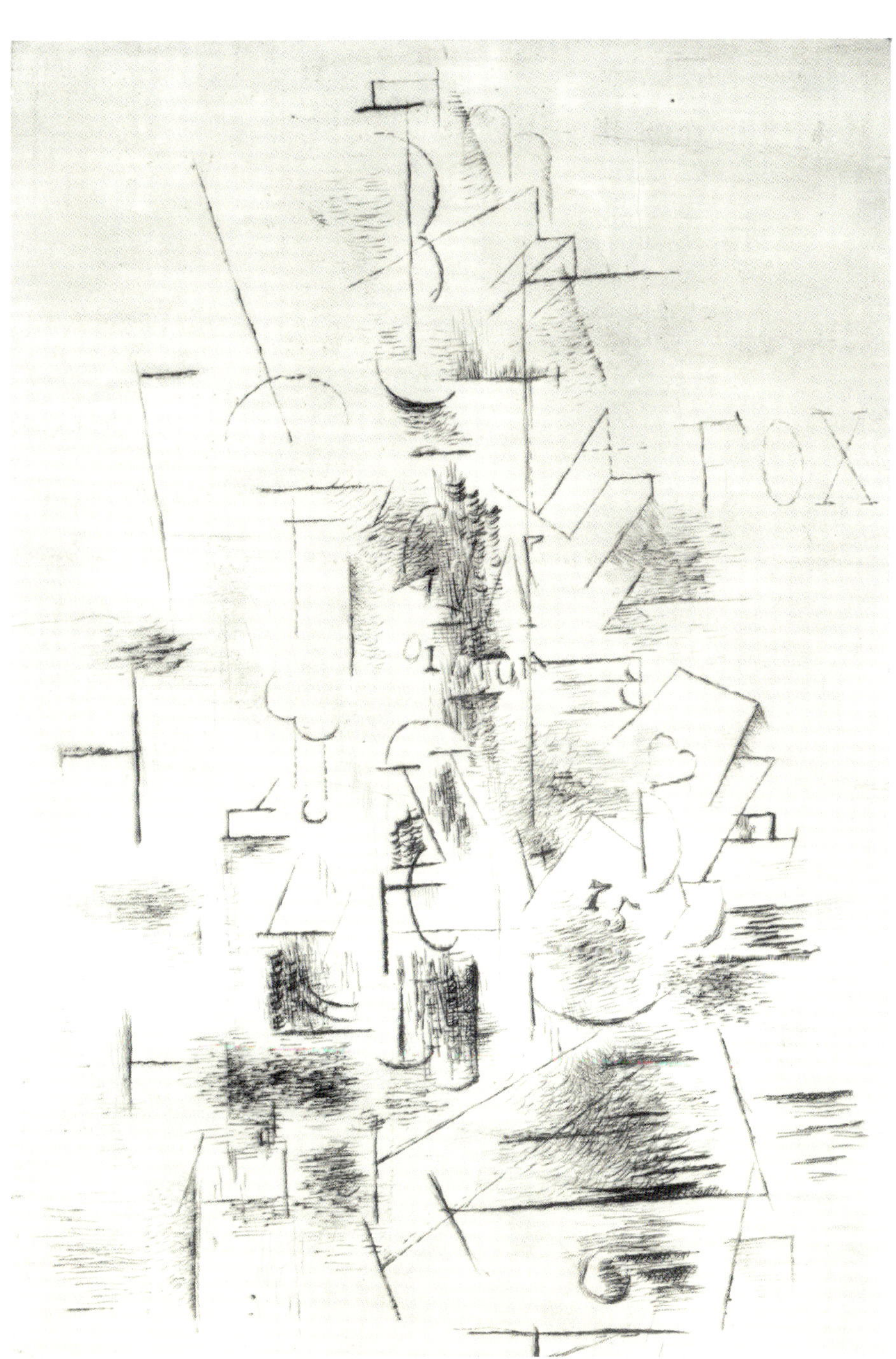

Braque produced 11 etchings between *c.*1907 and 1912 before abandoning printmaking for several years. He made a few woodcuts and lithographs in the 1920s, but returned to etching only in 1932. Of these early etchings, ten form a series of still-life subjects drawn in the Cubist manner. Only two, commissioned by Daniel Kahnweiler, were published at the time: the present etching, issued in 1912 in an edition of 100, and another entitled *Job* (Vallier, no.5). Kahnweiler also published an etching by Picasso [cat.65] in the same large upright format as *Fox* (Geiser/Baer, no.33) as a companion to Braque's etching. Both prints feature bottles of alcohol: pomace brandy in Picasso's, Old Tom Gin in Braque's. Both also include playing cards, and both are etched in the same brisk manner with straight, incisive strokes, cylindrical forms and small patches of drypoint.

'Fox', the name inscribed on the plate, alludes to C. J. Fox. He was the proprietor of Austin's Railway Hotel, an English-style hotel and bar where Picasso first met Apollinaire in 1905, and which is still located on the rue Amsterdam in Paris. There is a table with a drawer on the lower right of the print on which there is an ace of hearts and a bottle labelled GIN OLD TOM, a sweet gin widely sold in nineteenth-century Europe by purveyors of British alcohol. Picasso's bottle, labelled *Eau de Vie*, is probably an allusion to the volume of poetry on which Apollinaire was working at the time. This was published with the title *Alcools* in 1913, but, as his friends at Fox's bar would certainly have known, the proposed title had been *Eau de Vie*.

65

PABLO PICASSO 1881–1973

Still Life with a Bottle of Marc (Nature morte à la bouteille de Marc), 1911

Drypoint on laid paper, 50 × 30.6 cm
Signed in pencil: *Picasso*
LITERATURE: Bloch (1968), 24; Gervis (1984), 16; Geiser/Baer 33b; Johnson (1991), no.37, ill. p. 103

Picasso, unlike Braque, made prints throughout his long career. Etching, which suited his mastery in pen drawing, first appeared in his work in 1904–5 and remained his favourite medium, at least until 1919 when he began to work in lithography. The print *Still Life with a Bottle of Marc*, printed by Auguste Delâtre and published by Kahnweiler in 1912, was the largest and most important of Picasso's prints to date. It was issued as one of a pair to Braque's *Fox* [cat.64], and corresponds to Braque's etching in so many details that one might believe they were the work of a single artist. Both prints are composed around a structure of circular motifs and straight lines, finely ruled in drypoint and strengthened with small, freehand touches. Both are shaded with scattered patches of tone and both contain similar allusions to the café society that inspired many of the Cubist works of Braque and Picasso. The details of Picasso's etching – the bottle of Marc, the glasses, the playing cards and the reference to Eau de Vie (a colourless brandy) – correspond to the playing cards, drinking glasses and reference to Old Tom Gin in its companion by Braque.

As often in Picasso's work, his etching probably contains covert allusions to his own life. Brigitte Baer has pointed out that the word 'Marc' might refer not only to a popular type of pomace brandy, but also to Marcelle Humbert, Picasso's mistress from 1912 to 1915.[1] She appears as *Ma jolie* (*My Pretty Girl*) in several works dating from this period, once in the company of a bottle of Marc.[2] Perhaps the conspicuous Queen of Hearts placed beneath the bottle of Marc was introduced in order to reinforce the allusion. The inscription *Eau de Vie* might also have a double meaning, referring both to the popular drink and the book of poems that Apollinaire was then compiling with the working title *Eau de Vie*.

From 1912 to 1914 bottles of Marc figure in several of Picasso's compositions.[3] Not all necessarily carry a punning significance. The names of several drinks appear in his compositions in the same years – Bass, Pernod, Suze, Rum – but Vieux Marc, the aged form of the spirit, seems to have been the favourite. Vieux Marc appears also in Braque's work in the same years and later,[4] and no doubt featured as often in the artists' lives around the café table as it did in their drawings and paintings in the two years before the First World War.

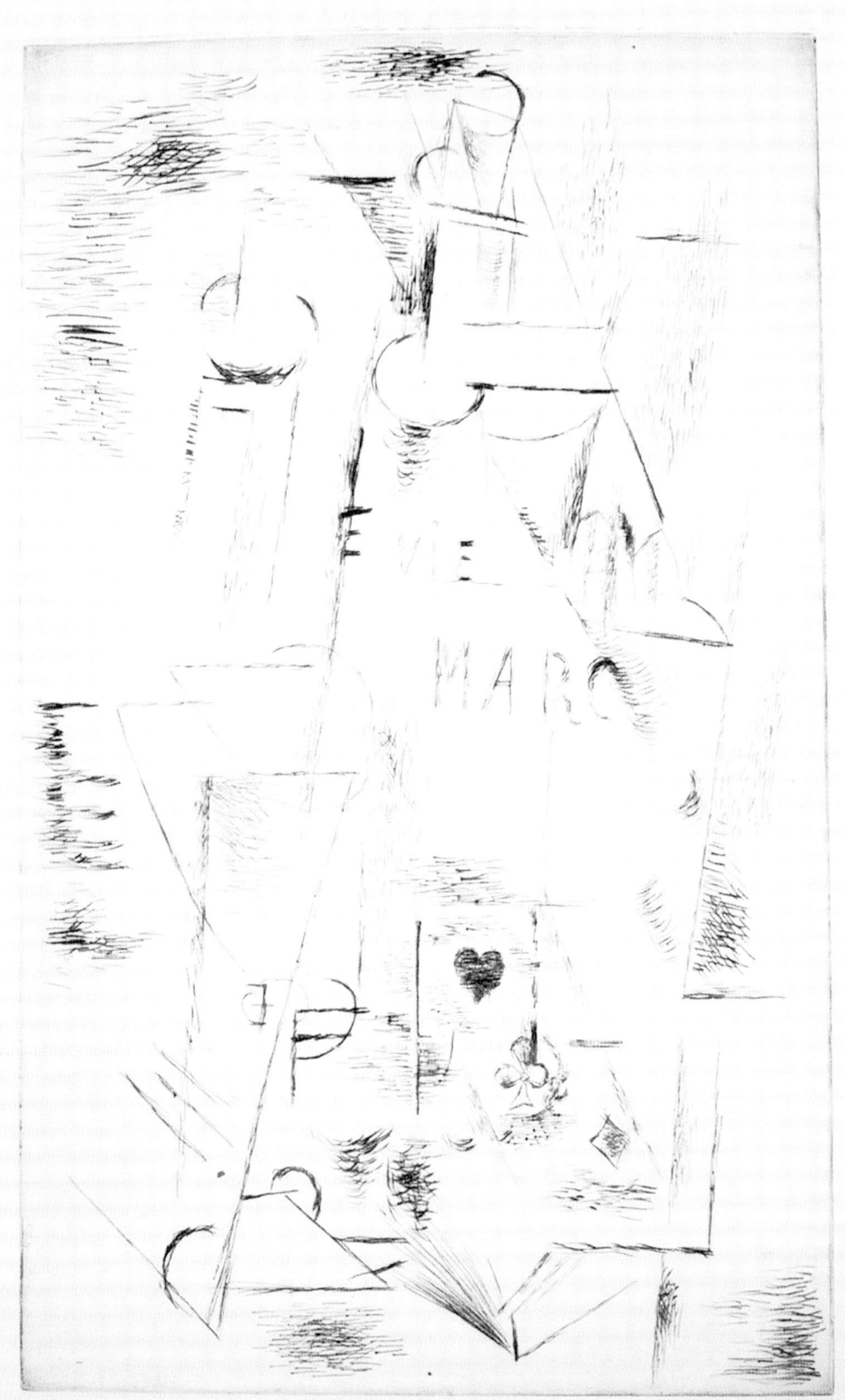

66

JEAN METZINGER 1883–1956

Study for 'The Cyclist', 1911–12

Charcoal on paper, 34.5 × 28 cm

Signed, lower right: *J Metzinger*

PROVENANCE: P. T. Nielsen, Copenhagen

LITERATURE: Moser (1985–86), no.50, ill. p.57; Johnson (1991), no.29, ill. p.87

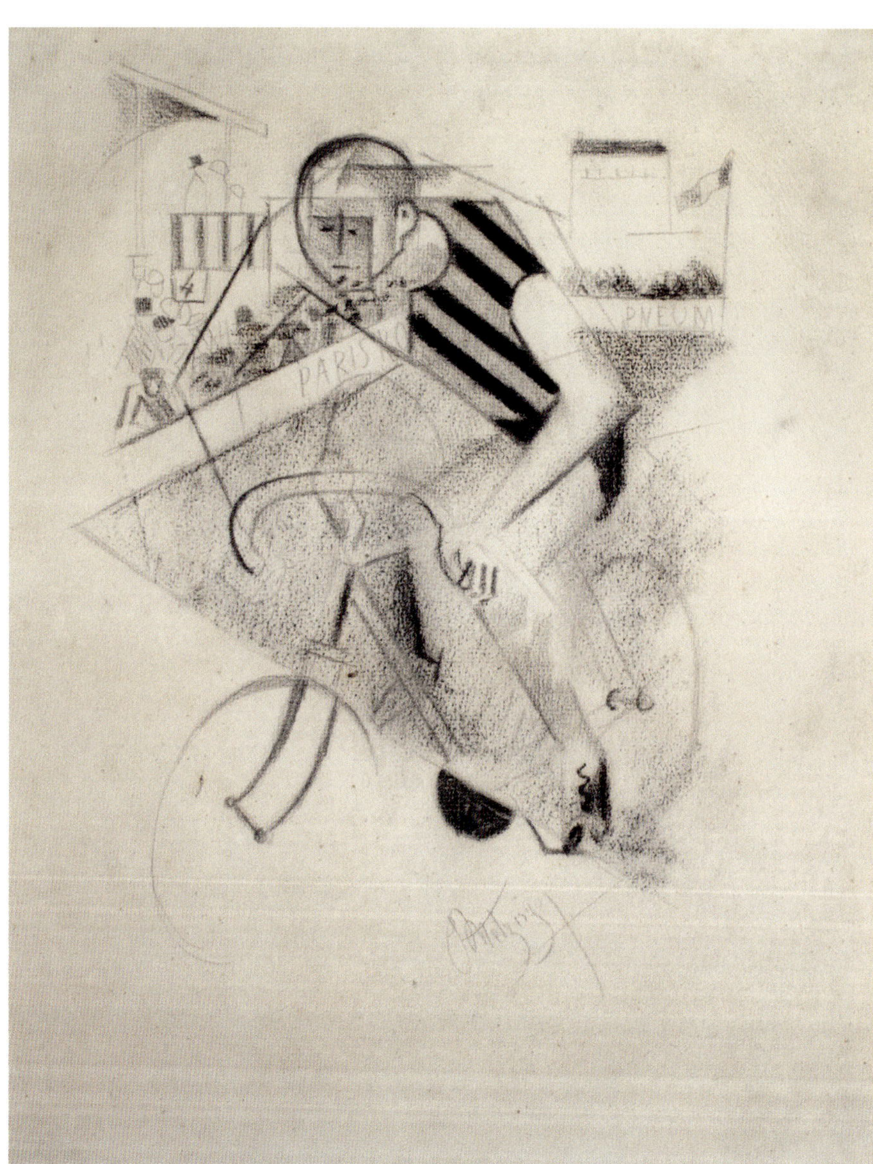

Jean Metzinger was central to the development of Cubism as it has been generally understood, both as a writer and as a painter – not least because, together with Albert Gleizes, he wrote and published the first text devoted to the movement, *Du Cubisme*, in 1912. The book appeared two years after an exhibition at the Salon des Indépendants, which included works by Robert Delaunay, Metzinger and Lhote, had made it clear that a new group had emerged. In Apollinaire's words, it marked 'the rout of Impressionism'.[1] The year after this exhibition, in 1911, a separate room at the Salon des Indépendants confirmed the emergence of Cubism as a movement, marked by elements including a clear structure and a combination of separate viewpoints, as well as an occasionally ambiguous combination of figurative and abstract elements.

The present drawing, produced in 1911–12, is a study for the painting of the same title (sometimes also known as *Au vélodrome*), now in the Peggy Guggenheim collection in Venice. The image evokes the visual language of the advertising poster, a pictorial element to which Léger was particularly responsive. However, Metzinger derives from it an image which fuses aspects of several different artistic currents of the period. For example, the work invites comparison with Delaunay's *Équipe de Cardiff*, the title of a series of pictures he showed at the Indépendants one year later.

In this marvellously concentrated drawing, a few straight lines suggesting shifting planes produce a work at once diagrammatic and dynamic. The effect is heightened by the excitement of the public glimpsed across the near-transparency of the racing figure – a popular sporting event almost without precedent in painting since Géricault's series of the *Race of the Riderless Horses*.

67

ANDRÉ LHOTE 1885–1962

The Harvest, ca.1912

Pencil and watercolour on off-white paper, 31.8 × 49.5 cm

Signed: *A. Lhote*

PROVENANCE: John Kodner Gallery, St Louis; Christie's, New York, 1 March 2006, lot 49

LITERATURE: Bermann Martin (forthcoming)

André Lhote and his Cubist colleagues in the 'Section d'Or' (or 'Golden Section') movement distanced themselves from the Cubism of Picasso and Braque by emphasising their links with tradition. Jacques Villon claimed to have given the 'Section d'Or' movement its name after reading Leonardo da Vinci's *Treatise on Painting* in a translation by Sâr Péladan, published in 1910. Without pursuing too closely the passage to which Villon alluded, it is enough to point out that Villon and his colleagues, like Leonardo, were attracted to the idea that there were certain mathematical ratios underlying the natural world that could be applied in a work of art. How far this mattered for Lhote is not obvious. In this watercolour Lhote reworked a traditional subject, a scene of harvesting, by reducing complex forms into simple geometrical shapes – rectangles, triangles and pyramids – in a manner that owes more to the example of Cézanne than it does to the theories of the Golden Section.

Along with his figure paintings, landscape occupies a large part of Lhote's output. In his influential book *Traité du Paysage* (*Treatise on Landscape*), published in 1939, he described the stages of painting landscape as a transposition of the reality of nature into the reality of art, and condemned landscape artists who attempted to conceal the two-dimensional character of art by introducing an illusion of recession. In this watercolour, Lhote has raised the horizon and flattened the appearance of space in a manner that is common to all his landscapes. The debt to Cézanne and Cubism suggests that this is an early work, dating from 1912 or shortly after when he was involved with the Section d'Or movement.

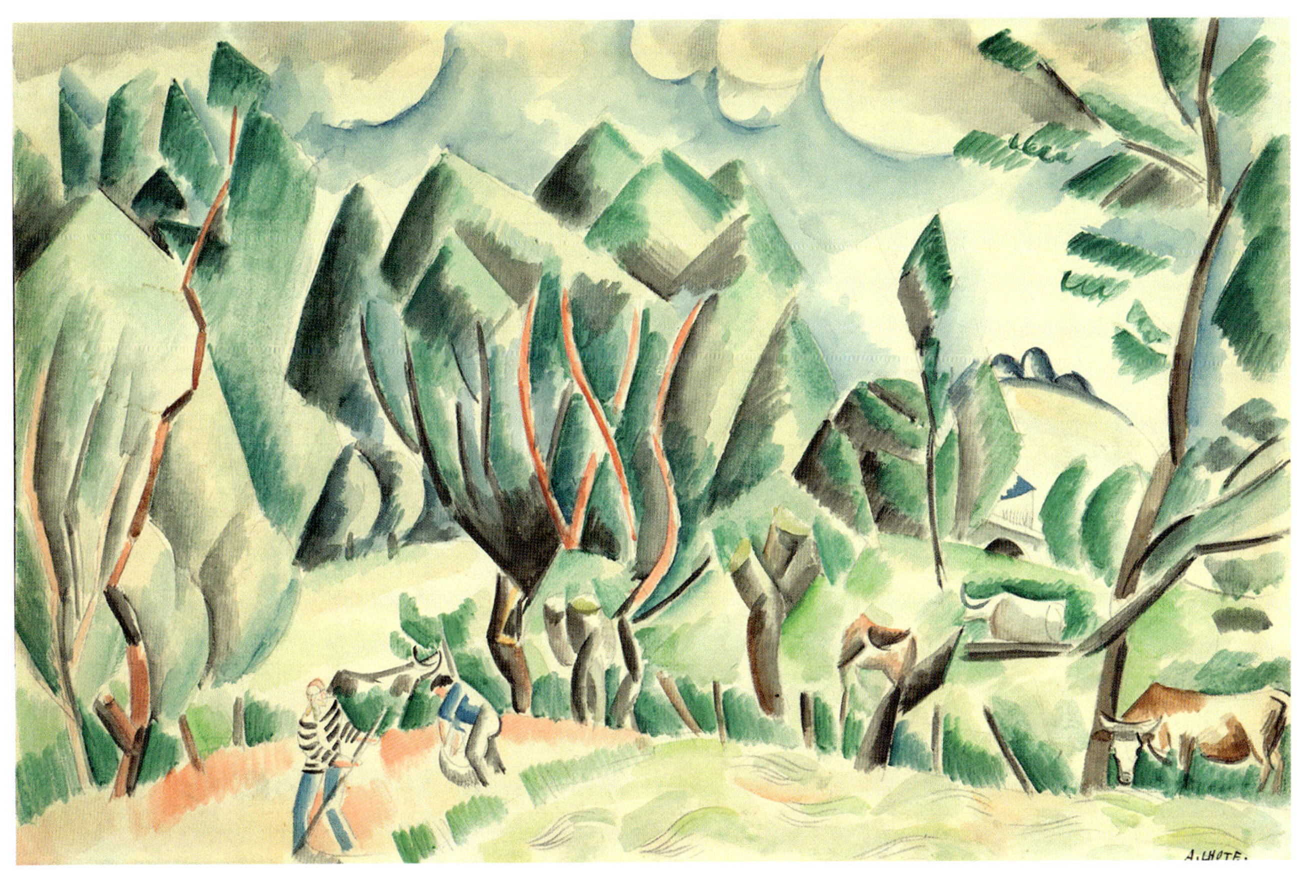

68

JACQUES VILLON 1875–1963

Soldiers Marching, 1912

Pencil and watercolour, 16 × 22.3 cm
Signed: *Jacques Villon*
LITERATURE: Johnson (1991), no.52, ill. p.129

Jacques Villon, brother of the artists Marcel Duchamp and Raymond Duchamp-Villon, was christened Gaston Duchamp. In the 1890s he adopted the name by which he is now known in tribute to *Jack*, a novel by Alphonse Daudet, and to François Villon, the sixteenth-century French poet. As Jacques Villon he made his reputation as a printmaker and illustrator in *fin-de-siècle* Montmartre. 1906 marked a break with his career as a commercial illustrator when Villon moved to Puteaux, a suburb in the west of Paris; here he became acquainted with Gleizes, Metzinger, Léger, Robert Delaunay and their Cubist colleagues. These artists, the so-called Puteaux group, met regularly at Villon's studio and formed the main exhibitors at the Salon de la Section d'Or ('Salon of the Golden Section') in 1912. The name was devised by Villon, who believed that the harmonious relationship between two quantities – known as the Golden or Divine Section – provided a key to creating art. It was a theory that could be applied in a general sense to the geometric shapes of Cubism and gave the movement a base in objective theory.

This watercolour is one of two preparatory studies for *Soldiers Marching* (Musée Nationale d'Art Moderne, Paris, which also owns the other preparatory study), a major composition painted in 1912 when Villon had become a committed Cubist. It is probably an early study since, by comparison with the final painting, it remains a recognisable image of soldiers wearing the blue coats and red breeches of the French infantry, marching away from the spectator with guns over their right shoulders. The perspective suggests that the artist is marching with them. Under the watercolour is a complex network of fine, straight lines joining an arrangement of dots that follow the contours of the soldiers and their equipment. The dotted composition was made before the watercolour, following a laborious stage of preparatory work involving the use of callipers to fix the points at which the lines converge.

In the Centre Pompidou in Paris is a photograph worked over with patches of wash; it appears to be a photograph of the present drawing before the watercolour was added. The wash on the photograph is more abstract than the watercolour in the present drawing – anticipating the appearance of the finished painting, in which the scene has been reduced to several V shapes radiating upwards. The major diagonals are interspersed with geometric shapes that contain an echo of the marching soldiers but are no longer recognisable as such, while the colours have been reduced to a scheme of pale uniformity.

What survives in the painting from the early study is a sense of movement, not characteristic of contemporary Cubism but a subject of major interest to the Futurists. At the time of the 1912 exhibition the Futurists had violently repudiated their Cubist heritage, causing a deep rift between the two camps. Villon had too much respect for his Cubist colleagues to join the Futurists. However, like his brother Marcel Duchamp in his painting *Nude descending a Stair*, 1912 (Philadelphia Museum of Art), he was attracted by the Futurists' attempt to represent movement, and *Soldiers Marching* added an element of dynamism to the static world of early Cubism.

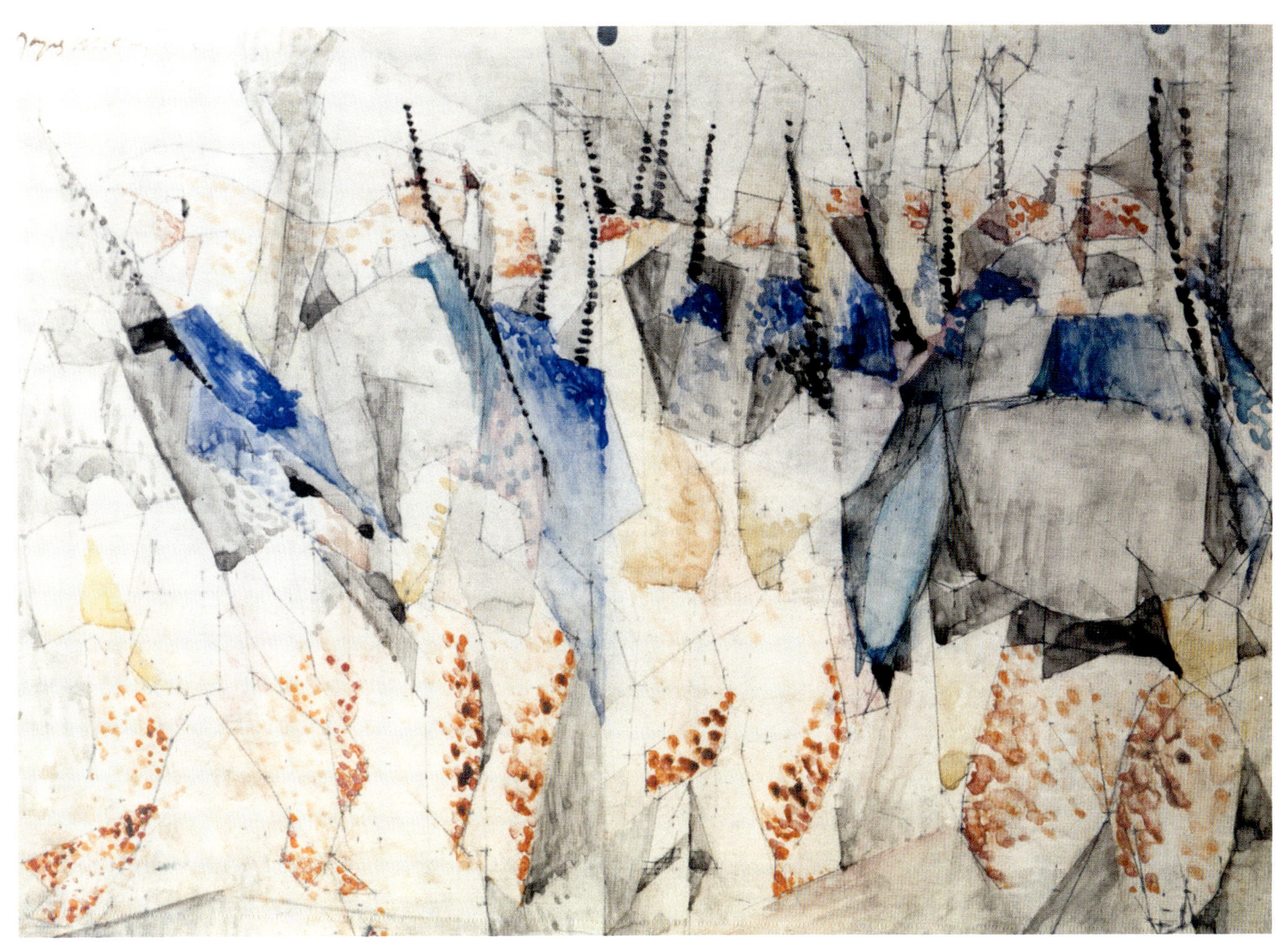

69

ALBERT MARCOUSSIS 1878–1941

Portrait of Guillaume Apollinaire, 1912–20

Etching, drypoint and aquatint on laid paper, 49.2 × 27.8 cm

Inscribed in the plate: GUILLAUME APOLLINAIRE / A PARIS CHEZ CAMILLE BLOCH RUE ST HONORE NO 366 / MARCOUSSIS / 1912–1920

Signed in graphite and numbered: Marcoussis 11/30

LITERATURE: La Franchis (1961), no.G.32; Millet (1991), no.33; Johnson (1991), no.28, ill. p.85

Ludwik Markus (better known as Albert Marcoussis) studied in his native Poland and in Paris, to which he moved in 1904. His early work was influenced by the Impressionists and the Fauves, and he supported himself by providing illustrations to popular magazines. His meeting in 1910 with his compatriot Wilhelm Apollinaris de Kostrowitzky (1880–1918), who worked from 1903 under the name Guillaume Apollinaire, completely changed his life and work. A poet, writer and art critic, Apollinaire was also the great champion of Cubism in its various forms. He persuaded Markus to change his name to Marcoussis, a village in the Essonne to the south of Paris, and also introduced him to Picasso (who ran away with his mistress, Marcelle Humbert) and to Braque. Having adopted their Cubist style, Marcoussis exhibited in the Section d'Or in 1912 and at the Salon des Indépendants in 1913, where Apollinaire praised his work.

Marcoussis' first portrait of Apollinaire was etched from life in 1912; it shows him sitting in an armchair reading his poem 'Zone'.[1] In the same year Marcoussis began this second portrait, but it was not completed until 1920, two years after the sitter's death from influenza. The preliminary drawing shows that originally the face was to have been less distorted, more in the manner of Metzinger, and the background to have incorporated the original title of Apollinaire's new collection of poems, Eau de vie, eventually published under the title Alcools.[2] The etching, which depicts Apollinaire with a bandage on his head as the result of a war wound, retains the fleshy face and double chin of the drawing, but also includes evocations of some of the writer's best known volumes, his original Polish name and a fictitious coat of arms.

After Apollinaire's death Marcoussis made three further portraits of his friend. In 1934 he published a suite of 18 illustrations for Alcools.[3]

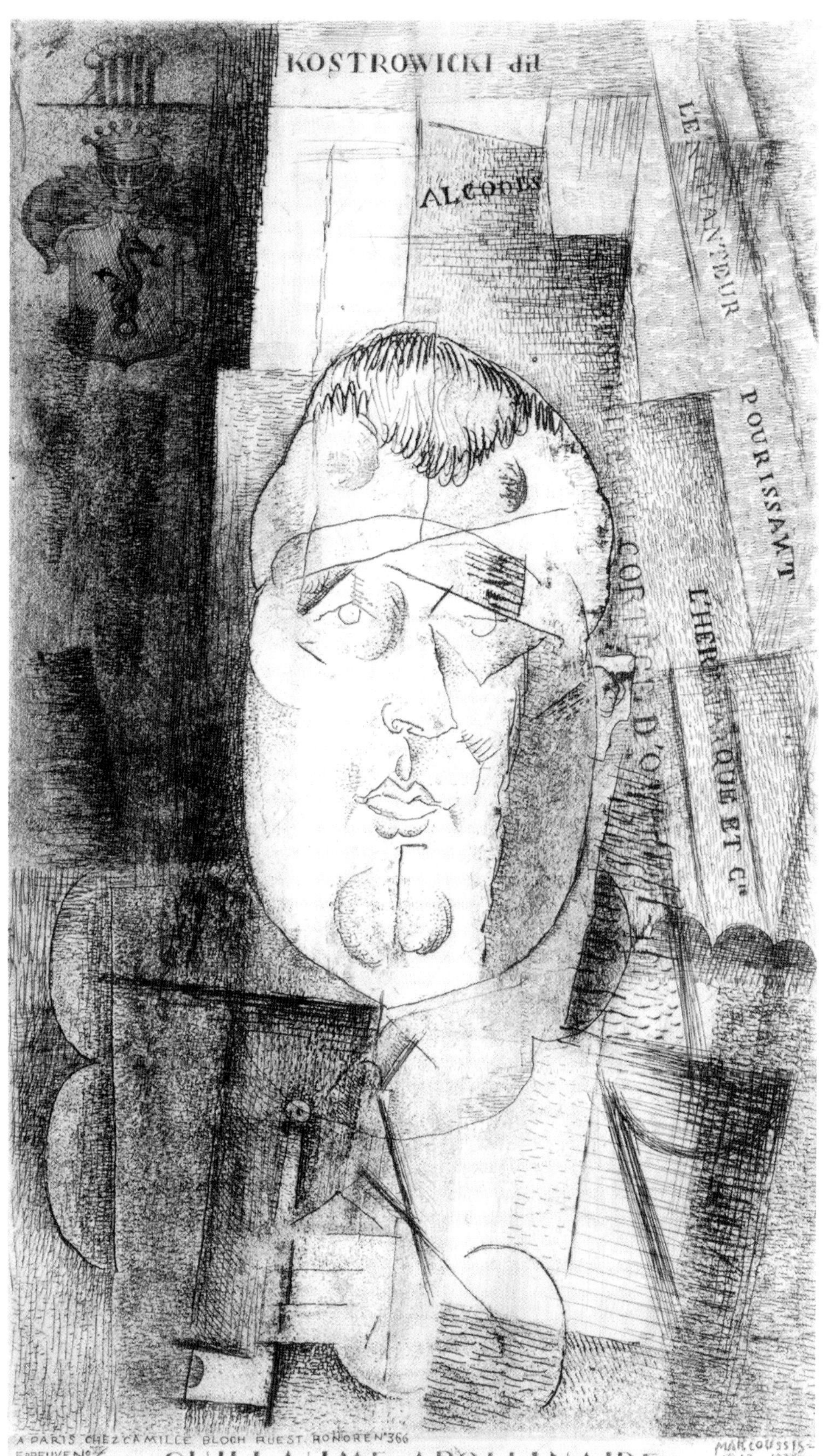
KOSTROWICKI dit
ALCOOLS
POURISSANT
A PARIS CHEZ CAMILLE BLOCH RUE ST. HONORE N°366
GUILLAUME APOLLINAIRE
MARCOUSSIS
1912–1920

70

JUAN GRIS 1887–1927

Head of Germaine Raynal, 1912

Charcoal on off-white wove paper with pin holes at top, 48 × 31.7 cm

PROVENANCE: the artist until 1927; Mme Josette Gris (the artist's wife); Gonzales Gris (the artist's son); Galerie Louise Leiris (Kahnweiler), Paris, 1965

LITERATURE: Kahnweiler (1968), no.228, ill; Cooper (1977). vol.1, p.50, no.28 bis; Johnson (1991), no.17, ill. cover and p.63; Tinterow (1985), no.120; Green, Maur and Derouet (1992), no.16; Leal (2005), no.177

Germaine Raynal was a composer of light music who came into contact with the world of the avant-garde through her husband, the critic Maurice Raynal - one of the most important advocates of Cubism in its early days. Juan Gris became a close friend of the Raynals, painting portraits of both in 1912 (private collection) and spending three days with them in Toulon in the winter of 1925. The portrait of Maurice is painted in a soft-edged version of Cubism while the portrait of Germaine is a far starker image, broken up through a network of lines, squares and rectangles imposed upon her features like a wall of bricks. There exists a second study for the portrait, dated July 1912,[1] which is in some respects closer to the finished painting. The present drawing is even more severely geometric and is an excellent example of the Section d'Or movement's deployment of mathematically-derived shapes. It also has greater circular emphasis and more frontality than is evident in the painting. The earrings, chin, nostrils and hair are drawn as circles, or parts of circles and ovals interspersed with squares and rectangles, in a manner that is modified in the painting; there the circles (which do not correspond to the reality of Germaine Raynal's long head) have been largely reduced. The dense charcoal in the drawing anticipates the dark tonality of the subject's hair in the finished work, framing and emphasising the pallor of her face.

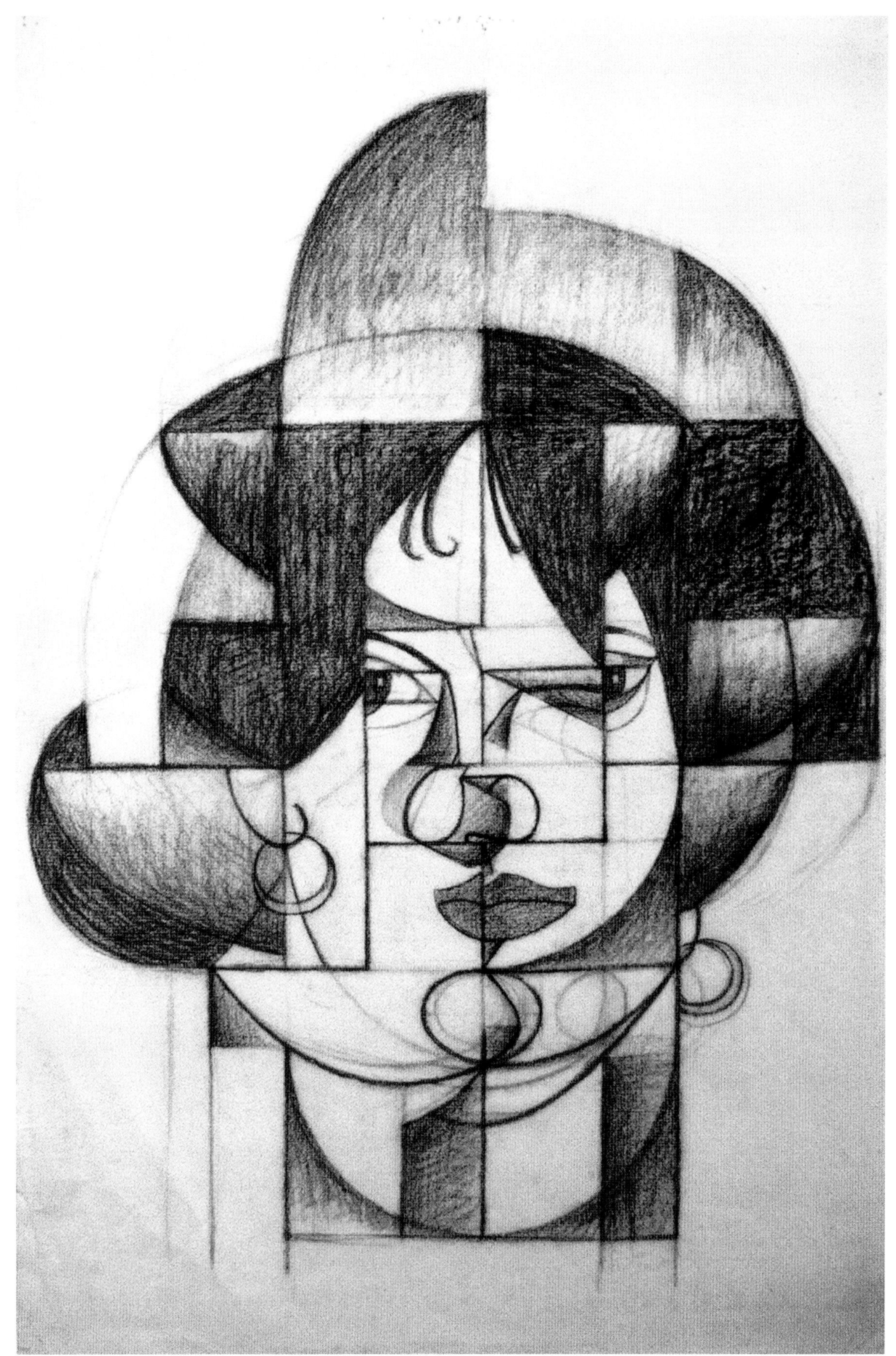

71

JUAN GRIS 1887–1927

The Guitar, 1912–13

Charcoal on paper, 31.6 × 48 cm

PROVENANCE: the artist until 1927; Mme Josette Gris (the artist's wife); Gonzales Gris (the artist's son); Galerie Louise Leiris (Kahnweiler), Paris, 1965

LITERATURE: Richardson and Kahnweiler (1965–66), no.106; Cooper (1977), vol.I, p.64, no.36a; Johnson, (1991), no.16, ill. p.65; Green, Maur and Derouet (1992), no.17; Leal (2005), vol.II, p.190, no.182

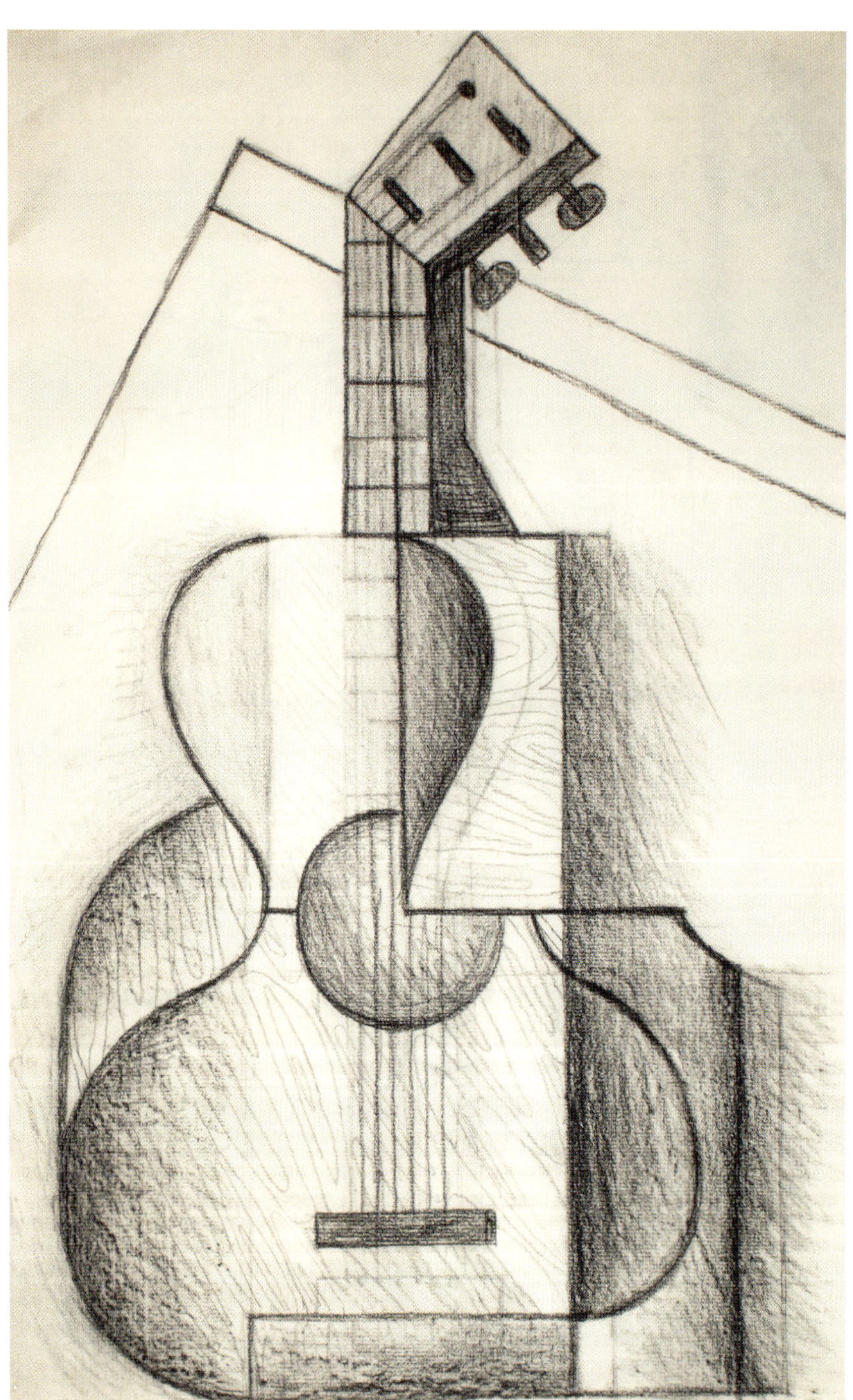

Gris, like Picasso, was born and raised in Spain. This must explain, at least in part, the frequency with which the Spanish guitar appears in the work of both artists. Unlike Picasso, however, Gris did not at first show much interest in the guitar, and was probably introduced to the idea of including it by the example of Braque. As Christopher Green has pointed out, only two paintings by Gris between 1910 and the end of 1912 feature guitars.[1] They are, however, common in his still-life paintings of 1913 and became one of his stock accessories thereafter.

This drawing is generally dated 1912–13, when the subject began to interest Gris. The idea of suggesting a guitar's wood grain by pasting a piece of oilcloth printed with imitation wood grain was first adopted by Braque in 1912. Although there is no collage in this drawing, the suggestion of wood grain inserted by Gris into this composition achieves the same purpose, eliminating the space between the surface of the guitar and the picture plane.

There is a general similarity between this drawing and several images of an upright guitar that appear in Gris' art. The direction of the pencil lines, from upper left to lower right when it is turned sideways, suggest that he drew the guitar in this direction, resting its head over the edge of the table. Kahnweiler also illustrated this drawing horizontally, but it is likely, however, that Gris intended to make use of the work in a vertical format, especially given that most of his paintings of guitars are in this latter format.

72

JEAN METZINGER 1883–1956

The Yellow Feather, 1912

Oil on canvas, 73 × 54 cm

Signed and dated lower left.

LITERATURE: Golding (1968), p.160; Moser (1985–6), exh.cat., p.43, ill. p.52 and front cover; Johnson (1991), p.14, fig.3

In his *Note sur la Peinture,* published in the journal *Pan* in October 1910, Metzinger identified what was for him the essence of the art of Braque and Picasso, at the same time relating it to the recent practices of his own friends Delaunay and Le Fauconnier. However, Picasso and, after 1909, Braque, both protégés of the dealer Daniel Kahnweiler, did not show their works in the public Salons; it was the little group surrounding Metzinger who had, since that autumn of 1910, recognised a common sense of purpose and made the notion of Cubism increasingly familiar to the public. They showed as a group at the Salon des Indépendants of 1911, and later in the year Metzinger exhibited his famous *Tea Time* (*Le goûter*), now in Philadelphia, at the Salon d'Automne – possibly as his own homage to Braque and Picasso, whose importance he had always understood.

That work was something of an exercise in style, by the following year, at the Section d'Or exhibition of 1912 (in which Juan Gris exhibited with the group for the first time), Metzinger had moved towards a more personal manner. He showed there the present work, *The Yellow Feather*, one of a small series of elegant images of women in which accessories form a crucial part of the subject. The multiple viewpoints that Metzinger had recognised as an essential element of the new painting, here suggested by the shifting and translucent planes, signal his adherence to what he has learned, but now contribute to the specific characterisation of a particular encounter. As Joann Moser has commented, the passing spectacle was a recurrent theme in his work.[1]

The Yellow Feather is brighter in tone than *Le goûter*, and the geometric elements smaller and more animated. It is generally supposed that the arrival of Gris in the group led Metzinger to make use, as in this case, of a grid-like structure of lines. However, as Golding comments, while Gris had evolved the technique in order to synthesise different aspects of a figure, in Metzinger's hands it became decorative.[2] Here it is entirely in keeping with the subject. The black lines take on a life of their own; they curve round the brim of the hat, provide an expressive eye, an earring, then retreat upwards, pointing to the feather of the title – an eruption of foggy yellow light with an effect not unlike that of Seurat's *Parade*.

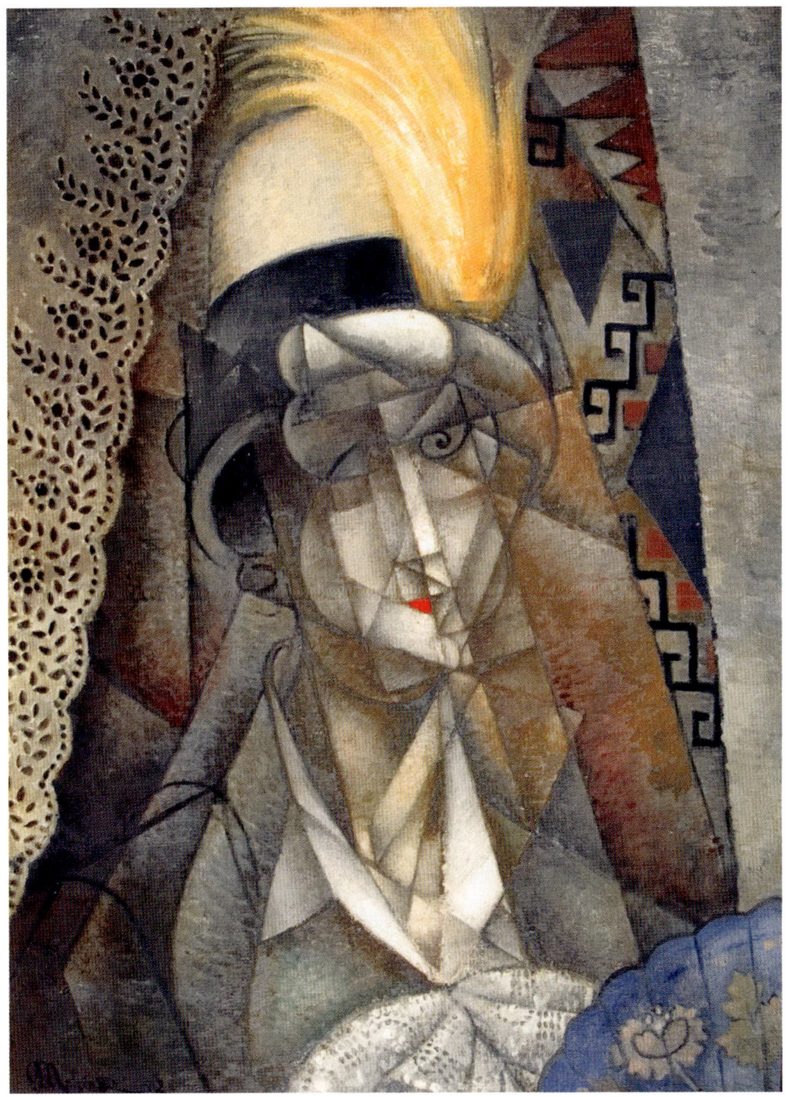

73

ALBERT GLEIZES 1881–1953

Still Life, 1911–12

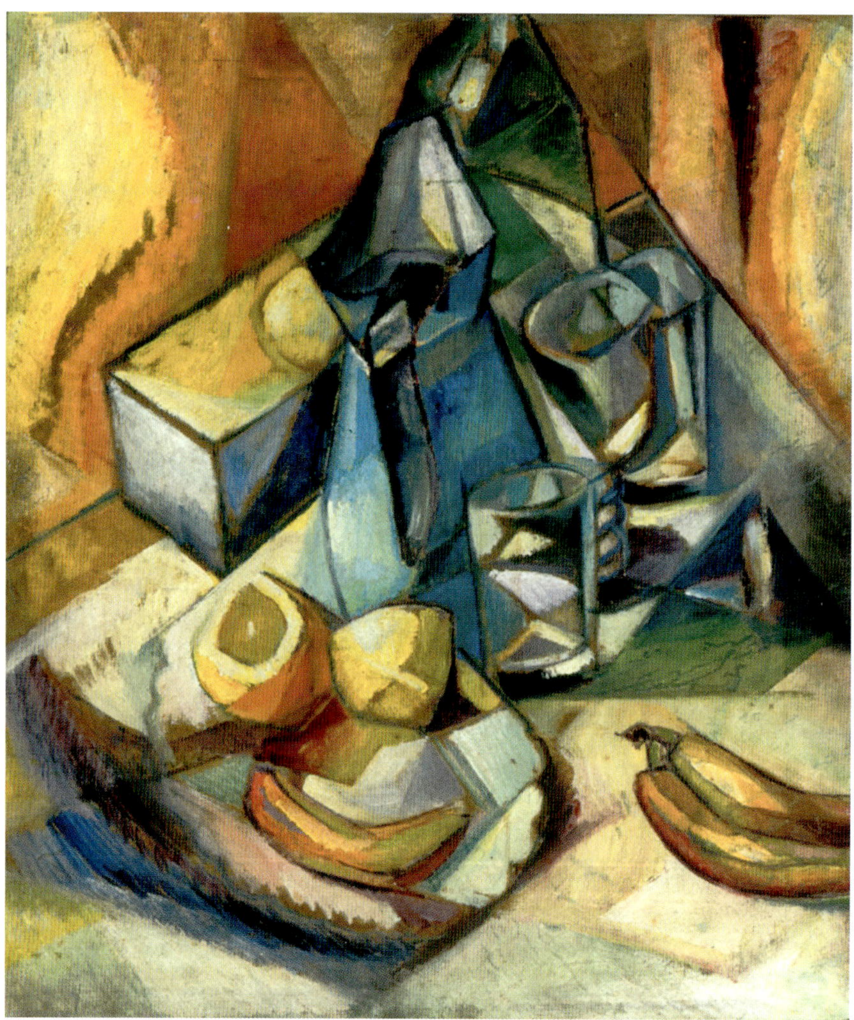

Oil on paper laid down on a cradled panel, 67.5 × 60 cm

LITERATURE: Varichon (forthcoming)

Apart from an apprenticeship in his father's fabric design studio, Gleizes had little formal training. After a period of Impressionism, he moved towards the Nabis (as a group of Gauguin's followers were known) and the Symbolists, then spent a brief period in 1908 experimenting with the colour of the Fauves. Like Metzinger and Le Fauconnier, both of whom he met in 1909–10, he worked in a style that was becoming increasingly structured and simple. By 1910 he had joined Metzinger, Léger, Delaunay and others who met regularly at Le Fauconnier's studio near the Boulevard de Montparnasse. Building on the example of Cézanne and the recent art of Braque and Picasso, they developed the style that was identified as 'Cubism' by a hostile press when they exhibited together in 1911 at the Salon des Indépendants.

This painting by Gleizes, dating from 1911–12, marks a moment in early Cubism as it developed out of its various sources. Cézanne's fragmentation and flattening of form are combined with a relic of Fauve colour. The objects are commonplace, as they often are in the still-life paintings of Cézanne, Braque and Picasso. They are also clearly identifiable, although the space they occupy is ambiguous. The high viewpoint serves to diminish the appearance of depth, and the surface is crossed with fault lines that disrupt the composition.

Following the controversy inspired by the exhibition of the Section d'Or in 1912, Gleizes and Metzinger collaborated in writing *Du Cubisme,* the first theoretical account of Cubism. This may not have dealt with all the concerns of their colleagues, but it provides a clear statement of the two authors' beliefs. While Gleizes' colleague Villon sought some geometrical basis for Cubism, Gleizes and Metzinger turned to more intuitive sources, declaring 'Geometry is a science; painting is an art'.[1] We should not, therefore, look too closely for any application of geometry in this painting. Both Gleizes and Metzinger believed in the autonomy of a work of art and in the possibility of a painting that represented nothing, even as they acknowledged that this could not be done 'at the first step'.[2] This is still a representational painting, particularly when compared with Gleizes' work over the following two or three years, as it evolved further towards abstraction.

74

FRANTIŠEK KUPKA 1871–1957

Study for 'Localizing Graphic Mobiles', 1912–13

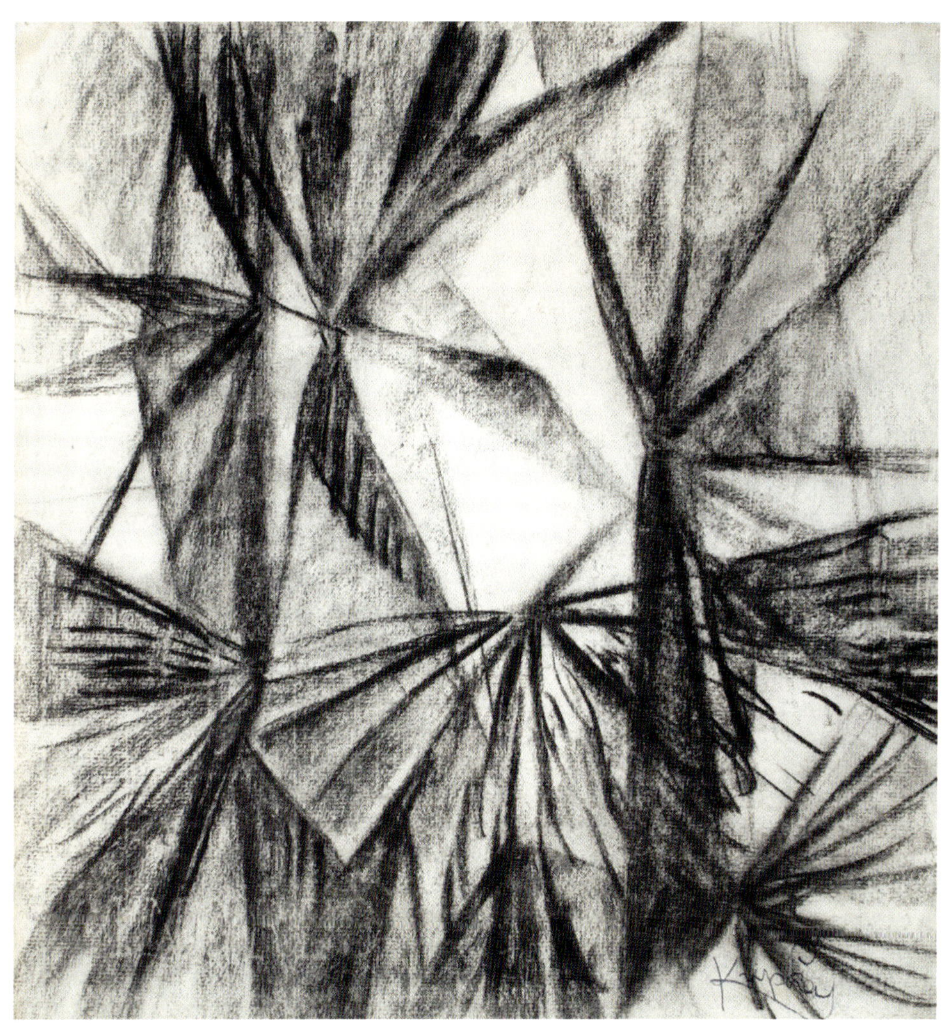

Charcoal on paper, 33 × 31.4 cm

Signed: *Kupka*

PROVENANCE: Eugénie Kupka (the artist's wife); Mira Jacob, Galerie le Bateau-Lavoir, Drouot-Montaigne, Paris, 23 September 2004, lot 111 and ill. p.122

Kupka was born in Opočno in Bohemia and trained in Prague and Vienna before migrating to Paris in 1895, where he spent the rest of his life. He arrived as a fully-fledged painter, well versed in the academic and Symbolist styles of Central Europe. Although he abandoned figure painting within a few years of his arrival, he continued to explore some of the philosophical concerns of the Vienna Symbolists and remained an outsider among his colleagues in the French avant-garde. Despite his conversion to a form of radical modernism in *c.*1909, Kupka took from the Fauves and the Cubists only those elements that suited his distinctive manner. At the Salon d'Automne of 1912 he exhibited a huge canvas, *Amorpha: Fugue in Two Colours* (National Gallery, Prague), that marked the first public appearance in France of a work of pure abstraction. This was followed in 1913 by the exhibition of two equally ambitious works, *Localizing Graphic Mobiles I* and *II* (Museo Thyssen-Bornemisza, Madrid, and National Gallery of Art, Washington). These, like *Amphora,* represented the final rejection of what Kupka called the 'fetishism' of representational art.

This drawing, with its arrangement of lines exploding like fireworks across the surface of the paper, is an early study for the two paintings that appeared at the Salon d'Automne in 1913. Like *Amphora,* these works derived their abstract character from an analogy with music, providing Kupka, as it did Kandinsky, with a model of a non-representational art. Both works were prepared with many studies in which radiant and curving lines represent a sense of musical rhythm. Kupka described these lines as 'stereoscopic bridges', suggesting an illusion of the third dimension.[1] They appear in the paintings in a vertiginous vortex of overlapping forms, encircling a central explosion of light. The luminous centre is indicated in the drawing by the white triangle that shines out in the midst of a forest of dark forms.

75

FERNAND LÉGER 1881–1955

Contrasts of Forms, 1913

Gouache, 37 × 28 cm

Initialled and dated: *F.L. 13*

PROVENANCE: Galerie Louise Leiris (Kahnweiler), Paris n. 14381/39488

LITERATURE: Johnson (1991), no.22, ill. p.73

This work of 1913 relates to a series of oil paintings grouped under the same title and dating from the period 1913–14. It departs from the Cubism of certain of Léger's contemporaries both in its range of bright primary colours and its sense of perpetual motion – an aspect that relates it, though in that respect only, to Futurism. This is what Léger meant by realism; it was a language in which to express the multitude of impressions, and thus the dynamism, of modern existence. It appears as a disintegration of form or, rather, a series of constant interruptions and eruptions.

Here the old forms of classic draughtsmanship, such as the cube, cone and cylinder, strongly outlined (a lesson Léger absorbed from Cézanne) and given volume simply by the effective use of white, meet and collide. The red/blue cubes, joining together, tumble down across the bell-like movements of the blue/yellow cones, evoking the rhythms of dance quite as much as the machine and perhaps indicative of Léger's later interest in the ballet. This found expression in both his important work for the *Ballets suédois* in the 1920s and, especially, the experimental film he devised and co-directed in 1924, *Ballet mécanique*. The present work differs a little in its effect from several other versions in oil (Centre Pompidou, Paris; Museum of Modern Art, New York) in which the conic bell-like forms dominate. A tendency to read some kind of figuration into these exhilarating forms may not be entirely misplaced: within a year Léger had painted several compositions in which the same forms do, indeed, come to life – most famously in *l'Escalier* (1914, Kunstmuseum, Basel), but also in *La sortie des ballets Russes* (1914, Museum of Modern Art, New York).

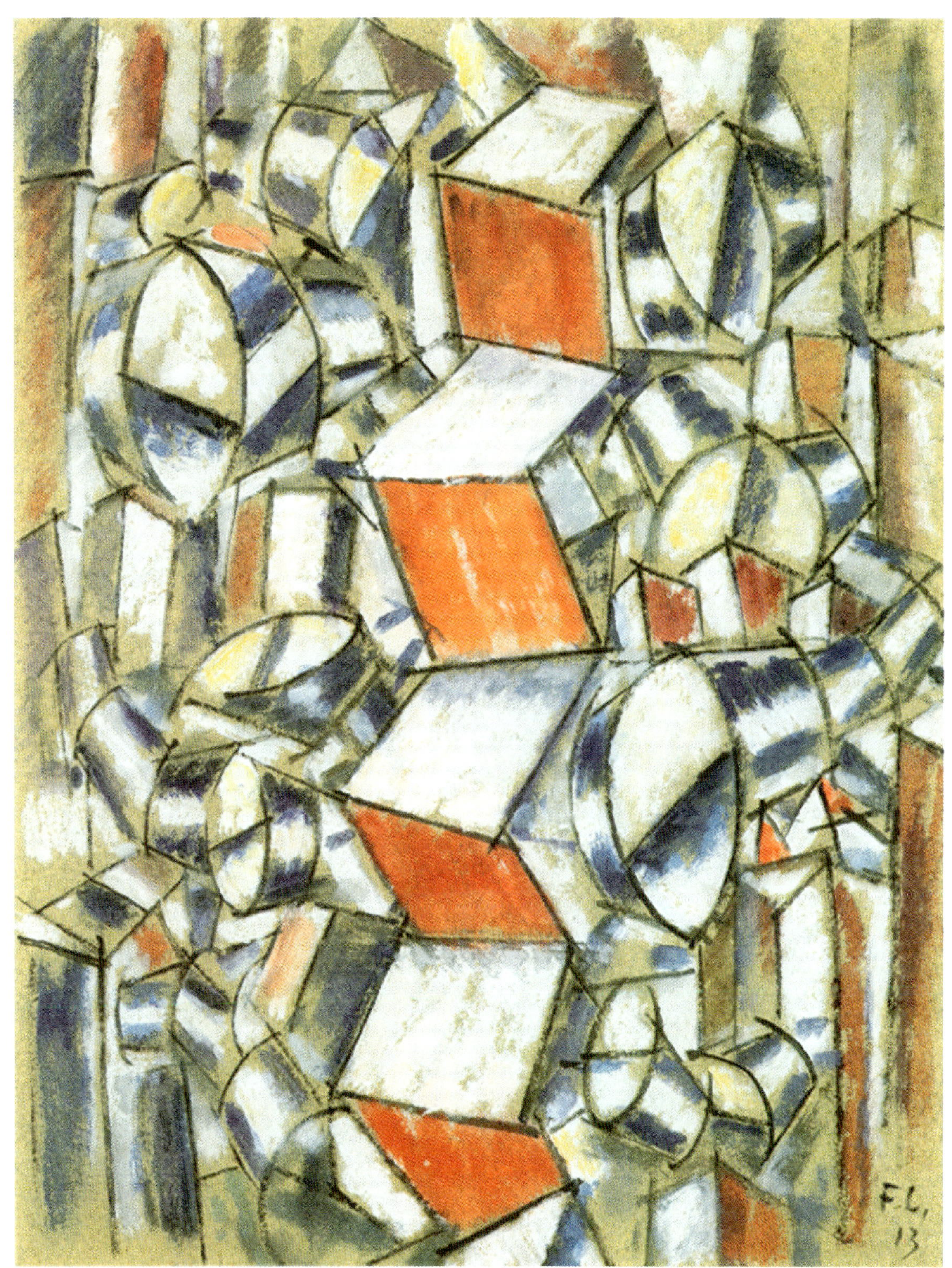
F.L.
13

76

RAOUL DUFY 1877–1953

View of Vence, ca.1908

Black crayon and watercolour on laid paper, 50 × 64.4 cm

Signed: *Raoul Dufy*

PROVENANCE: Galerie Delaive, Amsterdam

LITERATURE: Guillon-Laffaille (forthcoming)

Following Dufy's arrival in Paris from his native Normandy in 1900, he worked for a time in the manner of the Impressionists. This early period lasted until 1905, when he switched allegiance to the Fauves after seeing their work at the Salon des Indépendants. In 1907, impressed by the exhibition of Cézanne's work at the Salon d'Automne, Dufy changed course again, bringing a new clarity and sense of structure into his art. The impact of Cézanne was not immediately obvious, but surfaced in the course of 1907–8 while he worked alongside Braque on the French Riviera.

During his visit to the south of France, he made his first trip to the hill town of St-Paul-de-Vence. This view of the terraces located beyond the ancient ramparts of Vence was taken from the window of his room. Dufy painted a view corresponding to this drawing (Musée de la Ville de Paris) dated 1908, and a second painting of the interior of his room with part of the same view framed by the window (Musée de la Loire, Cosne-sur-Loire). The organisation of the shapes, flattened in a decorative pattern against the surface of the paper, follows the example of Cézanne, although the colour is brighter than in his work, partly because of a lingering debt to Matisse and the Fauves and partly because of the colour and light of Provence.

Dufy did not return to Vence until 1919, when it became a source of many of his drawings and paintings. The debt to Cézanne is less evident in these later works than the impact of Matisse, who had recently moved to the nearby port of Nice. Contact with Matisse contributed an essential part to the development of the colourful, calligraphic manner that is now universally associated with Dufy's work.

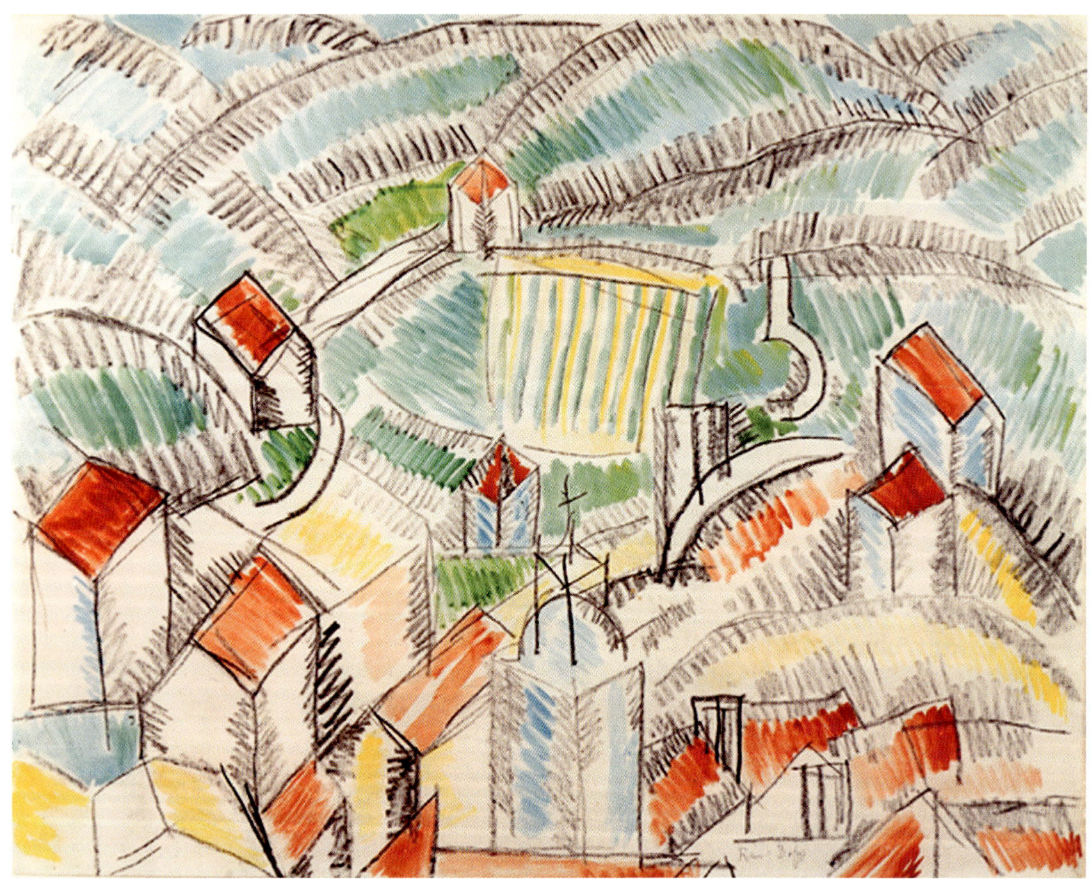

77

ALBERT GLEIZES 1881–1953

The City and the River, 1913

Oil on canvas, 80.6 × 64.6 cm

Signed and dated: *AlbGleizes / 13*

PROVENANCE: the heirs of Gottfried Graff, Stuttgart

LITERATURE: Antliff (1993), pl. 6 and cover; Varichon (1998), no.415, ill.

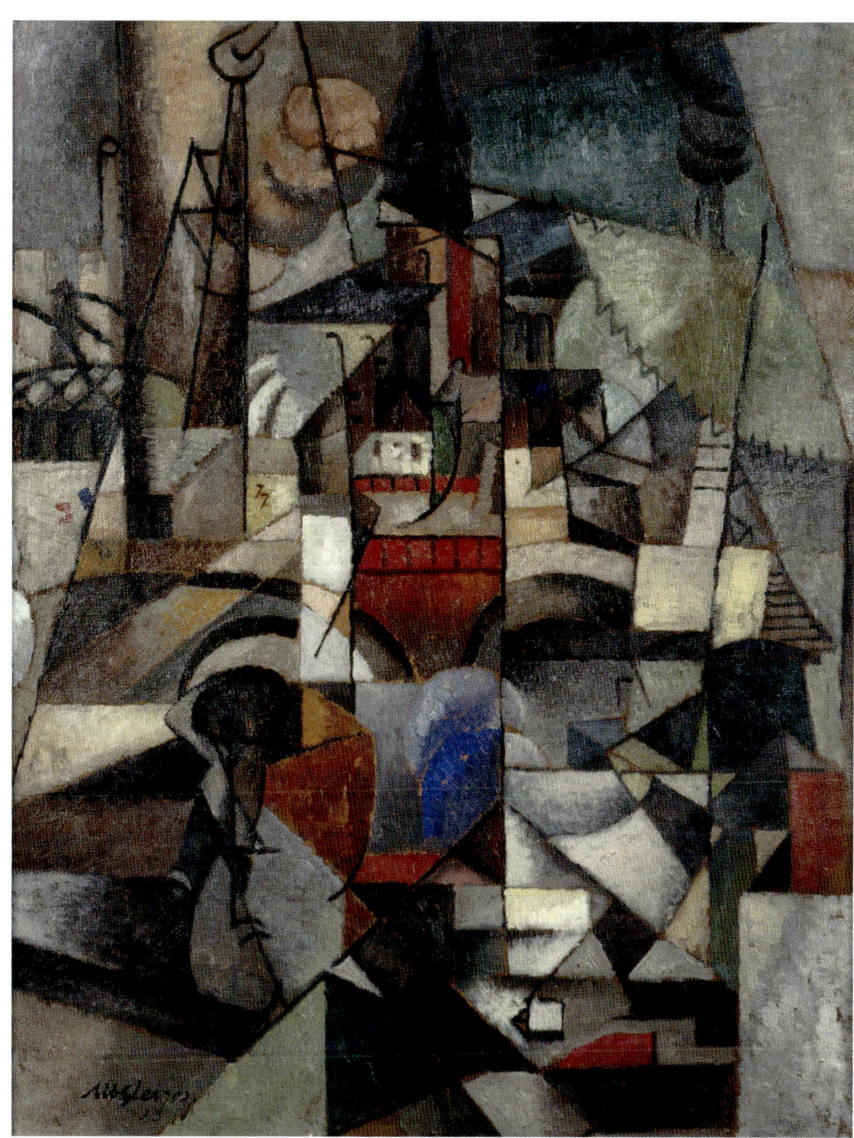

With the help of a preparatory drawing, also dated 1913,[1] the details of this painting can be mostly identified. It represents a view, presumably taken from an upstairs window, looking along a river towards a bridge of two arches with buildings, clouds and a church with tower and spire in the background. These details are inserted within a framework of straight, dark lines that cross the surface of the painting, disrupting the elements and marking changes in the colours. The shifting shapes and colour suggest Gleizes' belief that objects have no absolute reality, but exist in a state of change and motion, depending on the spectator's point of view.

The rectangle tilted across the composition introduces an element of movement and seems to represent a window frame. In front of this is some indication of the head and shoulders of a figure leaning forward, but with details of a face looking inwards towards the lower left corner.

78

JACQUES VILLON 1875–1963

Portrait of Monsieur Duchamp (Portrait de Monsieur Duchamp père), 1913

Oil on canvas, 116 × 89 cm
Signed: *Jacques Villon*
PROVENANCE: Jean Bauret, Paris.
LITERATURE: Cassou (1951)

Villon's father, Justin-Isidore Eugène Duchamp (1848–1925), is a frequent subject in Villon's art. This portrait of his father is undated, but is probably contemporary with the etching and drawing of the same seated figure that date from 1913 [cats 79 and 84]. All three works exemplify the synthesis of Cubism and geometric form that marked the artist's passage from the influence of Cézanne to the art of the Section d'Or. There is also a relationship with a portrait of the artist's father, seated with one leg crossed over the other and reading a paper (Musée des Beaux-Arts, Rouen), that is dated 1913, although this is painted with more naturalism than the other works and is clearly earlier. The present work retains elements of the Cézanne-like faceting of the head that is a striking feature of the Rouen portrait. The pose, too, is similar, although the sitter's slippered feet are not visible in the earlier work and the chair has been altered. Despite the similarities, this painting is not directly based on Villon's earlier work. It is rather a new, ambitious composition on a well-tried theme.

The significant novelty in this second portrait by comparison with Villon's earlier portraits lies in the bold deconstruction of the form that divides the surface into jagged shapes. Straight, dominant lines, scored across the picture plane, disrupt the image in a manner that is not found in Cézanne's art, nor in Villon's own work before 1911. By the time he painted the oval version of his father's portrait (private collection, Paris), also dating from 1913, his new style had reached its fullest resolution.

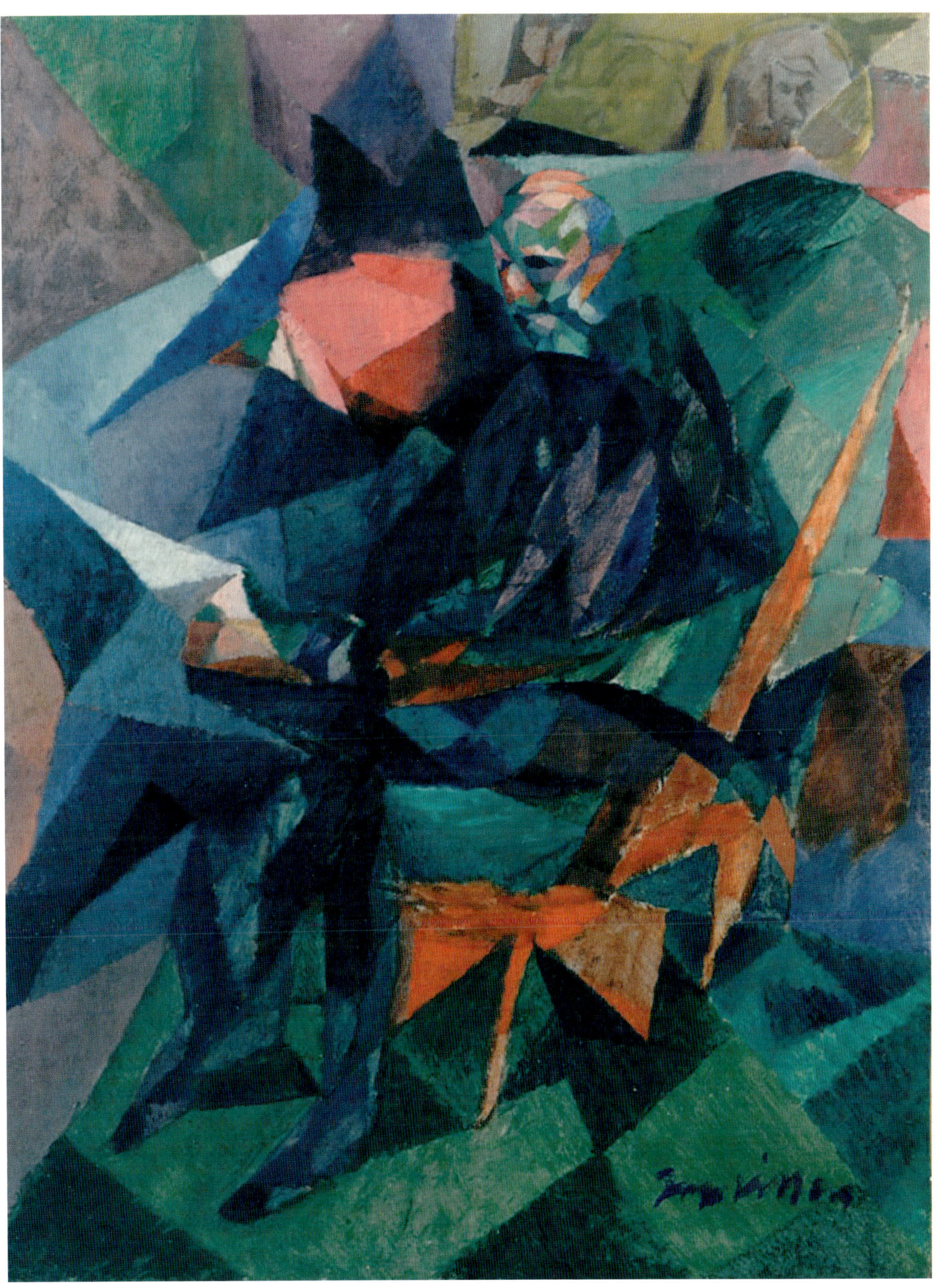

79

JACQUES VILLON 1875–1963

Monsieur D. reading trial proof, 1913

Drypoint on wove paper 39 × 29.5 cm
Signed with initials: *J. V.* and annotated in pencil: *essai*

LITERATURE: Ginestet and Pouillon (1979), E284; Johnson (1991), no.58, ill. p.141

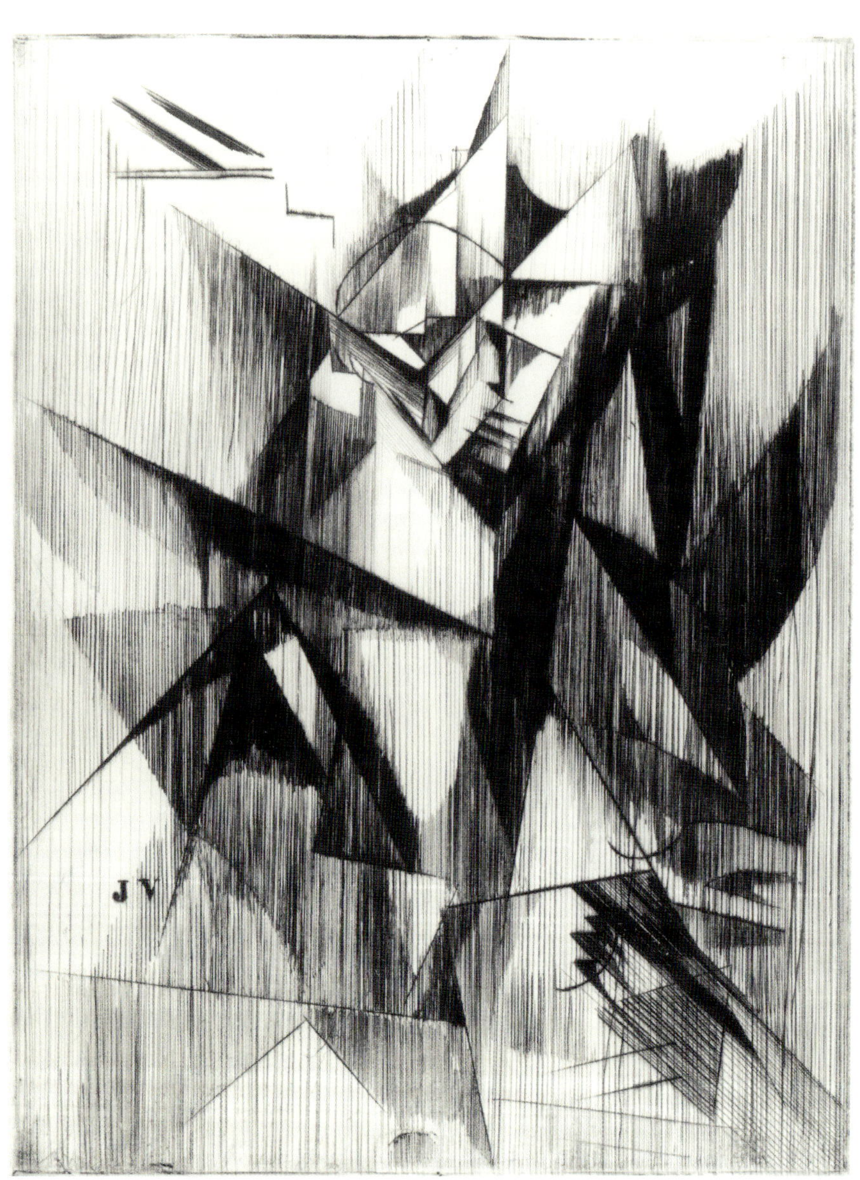

Villon's evolution towards the Cubist print began in 1913 with an etched study of his father's head[1]. His technique developed though portraits of his sister[2] to reach a final resolution in the near-abstraction of the portrait of Félix Barré[3] and the present portrait of Villon's father. The image of Villon's father, Justin-Isidore Duchamp, originated in a drawing of 1912 (St Louis Art Museum) and in a related painting (Musée des Beaux-Arts, Rouen), both of which represent Monsieur Duchamp seated in the same pose and reading a paper.

From the painting in Rouen, Villon produced a fragmented and less legible drawing of his father [cat.84]. This drawing became the basis of an oval painting (private collection) that became in turn the basis of the present print, one of only two trial proofs made before the plate was steel-faced. By this stage, the elements can barely be identified. The sitter's left hand (which has become his right hand in the print) is marked by a contrast between a pale area and a burst of dark, dynamic lines leading to the lower right. His head is composed from a series of squares and triangles in sequence of diminishing shapes that resemble diagrams of the Golden Section, while his body is indicated with lines and larger planes thrusting inwards from the margins. The concentration of form towards the centre carries a trace of the oval format of the painting on which the print was based.

80

ALBERT GLEIZES 1881–1953

Cubist Landscape, 1914

Watercolour, bodycolour and black ink over pencil on paper, 26.8 × 34.2 cm

Signed and dated: *Alb Gleizes 14*

PROVENANCE: Sotheby's, London, 1 July 1992, lot 173

LITERATURE: Varichon (1998), no.496

In August 1914 Gleizes was called up to serve in the 176th Infantry regiment based in Toul in north-eastern France, close to the main theatre of the war. Until early 1915, while organising entertainment for the troops, he painted a series of views of Toul and its vicinity, working mostly in gouache and watercolour. During these months in Toul Gleizes' work became increasingly abstract, leading up to his first works of complete abstraction in 1915. In this view, drawn during his months in Toul, there are few recognisable details. The bridge and the indication of water in the centre, and on the left, suggest the river Moselle or the canal that runs into the river at Toul, but the motifs are not significant.

There exists another, almost identical gouache study for this composition (Hôtel Drouot, 13 June 1994, lot 14). This work, along with the present gouache, was used for a finished, very similar painting, known now only in a photograph.[1]

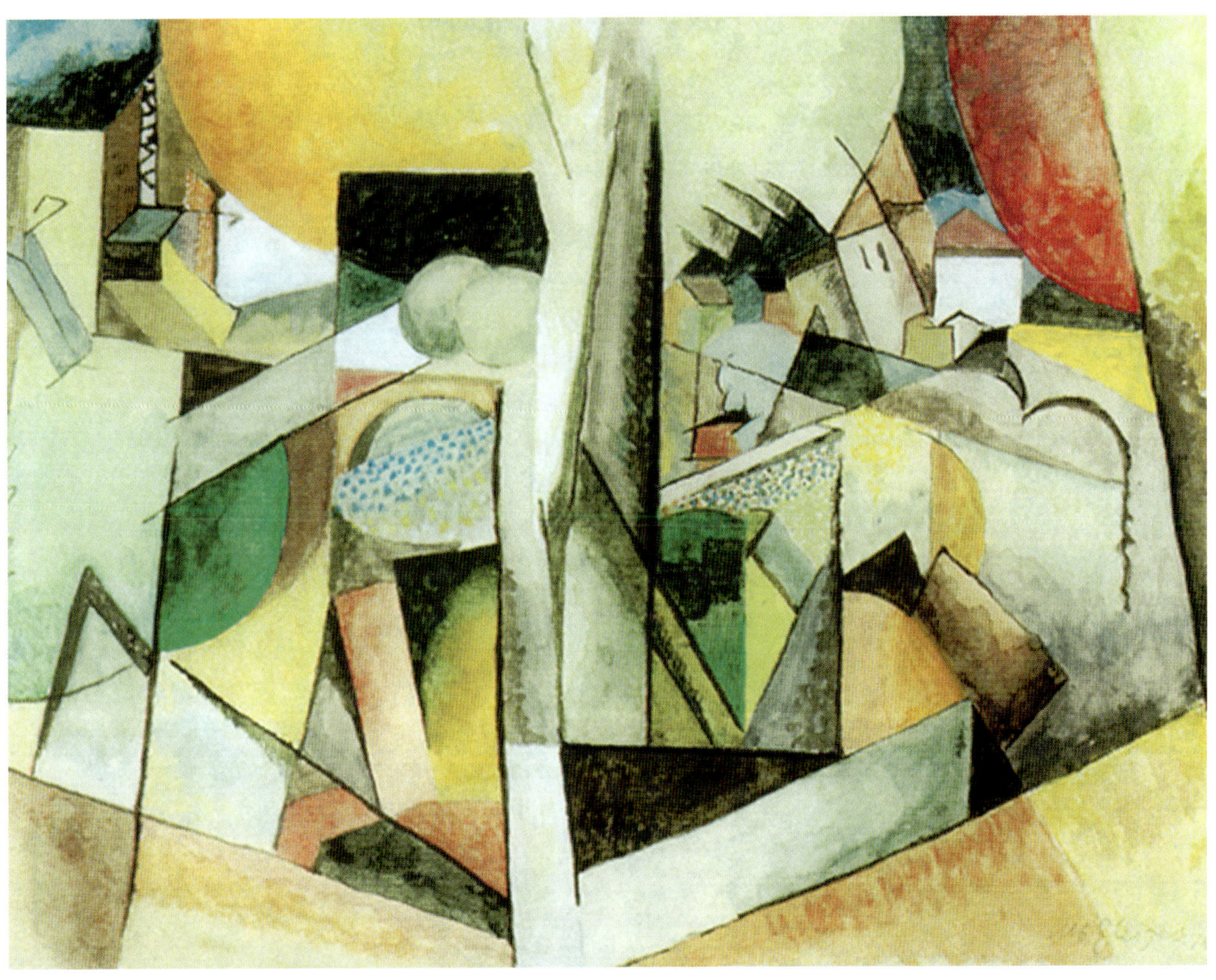

81

ALBERT GLEIZES 1881–1953

Figure with Buildings in the City of Toul, 1914

Pen and black ink, 24 × 17.5 cm

Signed, dated and annotated: *Toul 14 AlbGleizes*; and (indistinctly): *a Boiseo* ... (?)

LITERATURE: Johnson (1991), no.11 , ill. p. 51; Briend (2001), no.63

Following his posting to Toul in August 1914, Gleizes was put in charge of entertaining the troops. This role, which saved him from serving at the front, left him ample time to make drawings in pen and ink, pencil and gouache. Although these always began with a landscape or a sitter, he increasingly submerged his subject under a framework of lines, shapes and colours that gave the finished work an appearance of near abstraction. This striking image, like several of Gleizes' drawings from this period, is drawn with an arrangement of curves and straight lines that divide the surface into simple, strongly outlined shapes. There is a close resemblance to the technique of etching used in a print titled *La ville de Toul*[1] and a more general resemblance to the composition of the print. However, the etching and the related drawings are unambiguous views of a town, whereas the present drawing represents the figure of a man, seated at a table and holding a smoking pipe in his left hand. The wedge-shaped buildings in upper left, seen from a high vantage point, are perhaps the fortifications of Toul.

The same reduction of detail to a minimum, and the same division of the surface into jagged shapes, are found in the one major painting undertaken by Gleizes during his period at Toul. The *Portrait of an Army Doctor* (Salomon R. Guggenheim Museum, New York) is based on a series of drawings similar to this work. The lines that slice across the portrait of the doctor divide the surface into different coloured units. Here in the present drawing the difference between the adjoining shapes, created by the intersection of the straight lines, is defined by a strong contrast of black and white. Initially Gleizes drew his composition with a relatively light pen line, shaded with small touches of ink, but then went over the parts of the composition with dense, compacted lines. The result is a harmonious arrangement of shapes, tones and lines that comes close to concealing the subject of the drawing.

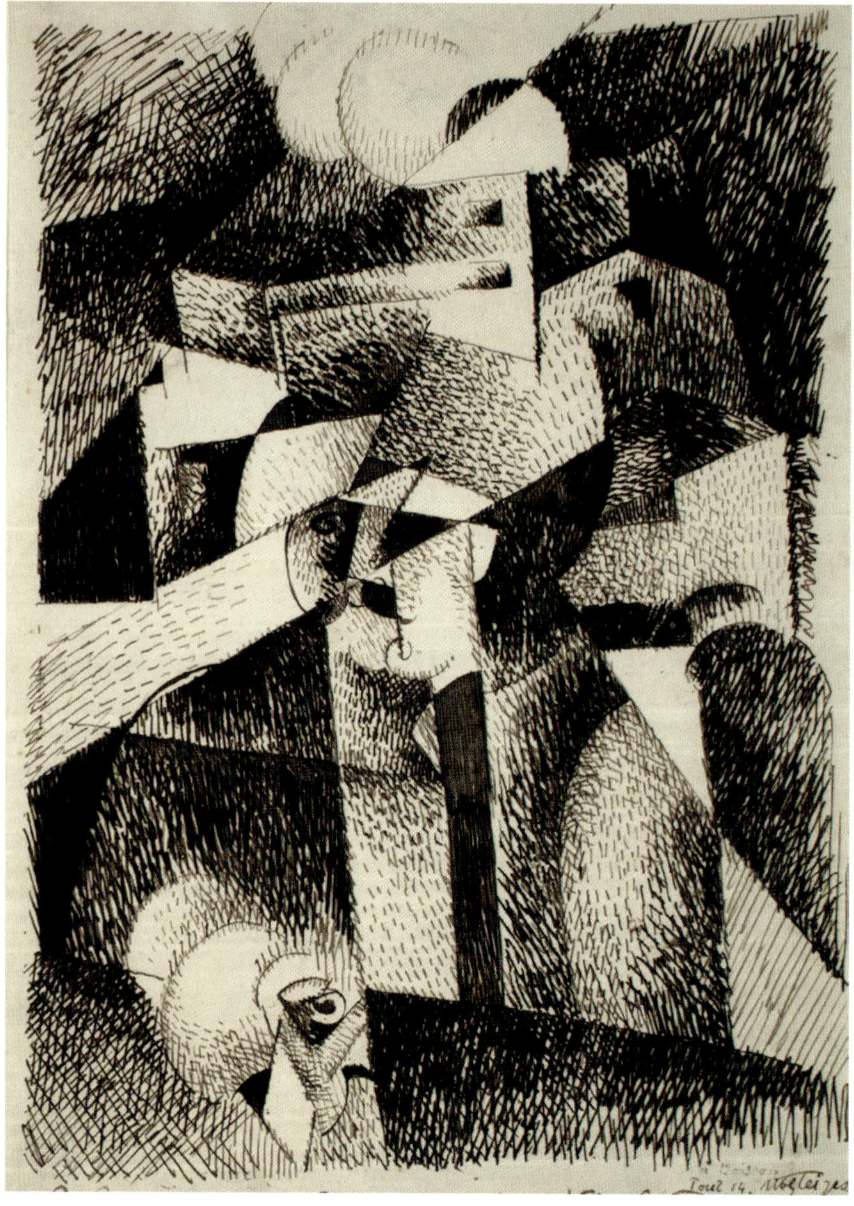

82

ALBERT GLEIZES 1881–1953

Toul, Landscape, 1914

Watercolour and bodycolour on buff card, 35 × 27.5 cm

Signed and dated: *Alb Gleizes / 14*

PROVENANCE: Raymond Vincent; private collection, Paris

LITERATURE: Varichon (forthcoming)

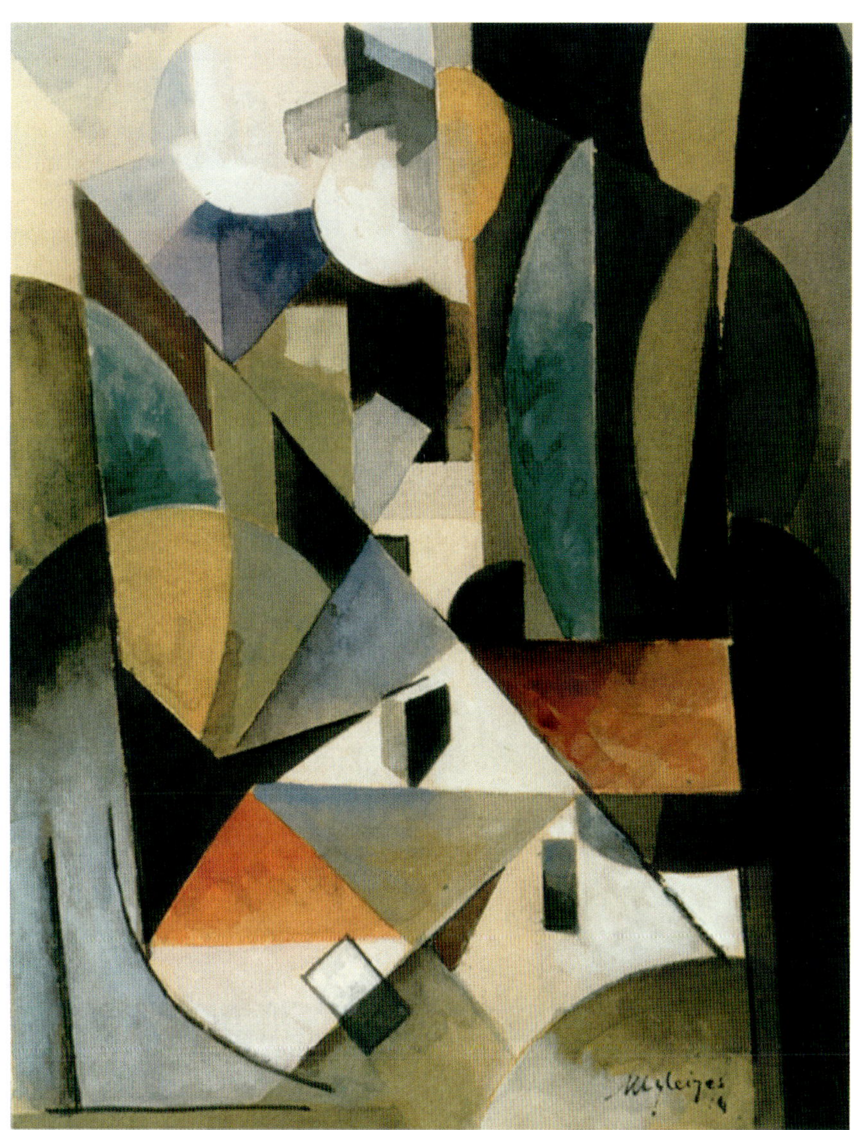

As Gleizes arrived in Toul in August 1914, he must have executed this gouache between August and the end of that year. In view of the extreme abstraction of the image, it may have been composed towards the end of that time as his work evolved towards the abstract compositions of 1915. It is closely related to a painting of 1916, formerly in the collection of Mr and Mrs Randall Schapiro in Chicago[1] and to a composition dated 1916 (Columbus Museum of Art, Ohio). Despite the date, however, this work must have originated in 1914–15 during Gleizes' months in Toul.

The pattern of straight lines, right angles and round shapes does not allow the subject to be identified easily. The circles in the upper part of the composition may suggest clouds, however, while the more rectangular elements lower down might refer to buildings. Yet any reading of the image as a view of nature is made difficult by the emphatic lines crossing the composition. These fragment the surface and act as a barrier to understanding the work as anything but a formal pattern of colour and shapes.

83

ALBERT GLEIZES 1881–1953

Portrait of Igor Stravinsky, 1914

Gouache and black ink on paper, 29 × 24.5 cm

Signed and dated: *Albert Gleizes / 14*

PROVENANCE: Georges Duhamel, Paris; private collection, France

LITERATURE: Varichon (1998), no.457; Briard (2001), no.49

It is not known for certain where or when Gleizes first met Stravinsky, although the men moved in similar circles and had a number of friends in common, notably Cocteau and Picasso. In 1913 both Stravinsky and Gleizes contributed to Canudo's Cubist review *Montjoie*, although Stravinsky's long absences in Switzerland would have limited the occasions for contact. The present portrait must have been made in the summer of 1914, after Stravinsky had returned to Paris for the opening of *Le Rossignol* at the Paris Opéra on 26 May. An earlier preparatory drawing is dated June 1914 and a large oil sketch, whose whereabouts are now unknown, is said to have been inscribed with a reference to Petrushka which was running at the Opéra in May and June.[1]

The sequence of studies for this portrait, illustrated in Anne Varichon's *Catalogue raisonné* of Gleizes' work,[2] shows a distinct development from the first, more representational study to the fragmented and abstracted image in the final painting (Museum of Modern Art, New York). In the first studies of the full-length figure the composer is shown clearly holding a sheet of paper in his right hand and a cane in his left. As the subject developed the paper became detached, the cane disappeared and the figure was reduced to a rigid kite shape, still recognisable by the black of his jacket and the buttons on his shirt. In this study the sheet of paper is inscribed with a few lines of musical notation, written on the picture surface in a classic Cubist blurring between the object represented and its representation. This study is almost identical to the finished painting and must have been made late in the preparatory process.

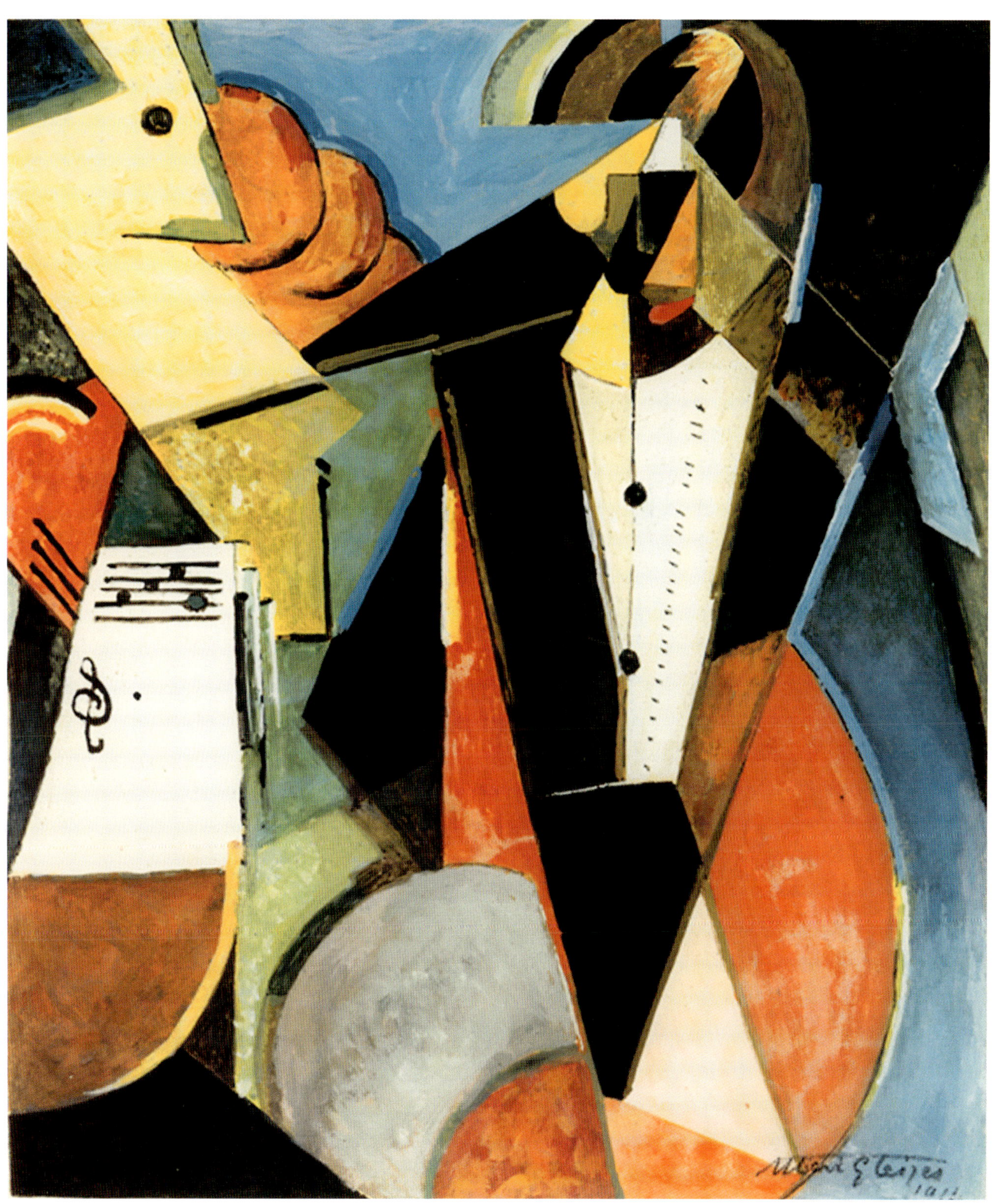

84

JACQUES VILLON 1875–1963

Monsieur Duchamp reading, 1913

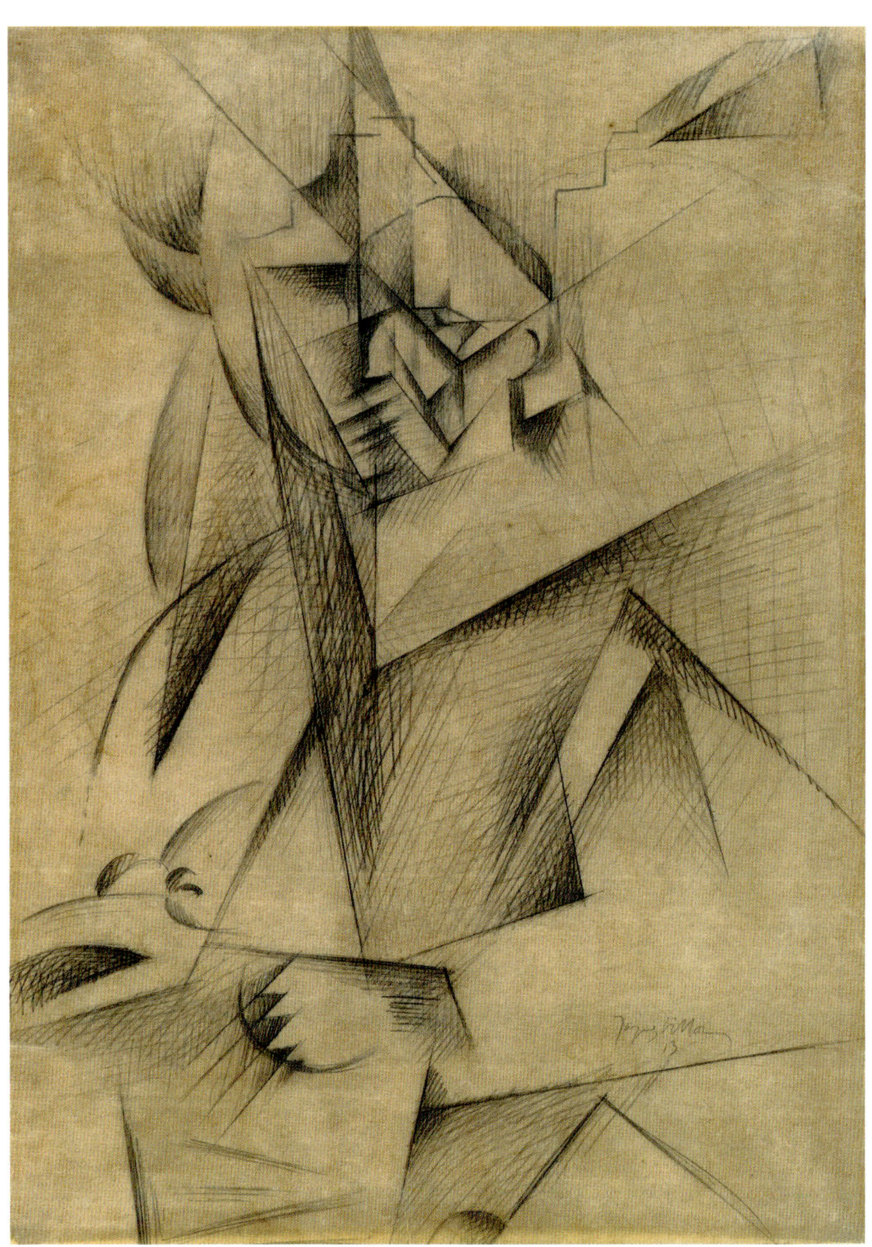

Pencil on paper, float mounted, 55.9 × 40.6 cm

PROVENANCE: Francey and Dr Martin L. Gecht, Chicago; Christie's, New York, 3 May 2006, lot 168

LITERATURE: McCullagh (2003–4), p.151, no.124, ill.; Silver (2008), no.48

Jacques Villon's first etching, made at the age of 16, was a portrait of his father, Justin-Isidore Duchamp – a notary at Blainville-Crevon in Normandy, where Villon spent his childhood. Over the following 30 years Duchamp *père* appeared in many of his son's etchings, drawings and paintings. The present drawn portrait, a related oval painting of 1913 (private collection, Paris) and a drypoint etching [cat.79], are all in the style of geometric Cubism that developed in Villon's art in 1912–13. The strong triangular shapes that fragment the forms like a prism appeared in his art after he had read Leonardo's account of how form is transmitted to the eye by means of a pyramid of lines. There exists a drawing related to his etched portrait of Félix Barré (Philadelphia Museum of Art) in which the distance of the sitter from the artist is established through a dense arrangement of lines radiating from a central focal point. Leonardo's theory did not lead Villon to adopt the Renaissance practice of creating the appearance of space beyond the picture plane; instead it allowed him to introduce allusions to the third dimension that respected the flatness of his canvas or paper.

Following Villon's practice, it seems that the oval painting of 1913 was made first and the etching [cat.79] was based on it. The present drawing was probably made as a study for the oval painting. It may not have been drawn from life, but rather developed from a more naturalistic portrait of his father, seated in a green armchair reading a paper (Musée des Beaux-Arts, Rouen). The Rouen painting also seems to be a precursor to the strongly coloured, highly fragmented painted portrait of the elder Duchamp in the current exhibition [cat.78] that is probably contemporary with the drawing, but that develops the Rouen painting and the present drawing's compositions into new and ambitious directions.

85

PABLO PICASSO 1881–1973

Woman with a Zither, 1912–14

Graphite on white paper, 64 × 47 cm

Signed on verso

PROVENANCE: Galerie Louise Leiris (Kahnweiler), Paris; G. David Thompson, Pittsburgh; Galerie Beyeler, Basel; Waddington & Tooth Galleries, London; Mr and Mrs Ahmet Ertegun

LITERATURE: Zervos (1932–78), vol.29, no.140; Daix and Rosselet (1979), p.137; Johnson (1991), no.38, ill. p. 105

In 1912, as so-called Analytic Cubism gave way to Synthetic Cubism, Picasso's compositions became simpler and more geometric. Along with Braque, he inserted printed materials into his compositions and eliminated the illusion of depth that had survived residually in his first Cubist works. References to the natural world were reduced to a few token marks and, although Picasso never abandoned the idea of representation, many of his works between 1912 and 1914, including the present drawing, appear at first glance to be wholly abstract. Only a few vestigial traces of a woman holding a stringed instrument allow this drawing to be identified as a representation of a musician. In other respects, too, it is an opaque image, particularly by comparison with Picasso's *Old Guitarist* of 1903–4 (Art Institute of Chicago), whose wretched condition evokes a sympathetic response in the viewer. *Woman with a Zither*, by comparison, suggests nothing about the condition of its subject. She is deprived of identity or personality, and the severe reduction of the image gives no idea of the artist's feelings and intentions.

This drawing is a study for a painting of 1914, now in the Kunstmuseum in Basel. The pattern of straight lines with a few curves that join but rarely cross is repeated in the painting, while the white of the paper anticipates the white background of the finished work. The artist has made extensive use of a ruler and strengthened the lines with short, free-hand strokes in the drawing. Initially he followed this arrangement in the painting, but made many revisions on the canvas before completing it.

In neither the drawing nor the painting is it clear what instrument the woman holds. It could be a mandolin or guitar, although there is no indication of a neck, and the position of the subject's arms (reversed in the painting) supports the idea that it is an instrument of the zither type.

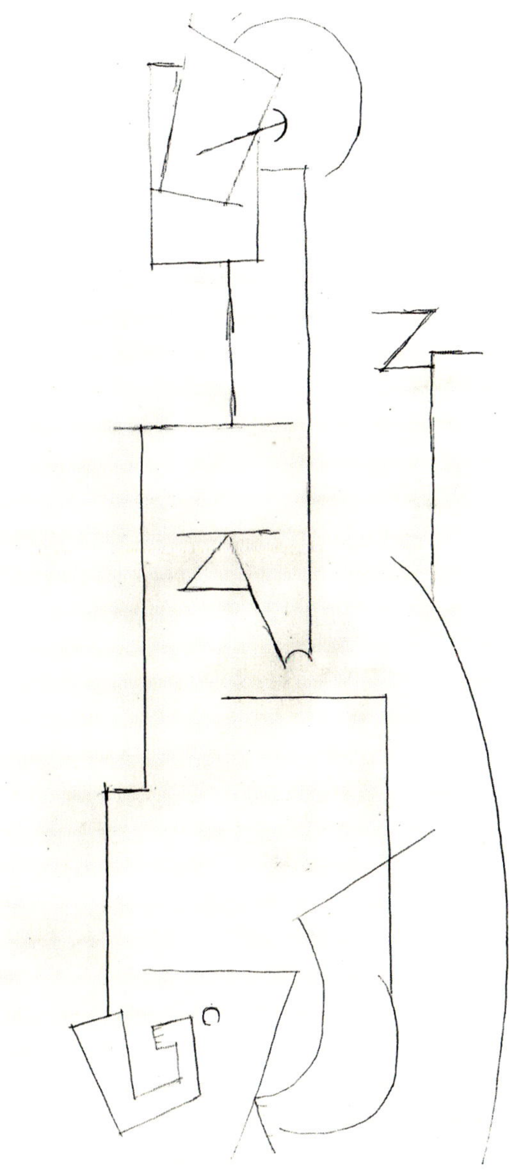

86

MARCEL GROMAIRE 1892–1971

The Relief Column, 1916

Pen and black ink over pencil on off-white paper, 27.7 × 20.8 cm

Signed and dated: *Gromaire 1916*

LITERATURE: Art in America (1977), ill. p.28; *Art News*, no.76, March 1977, p.88; Paris (1980), no.212, ill.; Sobel (1986), no.19, ill. p.9; Johnson (1987), no.1, ill.; Johnson (2007), no.2, ill., p.21

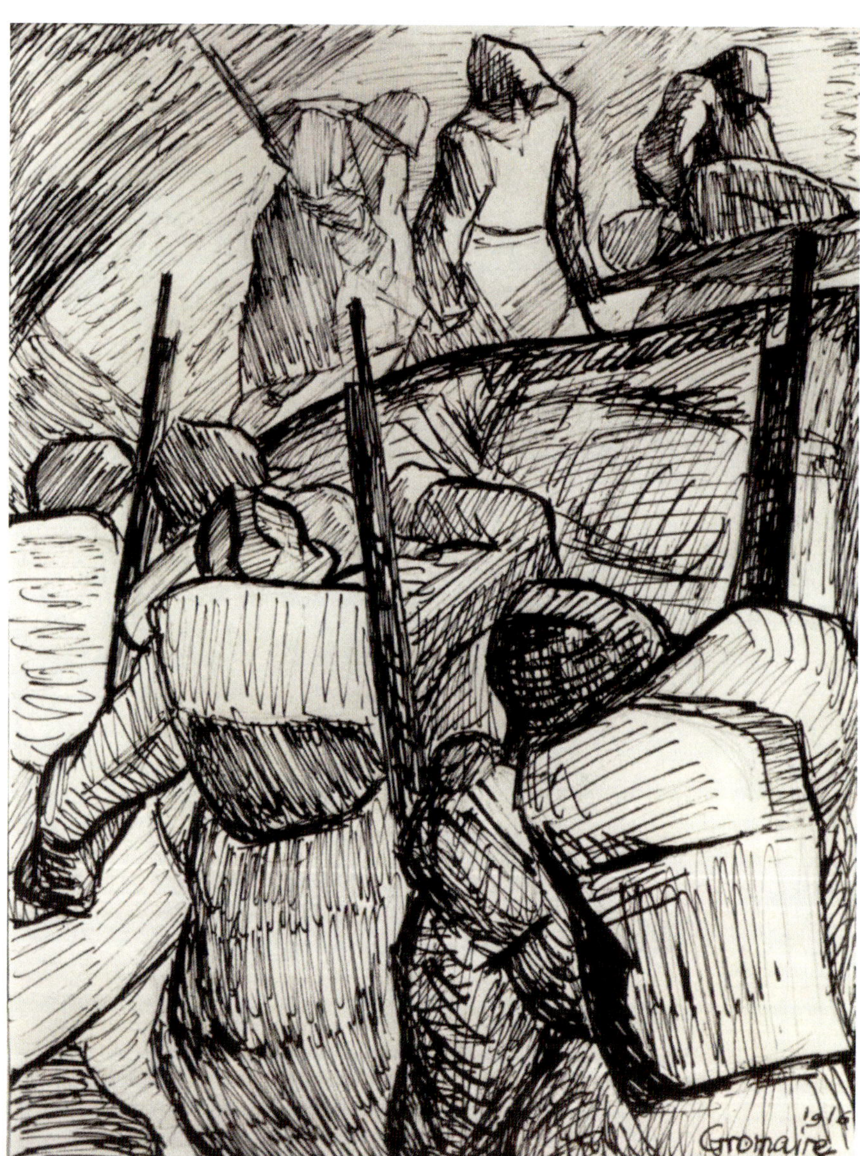

In 1911 Marcel Gromaire, having recently abandoned plans for a legal career, showed six works at the celebrated Salon des Indépendants. Le Fauconnier had recently become head of the Hanging Committee at the Salon, and for the first time the Cubists were able to exhibit together in one room, the famous room no.41. Gromaire, aged 19, thus found himself within a circle of artists, including Gleizes and Metzinger, who were at the forefront of an entirely new approach to painting. However, though he continued to frequent the studios of Montparnasse, including the Académie de la Palette, of which Le Fauconnier had become head in 1912, he retained an independence of outlook – influenced by no-one, as he later recalled, except by Matisse as a draughtsman, and by the enduring example of Cézanne and the old masters.

Gromaire was called up for military service in 1913, choosing to be based in Lille, in his native north, and was happy to find himself far away from the 'aesthetic chatter' of Paris. 'Tout changea', however, as he laconically wrote, and by the end of 1914 he was engaged in the infantry on the Western front. The strongly executed black lines of the *Relief Column* of 1916 powerfully evoke his experience of war. The heroism of Roger de La Fresnaye's pre-war *Cuirassier* [cat.60] has no place in this image of dogged endurance. Neither did Gromaire record the day to day experience of trench warfare; this toiling advance of burdened figures has a timeless gravity, enhanced by the transformation of the sou'westers of the smaller figures above into something that nearly resembles the garb of the 'weepers' sculpted on a fifteenth-century Burgundian tomb.

87

MARCEL GROMAIRE 1892–1971

War, 1924

Pen and black ink on buff paper, 32.5 × 24.8 cm

Signed and dated: *Gromaire 1924*

LITERATURE: Johnson (2007), no.9, ill., p.35

Often associated with the international postwar movement later known as Expressionism, a label he always rejected, Gromaire never abandoned his commitment to considerations of form. His powerful 1924 drawing *War* is the only known study for the painting of the same title (Musée de l'Art Moderne de la Ville de Paris) of 1925. The men's helmets and armoured garb give the soldiers a mechanical appearance, although their physical closeness and a certain droop in the pose retain the potential for pathos. Gromaire again seems to draw on the classic language of the past – perhaps that of the artist so admired by Seurat, Piero della Francesca.

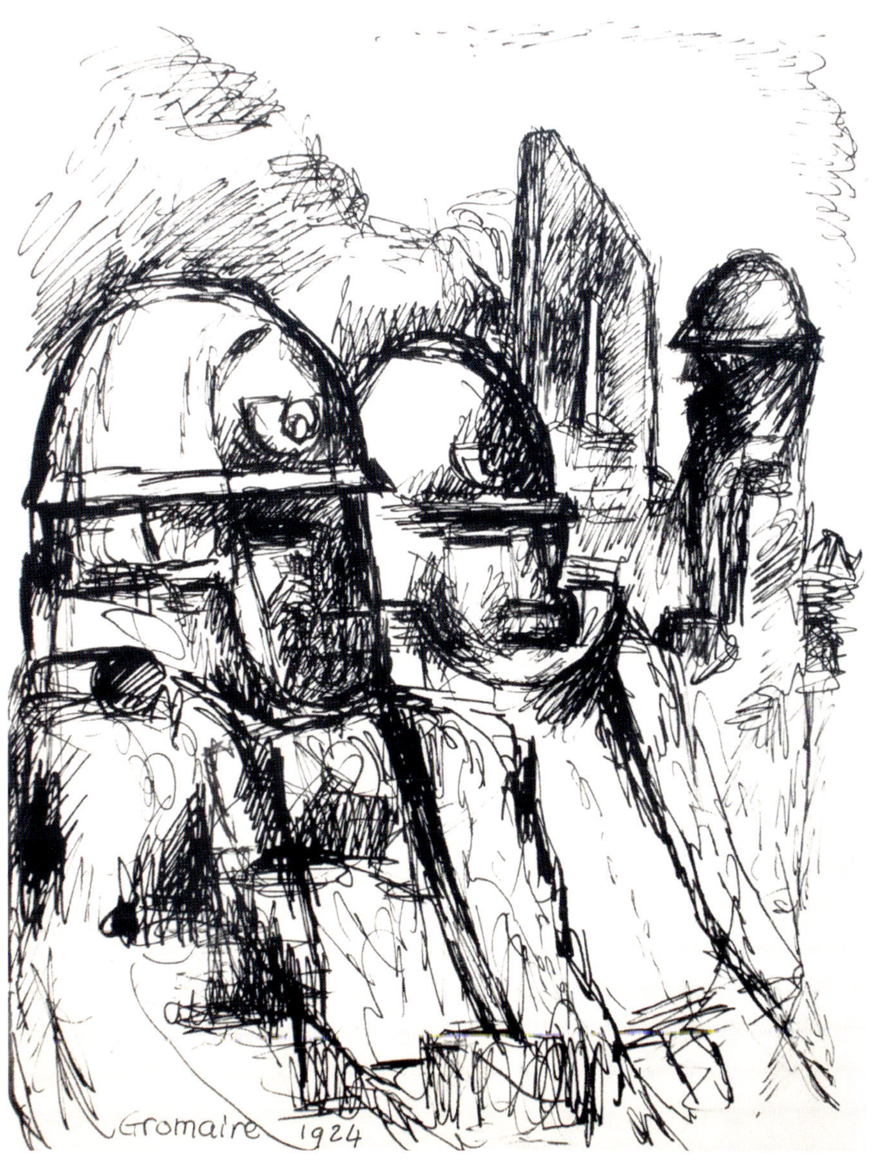

88

ROGER DE LA FRESNAYE 1885–1925

Composition with Drum and Trumpet, 1917–19

Watercolour with brush and india ink, 26 × 20 cm

LITERATURE: Johnson (1991), no.20, ill. p.69

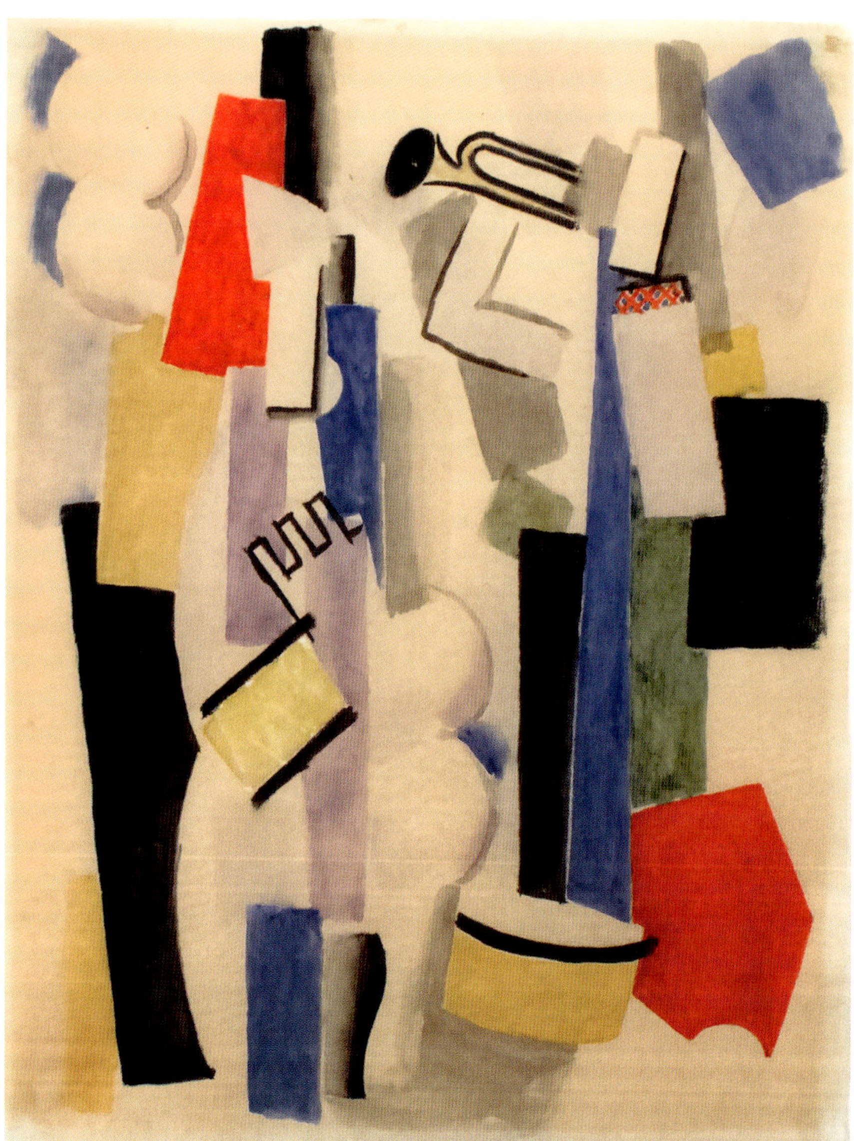

A less abstract, uncoloured version of this composition[1] was used as one of six illustrations in the first published edition of Jean Cocteau's *Tambour*, issued by the Fata Morgana imprint in 1989. The text was written by Cocteau between 1917 and 1919 to accompany a series of illustrations by La Fresnaye. The present drawing is probably contemporary with two other almost identical drawings, one dated (1917),[2] the other dated January 1918, formerly in the Winston collection,[3] all drawn perhaps in response to his first conversations with Cocteau about the project in the previous November. Writing the text, however, gave Cocteau 'a great deal of trouble' and, as La Fresnaye could not begin the illustrations until he had received the text, progress on the drawings was delayed by over a year. In 1919 La Fresnaye seems to have begun work, but in June he wrote to Cocteau to say he had been much hampered by illness.[4]

How much La Fresnaye completed is difficult to say. None of his illustrations has been identified, and those used in the 1989 edition were selected somewhat randomly from his surviving drawings. There exist several drawings from 1917–20 with themes that relate to Cocteau's text: drums,[5] the American intervention in the war[6] and Paris.[7] But works such as this would have been familiar to Cocteau, who clearly composed his text in keeping with La Fresnaye's thoughts about the war. It is not unlikely, however, that two or three of the known drawings, may have been made for the book. A highly abstracted version, dated 1919, inscribed with the letters PAR (for Paris), seems a possible candidate, [8] but there is as yet no firm evidence.

Comparison with the drawing used in *Tambour* makes it clear that the present watercolour represents a soldier looking down at a rectangle held in his left hand, perhaps a sheet of music, while he carries a drum at his waist. In the uncoloured drawing the trumpet appears somewhat disembodied on the left, while in the watercolour the instrument is played by a second figure on the right. La Fresnaye may have been thinking of the trumpeters and drummer who feature, more realistically, in his *Artillery* (Metropolitan Museum of Art, New York), painted in 1911.

89

FERNAND LÉGER 1881–1955

Factory, 1918

Gouache, 23 × 31 cm
Initialled and dated: F.L. 18
PROVENANCE: Galerie Louise Leiris (Kahnweiler), Paris
LITERATURE: Johnson (1991), no.23

This image of the factory, dated 1918, could be seen as the very archetype of Léger's take on this theme in this period. In spite of the horrors of the war, including many that were directly caused by the use of hideous machinery, Léger pursued a positive language of machine-made form. This picture, however, which combines figurative and abstract elements, though austere in colour, suggests a harmonious balance between the orders, mechanical and human. The staircase on the left translates (as staircases often did in those years) into abstract form on the right. The figure descending the staircase is not a robot. Without the wholly geometric form seen in Léger's slightly later and more stylised work, by means of soft shading the figure seems to retain an autonomy, even a sense of purpose. The left side of the picture is rich in atmosphere, animated, suggestive in the manner of a film still, while on the right elements break up, as cylinders and circles embody the rhythmic motion of wheels and pistons. Yet the two parts are held in a classic balance by means of strong vertical and horizontal emphases.

The work offers an interesting variant on the theme explored in *Dans l'usine* (1918; formerly Yves Saint-Laurent collection). There, in a brilliantly coloured composition, only the mechanical components appear, integrated in a complex and seemingly autonomous configuration of contrasting forms.

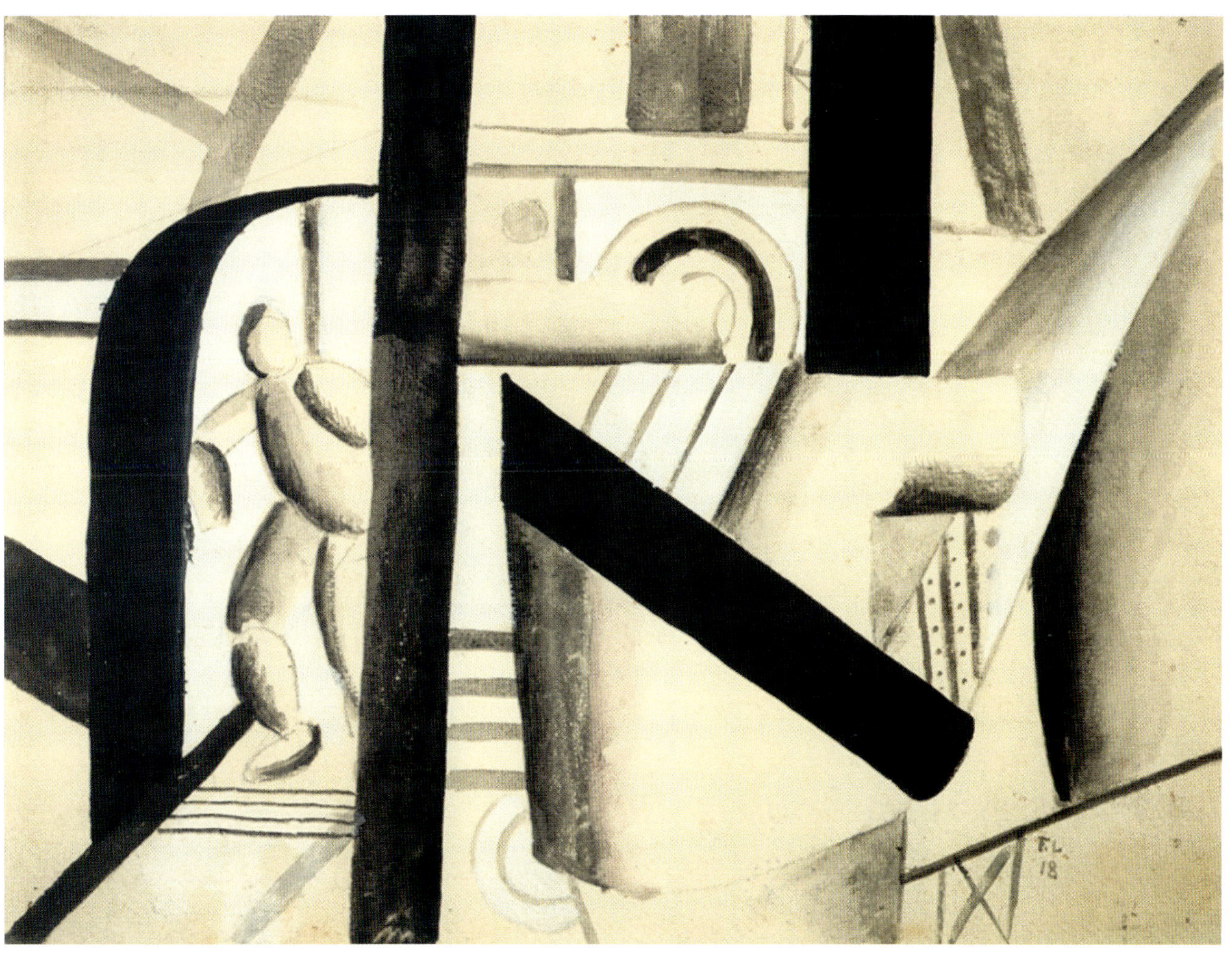

90

JEAN METZINGER 1883–1956

Woman with Earrings, ca.1919

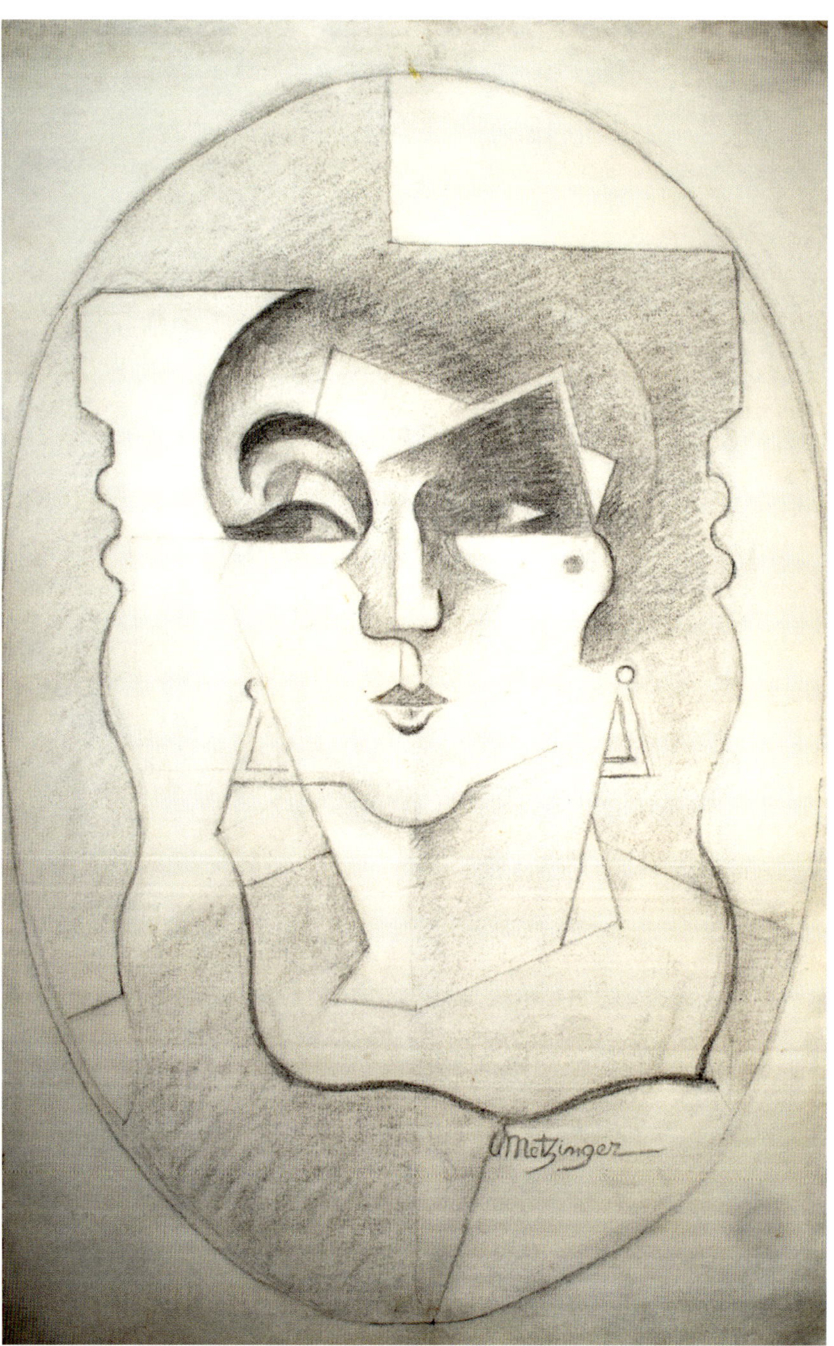

Charcoal drawing in oval form, 46.5 × 31.2 cm

Signed lower right: (?J) Metzinger

LITERATURE: Johnson (1964), ill. p.1; New York (1967), ref. 67, 1322; Johnson (1991), no.30, ill. p.89

Although Mme Metzinger, the artist's widow, in about 1960 dated this drawing to 1912, it has subsequently been dated by Johnson to about 1919 and compared with two oval paintings and two other oval drawings.[1]

As Moser has pointed out, the oval format does not appear in his work before 1918.[2] The decorative character of Metzinger's art at this time relates perhaps to a wider response in Cubist circles to developments in theatrical design. On 26 May 1917, shortly after the première in Paris of Diaghilev's ballet *Parade* (a collaboration between Eric Satie, Jean Cocteau, Leonide Massine and Picasso), Metzinger commented to his dealer, Léonce Rosenberg, 'It's the first time Cubism had had to face the crowd, and it emerged unharmed from the encounter'.[3] The ballet was not a success, however, and it is not suggested here that the lighthearted, somewhat brittle *chic* of this drawing was in any way related to that event. Yet the face has something of Cocteau's arch elegance, while the overlapping planes, the asymmetry of the shading and the playful reversals of the baluster-like forms contribute to a decorative effect not altogether unlike Picasso's essentially Cubist work for the theatre at that time.

91

JEAN METZINGER 1883–1956

Landscape, ca.1919

Oil on canvas, 92 × 60 cm

Signed: *Metzinger*

PROVENANCE: Howard Warren collection, Chicago

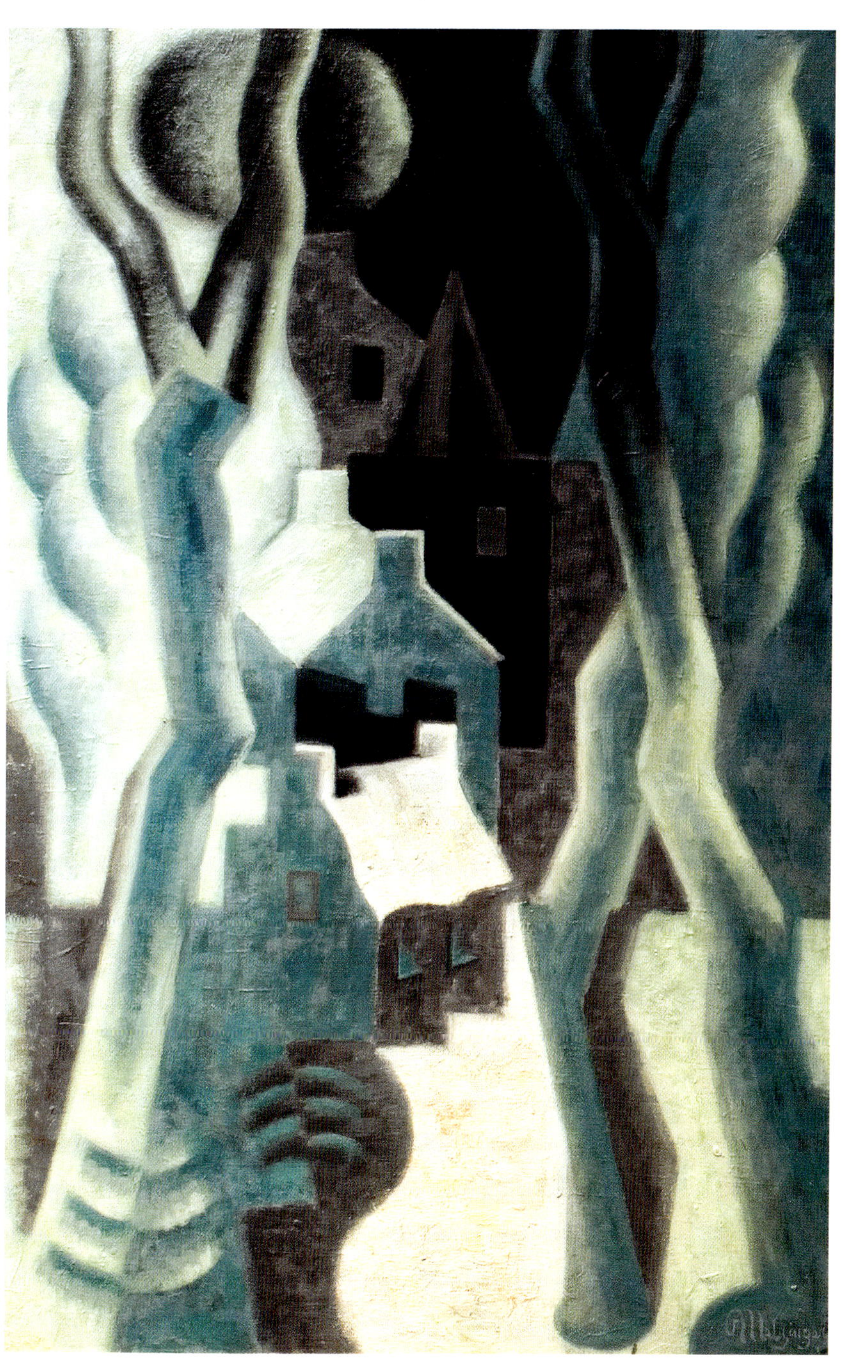

Landscape of this type was for a time a recurring theme in Metzinger's work. The winding downhill road recalls the manner of some of Cézanne's early landscapes, made while working with Pissarro at Auvers, in which the solid geometric forms of buildings are offset by the closely pressing, organic forms of trees. It is likely that Pissarro absorbed this kind of composition from Corot, who often used this type of classically satisfying arrangement.

This, though, is a nocturnal and faintly dream-like scene, fitfully lit from the front by two unidentifiable sources. The buildings are minimally described, though the extensive use of white succeeds in giving them a feeling of volume. The extended use of white overall may be a response to Cézanne's own comparable use of the colour, so amply seen in his *Study of Pines Trees* [cat.53]. Here the other forms, including the trees, are faintly ambiguous, but with a lyrical freedom that is matched by the colour. The undulating forms to the left and right serve to frame the scene, comparable with the similarly placed and purely decorative elements in *The Yellow Feather* [cat.72], a work which in this respect, as well as in its oblique pose, may derive, albeit unconsciously, from one of Cézanne's portraits of his wife Hortense. We might remember that Metzinger, like Gleizes and Le Fauconnier (and differing in that respect from Braque and Picasso), never ceased to find an absolute continuity between Cézanne's work and the innovations of his own generation.

92

FERNAND LÉGER 1881–1955

Study for 'The City', 1919

Gouache, 38.3 × 28 cm

Initialled, dated and annotated: *F.L. 19 étude pour la ville*

PROVENANCE: Galerie Louise Leiris (Kahnweiler), no.017179/30812

LITERATURE: Johnson (1991), no.24, ill. p.77

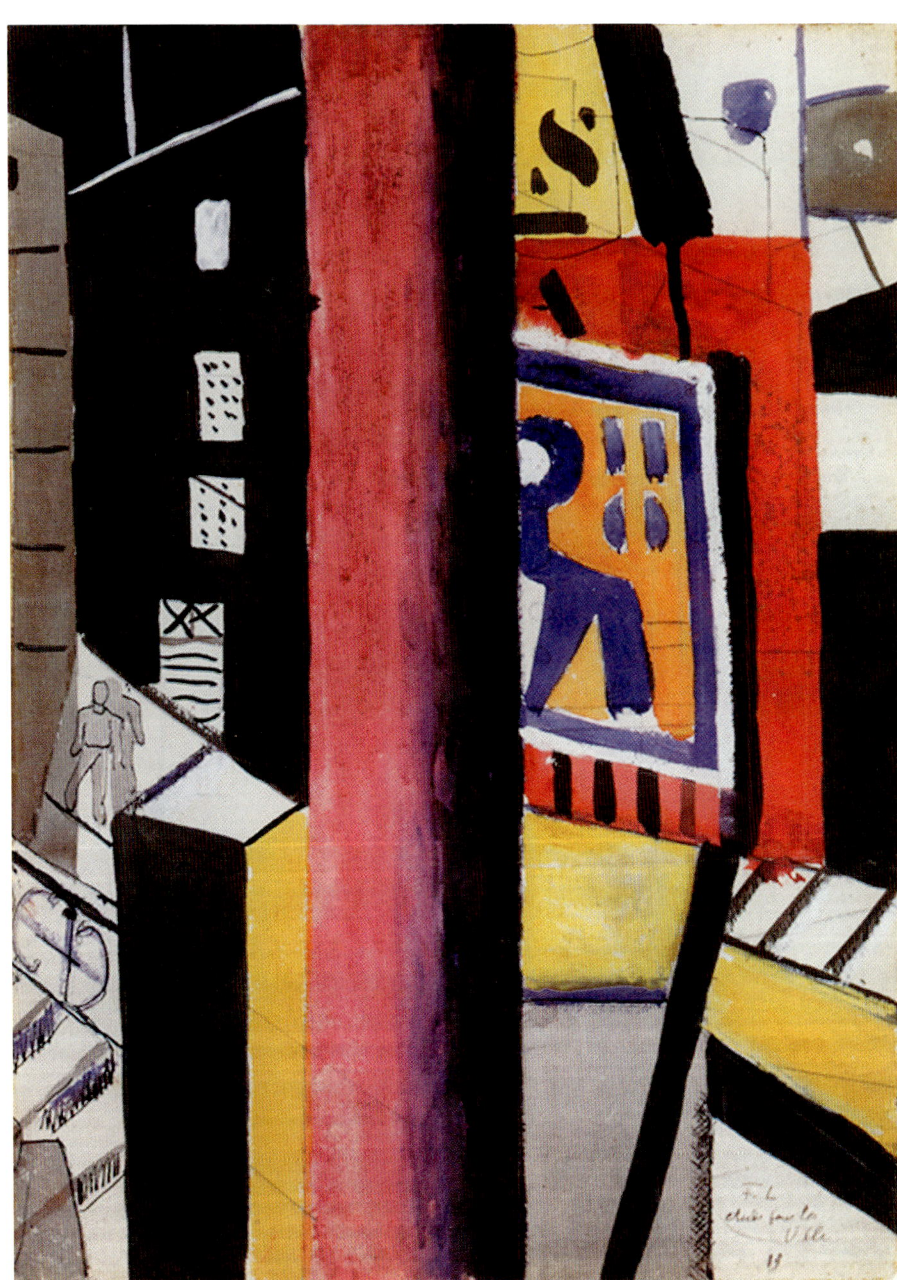

When Léger returned from the front in 1917, he took up painting again and began to explore the subject of the modern city in a series of brightly coloured compositions that evolved out of the flat, fragmented manner of Synthetic Cubism. This gouache, dated 1919, is a study for the right-hand side of *La Ville*, the most ambitious and elaborate of these paintings (Philadelphia Museum of Art), also completed in 1919. He prepared *La Ville* through a sequence of preparatory studies, including a companion gouache for the left-hand side (Musée Fernand Léger, Biot) and a large oil painting of the whole composition (Museum of Modern Art, New York).

Léger described *La Ville* as a 'plastic revolution', by which he meant that it was 'composed exclusively with pure, flat colours' while indicating 'depth and dynamism' without light and shadow.[1] The strong black, yellow and red in this study and the somewhat different colours used in the finished painting are applied in flat areas of overlapping planes, although the post that divides the composition vertically is still conventionally shaded. The elements in the drawing and in the painting are nearly identical, but they are treated in a slightly more descriptive manner in the study, which more clearly represents a city at night, brightly lit, with two figures dwarfed by the buildings. In the painting the suggestion of billboards, lights, smoke, stairs and girders is reduced to circles and flat shapes with straight sides and sharp angles, evoking the experience of city life without representing it from any particular point of view.

93

ALBERT GLEIZES 1881–1953

Composition, 1920

Mixed media on canvas, 89 × 72 cm

Signed and dated: *AlbGleizes 20*

PROVENANCE: Beaudoin de Grunne, Brussels; La Galerie Monique de Groote, Paris

LITERATURE: Varichon (1998), vol.I, no.936, ill., p.322; Massenet (1999), cover ill.

In the years following the First World War, Gleizes reached a point where he could eliminate all references to the subject that might conflict with 'pictorial expression'. This did not mean that he invariably eradicated indications of natural forms; he reduced them to flat, brightly coloured shapes that interlocked with one another in a vivid, decorative harmony. Framing lines that surround the central motif with differently coloured strips are common in Gleizes' work from this period. On the right side of this image, painted in 1920, the colours tend to be dark; on the left side they are brighter. To the left of a central vertical division a strong blue dominates, while the right side is coloured with the hues of night. The central image, only partly bisected by this division, represents a central figure flanked symmetrically by figures on the left and right.

The subject becomes easier to identify through comparison with a series of compositions dating from 1920 to 1929 that appear to represent the Virgin with two unidentified companions (for example, see Varichon, no.946). In 1918 Gleizes had an intimation of his eventual conversion to Roman Catholicism, finding in religion the sense of organisation that he had imposed upon his art. Although he did not participate in the work of the Studios of Sacred Art, co-founded by Maurice Denis in 1919, he shared many of the formal and spiritual concerns that motivated Denis and his followers.

Anne Varichon's catalogue features an early photograph[1] showing *Composition* in an earlier state. The image was flatter, clearer and simpler before the artist reworked it, introducing additional forms and dots and creating a sense of relief along the edges of the step shapes at the centre and in the upper left. The image in its present state is more complex. It has a greater sense of shifting pattern, in keeping with Gleizes' theory of movement, published in 1923 in his defence of Cubism, *Painting and its Laws*. Gleizes also reworked a similar composition, *The Horsewoman* (on deposit at the Musée des Beaux-Arts, Rouen), first painted in 1920 but revised in 1923 with similar additions. The reworking on the present painting may date from the same time.

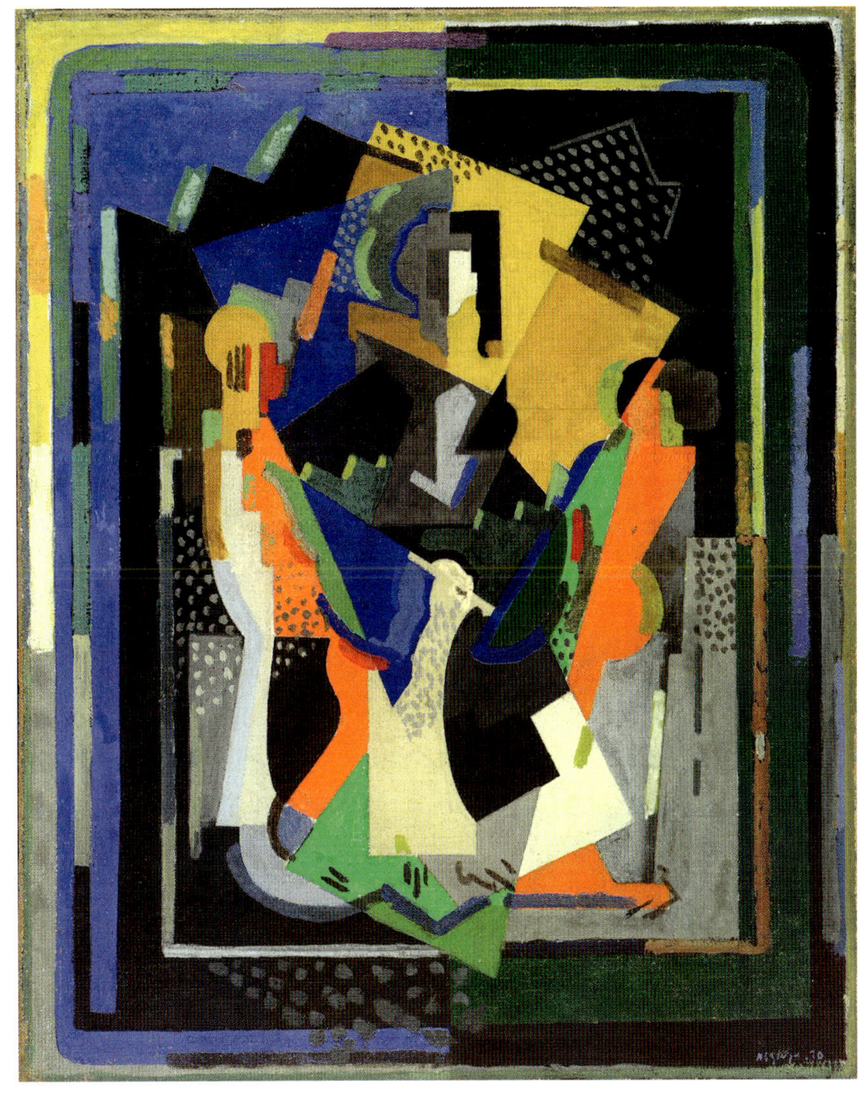

94

FERNAND LÉGER 1881–1955

Study for 'Le Grand Déjeuner', ca.1920

Pencil on off-white paper, 37 × 28.2 cm

Signed with initials, lower right: F.L.

PROVENANCE: André Lefèvre, Paris (Quatrième vente, André Lefèvre, 24 November 1967, no.29)

LITERATURE: Johnson (1991), no.26, ill. p.81

The notion of a return to classicism in the period after 1920, though variously interpreted, is generally associated with the work of a number of young artists who had been involved with Cubism. Léger, it seems, was not directly influenced by Greek and Roman art but responded to it indirectly through his admiration for artists for whom antiquity had been important, notably Poussin, David and Ingres. In the present study, the gesture of the young woman and the objects on the table suggest that it is a version of a classic nineteenth-century theme, *La Toilette*. It might be compared with *La Poudreuse* by Georges Seurat, another artist who had looked closely at ancient art and who had once observed that he would like to paint people as if they were figures on the Parthenon frieze.

This finely controlled drawing's composition was later to find its way into several paintings, including *Le Corsage Rouge*,[1] the slightly later *Nudes against a Red Ground* (Kunstmuseum, Basel) and, most obviously, into the *Grand Déjeuner* (Metropolitan, New York). All were works in which Léger engaged in an exchange with artists who were by then classics of the French tradition. He names them in a letter of 1922 as Renoir, Seurat, Ingres and David. Although Manet is not mentioned, Léger quite clearly evoked his *Olympia* in *Le corsage rouge* and in the *Grand déjeuner.*

This drawing, then, might be seen as a kind of *académie*, admittedly an odd one, in the classic French sense: a stock pose that might serve a number of separate purposes. But, like Seurat, Léger maintains a remoteness from his subject, both in this study, and in the paintings that draw on it, by composing this clearly recognisable figure of a young woman from a series of cones and spheres set against a grid. However, this refined drawing marks a distinct change in Léger's manner: the figure here has little of the hard-edged character of his earlier figures, composed of geometric elements. In the upper left rectangle we find something of the kind of gently modulated shading associated with Delaunay's use of colour (and maintained in the upper right of *Le Grand Déjeuner*, together with the little table and pots). The odd dislocation of the limbs, particularly striking in *Le Grand Déjeuner*, anticipates in this drawing some of the later inventions of Surrealism. However, the overall impression here, with the rounded forms of the figure evoking a sense of animation blowing from within, may have more in common with Picasso's classicising *Deux femmes courant sur une plage* (1922, Musée Picasso, Paris) than is apparent at first sight.

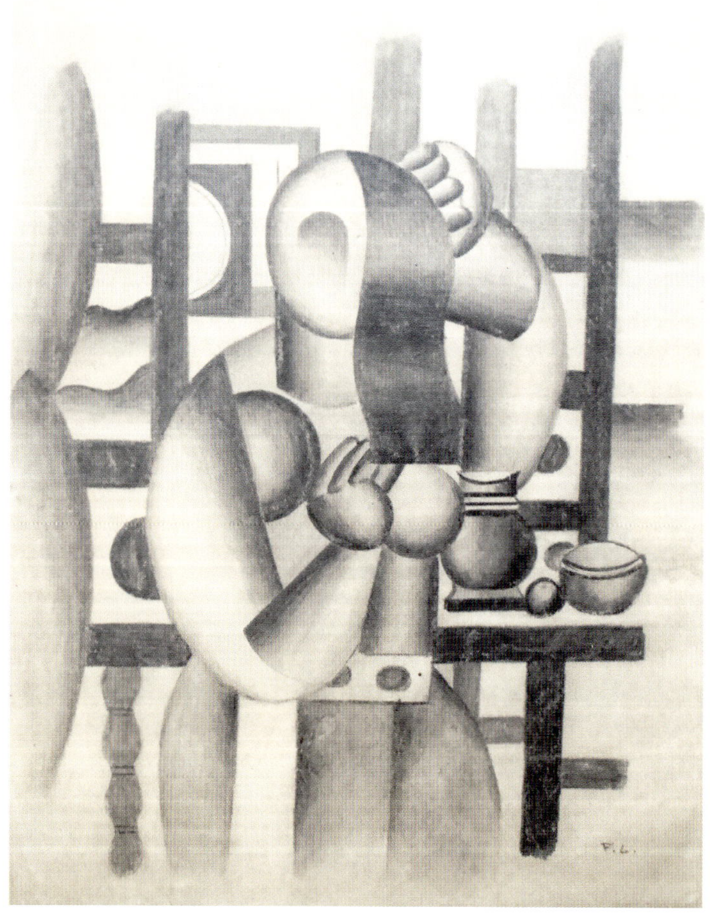

95

FERNAND LÉGER 1881–1955

Figures in a Landscape, 1921

Pencil on white paper, 37 × 26.5 cm

Initialled and dated: F.L. 21

Verso: a pencil sketch of figures in a landscape

LITERATURE: Johnson (1991), no.27, ill. p.83

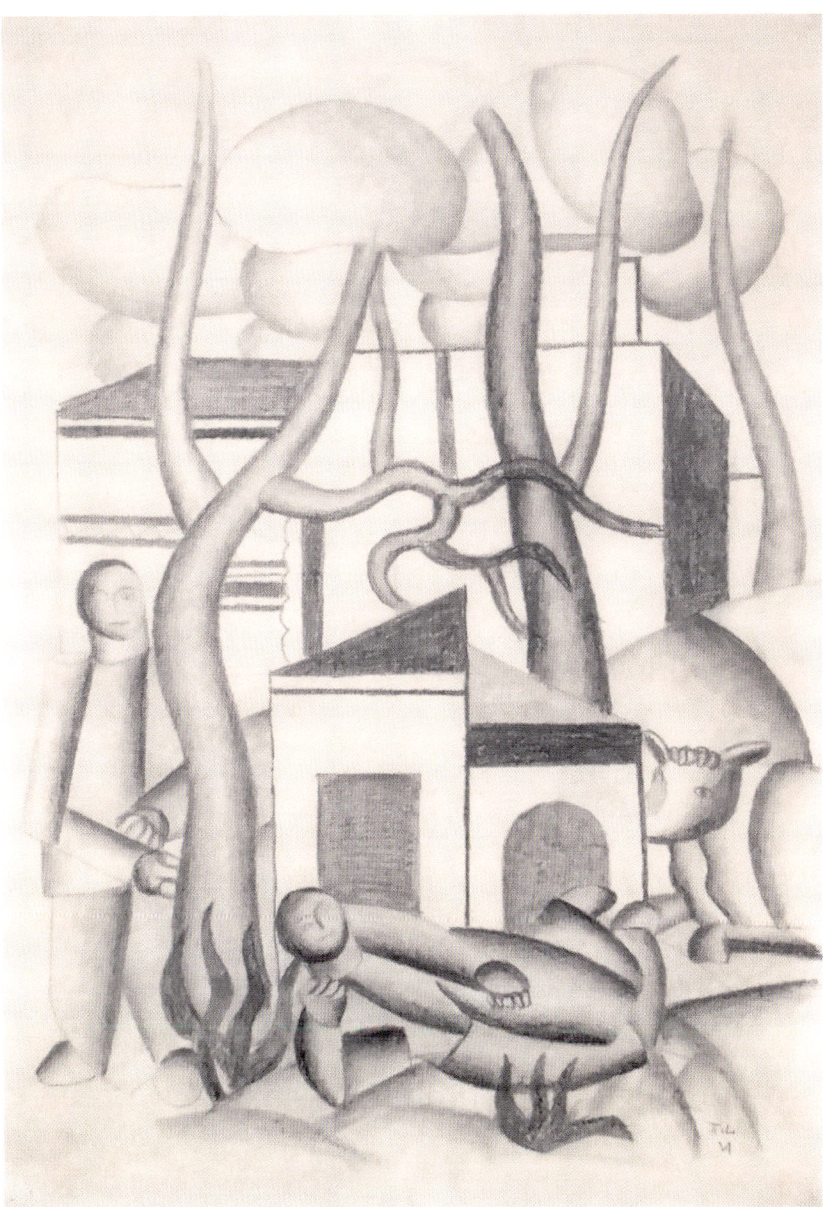

From 1918 onwards, the human figure became a major element in Léger's art. Alongside works of near abstraction, he took up several traditional subjects – nudes, mothers and children, figures in a landscape – that he drew and painted with a new simplicity. Whereas Cubism had originally fragmented the human figure to the point of dissolution, Léger now used the simplified forms of Cubism, along with the tubular shapes that he had introduced into his earliest Cubist works, to make his subjects recognisable.

The direction of his art towards a new humanism and legibility is evident in the present landscape, one of a sequence of stylised drawings and paintings titled 'paysages animés' ('animated landscapes') that he executed in 1921–22. These usually include two men, one of whom is seen reclining, fishing, standing or leaning against a cow. There is generally a farm animal in the composition and the figures face outwards, set against a background of trees and buildings. The figures, animals and trees are modelled with simple, rounded forms, contrasting with the severe geometry of the buildings – constructed from triangles and rectangles resembling toy bricks, with flat rectangular and arched openings.

The reclining man who appears here and in other works in this series suggests a kinship between himself and the world of nature. Women reclining in a landscape are more common in Western art than men, but there are notable exceptions. Samuel Palmer made use of a similar motif in a drawing that is executed in a similarly naïve manner.[1] There is no evidence that Léger had any knowledge of Palmer or his work, but both artists drew upon a pastoral tradition of idyllic imagery that celebrates the pleasures of the country. Léger, like Jean-François Millet, was born in rural Normandy and, again like Millet, may have turned to rustic themes through nostalgia for his childhood. Despite his commitment to the beauty of machines, there is an element of old-fashioned nature worship in Léger's work.

96

PABLO PICASSO 1881–1973

Study for 'Three Musicians', also known as The White Coffee Table (Le Guéridon Blanc), 1920

Gouache on brownish paper, 26.1 × 21 cm

Signed and dated: *Picasso 29-8-20*

PROVENANCE: R. Pellequer, Paris; Valentin Gallery, New York: Henry P. McIlhenny, Philadelphia; Mrs John Wintersteen, Villanova; Galerie Jan Krugier, Geneva

LITERATURE: Level (1928), p.58; Johnson (2004), p.30

In his book on Picasso of 1928, André Level called this work of 1920 *Le Guéridon Blanc* (*The White Coffee Table*).[1] Level's title is not unreasonable, as the drawing seems to represent a table with a baluster-shaped pedestal of a type that is recurrent in Picasso's art from *c.* 1917 to the early 1920s.[2] Picasso's pedestal tables usually support a still-life composition. In this case, the details are difficult to decipher although the white oblong with a blue extension could represent the guitar that figures frequently in his pictures of this type. It has been suggested that this is a study for the figure of Pierrot, seated on the right side of *Three Musicians* (Museum of Modern Art, New York), one of two closely linked works painted in 1921.[3] The similarities between the present study and the painting in New York are not immediately obvious although the stylistic links are clear enough. The flat areas of bright colour and fragmented shapes, juxtaposed like paper cut-outs, derive from Synthetic Cubism, but are clearer and simpler than they would have been in Picasso's earlier Cubist compositions.

The musician on the right of the painting has been identified as Picasso's friend, the poet and painter Max Jacob, dressed as a monk. Jacob introduced the artist to Guillaume Apollinaire who appears in the centre, dressed as Harlequin playing a guitar. Apollinaire had died in 1918, and it has been suggested that Picasso painted the *Three Musicians* in memory of their friendship. Perhaps this explains the areas of dense black in the present study and the painting that add a dark, elegiac note to the otherwise bright colours of both works.

The motif of a small coffee table on a tripod pedestal was taken up by Braque in 1922[4] and repeated by him more than a dozen times over the following nine years. The form and small size of the table allowed both artists to make still-life compositions in an upright format using a play of curves and contrasting rectangles.

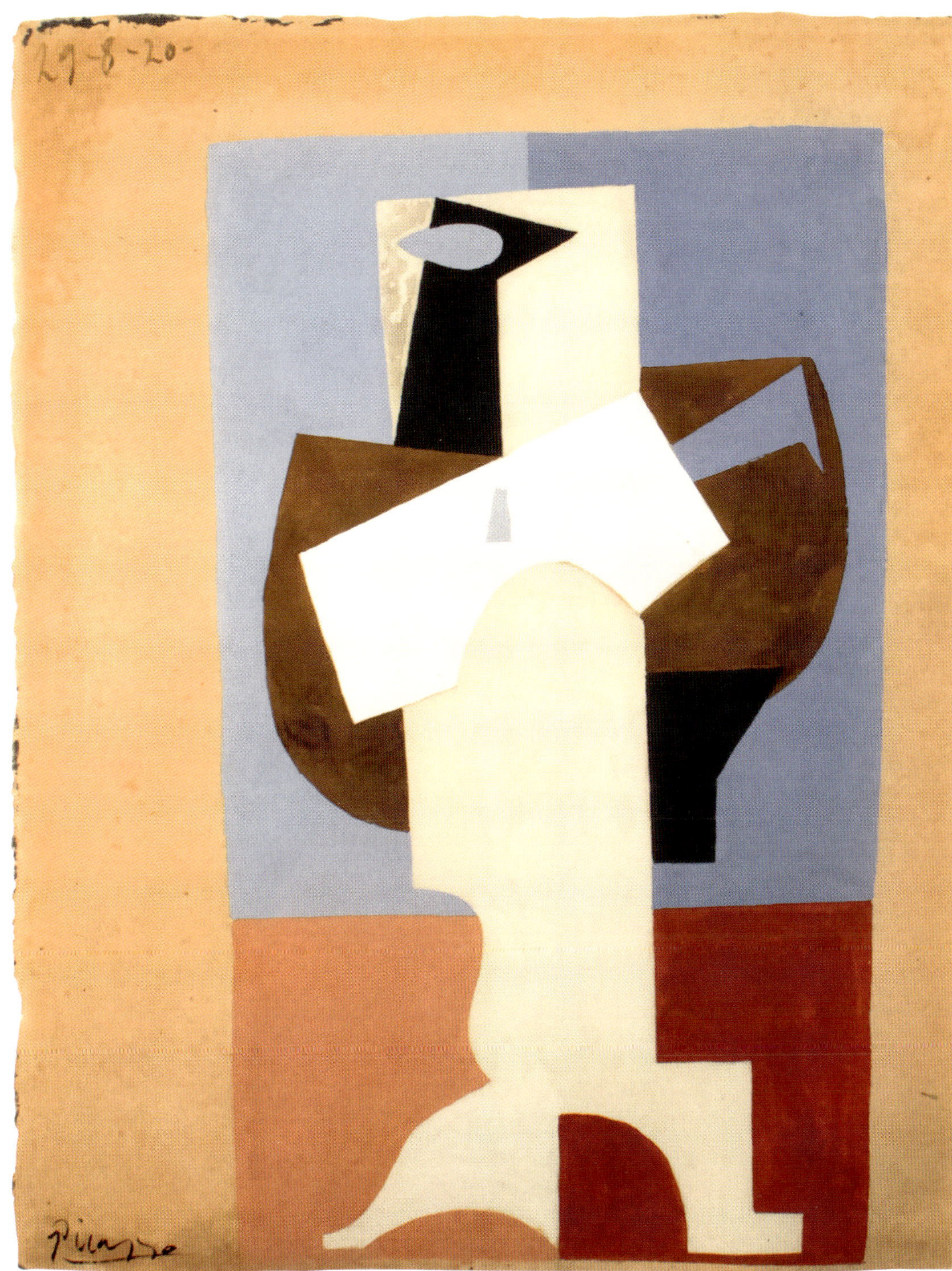

97

PIERRE BONNARD 1867–1947

Nude in an Interior, 1920–22

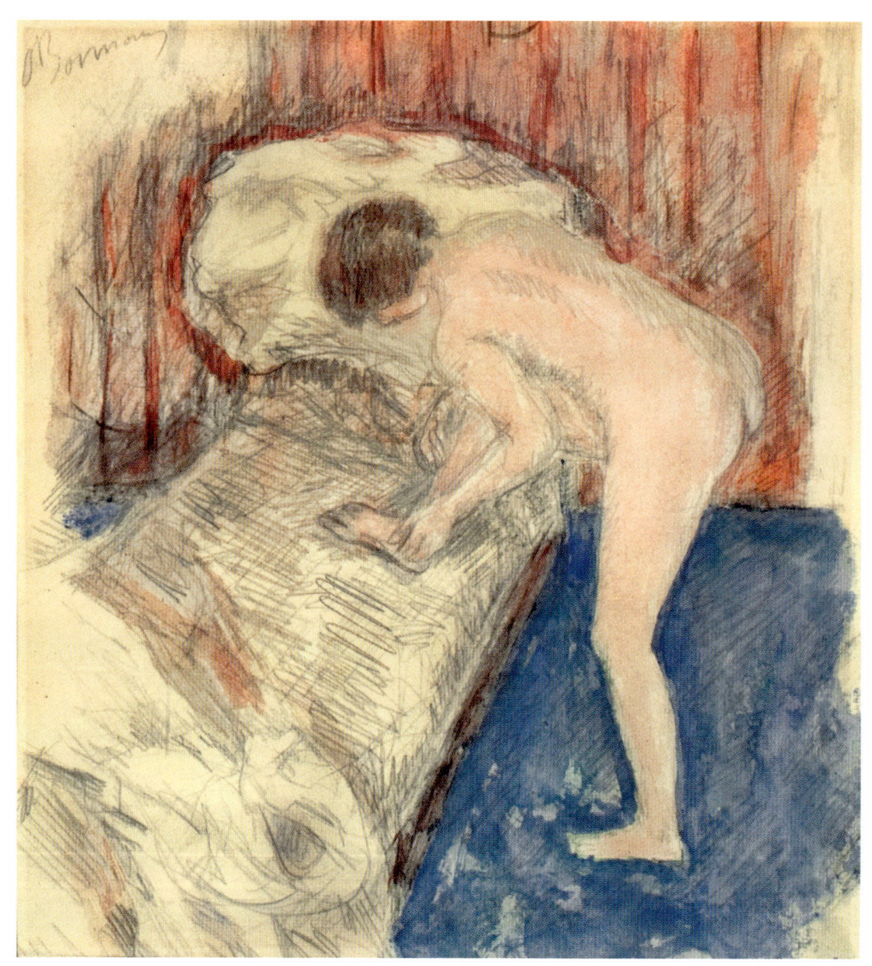

Graphite and watercolour on paper, 24.3 × 22.7 cm

Signed: *Bonnard*

PROVENANCE: Louise Hervieu, Paris (gift of the artist); Gilbert Gruet, former director of Bernheim-Jeune, Paris; Christie's, Paris, 1 December 2006, lot 112

LITERATURE: Coquiet (1922), ill. on cover

From an early date Bonnard painted nudes in contemporary interiors. By 1908 his treatment of the subject had evolved into a concentration on the single nude woman, bathing in a tub or standing at her toilette. The debt to Degas is obvious, although Degas approached his bathers with ruthless detachment while Bonnard painted them with affection – no doubt because he almost always used his mistress, Marthe (whose real name was Maria) Boursin, as his model. During the decades in which they were together, Marthe never aged in Bonnard's art. In the present watercolour, dating from *c.*1920–22, she would have been in her early fifties. Her informal pose, seen from a high viewpoint, and the rich streaks of colour owe much to Degas' late pastels. Bonnard clearly liked the pose, which appears in his art in a number of variations in the 1920s – notably in a drawing of Marthe, dated 1925, that was on the art market in 2012.[1]

The watercolour is undated, but was used on the cover of Gabriel Coquiot's *Bonnard,* published by Bernheim-Jeune in 1922 with seven vignettes supplied by the artist. Colour is uncommon in Bonnard's drawings, and this one was presumably made specifically for the book. A similar watercolour recently on the market is probably a copy of the present work.[2]

98

JACQUES VILLON 1875–1963

Olympia (after Manet), 1926–27

Watercolour over graphite, partly squared for transfer, 20.5 × 27.5 cm

Signed, dated and annotated: *d'aprés Manet Jacques Villon*

PROVENANCE: Louis Carré; Olga Carré (née Burel); *Collection Olga Carré,* Hôtel Dassault, Paris, 10 December 2002, lot 86

LITERATURE: Bongers (forthcoming)

Between 1922 and 1930 Villon made 34 aquatints for the firm of Bernheim-Jeune after works by Impressionist and contemporary artists. These ranged from Bonnard to Maurice de Vlaminck and included Braque, Dufy, Matisse, Picasso and many others. Villon's skill as a draughtsman and his early mastery of the technique of aquatint allowed him to reproduce the originals with a lively fidelity. This was commercial work of a type that he had left behind when he left Montmartre in 1908, but he took it up again at a time when he needed to supplement his income.

Manet, as the acknowledged father of modern art, was one of the oldest artists in the series. His *Olympia* provoked much hostile comment from uncomprehending critics when it appeared at the Salon of 1865, but by the 1920s it had become one of the most celebrated of nineteenth-century French paintings. Villon's spirited copy was prepared for an aquatint, issued in 1926–7 in an edition of 100 and printed in the same direction.[1] Two years later he produced an aquatint of Manet's equally controversial *Déjeuner sur l'herbe* in an edition of 300.[2] The series was largely intended to promote artists whose work was sold by Bernheim-Jeune. In 1910 the firm had been involved, along with Cassirer and Durand-Ruel, in acquiring 35 works by Manet from the collection of Auguste Pellerin – confirming its place as one of the major dealers of the Impressionists and their followers.

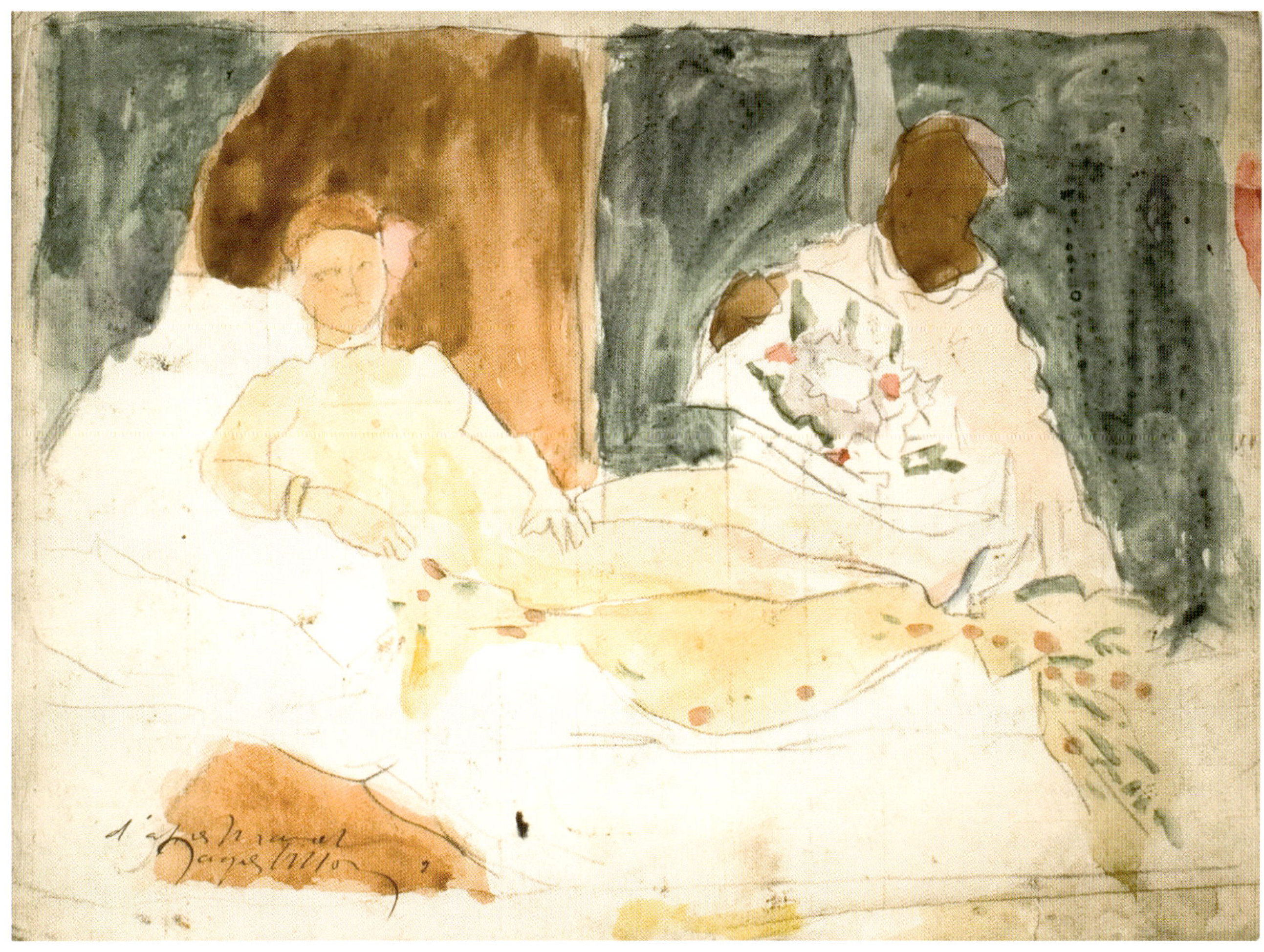

99

FERNAND LÉGER 1881–1955

Study for 'The Three Musicians', 1932

Pen and ink on white paper, 38 × 36 cm

Initialled and dated: *F L 32*

Verso: a pencil sketch of figures in a landscape

PROVENANCE: Louis Clayeux, Paris

The various versions of Léger's *Three Musicians* all derive from a drawing dated 1924 (private collection, USA) and culminate in a painting of 1944 (Museum of Modern Art, New York). According to Léger, he based the painting on a drawing of 1925 that he took with him when he moved to New York in 1940. Between 1924 and 1944 Léger repeated the composition in a series of drawings and in a near-monochrome painting dated 1930 (Von-der-Heydt Museum, Wuppertal) that closely resembles the work in this exhibition. The painting was probably based on an undated drawing formerly in the collection of Picasso's friend, Lionel Prejger[1]. The present drawing, dated 1932, must have been based either on the painting of 1930, which it closely resembles or on the related drawing.

Léger drew the first version in 1924 – a time when he was developing a vein of popular subjects, based on common life and modelled in a monumental and simplified manner. He discovered the music-making theme at a popular Parisian dance hall, or *bal musette*, in the rue de Lappe. The boy in the centre plays an accordion, the instrument *par excellence* of Parisian dance halls. He is flanked on the right by a tuba player and on the left by a musician playing a 'cello-sized instrument, waisted and strung like a guitar, with an extremely low sound hole. The guitar-like head has been turned round and is seen from the side. In the first version, and in the other early drawings, the instrument has a scroll.

Léger's choice of subjects shows an interest in ordinary people, yet he depicted them with unfailing detachment. There is a striking dissonance between the gaiety of the subject and the expressions of indifference on the faces of the musicians. In the work of another artist, this might have been intended as an ironic comment. Léger, however, did not allow his feelings to affect his art. He treated human subjects as if they were objects of still life. Abstraction, as he noted in 1952, made it possible 'to see the human figure in terms of its plasticity only, and without evaluating it in terms of sentiment. That is why it remained deliberately inexpressive in the development of my art from 1905 to the present'.

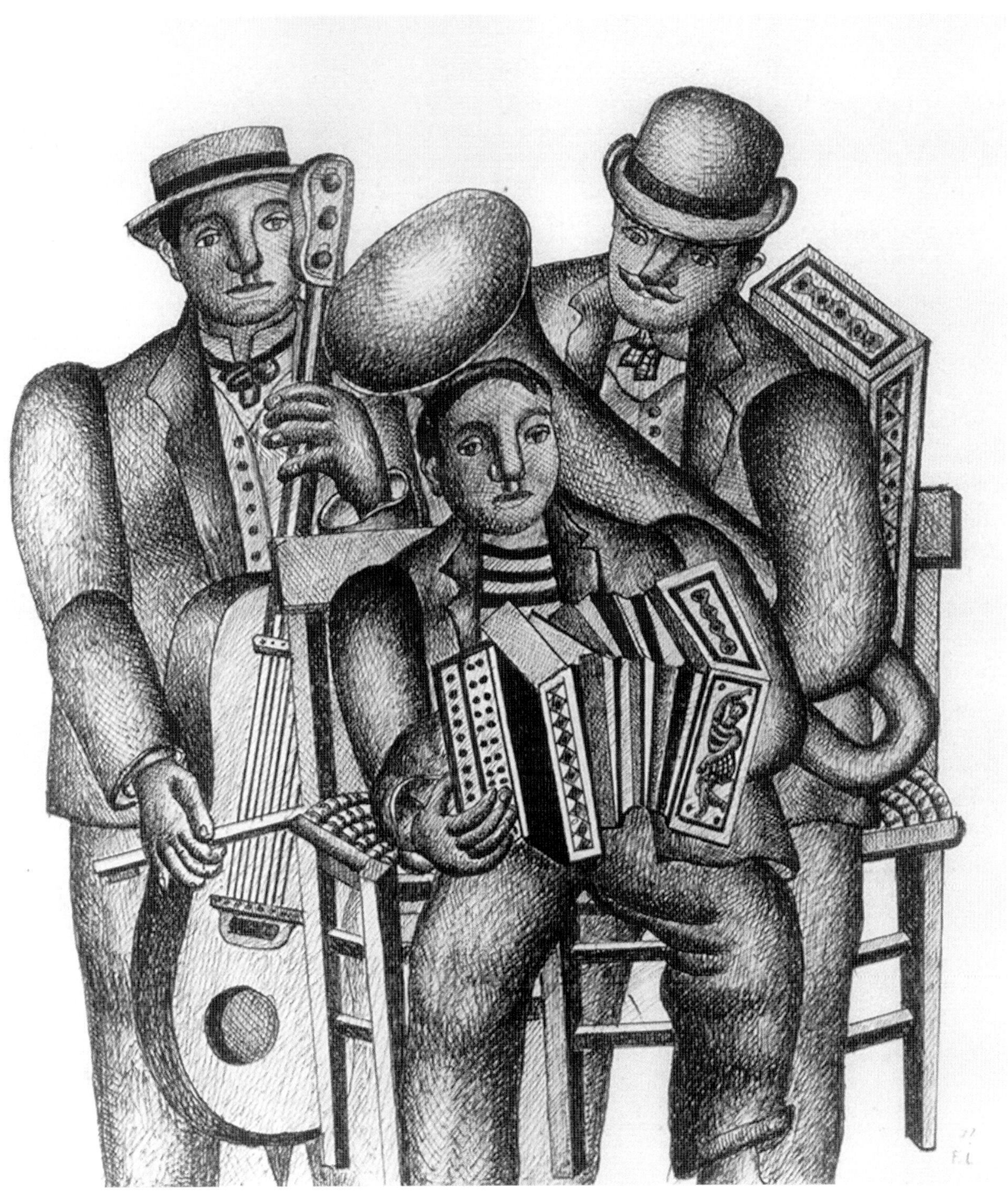

100

GEORGES ROUAULT 1871–1958

Two Judges, 1912

Bodycolour on vellum paper, 43.7 × 35.7 cm

Signed and dated lower right: *G.Rouault 1912*

PROVENANCE: Karl Spoonagel collection, Zurich (acquired 1935); private collection, Zurich; Kornfeld, Bern, June 2012

LITERATURE: Johnson (2014), no.14, p.31, ill.; Dorival and Rouault (1988), no.401, ill.

The son of a cabinet-maker, Georges Rouault began work as an apprentice to a stained-glass maker. He thus gained an early familiarity with religious subject matter, as well as an admiration for the expressive forms and rich colours of medieval stained glass, regularly brought into the studio for repair. During his apprenticeship Rouault attended evening classes in drawing, and in 1891, on choosing painting as his future career, he enrolled at the École des Beaux-Arts, shortly afterwards entering the studio of Gustave Moreau. Clearly a promising pupil, he won the studio prize the following year with a series of religious subjects, marking the beginning of a developing and eventually lifelong attraction to spiritual themes.

However, other early events were also to help determine the future course of Rouault's work.

In Moreau's studio he had been a fellow pupil of Matisse (who became a close friend), as well as the painters Albert Marquet and Étienne-Adolphe Piot, and in 1903 they formed part of the group that founded the Salon d'Automne. At the Salon of the following year, to which Rouault sent eight oils and numerous pastels and watercolours, an entire room was devoted to Cézanne, whose name also appeared on the list of founder members.

From about 1903, the religious themes from the early years of Rouault's career for a time gave way to a vein of popular life and entertainment. In depicting essentially tragic acrobats, Pierrots and clowns, he took up themes explored by Daumier in a technique that owed something to Cézanne's use of watercolour. At the 1905 exhibition of the Salon, one chiefly associated with the appearance of the Fauves, Rouault showed a triptych of three prostitutes entitled *Filles*. This proved an early appearance of a form he was to find congenial for the treatment of stock characters, exemplified in his depictions of judges – a theme he first began to work with some three years later, after attending hearings at the Tribunal de la Seine for the best part of a year.

The present work, dated 1912, though showing only two figures, appears to be a first working-out of the tripartate composition of *The Three Judges* of 1913 (New York, Museum of Modern Art). In the present piece, however, the colours are of a quite different glow and intensity, and a comparison with stained glass could be made. The figures themselves, unlike those of the triptych, have the immobility of stone carvings, also suggested in the sharply chiselled features of the figure on the left. Such a striking simplification of form was common to several of Rouault's contemporaries in those years, though in his case the influence is more likely to be early Christian art than the exotic.

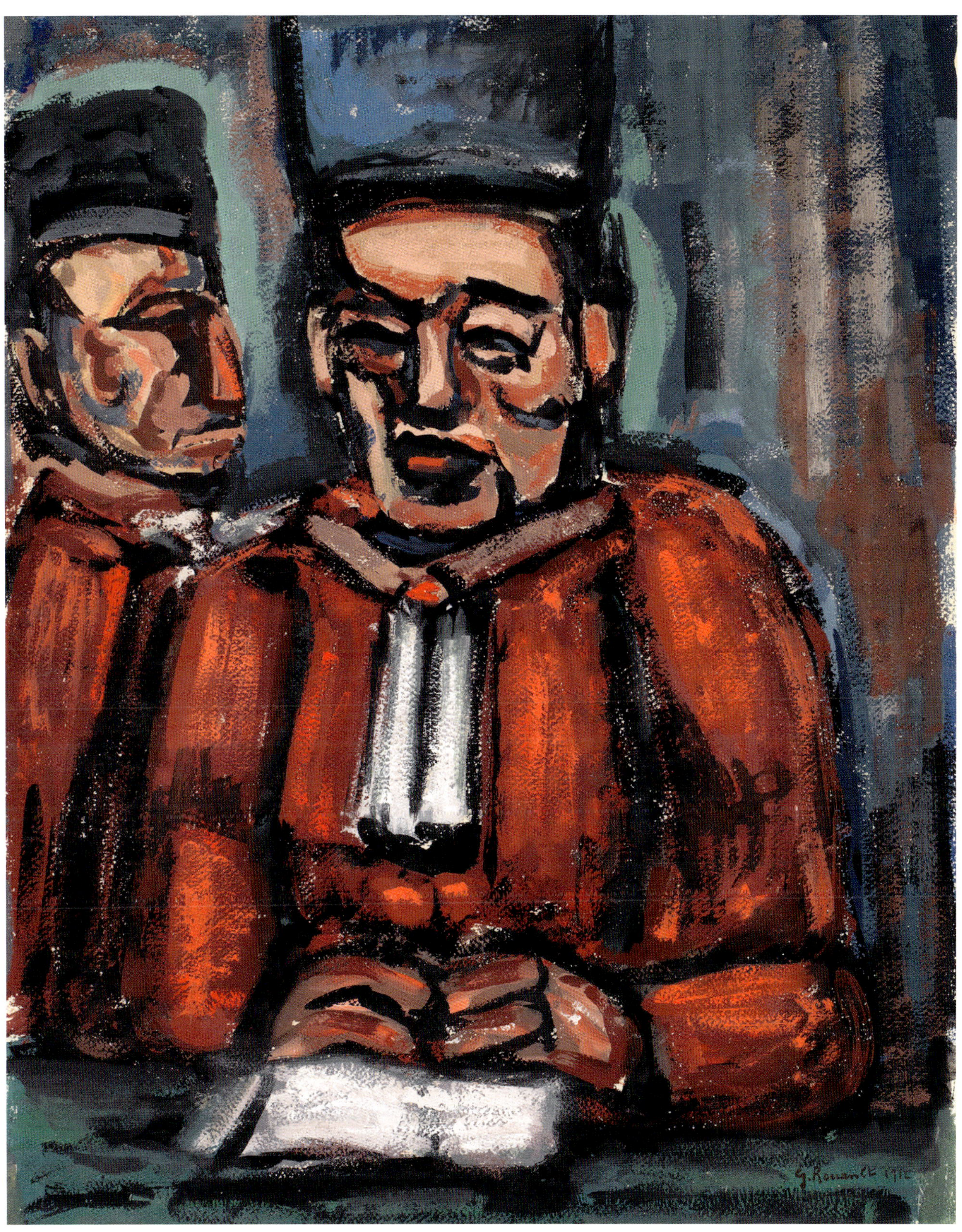

101

GEORGES ROUAULT 1871–1958

Three Nudes, 1914

Brush and watercolour on white paper, 40.4 × 62 cm

PROVENANCE: Kornfeld, Bern

LITERATURE: Dorival and Rouault (1988), vol.1, no.469, ill.

The founding of the Salon d'Automne in 1903 provided a certain context for the exhibition of Rouault's work, but his art was to remain distinct from the practices of his contemporaries. In 1905, though exhibiting with the Fauves, his own work, somewhat dark in comparison, appeared in a separate room. Rouault's own view, as he later expressed it to Ambroise Vollard, was 'Le fond humain ne les intéresse pas. Moi, c'est ma vie' ('The human background does not interest them. As for me, it is my life!').[1]

However, from about 1906 Rouault once again took part in the activities of a group of young painters, this time working on the decoration of ceramics in the studio of André Methey at Asnières. Methey was a friend of Vollard, and at least two of the painters involved, Matisse and Maurice de Vlaminck, had already been taken up by the dealer, who strongly encouraged their work in this field. In 1907 Derain produced a piece entitled *Large Plate with Bathers,* and at about the same time Matisse decorated a vase with dancing nude figures. Dufy took up the theme of bathing women in paintings from 1913 to 1914 and Rouault also had painted a number of pictures on the theme before 1914.

The title of the present work makes no specific reference to bathers, however, and, although it is thought to be a study for a ceramic piece, it is of an altogether different order from the others. While owing something to Cézanne, and just a little to Matisse himself, it has a gently lyrical character quite unlike the energetic Fauve manner of Matisse's work in those years, or of Rouault's earlier bathers. This character is most evident in the graceful continuous form of the figure on the left, in part derived from Ingres' *Grande Odalisque* but unmistakably Rouault's own. The limited range of colour, a wonderful concentration of blue, grey and black, with just a touch of brown, may have been determined by considerations of firing, and the compactness that contributes so much to the satisfyingly cameo-like quality of the composition may have been similarly determined by its function as a ceramic design.

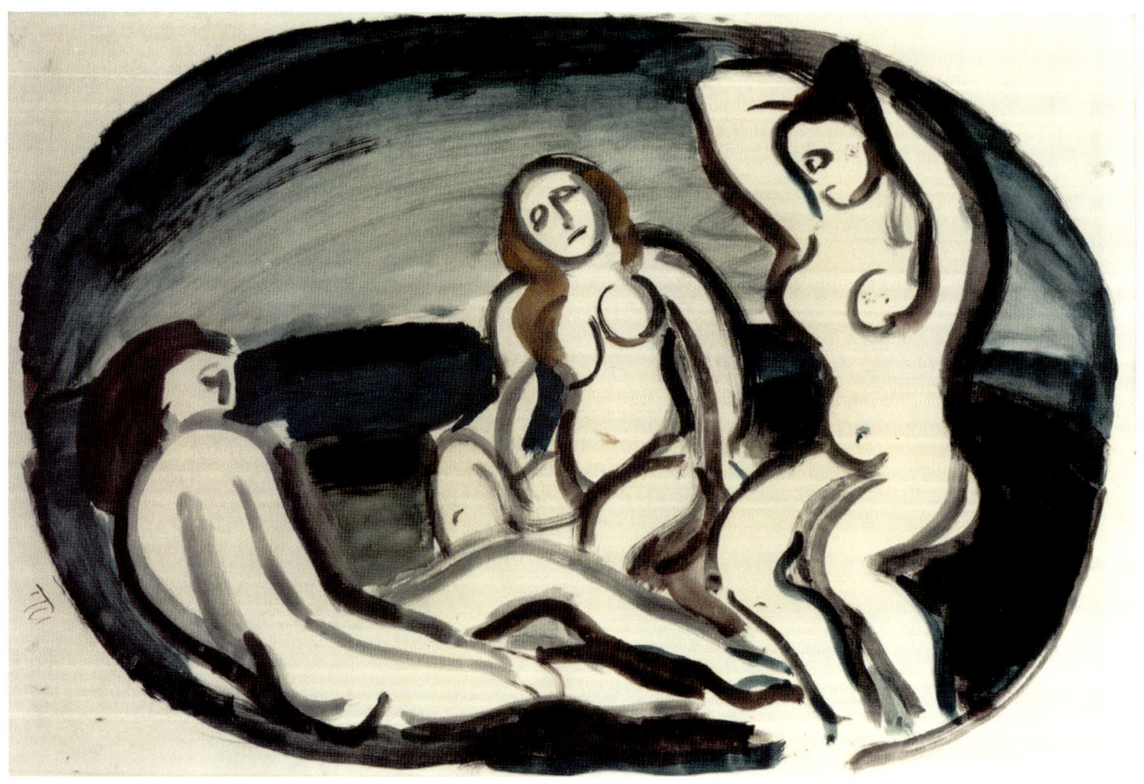

102

GEORGES ROUAULT 1871–1958

The Way is Long, 1929

Crayon, overworked with pastel, watercolour and gouache, 50 × 34.3 cm

Signed and dated lower left: *Georges Rouault 1929*

Verso: Written in pencil in the hand of the artist: *La route est longue*,

after which is added: *chétifs humains / et la mort / au tournant / du chemin; (miserable humans / and death / at the turning / of the road)*

PROVENANCE: Hedi Hahnloser, Zurich; John D. Rockefeller, Jr., New York; private collection, Switzerland; Ebi Kornfeld, Bern, 2005

LITERATURE: Courthion (1962), p.204, ill.; Dorival and Rouault (1988), vol.II, no.1197

In 1913 Ambroise Vollard, long an admirer of Rouault, bought all the pictures in his studio, some 700 works. By 1917 he had become Rouault's sole agent, engaging him to complete the many unfinished works he had acquired and to embark on a series of illustrations for his own series of very beautiful *livres d'artiste*, a project particularly dear to Vollard. For Rouault, this was to take precedence over painting for the next ten years. A deeply religious man, he had his own plan for an illustrated work, *Misèrere et Guerre* (or *Miserere*, as it was to become), an extended meditation on the theme of death, which Vollard engaged to publish. Several plates in this work depict suburban scenes representing a desolation both physical and moral – possibly, as Waldemar George has suggested, a transposition of Rouault's Belleville childhood into tragic mode.[1]

1929, the year in which the present work was made, marked the resuming of a wider range of activities, including painting. Rouault had completed his only commission for Diaghilev, sets and costumes for the ballet *The Prodigal Son*, and in the same year produced a series of six lithographs entitled *Petite banlieue*, as well as a number of lithographs and drawings for a project entitled *Paysages légendaires.* The present work,dating from the same year, is an anti-naturalistic landscape of the imagination. It may owe something to Rouault's recent exploration of new forms of representation: the grim pyramids, the triple, shattered chimneys, the road winding upwards only to meet death at the turning. In this painted scene, the backdrop to one of the darkest of Rouault's images, irony and pathos are concentrated in the huddled group low in the foreground – the *Faubourg des longues peines*, indeed, to take the title of plate 10 of the *Miserere*.

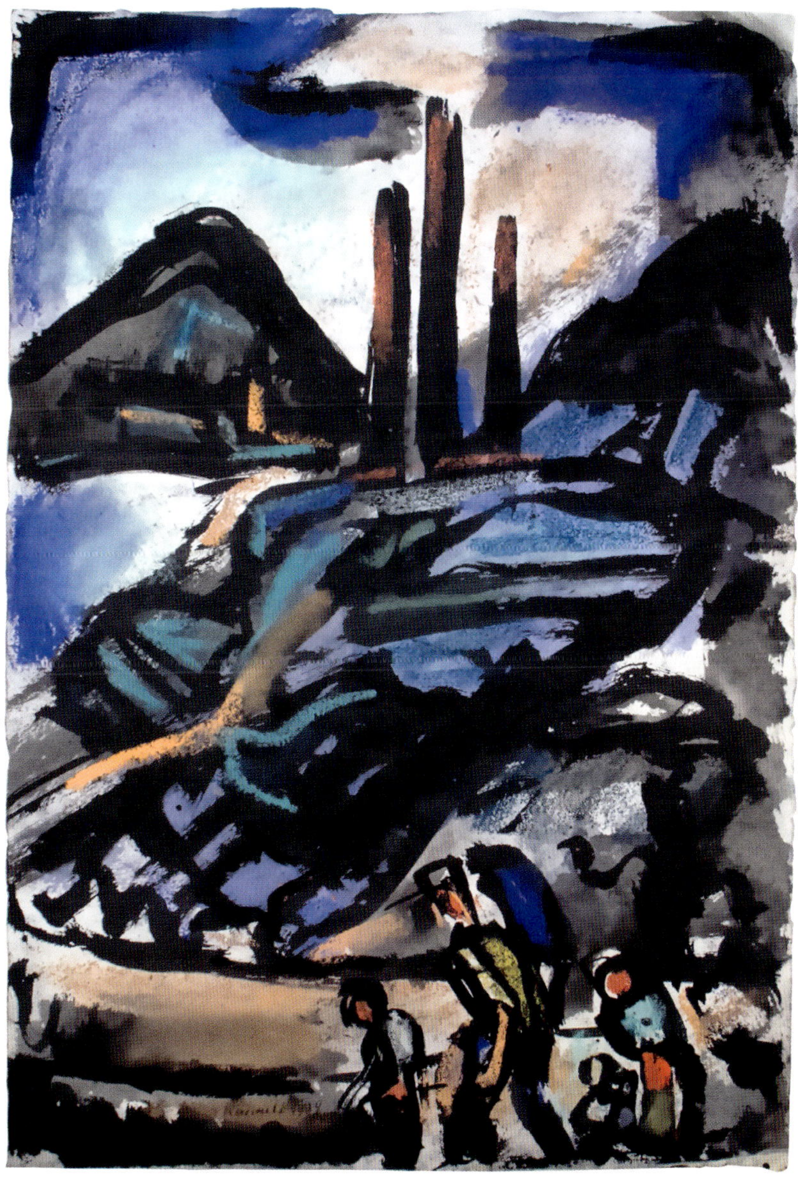

103

MARC CHAGALL 1887–1985

The Little Fish and the Fisherman, 1927

Watercolour and bodycolour on buff paper, 50.7 × 41.2 cm

Signed in pen and ink: *Chagall*

PROVENANCE: Gallery Kenneth Aberg, Gothenburg; private collection, 1980

LITERATURE: Meyer (1963), p.332

In his *Recollections of a Picture Dealer*, Ambroise Vollard (1936) remembered that:

One of my most cherished ambitions had been to publish a La Fontaine, worthily illustrated. When the time came, it was the Russian painter Marc Chagall that I thought of for the illustration of the book. I was sharply criticised for it. People could not understand the choice of a Russian painter to interpret the most French of all our poets. But it was precisely on account of the Oriental sources of the fabulist that I had pitched on an artist whose origins and culture had rendered him familiar with the magic east. My hopes were not deceived: Chagall did a hundred dazzling gouaches. But when it came to putting them on copper, so many technical difficulties arose that the artist decided to substitute etchings in black.[1]

Chagall had first visited Paris in 1911. Having been rejected for the Salon d'Automne that year, he enjoyed success at the Salon des Indépendants in 1912, 1913 and 1914. He spent the First World War in Russia and only returned to Paris at the suggestion of his friend, the Swiss-born poet Blaise Cendrars, who told him that he was sufficiently well known for Vollard to want to commission work from him. Vollard became Chagall's most important patron, for whom the artist made three major suites of etchings: Gogol's *Les ames mortes* (printed 1927), La Fontaine's *Fables* (1928–31) and the Bible (1931–9). None of the three titles were published until after the Second World War.

For the La Fontaine commission Vollard had originally envisaged colour reproductions, but this proved technically impossible. Chagall worked on the gouaches illustrating La Fontaine between 1926 and 1930. In order to immerse himself in the French countryside, he travelled extensively in central and southern France. He stayed first in a fishing village near Toulon, where he was dazzled by the light on the sea, and later lived for several months in a house in the main square of Chambon-sur-Lac in the Auvergne. Here the artist painted some 30 gouaches for the La Fontaine project. The completed series was exhibited at the Galerie Bernheim-Jeune in February 1930, and subsequently in Brussels and Berlin. The works were poorly received.

Chagall's illustrations are generally evocative rather than literal. Book V, fable 3 (*Le petit poisson et le pêcheur*), for example, tells how a young carp remonstrated with the fisherman, asking that he should throw him back so that he might grow to maturity. The fisherman refused, arguing that a fish in the basket is better than two yet to catch (the same sentiment as the English proverb 'a bird in the hand is worth two in the bush'). Chagall's evocation, with only the sneering face of the fisherman and his right hand holding the rod visible on the right, is characteristically quirky, with the river occupying the greater part of the composition.

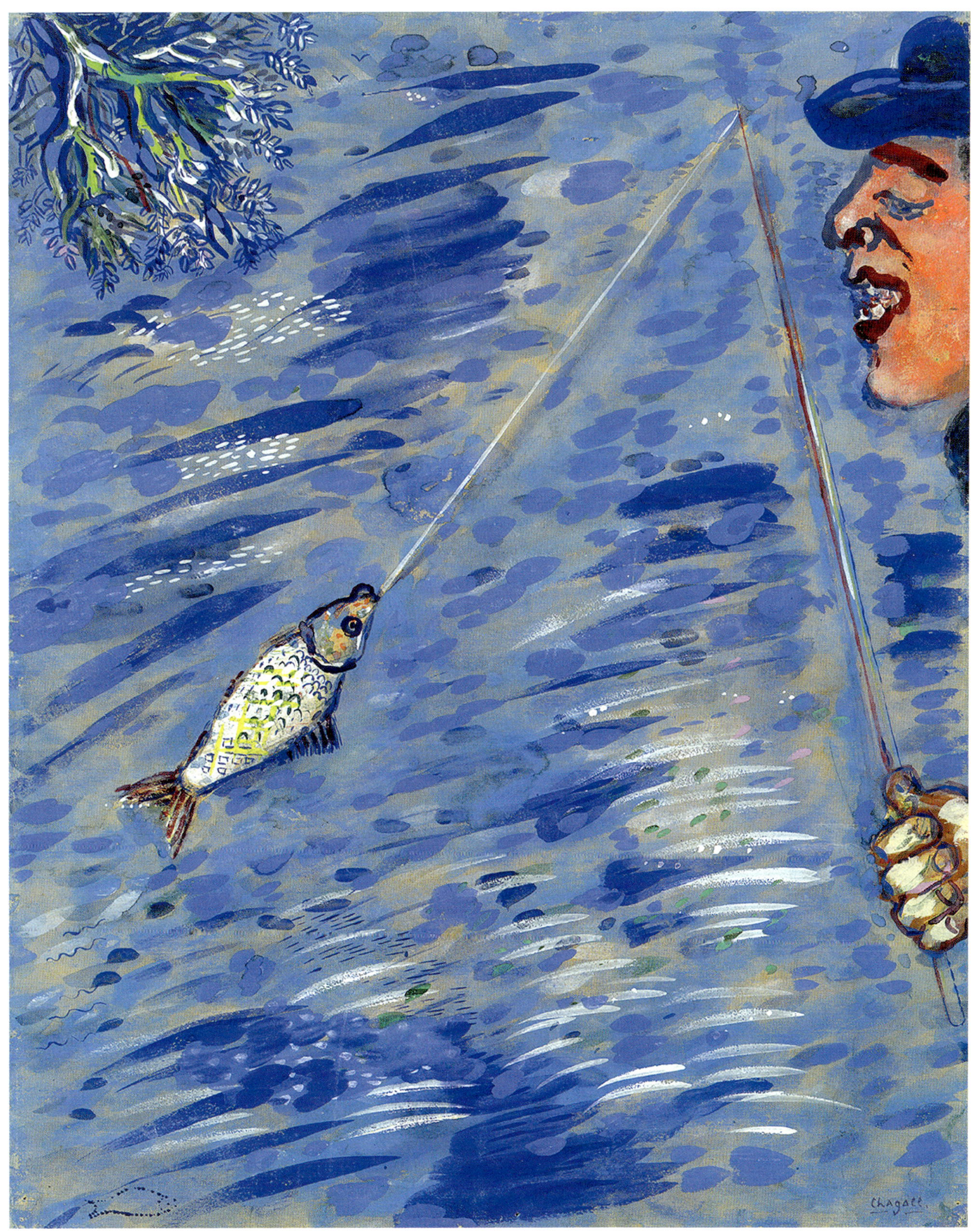
Chagall

104

JACQUES VILLON 1875–1963

Self Portrait, 1935

Watercolour with pen and red and black inks on paper, 28 × 23 cm

Signed and dated: *Jacques* VILLON / 35

PROVENANCE: Louis Carré

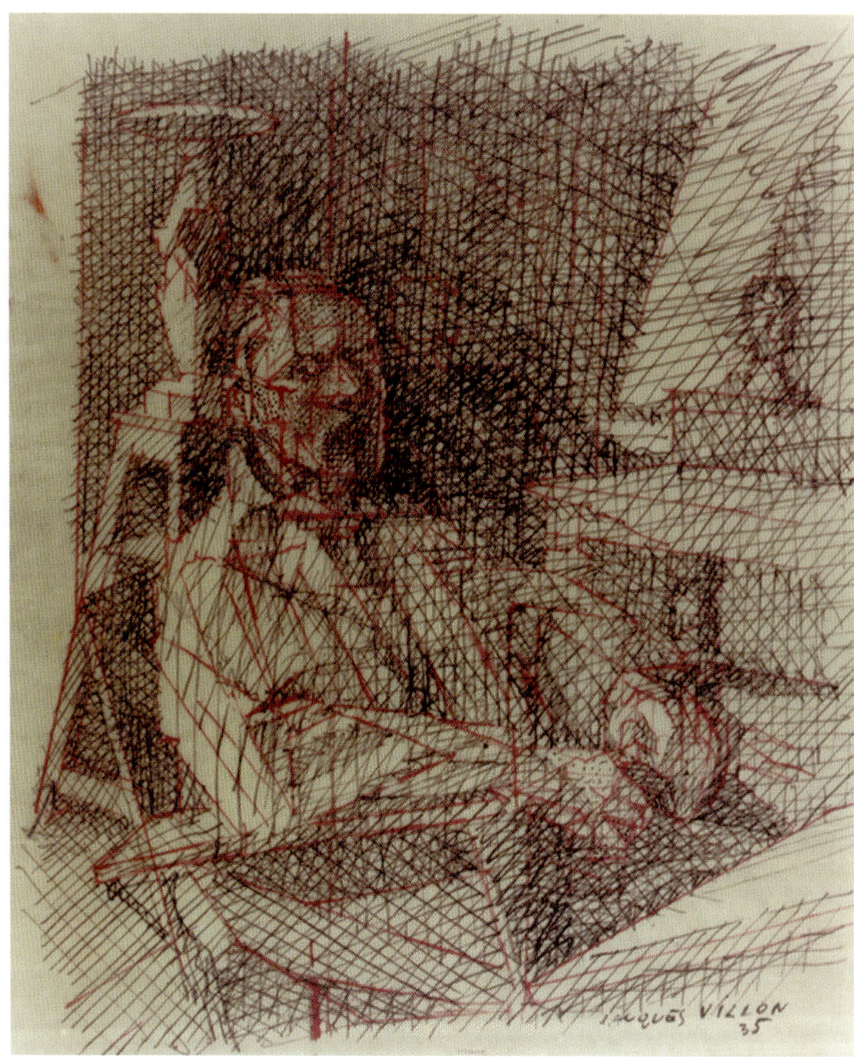

Towards the end of the 1920s Villon's portraits became more naturalistic. This tendency is found in the work of several of his fellow Cubists, responding perhaps to a sense that the purposes of a good likeness were not ideally served by Cubism. Like other artists, Villon frequently used his own features as a model. His prints, in particular, provide an overview of the many phases of his art as it evolved from the colourism of the Nabis through Cubism to the greater realism of his late portraits.

This drawing was the model for an etching of 1935, known as *Le grand dessinateur* (Ginestet and Pouillon, E385), printed in reverse. The artist is seated in front of his drawing paper in his studio at no.7 rue Lemaître in Puteaux, observing his features in a mirror. In the background, on a modelling stand, is the *Decorative Basin*, a work of 1911 by his late brother, Raymond Duchamp-Villon; on the table in front of the easel is Duchamp-Villon's bust of Baudelaire. These two works must have been included as a tribute to Raymond, whose death in 1918 had affected Villon deeply. This loss may also explain the air of melancholy that seems to pervade the image. The intensity of the artist's expression, however, may be no more than the result of his concentration on the work in hand.

The main outlines of the drawing were done first in red ink. The artist then hatched most of the surface with brown ink to create the effect, more clearly rendered in the print, of a figure emerging from the shadows. These two stages conform to the changes made by Villon to the print between the first state, drawn in simple outline, and the final state, densely worked over with hatched lines. The essential details – the artist's head, his right hand and the drawing paper – are picked out by the light. In the print, the hatching is regularised into a network of fine, straight lines imposed upon the image like a covering of thin, woven material. The device of over-laying the image with a thin grid of lines was used by Villon in his Cubist prints, but here the effect is more naturalistic and reminiscent of Rembrandt.

105

MARCEL GROMAIRE 1892–1971

The Town of Aubusson, 1940

Pen, black ink and watercolour within delineated border, 42 × 48 cm

Signed and dated 1940 in ink in the margin, lower right; annotated lower left in pencil: *First study for the tapestry Aubusson (1er projet pour la tapisserie Aubusson)*

Gromaire's interests had long ranged beyond the confines of easel painting: they included ceramic decoration, stained glass and wallpaper design, as well as an early and deeply serious interest in the potential of cinema. An active member of the Popular Front, an alliance of the left during the inter-war period, he approached all his interests in a way consistent with a fundamental principle close to his heart – an ideal of a social art, not unlike that of William Morris. For Gromaire, the strength of art in the Middle Ages and later lay in its popular foundations; this was a time when the 'people built their cathedrals and when free spirits, responding to a movement of unanimous revolt, in one century prepared the way for the revolution. In the thirteenth century and in the eighteenth century, a vibrant and passionate national art thrust its roots into every little village'.[1] Northern Gothic tapestries, which, like Morris, he passionately admired, gave him a model for reviving tapestry as a form of contemporary mural art.

In 1938 Guillaume Jeanneau, director of the Mobilier National, which included the tapestry works of the Gobelins, invited Gromaire, Pierre Dubreuil and Jean Lurçat to make cartoons for tapestries. These were to be woven at the Gobelins according to the old practices, abandoned in the eighteenth century, when tapestries had become simply copies of paintings. The war interrupted this scheme, but the following year Jeanneau invited them to make cartoons for the works at Aubusson and nearby Felletin, also under Royal Warrant. His scheme was partly intended to revive morale in these depressed areas, situated as they were in the Limousin region – one of the chief centres of the French Resistance, and therefore a place that had suffered particularly savage acts of reprisal during the German Occupation. Perhaps Gromaire also knew of the court troubadour Joan d'Aubusson. In any case it is difficult not to see this brilliant watercolour study for a tapestry cartoon as expressing an enduring spirit of old France, the huddle of pointed roofs of Aubusson appearing between its encircling rivers as if on an ancient map.

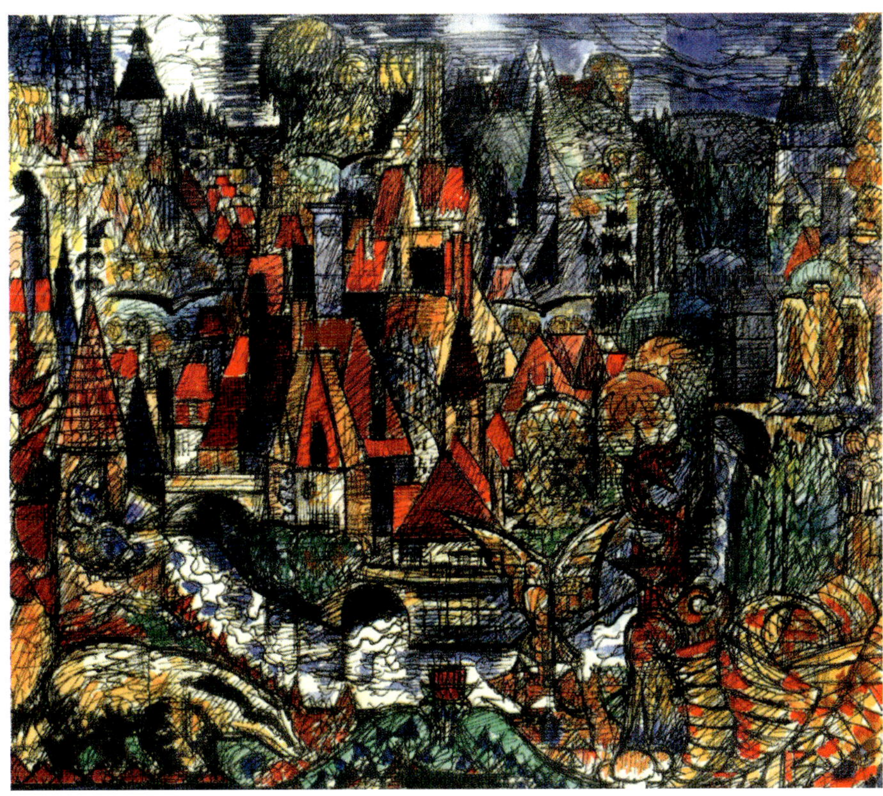

106

HENRI MATISSE 1869–1954

Portrait of Henry de Montherlant, 1943

Charcoal on paper, 27 × 20.2 cm
Signed and dated in graphite: *Henri Matisse 4/43*
PROVENANCE: by descent from the artist

As a young man Matisse developed his facility as a portrait draughtsman by doodling while he was waiting in the queue at the post office. His portraits were habitually executed in pen and ink or crayon, giving a spare but dynamic outline; or in charcoal, which offered much more painterly possibilities for modelling and the evocation of light and shade. Matisse used both techniques throughout his mature life; among the earliest examples of the latter is his 1912 portrait of the artist and writer André Rouveyre.[1] In the winter of 1935–6 Matisse met the writer Henri de Montherlant (1895–1972), who approached him to illustrate one of his texts. The most important fruit of their collaboration was the edition of *Pasiphae: Chant de Minos*, published by Martin Fariani on 20 May 1944, with 18 full page linoleum engravings and numerous decorations.[2] While he was working on the project, Matisse made a total of 17 portraits of Montherlant. In an interview published in 1938, the artist explained his fascination with Montherlant's features.

I was interested by Montherlant's face, and asked him to pose for me, and during seven sittings I was able to make some drawings that were simply responses to his face. An artist must be able to forget everything about the life and the work of whoever poses for him ... The whole time Montherlant posed, my reading of his work, which I love, was far from my mind; only his expression, whose originality is what made it worthwhile, was used to make his portrait. At the eighth sitting, it was impossible for me to see anything at all in Montherlant. He was impossible to capture. He wasn't there.[3] When this portrait was drawn, in April 1943, Montherlant had become an enormously controversial figure. Having staunchly advocated French rearmament throughout the 1930s, he felt vindicated when Paris fell to the Germans on 14 June 1940. In *Le solstice de juin*, published in the following year, he tried to put the defeat into a longer perspective of renewal and consolidation, which caused left-wing writers to accuse him of being a collaborator.

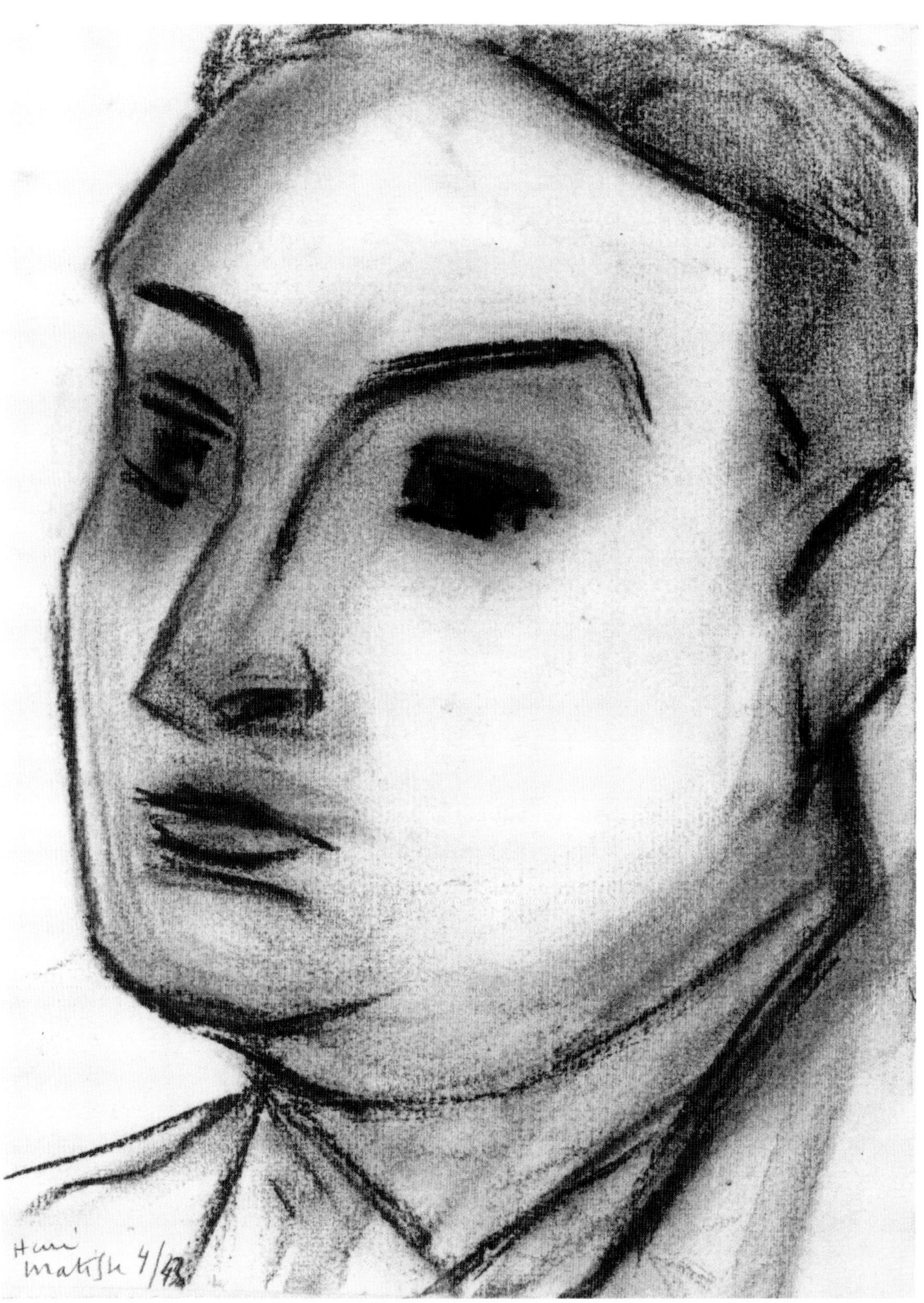
Henri
Matisse 4/42

107

FERNAND LÉGER 1881–1955

Mother and Child (Mère et enfant), ca.1949

Gouache, 58.5 × 50 cm

Signed with initials: F.L.

PROVENANCE: Galerie Louise Leiris (Kahnweiler), Paris, December 1975

Better than any other work by Léger, this image of a mother and child illustrates his ambition to create a humane, uncomplicated and accessible art with a popular appeal and a subject based in common experience. It is the female equivalent of the paintings of builders that occupied him in the 1950s. The style of the work, with its heavy, simple outlines and empty background, originated in Léger's *Nude in a Red Background* of 1927 (Hirschorn Museum, Smithsonian Institute, Washington DC) and evolved through the 1930s into a style of descriptive figure drawing in which all trace of Cubist fragmentation has been eliminated. Contours are thick like the lines of a woodcut, and shading has been removed.

The pair represent a secular version of the Madonna with the Christ Child. The plant that the child carries is reminiscent of the emblems traditionally carried by the Christ Child in the presence of his mother. It reappears invariably in the many images of women made by Léger between *c.*1949 and 1955. In Léger's art, the image of the plant seems to affirm a commitment to the saving grace of the natural world, in the face of the dehumanising forces of post-war society. Léger, who had joined the Communist Party in 1945, used a sprig or a flower in the manner of Picasso's dove as an emblem of his desire for a just and peaceful world.

The drawing of the figures is realistic while the added colour is wholly abstract. The three primary colours, including two shades of blue, have been added in near-rectangular blocks that take no account of the contours except where they abut the faces, the child's hand and the plant. This combination of arbitrary colour and representational drawing was an established feature in many of Léger's late works. In the *Two Women* of 1954 (Tate Modern, London), the outlines were painted over the blocks of colour. In this gouache the artist has drawn the contours first, then carefully inserted the colour up to the edges of the black lines. The effect is striking in its simplicity. Léger liked so-called primitive or naïve art and made use of its imagery in his late work. The *Mother and Child*, however, is a work of passionate intensity and sophistication that is artless only in appearance.

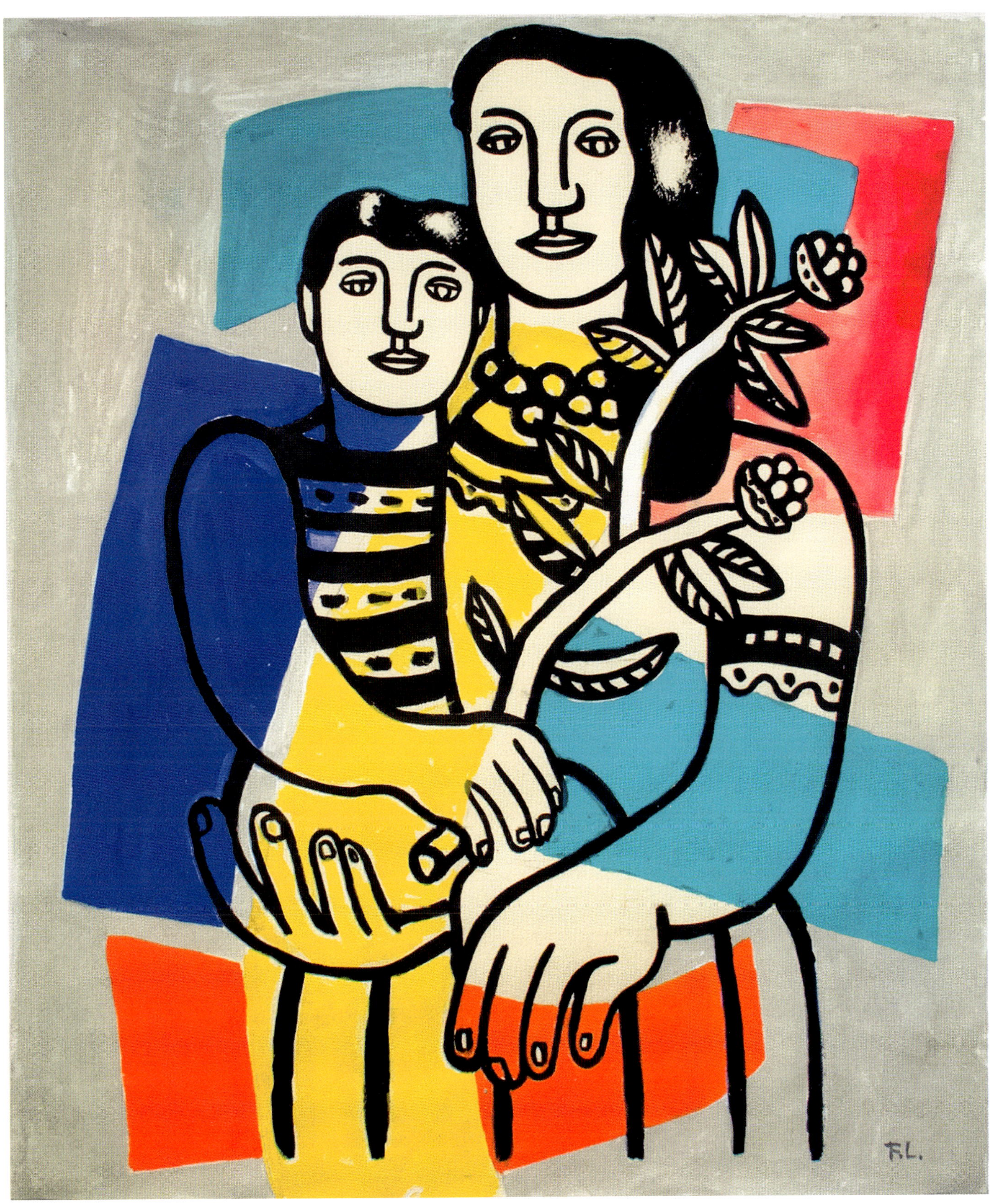
F.L.

108

ANDRÉ MASSON 1896–1987

A Celebration, 1958

Pastel on orange/brown paper; blind-stamped: STRATHMORE ARTIST, 64.1 × 48.2 cm

Signed: *André Masson;* dated 1958 and titled on the verso

PROVENANCE: Dr and Mrs Philip Falk, Chicago

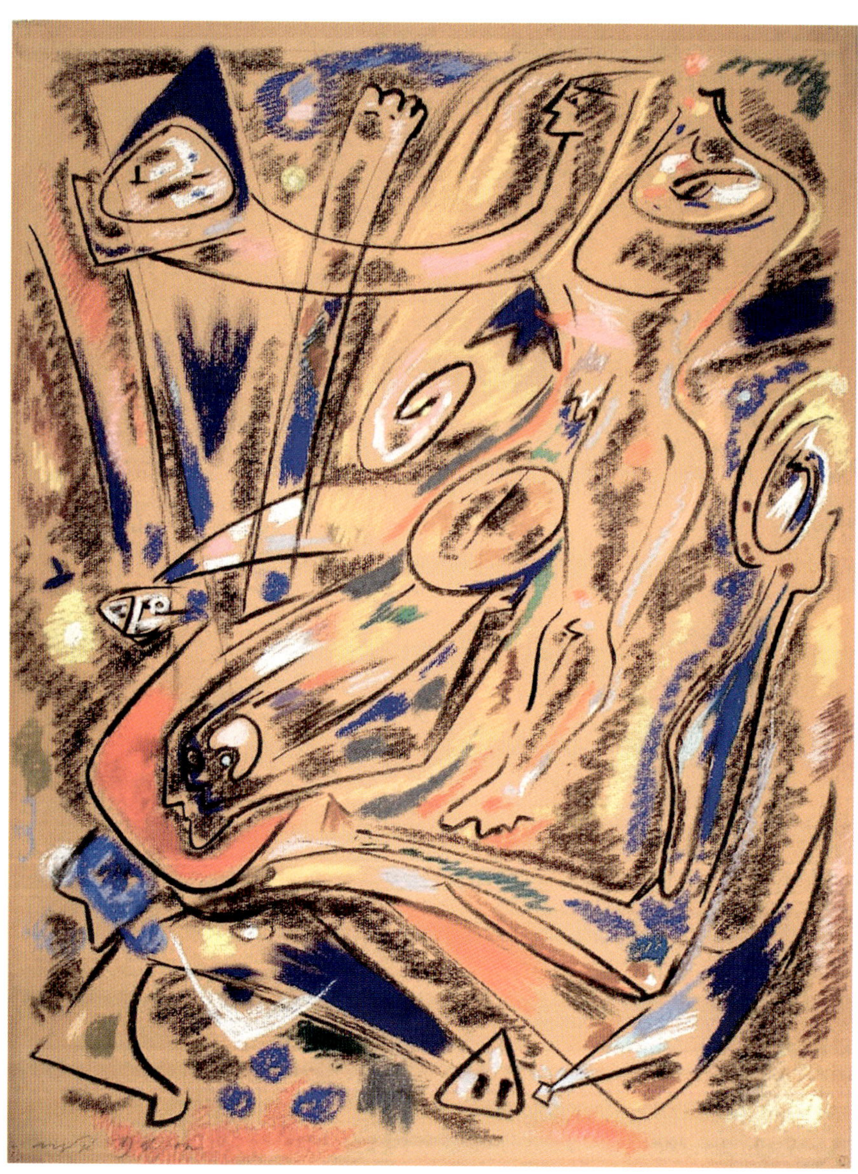

In 1924, after working for several years with the Cubists, André Masson turned to the Surrealists and found a new source of inspiration in their exploration of dreams and the irrational. Along with Joan Miró, he developed a form of unpremeditated or 'automatic' drawing that was intended to give access to a subconscious liberated from the restraints of reason. Although he disengaged himself from the Surrealists in 1929 following a quarrel with André Breton, Masson's art continued to make use of images drawn from his subconscious that were often violent and disturbing.

In the 1950s he returned to a form of freely improvised art that evolved out of his earlier work. The present pastel, executed in 1958 with the spontaneous vigour of the automatic drawings, has a festive theme that recurs from time to time in his paintings and prints of the 1950s and 60s. As the writer Georges Limbour noted in an essay on Masson's 'Fêtes', published in 1947,[1] his art sometimes exhibits an unexpected *joie de vivre*. These festive compositions as well as the images of violence have a mythic character that they share with the themes of Georges Bataille's publication *Acéphale*, on which Masson collaborated from 1936 to 1939. The fragmented figures, hot colours and frenzied movement in the pastel suggest some primordial bacchanal, mirroring the imagery of Bataille's magazine and its cult of the instinctive and irrational.

109

PABLO PICASSO 1881–1973

Bathers, 1961

Graphite on wove paper, 32.5 × 49.5 cm

Signed, dated and numbered: *Picasso 4.6.61 x*

PROVENANCE: Galerie Louise Leiris (Kahnweiler), Paris, 1971

LITERATURE: Zervos (1932–1978), vol.20, no.11; D'Alessandro (2013), ill. p.92

This drawing of two figures, one standing in a robe, the other a female nude sleeping on the ground, was made in June 1961 when Picasso was working on an extensive series of drawings, paintings and prints based on Manet's *Déjeuner sur l'herbe* (Musée d'Orsay, Paris). He reinterpreted Manet's composition as an image of a seated male contemplating a nude woman, a recurrent theme in Picasso's late work. It is difficult, however, to identify a link with Manet's painting here. If the standing figure is wearing oriental costume, Picasso may have been thinking back to the series of paintings and drawings that he made in the 1950s, based on Delacroix's *Women of Algiers*, although these featured two women, one in arab dress, the other nude. The figure on the left, however, seems to be a man. The sleeping woman also differs from the sprawling nude in Picasso's version of *The Women of Algiers.* She does, however, somewhat resemble the reclining nude in Ingres' *Odalisque and the Slave* or in several of the odalisques painted by Matisse. In all probability the composition is an invention, drawn at a time when Picasso's imagination was filled with many images of earlier works.

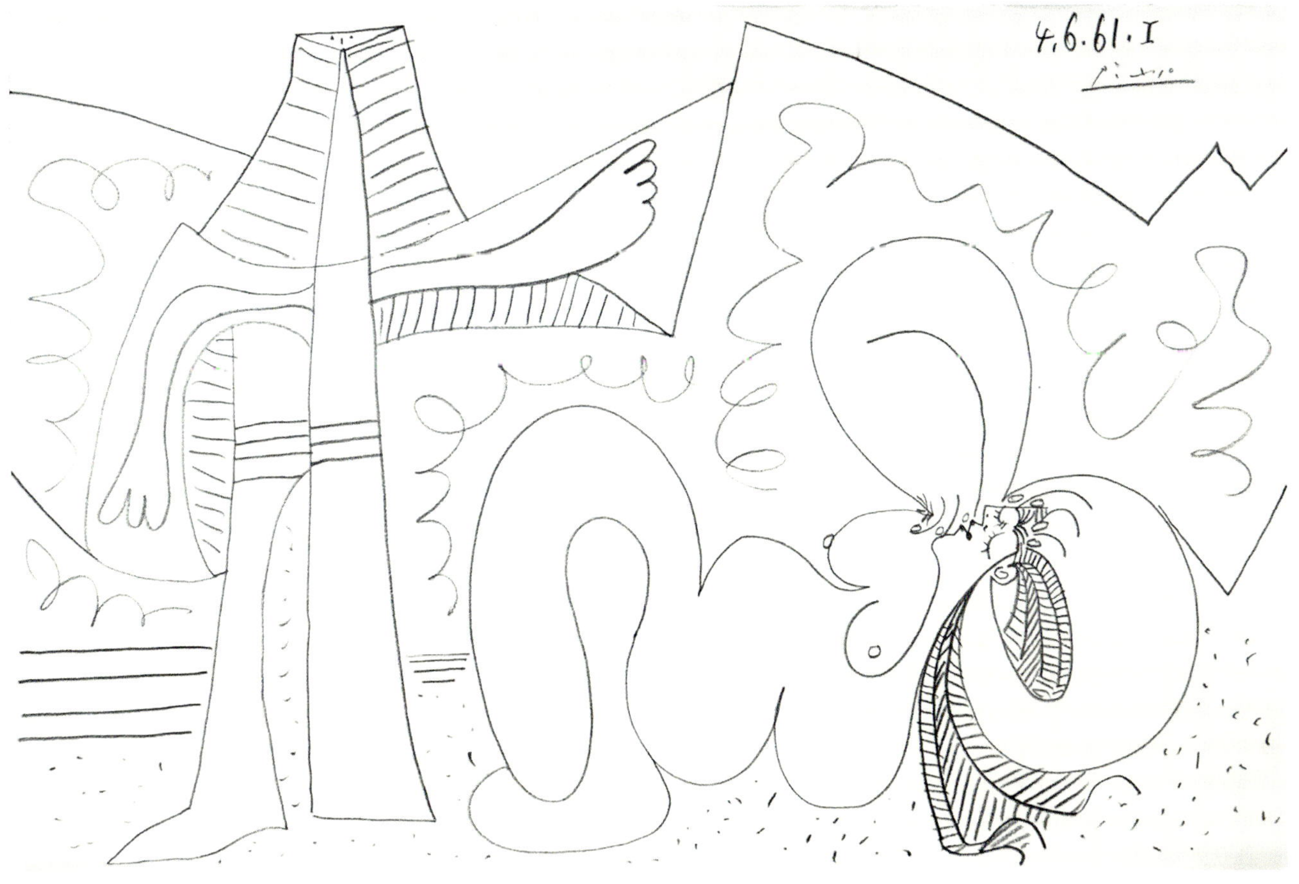

110

PABLO PICASSO 1881–1973

Head of a Woman, 1962

Graphite on white paper, 42.5 × 26.5 cm
Signed and dated: *Picasso 3.6.62*
PROVENANCE: Galerie Louise Leiris (Kahnweiler), Paris, 1971
LITERATURE: Zervos (1932–78), vol.20, no.247; Cooper (1962), no.34; D'Alessandro (2013), ill. p.95

In April 1963 the architects of the new Chicago Civic Center, William Hartmann, Charles Murphy and Richard Bennett, approached Picasso's friend, Roland Penrose, to ask him if Picasso might accept a commission to design a sculpture for the plaza in front of the new building. Picasso accepted the commission willingly, donating it without a fee in gratitude to a city where his work had been exhibited as early as 1913.

Picasso, it seems, had been recently thinking about a three-dimensional work based on a schematic, wedge-shaped face with flowing hair, parted in the centre. He developed this idea in a maquette, or model, which he sent to the city in 1965. After some minor revisions the steel sculpture, 50 feet in height, was constructed at a steelworks in Indiana and unveiled in May 1967.

This drawing belongs to a sequence of sketches, nine of which are dated May 1962[1] - one year before he was approached by the architects. These show only minor differences from the sculpture as executed. Each of the nine includes a flat support with a baluster-shaped outline similar to the support in the final work. This drawing, dated one month later, shows the artist thinking about an alternative dome-shaped support, but retaining the profile of the pedestal on the edge of the subject's hair. That Picasso had in mind the lips of a classical head in profile is evident from the study on the left. Although he returned to his first thoughts about the support, the study confirms that the pedestal represents the lips and chin of a human face. There is a general but telling resemblance to a number of portraits painted at this time of his wife, Jacqueline Roque (1927–86).

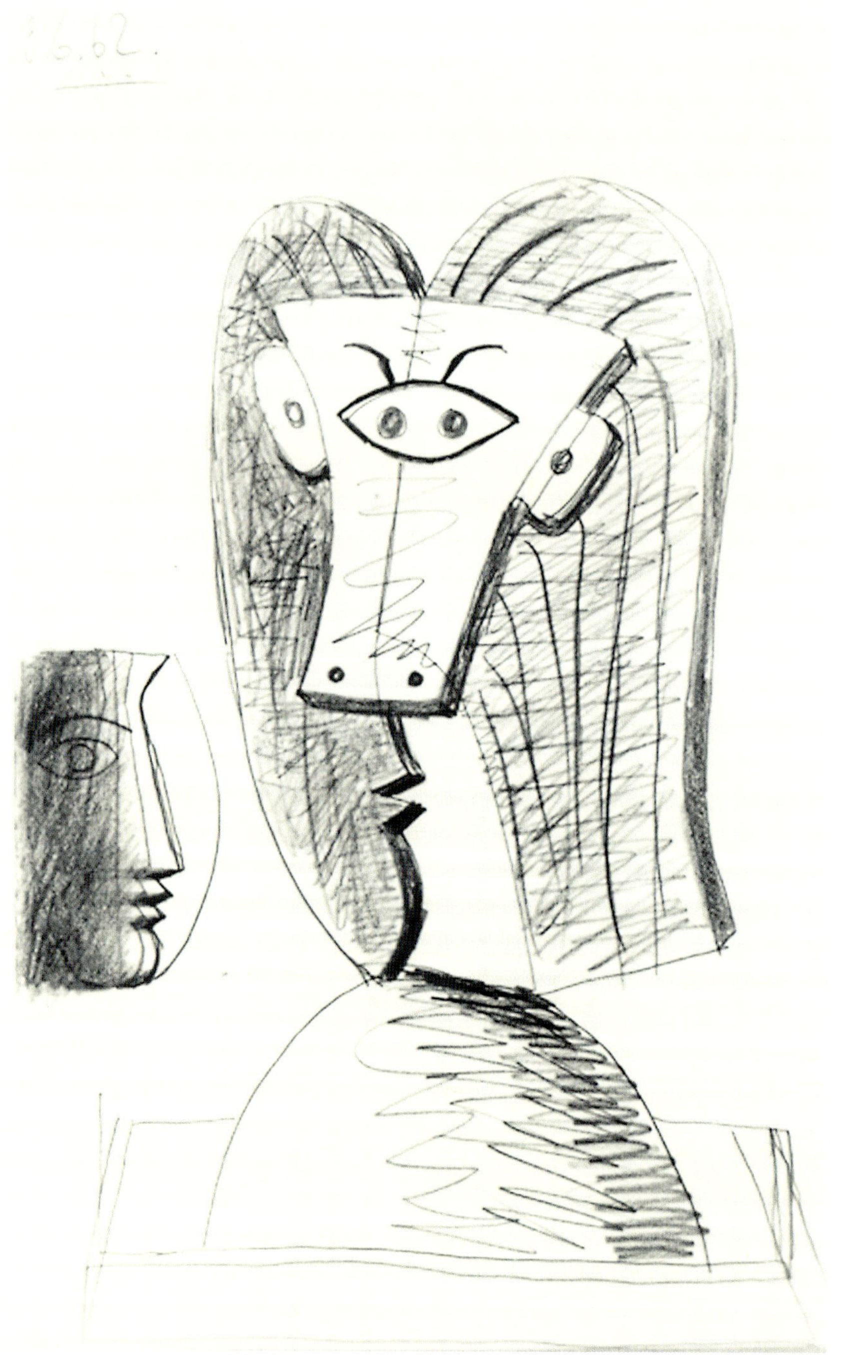

111

PABLO PICASSO 1881–1973

Cockerel, Woman and Young Man, 1967

Pencil, blue crayon and yellow wash on paper, 56.5 × 75 cm

Signed and dated: *Picasso 4.9.67*

PROVENANCE: Galerie Louise Leiris (Kahnweiler), Paris, 1968

LITERATURE: Zervos (1932–78), vol.27, no.514; D'Alessandro (2013), ill. p.98

In the 1920s Picasso began to work in a manner of drawing that was strongly linear, based partly on the work of Ingres and partly on Greek vase painting. While he used several styles of painting and drawing at the same time, the outline style remained the basis of most of his drawings from this date onwards. It was a style that he used in particular when drawing nudes, and it was well adapted for etching.

The simplicity and naturalism that mark much of Picasso's graphic work in the 1920s and early 1930s modified in the later 1930s. As his figures became increasingly distorted and less representational, Picasso retained the same linear manner of drawing. The anatomy of the reclining nude in this drawing of 1967 is not naturalistic. There is a memory of Cubism in the use of more than one viewpoint, but the hard outline, the lack of shading or modelling, the Greek profile of the woman and the simplicity of the drawing all derive from a Neo-Classical tradition.

The significance of the cockerel on the left is not clear. Picasso's images of cockerels do not usually include other figures. It is often said that they represent the image of France, particularly during the Occupation and Liberation, but it need not always be so. The cockerel may have been introduced to add a note of domesticity to a composition which, perhaps, represents a mother and son and not a pair of lovers. Whatever he had intended, Picasso thought better of this detail and scored it out. He also changed his mind about the upper left arm of the reclining woman, which is heavily reworked.

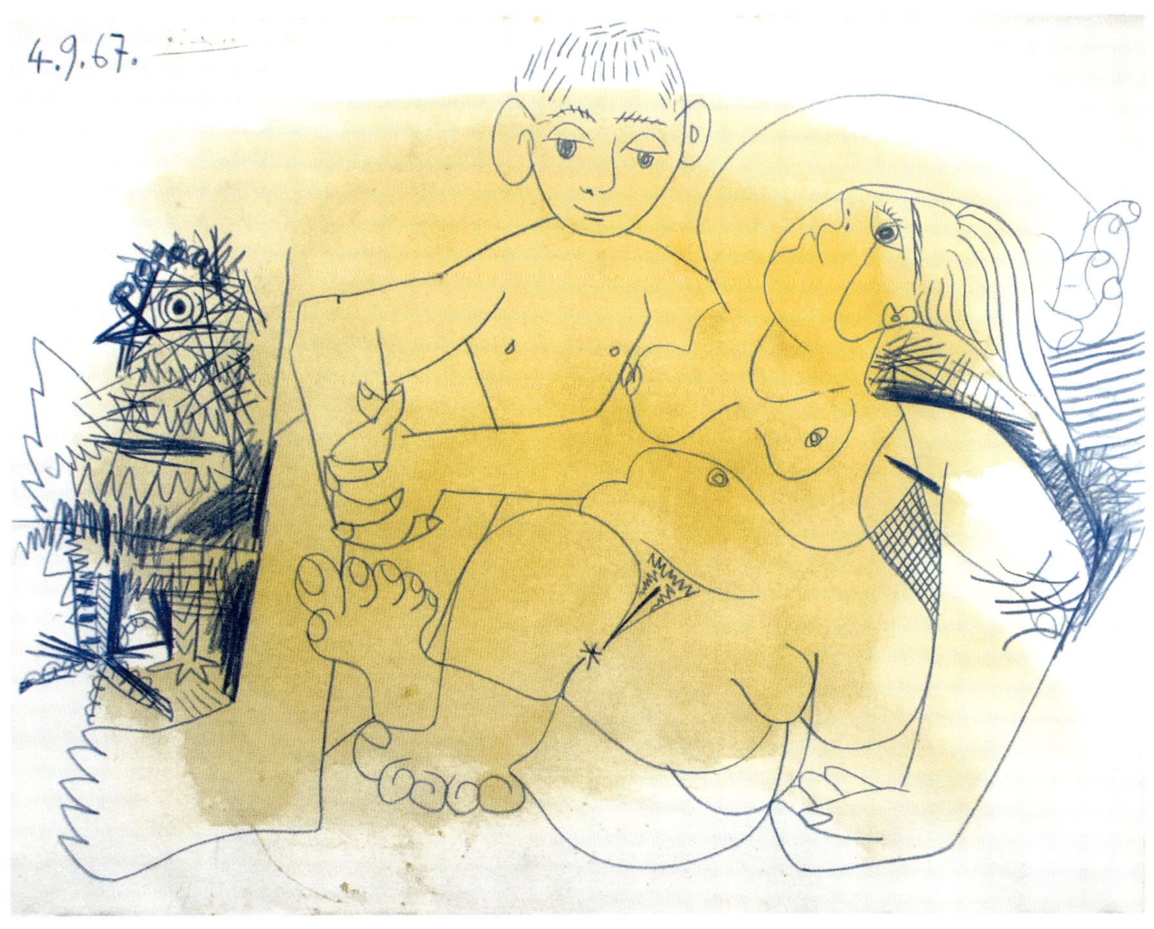

112

PABLO PICASSO 1881–1973

Female Nude, 1969

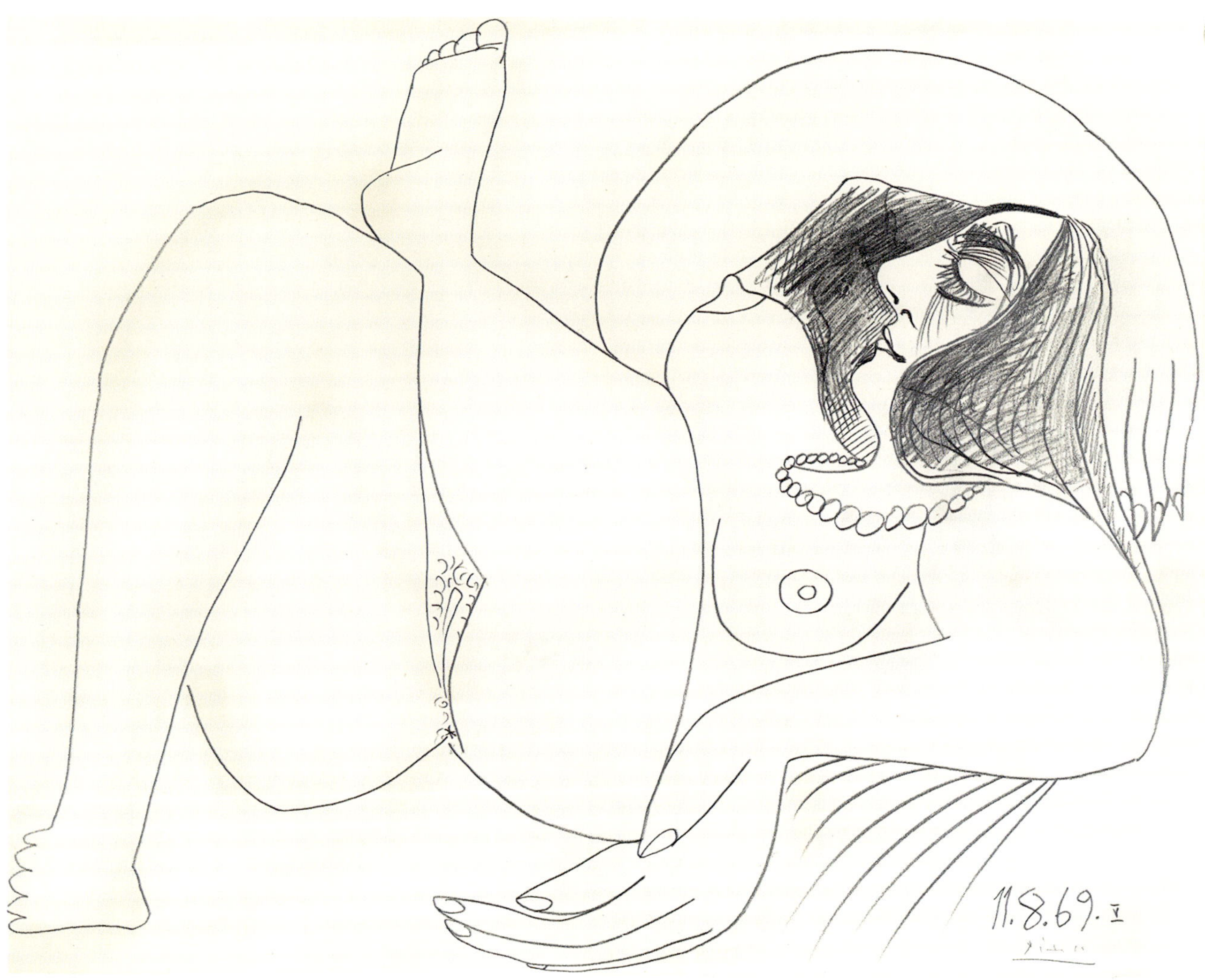

Graphite and pastel on off-white wove paper, 50.5 × 65.5 cm

Signed, dated, and numbered: *Picasso 11.8.69 V*

PROVENANCE: Galerie Louise Leiris (Kahnweiler), Paris, 1971

LITERATURE: Zervos (1932–78), vol.31, no.370

Throughout his life Picasso made images of the female nude, and by the 1960s it had become the major subject of his art. This study of a sleeping woman was one of a group of 19 similar drawings of a nude model, reclining with legs crossed, that he made on 10–12 August 1969.[1] By the end of the month he had begun work on a series of etchings, based on Ingres' painting of *Raphael and the Fornarina*, in which the elements of Ingres' composition were reworked with such licence that his dealer, Daniel Kahnweiler, felt unable to put them on exhibition. The suite, which explores the theme of art and its relationship to desire, provides a key to the other images of nude women that he drew in large numbers in the 1960s.

The models who posed for Picasso's nude studies are generally difficult to identify. In this case, however, it is easy to recognise the features of his wife, Jacqueline Roque, who posed for him more often than any other model in his later years. Her upper arm was originally thicker, but it has been reduced in size and the change concealed under dense hatching.

113

PABLO PICASSO 1881–1973

Harlequin with Mask, 1971

Ink and coloured chalks on paper, 24.1 × 18 cm

Signed, dated and numbered: *Picasso 10.1.71 VI*

PROVENANCE: Galerie Louise Leiris (Kahnweiler), Paris, 1971; private collection, Texas, 1971

LITERATURE: Zervos (1932–78), vol.33, no.27

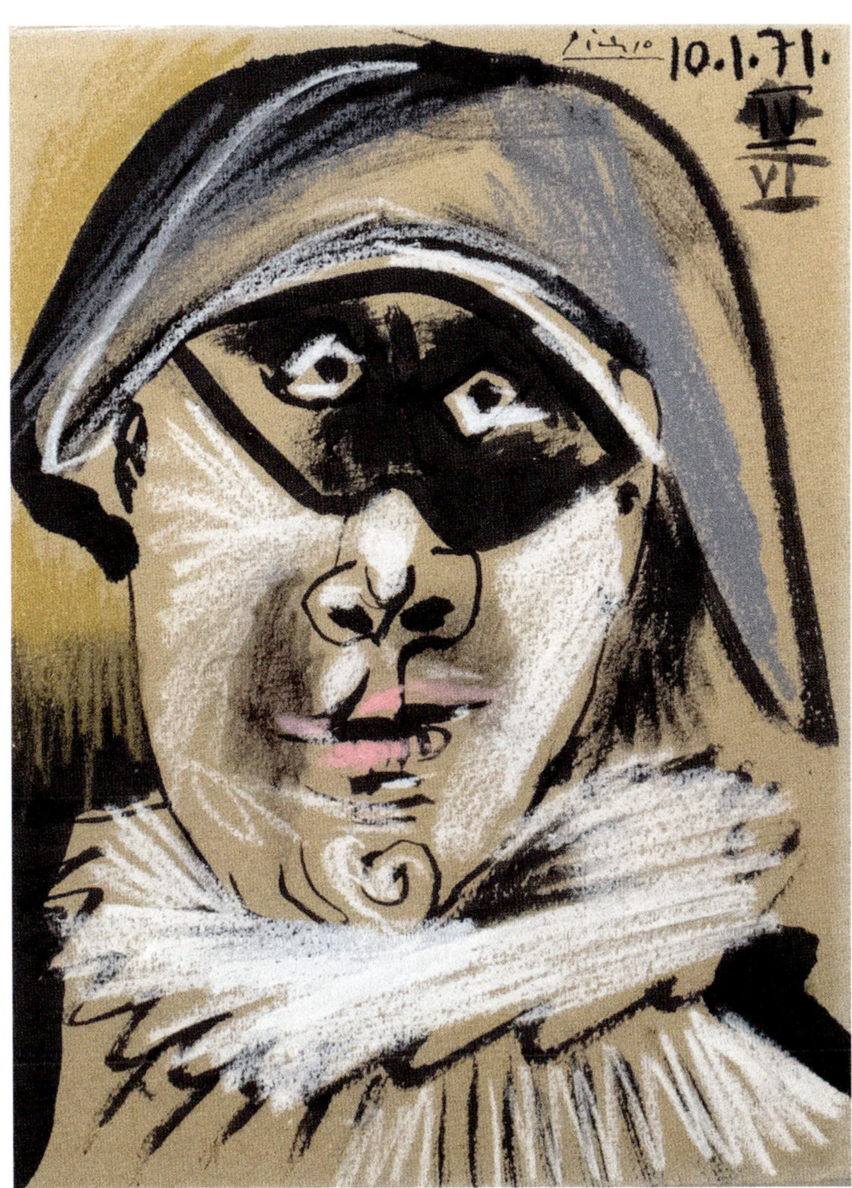

The theme of the Commedia dell'Arte was common in nineteenth-century art and literature. The characters of Pierrot, Harlequin and Columbine, taken from the popular theatre, became as recognisable as the deities of ancient Greece. Picasso was attracted to the Commedia dell'Arte from an early date, encouraged, perhaps, by street performances in his native Barcelona. The character of Harlequin appeared frequently in his art between 1901 and 1905 during the so-called Rose period, cast in the role of the alienated artist. Picasso produced only a handful of Harlequins in the following decade, but he remained attached to the theme. The costumes he designed for Diaghilev's production of Stravinsky's *Pulcinella* in 1920 seem to have reawakened his interest in the Commedia dell'Arte. Over the following four years he produced several pictures of Harlequins before his interest again subsided.

In the early 1960s Picasso returned to the theme of the clown, linking it to a conception of the artist as a role-player and performer recurrent in the art of his final years. During the winter of 1970–1 he made a large number of drawings of Harlequin, either alone or in the company of Pierrot.[1] In a sustained burst of creative energy in January 1971 he made a series of studies of Harlequin's head alone, including the present drawing, generally in a rather messy, childlike manner using coloured chalks.[2] Picasso represents the subject in a way that recalls his earliest work when Harlequin had appeared as the type of the sad clown. By the 1970s Harlequin was no longer depicted as rejected and poor, but he retained his role as a comedian who performs for the public while hiding his true persona behind a mask.

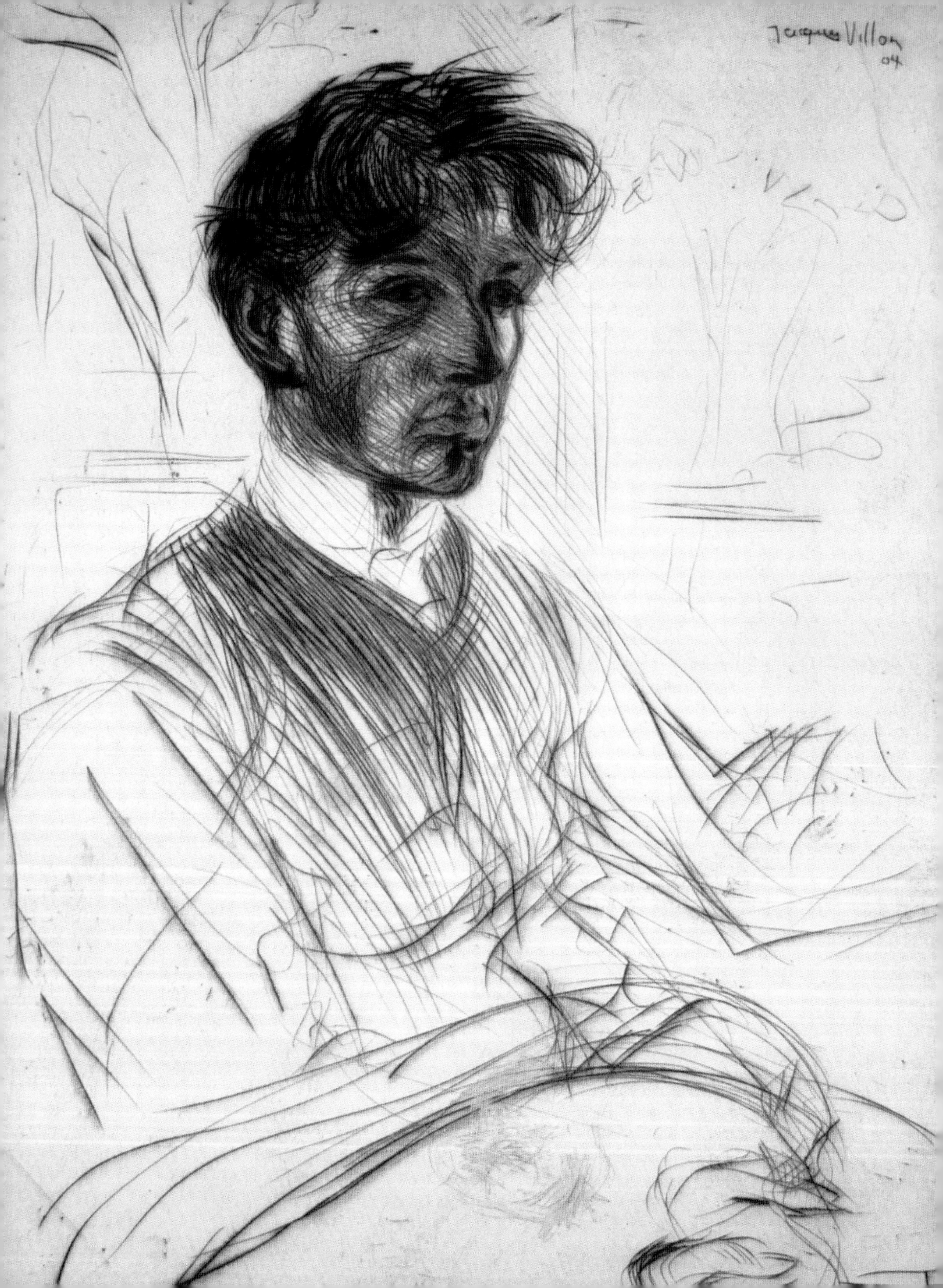
Jacques Villon
04

NOTES AND REFERENCES

Pages 9–19

1. 'Only with the heart can one see clearly.' Antoine de Saint-Exupéry, *Le Petit Prince*, Paris: Gallimard, 1945, p. 72.
2. 'Johnson is crazy! Everyone from Chicago is crazy!'
3. 'To Miss Isabelle, this beautiful mirabelle plum.'
4. See note 1 above.

Cat.1

1. Rosenberg (1987–8), p.508.
2. Rosenberg (1993), p. 7.

2

1. Basily-Kallimaki (1909), p.12.
2. Quoted in Lécosse (2005), p. 33.

4

1. Siegfried (1995), p.89.
2. ibid., p.91.

5

1. Chaudonneret (1980), no.62.
2. ibid., nos 3, 19, 58 and 78.
3. ibid., no.84.

6

1. Sérullaz (1989), p.549.

7

1. Bazin (1987–97), nos 782–3, 795.

8

1. Quoted in Athanassoglou-Kallmyer (2010), p.95.
2. Rouen; Bazin (1987–97), no.1462.
3. Clément (1879), pp.213–4.

9

1. Eitner (1983), p.218.
2. Bazin (1987–97), VII, p.32.
3. Delteil (1924), no.26; Bazin (1987–97), no.2338.

10

1. Quoted in Johnson, L. (1995), p.9.
2. Johnson, L. (1995), no.12.

opposite:
Detail from Jacques Villon 1875–1963 *Marcel Duchamp* [cat.56]

11

1. Johnson, L. III (1981–89), vol. 3, p.164.
2. Delacroix (2009), p.214.
3. Johnson, L. (1981–89), vol. 3, p.355 (private collection); cf. earlier versions 349, 351, 353 and later 367 (1844) and 376 (1847).
4. Johnson, L. (1981–89), vol. 3, p.355, footnote.
5. Béraldi (1885–1892), X, p.176, nos 50–51.

12

1. Salmon (2006), p.22.

13 & 14

1. Quoted in Foucart (2002), p.20.

15

1. Quoted in Guégan, Pomarède and Prat (2002), p.84.
2. Prat (1988), I, no.10.

16

1. Quoted in Guégan, Pomarède, Prat (2002), p.179.
2. ibid.
3. Prat (1988), no.1417.

17

1. Quoted in Loyrette (1999), p.125.
2. ibid., p.175.

18

1. Maison (1968), no.666; Stampfle and Denison (1975), no.85.

19

1. Maison (1968), nos 30, 319, 360–1.

20

1. Naegely (1898), pp.13–14.
2. Sotheby's, New York, 3 November 2015, lot 84.

21

1. Now in Cincinnati; Herbert (1975), no.57. The replica is in the Metropolitan Museum, New York.
2. National Gallery of Scotland, Edinburgh.
3. National Gallery, London; Herbert (1975), no.26.
4. Yamanashi Prefectural Museum of Art, Kofu and Louvre, Paris respectively; Herbert (1975), nos 37, 41 and 42.
5. Paine Art Center, Oshkosh; see Murphy (1984), no.8.
6. See Murphy (1984), nos 83 and 92–3.

22

1. Clapp (1983), p.18.
2. Quoted in Zafran (2007), p.126.
3. Quoted in Clapp (1983), p.49.
4. Quoted in Geyer (1993), p.59.
5. Cf. Favière (1983), nos 177–8 and 180.

23

1. Rouart and Wildenstein (1975), no.360.
2. ibid., no.306.

24

1. Quoted in Cachin, Moffett, Wilson Bareau (1983), p.237.
2. See Kopplin (1981), p.42.
3. http://gallica.bnf.fr/ark:/12148/btv1b8432399p/f21.highres

25

1. Quoted in Cachin, Moffett, Wilson Bareau (1983), p.273.

26

1. Quoted in Cachin, Moffett, Wilson Bareau (1983), p.302.
2. Mallarmé (2003), pp.151–2.
3. Musée d'Orsay, Paris; Rouart and Wildenstein (1975), no.179; Cachin, Moffett, Wilson Bareau (1983), no.130.

27

1. Rouart and Wildenstein (1975), no.574; Mauner et Loyrette (2001), no.46.

28

1. Quoted in Hamilton (1992), p.84.
2. Quoted in Jean-Aubry (1922), p.62.
3. Quoted in Cahen (1900), p.71
4. ibid., p.181

29

1. For example Wildenstein (1974–91), V, nos D26, 51.
2. ibid., nos D416–21.
3. Ganz and Kendall (2007), pp.87–96.

30

1. See Brettell and Lloyd (1980), no.44.
2. ibid., no.45.
3. ibid., nos 70–1; Snollaerts and Pissarro (2005), nos 365–6.
4. ibid., no.157.

31

1. Quoted in French in Brettell and Lloyd (1980), p.15.
2. ibid., nos 334–5.

32

1. Quoted in Breeskin (1979). p.13.
2. Segard (1913), p.86.

33

1. Breeskin (1979), nos 85–7.

34

1. Lemoisne (1946–9), no.34.

35

1. Quoted in Thomson (1987), p.15.
2. The first three remained together until sold in 1981. The other group is now dispersed, with the painting of Rosa-Adelaida now in the Thaw collection, exhibited in Boggs (1988), no.16.
3. Quoted in Boggs (1988), p.52.

36

1. Musée d'Orsay; Boggs (1988), no.58.
2. Quoted in Baumann and Karabelnik (1994), p.162.
3. Louvre; Boggs (1988), no.59.

37 & 38

1. Reff (1976), nb 18, p.55.
2. Degas's fourth sale, 2–4 July 1919, lots 23a and 202.

39

1. Reed and Shapiro (1984), p.98.
2. For example, *Mlle Bécat aux ambassadeurs* (Reed and Shapiro (1984), 31); *Chanteuse de café concert* (Lemoisne III, no.68).
3. Reed and Shapiro (1984), p.33.
4. ibid., p.48.

40

1. Reed and Shapiro (1984), p.132, n. 3.
2. ibid., p.126, fig.2 and p.128, fig.3.

41 & 42

1. Reed and Shapiro (1984), 61. I–VI
2. ibid., 62–6
3. ibid., 61. I, II and III
4. As Richard Thomson first suggested in *The Private Degas*, Whitworth Art Gallery, Manchester, 1987, p.124.

43

1. Reed and Shapiro (1984), 63–65
2. ibid. 66.I–V

44

1. Kendall (1996), pp 189–191, nos 11–15.

45

1. Fourth sale 2–4 July 1919, lot 327

46

1. Quoted in Distel and House (1985), p.263.
2. Toledo Museum of Art; Dumas and Collins (2005), pp.80–1.
3. Quoted in Distel and House (1985), p.280.

47

1. Duranty (1878), p. 24.

48

1. Ongpin (2016), no.43
2. Redon (1961), pp.26–27.

49

1. Musée d'Orsay, private collection, Musée d'Orsay respectively; Rewald (1996), nos 166, 164 and 171.

50

1. Rewald (1996), nos 259 (Geneva), 260 (private collection) and 261 (Barnes collection). For the convincing suggestion that the Barnes painting is not a sketch, see Richard Brettell in Moffett (1986), p.195.
2. Chappuis (1973), no.713 (Albertina, Vienna).
3. Rewald (1996), nos 252 (Rose Art Museum, Brandeis University, Mass.), 253 (private collection), 255 (private collection), 269 (Jasper Johns); and, for example, Chappuis (1973), nos 385–9.
4. Rewald (1996), no.370 (private collection).
5. Rewald (1996), no.555 (Museum of Modern Art, New York).

51 & 52

1. Quoted in Johnson, U. (1977), p.19.
2. Venturi (1936), no.1157.

53

1. Gleizes and Metzinger (1913), p.16
2. Cooper (1971), p.68

54

1. http://vangoghletters.org/vg/letters/let879/letter.html
2. Quoted in Distel and Stein (1999), p.100.
3. http://vangoghletters.org/vg/letters/let890/letter.html

55

1. See Carlson (1976) no.2 (Baltimore Museum of Art) and Daix, Boudaille, Rosselet (1967), nos D.III.4, D.III.1–2 (Kröller-Müller Museum, Otterlo)

57

1. Cleveland Museum of Art.
2. Metropolitan Museum, New York.
3. Museum of Modern Art, New York.
4. Philadelphia Museum of Art.

58

1. Rewald (1989), pp.84–6. The woodblock is in the Victoria and Albert Museum, London.

59

1. Metropolitan Museum of Art, New York, promised gift from the Leonard A. Lauder Cubist Collection.

60

1. Seligman (2000), no.438.

62
1. Golding (1968), pp 28–29

63
1. For a lively account of this farcical episode, see Peter Read (2008), pp.59–67.

65
1. Baer (1997), p. 32.
2. Picasso, *The Architect's Table*, 1912, Museum of Modern Art, New York.
3. Picasso, *Guitar, Wine-glass, Bottle of Vieux Marc*, 1913, Musée Picasso, Paris; *Bottle of Vieux Marc*, 1913, Musée National d'Art Moderne, Paris; *Paper, Glass, Bottle of Vieux Marc*, 1914, Guggenheim Museum, New York.
4. Georges Braque, *Bottle of Vieux Marc*, 1912, Metropolitan Museum of Art, New York; *Guitar and Bottle of Marc*, Cleveland Museum of Art.

66
1. Quoted in Cooper, 1971, p.68.

69
1. Art Institute of Chicago.
2. Art Institute of Chicago; McCullagh (2003–4), no.69.
3. Millet (1991), nos 38, 43 and 113.

70
1. Leal (2005), no.176, ill.

71
1. Green, Maur and Derouet (1992), p.151.

72
1. Moser (1985–6), p.21.
2. Golding (1968), p.160.

73
1. Gleizes and Metzinger (1913), p.46.
2. ibid., p.27.

74
1. Rowell (1975), p.338.

77
1. Varichon (1998), no.412.

79
1. Ginestet and Pouillon (1979) E277.
2. ibid. (1979) E277 and E280.
3. ibid. (1979) E282.

80
1. Illustrated in Varichon (1998), vol.1, p.177, no.497.

81
1. Loyer (1976), no.1.

82
1. Varichon (1998), no.470.

83
1. Varichon (1998), nos 455 and 447.
2. ibid., nos 447–458.

88
1. Seligman (2000), no.263.
2. ibid., no.264.
3. ibid., no.265.
4. Caizergues (1989), np.
5. Seligman (2000), nos 263–5, 284–8.
6. ibid., nos 242–3.
7. ibid., nos 285–6.
8. ibid., no.286.

90
1. Johnson (1991), p.88.
2. Moser (1985–6), p.46.
3. Derouet (1999), p.59.

91
1. New York (1998), quoted on p.177.

93
1. Varichon (1998), vol.1, p.322.

94
1. Impressionist and Modern Evening Sale, Christie's, New York, 14 May 2015, lot 9c.

95
1. Samuel Palmer, *The Valley Thick with Corn*, Ashmolean Museum.

96
1. Level (1928), p.58.
2. eg. Zervos (1932–78), vol.4, nos 79–88, 100–104; vol.6, nos 1383–1385, 1388–1390; vol.29, nos 450–454.
3. The other version of *Three Musicians* is in the Philadelphia Museum of Art.
4. Georges Braque,*Guitar and Still Life on a Guéridon*, Metropolitan Museum of Art, New York.

97
1. Ongpin (2012), no.43.
2. Artcurial, Hôtel Dassaut, Paris, 20 October 2007, lot 74.

98
1. Ginestet and Pouillon (1979), E647.
2. ibid., E668.

99
1. Cassou and Leymaire (1972–3), no.205.
2. Quoted in Francia (1983), p.115.

102
1. George and Nouaille-Rouault (1971), p.51.

103
1. Vollard (1936), pp.260–1.

105
1. Paris (1980), p. 25.

106
1. Reproduced in Klein (2001), p.138.
2. Duthuit and Garnaud (1988), no.10.
3. Translated from Matisse (1972), p.179.

108
1. Limbour (1947), pp.185–89.

110
1. Art Institute of Chicago, restricted gift of William E. Hartmann.

112
1. Zervos (1932–1978), vol.3, nos. 356–374.

113
1. Zervos (1932–78), vol.32, nos 318–333.
2. ibid., 33, nos 1–7, 11–27.

BIBLIOGRAPHY

ADHÉMAR (1974)
Adhémar, Jean, *Degas, the complete etchings, lithographs and monotypes*, London 1974

ALAOUI (1994–95)
Alaoui, Brahim, *Delacroix, le voyage au Maroc*, Institut du Monde Arabe, Paris 1994–95

ANTLIFF (1993)
Antliff, Mark, *Inventing Bergson: Cultural Politics and the Parisian Avant-Garde*, Princeton 1993

ART IN AMERICA (1977)
Art in America, no.65, March 1977

ATHANASSOGLOU-KALLMYER (2010)
Athanassoglou-Kallmyer, Nina, *Théodore Géricault*, London 2010

AUBERTY AND PERUSSAUX (1954)
Auberty, Jacqueline, and Perussaux, Charles, *Jacques Villon: catalogue de son oeuvre gravé*, Paris 1954

BAER (1997)
Baer, Brigitte, *Picasso the Engraver: Selections from the Musée Picasso*, Paris, New York/London 1997

BARTER (1998)
Barter, Judith, *Mary Cassatt, Modern Woman*, Art Institute of Chicago, 1998

BASILY-CALLIMAKI (1909)
Basily-Callimaki, E. de, *J.-B. Isabey, sa vie, son temps, 1767–1855, suivi du catalogue de l'oeuvre gravé par et d'après Isabey*, Paris 1909

BAUMANN AND KARABELNIK (1994)
Baumann, Felix and Karabelnik, Marianne, *Degas; portraits*, Kunsthaus, Zurich; Kunsthalle, Tübingen, 1994

BAZIN (1987–97)
Bazin, Germain, *Théodore Géricault: étude critique, documents et catalogue raisonné*, Paris 1987–1997, 7 vols

BÉRALDI (1885–1892)
Béraldi, Henri, Les graveurs du XIXe siècle; guide de l'amateur d'estampes modernes, Paris 1885–1892, 12 vols

BERMANN MARTIN (FORTHCOMING)
Bermann Martin, Dominique, *André Lhote: catalogue raisonné* (forthcoming)

BOGGS (1962)
Boggs, Jean Sutherland, *Portraits by Degas*, Berkeley 1962

BOGGS (1988)
Boggs, Jean Sutherland, "Degas et la maternité", in *Degas inédit*, ed. Henri Loyrette, Paris 1989, pp.35–45

BOGGS (1989)
Boggs, Jean Sutherland, "Les dernières années, 1890–1912" in *Degas*, Galeries nationales du Grand Palais, Paris; Musée des beaux-arts du Canada, Ottawa; The Metropolitan Museum of Art, New York, 1988–99, pp.481–499

BONGERS (FORTHCOMING)
Bongers, Patrick, *Jacques Villon: catalogue raisonné* (forthcoming)

BREESKIN (1970)
Breeskin, Adelyn Dohme, *Mary Cassatt, 1844–1926*, National Gallery of Art, Washington 1970

BREESKIN (1979)
Breeskin, Adelyn Dohme, *Mary Cassatt: A Catalogue Raisonné of the Graphic Work*, Washington 1979

BRETTELL AND LLOYD (1980)
Brettell, Richard and Lloyd, Christopher, *A Catalogue of the Drawings by Camille Pissarro in the Ashmolean Museum, Oxford*, Oxford 1980

BRIEND (2001)
Briend, Christian, *Albert Gleizes: le cubisme en majesté*, Museu Picasso, Barcelona; Lyons, Musée des beaux-arts, 2001

CACHIN, MOFFETT AND WILSON BAREAU (1983)
Cachin, Françoise; Moffett, Charles; Wilson Bareau, Juliet, *Manet 1831–1883*, Galeries nationales du Grand Palais; The Metropolitan Museum of Art, New York, 1983

CAHEN (1900)
Cahen, Gustave, *Eugène Boudin, sa vie et son oeuvre*, Paris 1900

CAIZERGUES (1989)
Caizergues, Pierre, "Un dialogue interrompu" in Jean Cocteau, *Tambour*, Marseille 1989, np

CARLSON (1976)
Carlson, Victor, *Picasso Drawings and Watercolours 1899–1907 in the Collection of the Baltimore Museum of Art*, Baltimore 1976

CASSOU (1951)
Cassou, Jean, *Jacques Villon*, Musée National d'Art Moderne, Paris 1951

CASSOU AND LEYMAIRE (1972–73)
Cassou, Jean and Leymaire, Jean, *Fernand Léger, dessins et gouaches*, Paris 1972

CHAPPUIS (1973)
Chappuis, Adrien, *The Drawings of Paul Cézanne: A Catalogue Raisonné*, New York 1973, 2 vols

CHAUDONNERET (1980)
Chaudonneret, Marie-Claude, *Fleury Richard et Pierre Révoil: la peinture troubadour*, Paris 1980

CHERPIN (1972)
Cherpin, Jean, *L'oeuvre gravé de Cézanne*, Marseille 1972

CLAPP (1983)
Clapp, Samuel F., *Gustave Doré, 1832–1883*, loan exhibition held on the centenary of the artist's death, Hazlitt, Gooden & Fox, London 1983

CLÉMENT (1879)
Clément, Charles, *Géricault: étude biographique et critique, avec le catalogue raisonné de l'oeuvre du maître*, 3rd ed., Paris 1879

COOPER (1962)
Cooper, Douglas, *Picasso: le Déjeuner sur l'herbe*, Galerie Louise Leiris, Paris 1962

COOPER (1971)
Cooper, Douglas, *The Cubist Epoch*, London 1971

COOPER (1977)
Cooper, Douglas, *Juan Gris: catalogue raisonné de l'oeuvre peint*, Paris 1977

COQUIOT (1922)
Coquiot, Gustave, *Bonnard*, Paris 1922

COURTHION (1962)
Courthion, Pierre, *Georges Rouault*, Paris 1962

DAIX, BOUDAILLE AND ROSSELET (1967)
Daix, Pierre; Boudaille, Georges; Rosselet, Joan, *Picasso, the Blue and Rose periods: A Catalogue Raisonné of the Paintings and Related Works*, London 1966

DAIX AND ROSSELET (1979)
Daix, Pierre and Rosselet, Joan, *Picasso, the Cubist years, 1907–1916: A Catalogue Raisonné of the Paintings and Related works*, London 1979

D'ALESSANDRO (2013)
D'Alessandro, Stephanie, *Picasso and Chicago*, The Art Institute of Chicago, 2013

DELTEIL (1908)
Delteil, Loys, *Ingres et Delacroix, Le peintre-graveur illustré*, vol. 3, Paris 1908

DELTEIL (1919)
Delteil, Loys, *Degas, Le peintre-graveur illustré*, vol. 9, Paris 1919

DELTEIL (1924)
Delteil, Loys, *Géricault, Le peintre-graveur illustré*, vol.18, Paris 1924

DELTEIL (1925–30)
Delteil, Loys, *Oeuvre lithographié de Honoré Daumier, 11 vols, Le peintre-graveur illustré*, vols 20 to 29 bis, Paris 1925–30

DELTEIL, HYMAN AND JACKSON (2010)
Delteil, Loys; Hyman, Alan; Jackson, Geoffrey, *Théodore Géricault, the Graphic Work/ l'oeuvre gravé: A Catalogue Raisonné*, San Francisco 2010

DELTEIL AND STRAUBER (1997)
Delteil, Loys and Strauber, Susan, *Delacroix, the Graphic Work: A Catalogue Raisonné*, San Francisco 1997

DEROUET (1999)
Derouet, Christian, ed., *Juan Gris: correspondance avec Léonce Rosenberg, 1918–1927*, Paris 1999

DISTEL AND HOUSE (1985)
Distel, Anne and House, John, *Renoir*, Hayward Gallery, London; Galeries nationales du Grand Palais, Paris; Museum of Fine Arts, Boston, 1985–86

DISTEL AND STEIN (1999)
Distel, Anne and Stein, Susan, *Un ami de Cézanne et Van Gogh, le docteur Gachet*, Galeries nationales du Grand Palais, Paris; Museum Van Gogh, Amsterdam; The Metropolitan Museum of Art, New York, 1999

DORIVAL (1964)
Dorival, Bernard, *Georges Rouault: oeuvres données à l'Ètat*, Paris 1964

DORIVAL AND ROUAULT (1988)
Dorival, Bernard and Rouault, Isabelle, *Georges Rouault, l'oeuvre peint*, Paris 1988, 2 vols

DRUICK (1978)
Druick, Douglas, "Cézanne's lithographs" in *Cézanne, the Late Work*, The Metropolitan Museum of Art, New York, 1978, pp.119–137

DUMAS AND COLLINS (2005)
Dumas, Ann, and Collins, John Bruce, *Renoir's Women*, London 2003

DUPUY-VACHEY (2003)
Dupuy-Vachey, Marie-Anne, *Fragonard et le Roland Furieux*, Paris 2003

DURANTY (1878)
Duranty, Louis-Émile, *La nouvelle peinture: à propos du groupe d'artistes qui expose dans les galeries Durand-Ruel*, Paris 1878

DUTHUIT (1983)
Duthuit, Claude and Matisse-Duthuit, Marguerite, *Henri Matisse: catalogue raisonné de l'oeuvre gravé*, Paris 1983, 2 vols

DUTHUIT AND GARNAUD (1988)
Duthuit, Claude and Garnaud, Françoise, *Henri Matisse, catalogue raisonné des ouvrages illustrés*, Paris 1988

EITNER (1983)
Eitner, Lorenz, *Géricault: his Life and Work*, London 1983

FAVIÈRE (1983)
Favière, Jean, ed., *Gustave Doré 1832–1883*, Musée d'art moderne, Strasbourg, 1983.

FEIST (1963)
Feist, Peter, *Paul Cézanne*, Leipzig 1963

FISHER (1979)
Fisher, Jay McKean, *Théodore Chassériau: Illustrations for Othello*, Baltimore Museum of Art, Baltimore 1979

FOUCART (2002)
Foucart, Jacques, *Ingres: les cartons de vitraux des collections du Louvre*, Musée du Louvre, Paris 2002

FRANCIA (1983)
Francia, Peter de, *Fernand Léger*, New Haven/London 1983

GANZ AND KENDALL (2007)
Ganz, James A. and Kendall, Richard, *The Unknown Monet. Pastels and Drawings*, Royal Academy of Arts, Sterling and Francine Clark Institute, Williamstown, 2007

GEISER/BAER (1933–72)
Geiser, Bernhard and Baer, Brigitte, *Picasso, peintre-graveur, catalogue raisonné de l'oeuvre gravé et des monotypes*, Berne 1933–1972, 7 vols

GEORGE AND NOUAILLE-ROUAULT (1971)
George, Waldemar, and Nouaille-Rouault, Geneviève, *Rouault*, London 1971

GEYER (1993)
Geyer, Marie-Jeanne, *Gustave Doré: une nouvelle collection*, Palais Rohan, Strasbourg 1993–94

GINESTET AND POUILLON (1979)
Ginestet, Colette and Pouillon, Catherine, *Jacques Villon: les estampes et les illustrations: catalogue raisonné*, Paris 1979

GLEIZES AND METZINGER (1913)
Gleizes, Albert and Metzinger, Jean, *Cubism*, translated, London 1913

GOLDING (1968)
Golding, John, *Cubism: A History and an Analysis, 1907–1914*, London 1968

GREEN, MAUR AND DEROUET (1992)
Green, Christopher; Maur, Karin von; Derouet, Christian, *Juan Gris*, Whitechapel Art Gallery, London, 1992

GUÉGAN, POMARÈDE AND PRAT (2002)
Guégan, Stéphane; Pomarède, Vincent; Prat, Louis-Antoine, *Chassériau: un autre romantisme* Galeries nationales du Grand Palais, Paris; Palais Rohan, Strasbourg; The Metropolitan Museum of Art, New York, 2002

GUÉRIN (1944)
Guérin, Maurice, *L'oeuvre gravé* de Manet, Paris 1944

GUILLON-LAFFAILLE (FORTHCOMING)
Guillon-Laffaille, Fanny, *Raoul Dufy, catalogue raisonné des aquarelles, gouaches et pastels, supplement* (forthcoming)

HAMILTON (1992)
Hamilton, Vivien, *Boudin at Trouville*, London 1992

HANNOOSH (2009)
Hannoosh, Michèle, ed., *Journal de Delacroix*, Paris 2009, 2 vols

HARRIS (1970)
Harris, Jean C., Édouard Manet: Graphic Works: A *Definitive Catalogue Raisonné*, New York 1970

HARRISSE (1898)
Harrisse, Henry, *L.-L. Boilly, peintre, dessinateur et lithographe: sa vie et son oeuvre, 1761-1845; étude suivie d'une description de treize cent soixante tableaux, portraits, dessins et lithographies de cet artiste*, Paris 1898

HAUKE (1961)
Hauke, César de, *Seurat et son oeuvre*, Paris 1961

HAUPTMAN (2016)
Hauptman, Jodi and Armstrong, Carol, *Degas: A Strange Beauty*, Museum of Modern Art, New York, 2016

HERBERT (1975)
Herbert, Robert, *Jean-François Millet*, Galeries nationales du Grand Palais, Paris; Hayward Gallery, London, 1975–76

JEAN-AUBRY (1922)
Jean-Aubry, Georges, *Eugène Boudin d'après des documents inédits: l'homme et son oeuvre*, Paris 1922

JOHNSON (1987)
Johnson, R. Stanley, *Marcel Gromaire: works on paper*, Chicago, 1987

JOHNSON (1991)
Johnson, R. Stanley, *Cubism & la Section d'Or*, The Phillips Collection, Washington; The Dallas Museum of Art, Dallas; The Minneapolis Institute of Arts, Minneapolis, 1991

JOHNSON (2004)
Johnson, R. Stanley, *Pablo Picasso*, Chicago 2004

JOHNSON (2007)
Johnson, R. Stanley, *Marcel Gromaire, 1892–1971*, Chicago 2007

JOHNSON (2008)
Johnson, R. Stanley, 50 *drawings*, Chicago 2008

JOHNSON (2014)
Johnson, R. Stanley, *Aspects of Modern Art, 1880–1980*, Chicago 2014

JOHNSON (2015)
Johnson, R. Stanley, *Camille Pissarro: Important Works on Paper*, Alliance Française, Chicago 2015

JOHNSON L. (1981–89)
Johnson, Lee, *The Paintings of Eugène Delacroix: A Critical Catalogue*, Oxford 1981–89, 3 vols

JOHNSON, L. (1995)
Johnson, Lee, *Delacroix: Pastels*, London 1995

JOHNSON, S. (1964)
Johnson, Samuel E., *Metzinger: pre-Cubist works, 1900–1930*, International Galleries, Chicago, 1964

JOHNSON, U. (1977)
Johnson, Una E., *Ambroise Vollard*, Éditeur: Prints, Books, Bronzes, Museum of Modern Art, New York; Art Gallery of Ontario, Toronto; Krannert Art Museum, University of Illinois at Urbana-Champaign; Toledo Museum of Art, 1977

KAHNWEILER (1965)
Kahnweiler, Daniel, *Juan Gris, dessins et gouaches, 1910–1927*, Galerie Louise Leiris, Paris 1965

KENDALL (1996)
Kendall, Richard, *Degas: Beyond Impressionism*, National Gallery, London; The Art Institute of Chicago, 1996–97

KLEIN (2001)
Klein, John, *Matisse Portraits*, New Haven/London 2001

KOPPLIN (1981)
Kopplin, Monika, *Das Fächerblatt von Manet bis Kokoschka: Europäische Traditionen und japanische Einflüsse*, Cologne 1981

LA FAILLE (1970)
La Faille, Jacob-Baart de, *The Works of Vincent Van Gogh: his Paintings and Drawings*, Amsterdam, new ed., 1970

LAFRANCHIS (1961)
Lafranchis, Jean, *Marcoussis: sa vie, son oeuvre: catalogue complet des peintures, fixés sur verre, aquarelles, dessins, gravures*, Paris 1961

LAUNAY (1991)
Launay, Elisabeth, *Les frères Goncourt: collectioneurs de dessins*, Paris 1991

LEAL (2005)
Leal, Paloma Esteban, *Juan Gris, Paintings and Drawings 1910–1927*, Museo Nactional Centro de Arte Reina Sofia, Madrid, 2005

LÉCOSSE (2005)
Lécosse, Cyril, "Le parcours de Jean-Baptiste Isabey sous la Révolution" in *Jean-Baptiste Isabey, portraitiste de l'Europe (1767–1855)*, Malmaison, Musée des beaux-arts, Nancy, 2005–06, pp.29–38

LÉCOSSE (2006)
Lécosse, Cyril, "De l'intérêt d'être amis, ou le Bélisaire de Gérard et son portrait d'Isabey, peintre" in *Au-delà du maître. Girodet et l'atelier de David*, Musée Girodet, Montargis, 2003, pp.106–115

LEMOISNE (1946–49)
Lemoisne, Paul André, *Degas et son oeuvre*, Paris 1946–9, 4 vols

LEMOISNE (SUPP.)
Brame, Philippe and Reff, Théodore, *Degas et son oeuvre: A Supplement*, New York 1984

LEVEL (1928)
Level, André, *Picasso*, Paris 1928

LIMBOUR (1947)
Limbour, Georges, "Fêtes" in Michel Leiris, *André Masson et son univers*, Paris 1947, pp.185–89

LONDON (1980)
Abstraction: Towards a New Art. Painting, 1910–1920, Tate Gallery, London 1980

LOYER (1976)
Loyer, Jacqueline, "L'oeuvre gravé d'Albert Gleizes", *Nouvelles de l'Estampe*, no.26, March-April, 1976, pp.11–22

LOYRETTE (1991)
Loyrette, Henri, *Degas*, Paris 1991

LOYRETTE (1999)
Loyrette, Henri, *Daumier 1808–1879*, National Gallery of Canada, Ottawa; Galeries nationales du Grand Palais, Paris; Phillips Collection, Washington, 1999

LOYRETTE (2016)
Loyrette, Henri, *Degas: A New Vision*, Museum of Fine Arts, Houston 2016

MCCULLAGH (2003)
McCullagh, Suzanne Folds, et al, *Graphic Modernism, selections from the Francey and Dr. Martin L. Gecht collection at the Art Institute of Chicago*, Chicago 2003

MAISON (1968)
Maison, K. E., *Honoré Daumier: catalogue raisonné of the paintings, watercolours and drawings*, London 1968, 2 vols

MALLARMÉ (2003)
Mallarmé, Stéphane, *Oeuvres complètes*, ed. Bertrand Marchal, vol. 2, Paris 2003

MASSENET (1999)
Massenet, Michel, *Albert Gleizes, 1881–1953*, Paris 1999

MATISSE (1972)
Matisse, Henri, *Écrits et propos sur l'art*, Paris 1972

MAUNER AND LOYRETTE (2001)
Mauner, George and Loyrette, Henri, *Manet: les natures mortes*, Musée d'Orsay, Paris; Walters Art Gallery, Baltimore 2001

MEIER-GRAEFE (1922)
Meier-Graefe, Julius, *Cézanne und sein Kreis: ein Beitrag zur Entwicklungsgeschichte*, 3rd ed., Munich 1922

MEYER (1963)
Meyer, Franz, *Marc Chagall*, New York 1963

MICHEL (1991)
Michel, Régis and Laveissière, Sylvain, *Géricault*, Galeries nationales du Grand Palais, Paris, 1991

MILLET (1991)
Millet, Solange, *Louis Marcoussis, 1878–1941: catalogue raisonné de l'oeuvre gravé*, Copenhagen 1991

MOFFETT (1986)
Moffett, Charles, ed., *The New Painting: Impressionism 1874–1886*, Fine Art Museums, San Francisco; National gallery of Art, Washington, 1986

MOREAU-NÉLATON (1921)
Moreau-Nélaton, Étienne, *Millet raconté par lui-même*, Paris 1921

MOSER (1986-86)
Moser, Joann, *Jean Metzinger in Retrospect*, University of Iowa Museum of Art, Iowa City and elsewhere, 1985–86

MURPHY (1984)
Murphy, Alexandra R., *Jean-François Millet*, Museum of Fine Art, Boston, 1984

NAEGELY (1898)
Naegely, Henry, *J. F. Millet and Rustic Art*, London 1898

NATHANSON AND OLSZEWSKI (1980)
Nathanson, Carol and Olszewski, Edward, "Degas's Angel of the Apocalypse", *Bulletin of the Cleveland Museum of Art*, October 1980, pp.243–55

NEW YORK (1998)
Fernand Léger, The Metropolitan Museum of Art, New York, 1998

ONGPIN (2012)
Stephen Ongpin Fine Art, *Master Drawings 2012*, London 2012

ONGPIN (2016)
Stephen Ongpin Fine Art, *Master Drawings 2016*, London 2016

PALAU I FABRE (1981)
Palau i Fabre, Josep, *Picasso: The Early Years, 1881–1907*, Oxford 1981

PARIS (1980)
Marcel Gromaire, Musée d'art moderne de la ville de Paris, 1980

PISSARRO AND VENTURI (1939)
Pissarro, Ludovic-Rodo and Venturi, Lionello, *Camille Pissarro, son art- son oeuvre*, Paris 1939

PRAT (1988)
Prat, Louis-Antoine, *Dessins de Théodore Chassériau*, 1819–1856, Paris 1988

READ (2008)
Read, Peter, *Picasso and Apollinaire; The Persistence of Memory*, Los Angeles 2008

REDON (1961)
Redon, Odilon, *A soi-même, journal 1867–1915*, Paris 1961

REED AND SHAPIRO (1984)
Reed, Sue Walsh, and Shapiro, Barbara, *Edgar Degas: The Painter as Printmaker*, Museum of Fine Art, Boston, Philadelphia Museum of Art, 1984

REFF (1962)
Reff, Theodore, "Cézanne's Bather with Outstretched Arms", *Gazette des Beaux-Art*, 59, no.118, (March 1962), pp.173–190

REFF (1976)
Reff, Theodore, *The Notebooks of Edgar Degas: A Catalogue of the Thirty-Eight Notebooks in the Bibliothèque Nationale and Other Collections*, Oxford 1976, 2 vols

REWALD (1946)
Rewald, John, *Renoir's Drawings*, New York 1946

REWALD (1989)
Rewald, Sabine and Lieberman, William, *Twentieth-Century Modern Masters; The Jacques and Natasha Gelman Collection*, The Metropolitan Museum of Art, New York, 1989

REWALD (1996)
Rewald, John, *The Paintings of Paul Cézanne: A Catalogue Raisonné*, New York 1996, 2 vols

RICHARDSON AND KAHNWEILER (1965–66)
Richardson, John and Kahnweiler, Daniel, *Juan Gris*, Museum am Ostwall, Dortmund; Wallraf-Richartz-Museum, Cologne, 1965–66

ROBAUT (1885)
Robaut, Alfred, *L'oeuvre complet de Eugène Delacroix: peintures, dessins, gravures, lithographies*, Paris 1885

ROBIDA (1958)
Robida, Michel, *Le salon Charpentier et les impressionistes*, Paris 1958

ROSENBERG (1987–8)
Rosenberg, Pierre and Dupuy-Vachey, Marie-Anne, *Fragonard*, Galeries nationales du Grand Palais, Paris; The Metropolitan Museum of Art, New York, 1987–88

ROSENBERG (1993)
Rosenberg, Pierre, "Fragonard et David" in *David contre David*, acts of the colloquium organised at the Musée du Louvre from 6 to 10 December 1989, Paris 1993, pp.5–16

ROSENBERG AND PRAT (2002)
Rosenberg, Pierre and Prat, Louis-Antoine, *Jacques-Louis David, 1748–1825: catalogue raisonné des dessins*, Milan 2002, 2 vols

ROUART AND WILDENSTEIN (1975)
Rouart, Denis and Wildenstein, Daniel, Édouard Manet: catalogue *raisonné*, Lausanne 1975, 2 vols

ROWELL (1975)
Rowell, Margit, *František Kupka 1871–1957: A Retrospective*, Solomon R. Guggenheim Museum of Art, New York, 1975

RUSSOLI AND MINERVINO (1970)
Russoli, Franco and Minervino, Fiorella, *L'opera completa di Degas*, Milan 1970

SALMON (2006)
Salmon, Dimitri, *Ingres: la Grande Odalisque*, Paris 2006

SANDOZ (1974)
Sandoz, Marc, *Théodore Chassériau, 1819–1856: catalogue raisonné des peintures et estampes*, Paris 1974

SANDOZ (1986)
Sandoz, Marc, *Portraits et visages dessinés par Théodore Chassériau*, Paris 1986

SECKEL (1988)
Seckel, Hélène, *Les Demoiselles d'Avignon*, Musée Picasso, Paris; Museu Picasso, Barcelona, 1988

SEGARD (1913)
Segard, Achille, *Un peintre des enfants et des mères, Mary Cassatt*, Paris 1913

SELIGMAN (2000)
Seligman, Germain, *Roger de La Fresnaye with a Catalogue Raisonné*, rev. ed., London 2000

SÉRULLAZ (1989)
Sérullaz, Arlette and Schnapper, Antoine, *Jacques-Louis David, 1748–1825*, Musée du Louvre, Musée national du château de Versailles, 1989–90

SEZNEC AND MORGAN (1945)
Seznec, Jean and Morgan, Elizabeth, *Fragonard, Drawings for Ariosto*, New York 1945

SIEGFRIED (1995)
Siegfried, Susan, *The Art of Louis-Léopold Boilly: Modern Life in Napoleonic France*, New Haven/London 1995+

SILVER (2008)
Silver, Kenneth, *Paris Portraits: Artists, Friends and Lovers*, London 2008

SNOLLAERTS AND PISSARRO (2006)
Snollaerts, Claire Durand-Ruel, and Pissarro, Joachim, *Pissarro: Critical Catalogue of Paintings*, Milan 2006, 3 vols

SOBEL (1986)
Sobel, Dean, *Reactions to the War: European Art, 1914–1925*, University of Wisconsin, Milwaukee, 1986

STAMPFLE AND DENNISON (1975)
Stampfle, Felice and Denison, Cara D., *Drawings from the Collection of Mr. and Mrs Eugene Thaw*, Pierpont Morgan Library, New York, 1975

STUFFMANN (1987)
Stuffmann, Margret, *Eugène Delacroix: Themen und Variationen;rbeiten auf Papier*, Stuttgart 1987

TABARANT (1947)
Tabarant, Adolphe, *Manet et ses oeuvres*, Paris 1947

THOMSON (1987)
Thomson, Richard, *The Private Degas*, Whitworth Art Gallery, Manchester; Fitzwilliam Museum, Cambridge, 1987

TINTEROW (1985)
Tinterow, Gary, *Juan Gris 1887–1937*, Salas Pablo Ruiz Picasso, Madrid, 1985

VALÉRY (1965)
Valéry, Paul, *Degas, danse, dessin*, Paris 1965

VALLIER (1988)
Vallier, Dora, *Braque: The Complete Graphics: Catalogue Raisonné*, New York 1988

VAN HEUGTEN AND PABST (1995)
Van Heugten, Sjraar, and Pabst, Fieke, *The Graphic Work of Vincent van Gogh*, Zwolle 1995

VARICHON (1998)
Varichon, Anne, *Albert Gleizes, catalogue raisonné*, Paris 1998, 2 vols

VARICHON (FORTHCOMING)
Varichon, Anne, *Albert Gleizes, catalogue raisonné, supplement* (forthcoming)

VOLLARD (1915)
Vollard, Ambroise, *Paul Cézanne*, Paris 1915

VOLLARD (1936)
Vollard, Ambroise, *Recollections of a Picture Dealer*, London 1936

WILDENSTEIN (1974–91)
Wildenstein, Daniel, *Claude Monet: biographie et catalogue raisonné*, Lausanne 1974–1991, 5 vols

WILDENSTEIN (1992)
Wildenstein, Alec, *Odilon Redon: catalogue raisonné de l'oeuvre peint et dessiné*, Paris 1992–98, 4 vols

WILSON BAREAU (1977)
Wilson Bareau, Juliet, *Édouard Manet: l'oeuvre gravé*, Ingelheim am Rhein 1977

WILSON BAREAU (1978)
Wilson Bareau, Juliet, *Manet: dessins, aquarelles, eaux-fortes, lithographies, correspondance*, Huguette Berès, Paris, 1978

ZAFRAN (2007)
Zafran, Eric, *Fantasy and Faith: The Art of Gustave Doré*, New Haven/London 2007

ZERVOS (1932–78)
Zervos, Christian, *Pablo Picasso*, Paris 1932–78, 33 vols.

COPYRIGHT CREDITS

Bonnard, Pierre © ADAGP, Paris and DACS, London 2016: cat.97, p.170

Braque, Georges © ADAGP, Paris and DACS, London 2016: cat.64, p.129

Chagall, Marc ® / © ADAGP, Paris and DACS, London 2016: cat.103, p.179

Czóbel, Béla © DACS 2016: fig.6, p.12

Dufy, Raoul © ADAGP, Paris and DACS, London 2016: cat.59, p.123; cat.76, p.146

Gleizes, Albert © ADAGP, Paris and DACS, London 2016: cat.73, p.142; cat.77, p.147; cat.80, p.151; cat.81, p.152; cat.82, p.153; cat.83, p.155; cat.93, p.165

Gromairé, Marcel © ADAGP, Paris and DACS, London 2016: cat.86, p.158; cat.87, p.159; cat.105, p.181

Herbin, Auguste © ADAGP, Paris and DACS, London 2016: cat.62, p.127

Kupka, František © ADAGP, Paris and DACS, London 2016: cat.74, p.143

Léger, Fernand © ADAGP, Paris and DACS, London 2016: cat.75, p.145; cat.89, p.161; cat.92, p.164; cat.94, p.166; cat.95, p.167; cat.99, p.172; cat.107, p.185

Lhote, André © ADAGP, Paris and DACS, London 2016: cat.67, p.133

Masson, André © ADAGP, Paris and DACS, London 2016: cat.108, p.186

Matisse, Henri © Succession H. Matisse/ DACS 2016. Image: © Arts Council Collection, Southbank Centre 2016: cat.58, p121

Matisse, Henri © Archives H. Matisse 2016: cat.106, p183

Metzinger, Jean © ADAGP, Paris and DACS, London 2016: cat.66, p.132; cat.72, p.141; cat.90, p.162; cat.91, p.163

Picasso, Pablo © Succession Picasso / DACS, London 2016: cat.55, p.115; cat.57, p.119; cat.63, p.128; cat.65, p.131; cat.85, p.157; cat.96, p.169; cat.109, p.187; cat.110, p.188; cat.111, p.189; cat.112, p.190; cat.113, p.191

Rouault, Georges © ADAGP, Paris and DACS, London 2016: cat.100, p.175, cat.101, p.176; cat.102, p.177

Villon, Jacques © ADAGP, Paris and DACS, London 2016: cat.56, p.117; cat.68, p.135; cat.78, p.149; cat.79, p.150; cat.84, p.156; cat.98, p.171; cat.104, p.180